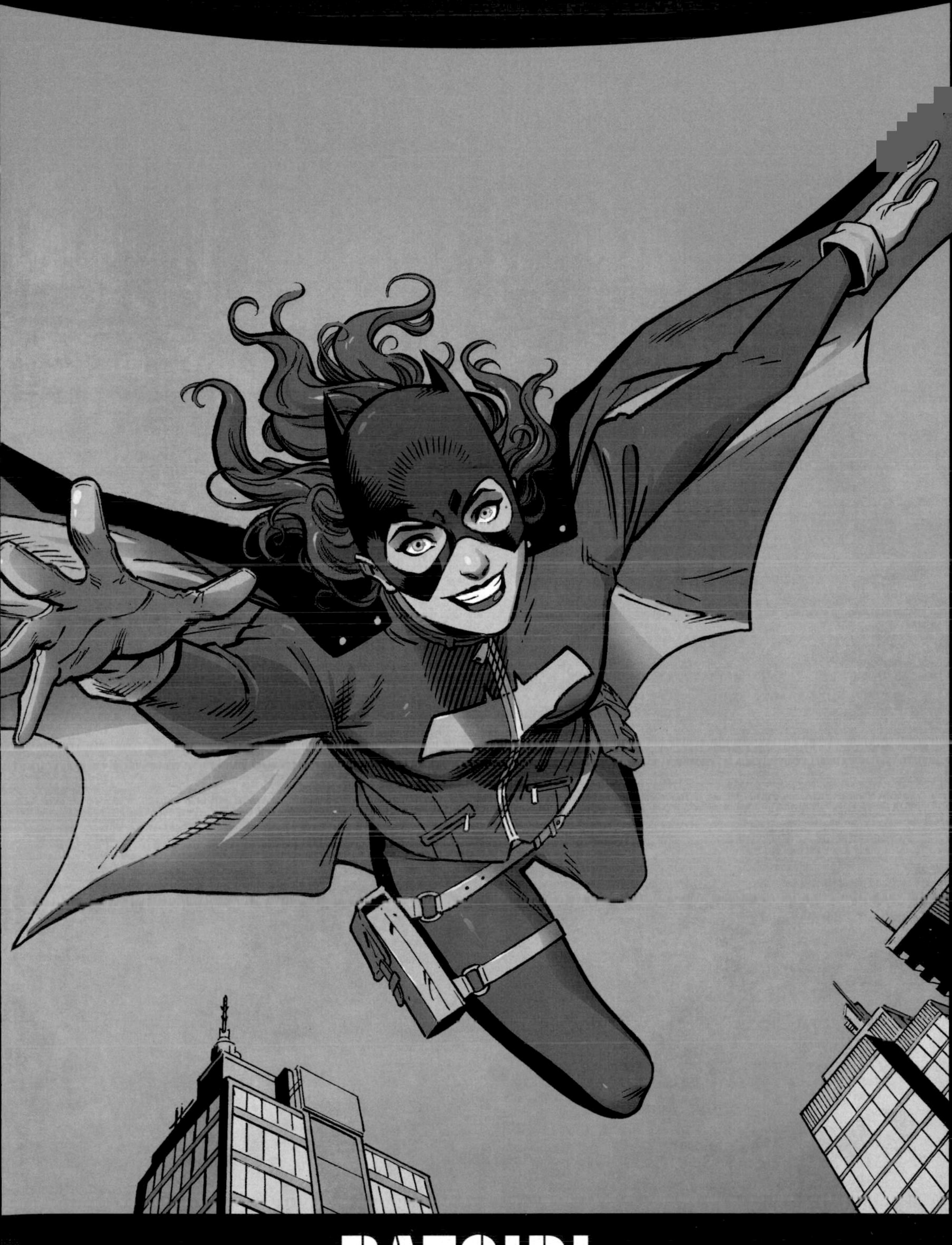

BATGIRL

VOL.4 STRANGE LOOP

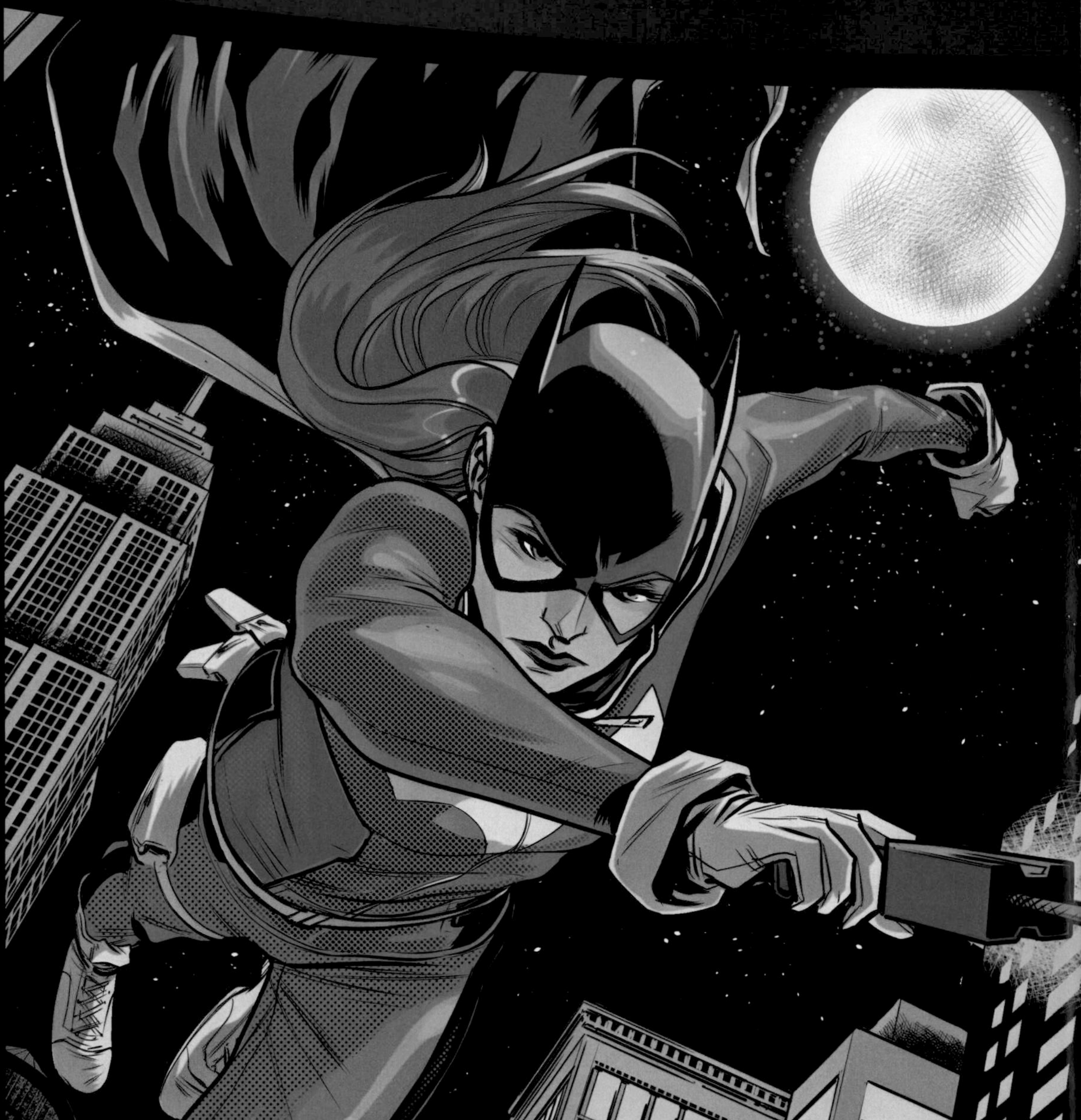

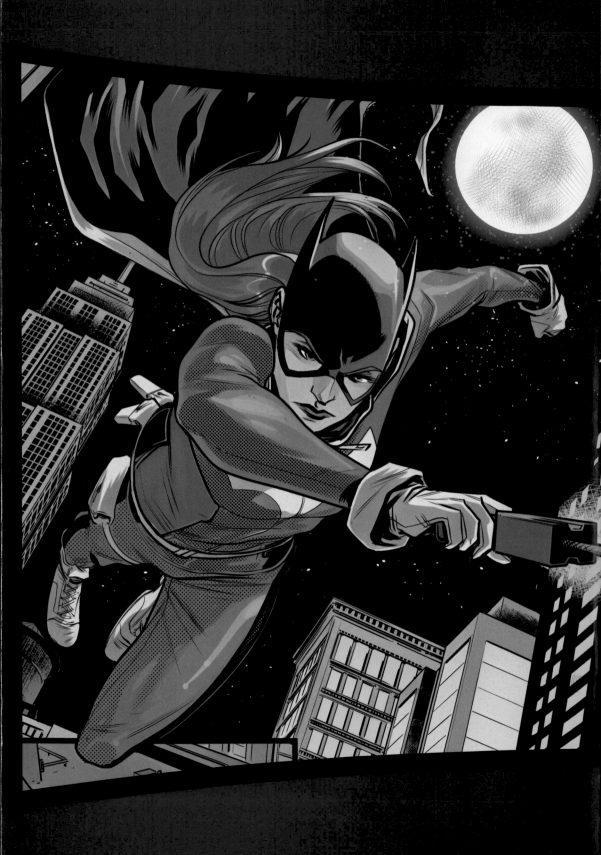

BATGIRL

VOL.4 STRANGE LOOP

HOPE LARSON
SHAWN ALDRIDGE * MAIRGHREAD SCOTT
PAUL DINI * MARGUERITE BENNETT
writers

SAMI BASRI * SCOTT GODLEWSKI
MINKYU JUNG * CHRIS WILDGOOSE
JOSE MARZAN JR. * TOM DERENICK * SEAN PARSONS
DAN PANOSIAN * EMANUELA LUPACCHINO * RAY McCARTHY
artists

MAT LOPES * JESSICA KHOLINNE
JOHN RAUCH * STEPHEN DOWNER * JORDIE BELLAIRE
colorists

DERON BENNETT
letterer

JOSHUA MIDDLETON
collection cover artist

BATMAN created by BOB KANE with BILL FINGER
HARLEY QUINN created by PAUL DINI and BRUCE TIMM
SUPERGIRL based on characters created by JERRY SIEGEL and JOE SHUSTER
By special arrangement with the Jerry Siegel family

BRITTANY HOLZHERR Editor - Original Series
JEB WOODARD Group Editor - Collected Editions ✱ **ROBIN WILDMAN** Editor - Collected Edition
STEVE COOK Design Director - Books ✱ **SHANNON STEWART** Publication Design

BOB HARRAS Senior VP - Editor-in-Chief, DC Comics
PAT McCALLUM Executive Editor, DC Comics

DAN DiDIO Publisher ✱ **JIM LEE** Publisher & Chief Creative Officer
AMIT DESAI Executive VP - Business & Marketing Strategy, Direct to Consumer & Global Franchise Management
BOBBIE CHASE VP & Executive Editor, Young Reader & Talent Development ✱ **MARK CHIARELLO** Senior VP - Art, Design & Collected Editions
JOHN CUNNINGHAM Senior VP - Sales & Trade Marketing ✱ **BRIAR DARDEN** VP - Business Affairs
ANNE DePIES Senior VP - Business Strategy, Finance & Administration ✱ **DON FALLETTI** VP - Manufacturing Operations
LAWRENCE GANEM VP - Editorial Administration & Talent Relations ✱ **ALISON GILL** Senior VP - Manufacturing & Operations
JASON GREENBERG VP - Business Strategy & Finance ✱ **HANK KANALZ** Senior VP - Editorial Strategy & Administration
JAY KOGAN Senior VP - Legal Affairs ✱ **NICK J. NAPOLITANO** VP - Manufacturing Administration
LISETTE OSTERLOH VP - Digital Marketing & Events ✱ **EDDIE SCANNELL** VP - Consumer Marketing
COURTNEY SIMMONS Senior VP - Publicity & Communications ✱ **JIM (SKI) SOKOLOWSKI** VP - Comic Book Specialty Sales & Trade Marketing
NANCY SPEARS VP - Mass, Book, Digital Sales & Trade Marketing ✱ **MICHELE R. WELLS** VP - Content Strategy

BATGIRL VOL. 4: STRANGE LOOP

Published by DC Comics. Compilation and all new material Copyright © 2018 DC Comics. All Rights Reserved.
Originally published in single magazine form in BATGIRL 18-25. Copyright © 2017, 2018 DC Comics. All Rights Reserved.
All characters, their distinctive likenesses and related elements featured in this publication are trademarks of DC Comics.
The stories, characters and incidents featured in this publication are entirely fictional.
DC Comics does not read or accept unsolicited submissions of ideas, stories or artwork.

DC Comics, 2900 West Alameda Ave., Burbank, CA 91505
Printed by LSC Communications, Kendallville, IN, USA. 11/2/18. First Printing.
ISBN: 978-1-4012-8465-7

Library of Congress Cataloging-in-Publication Data is available.

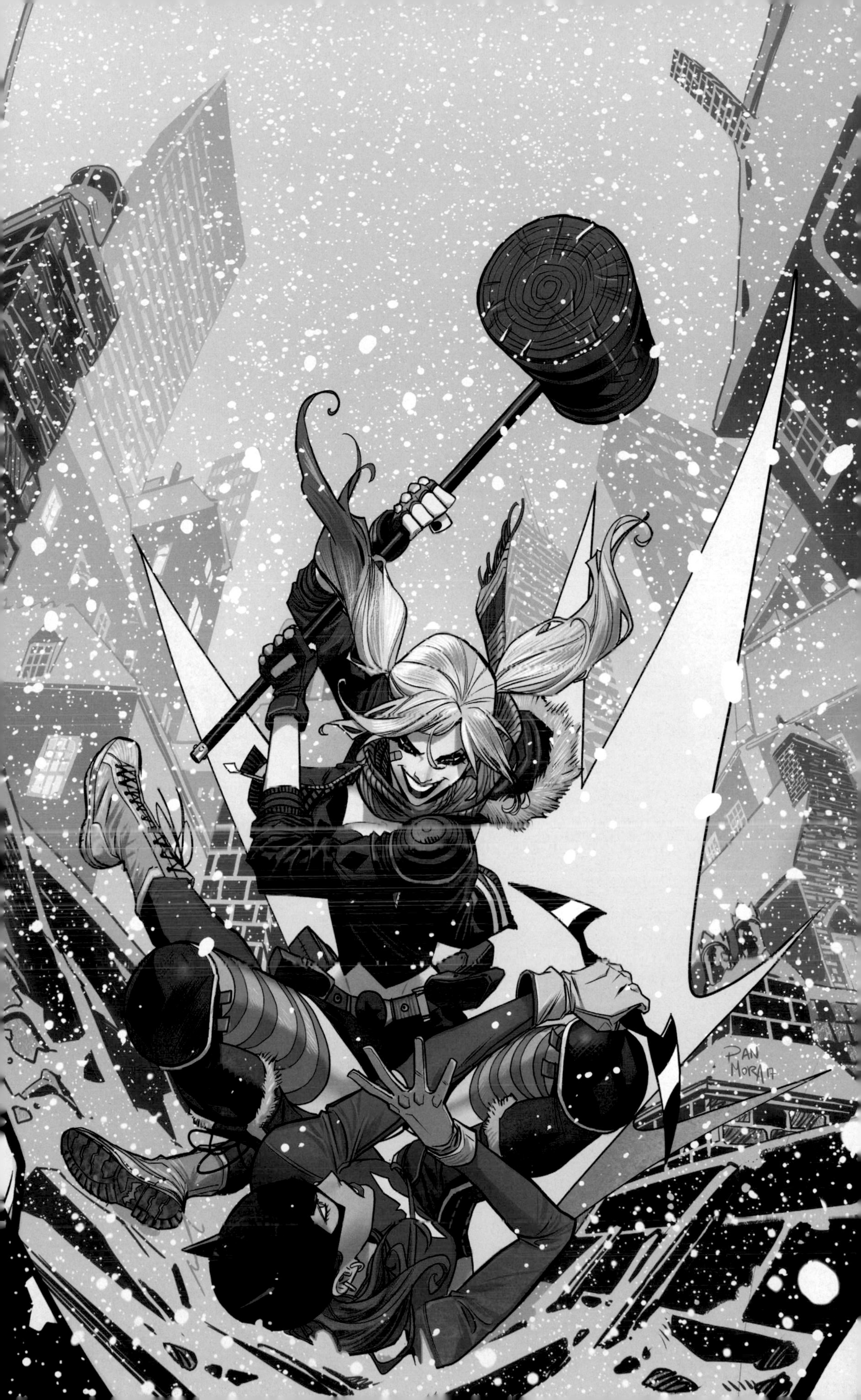
DAN
MORA 17

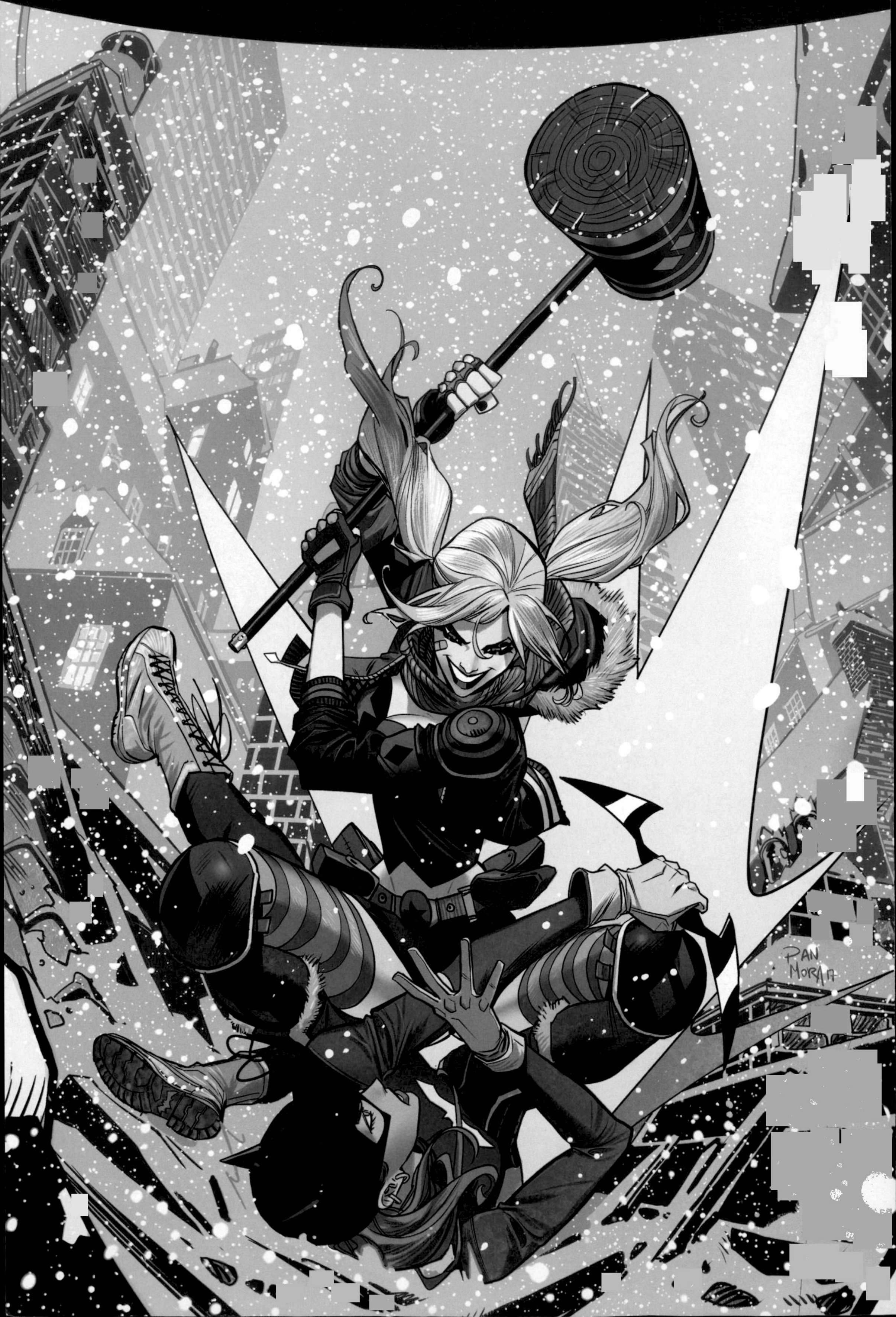

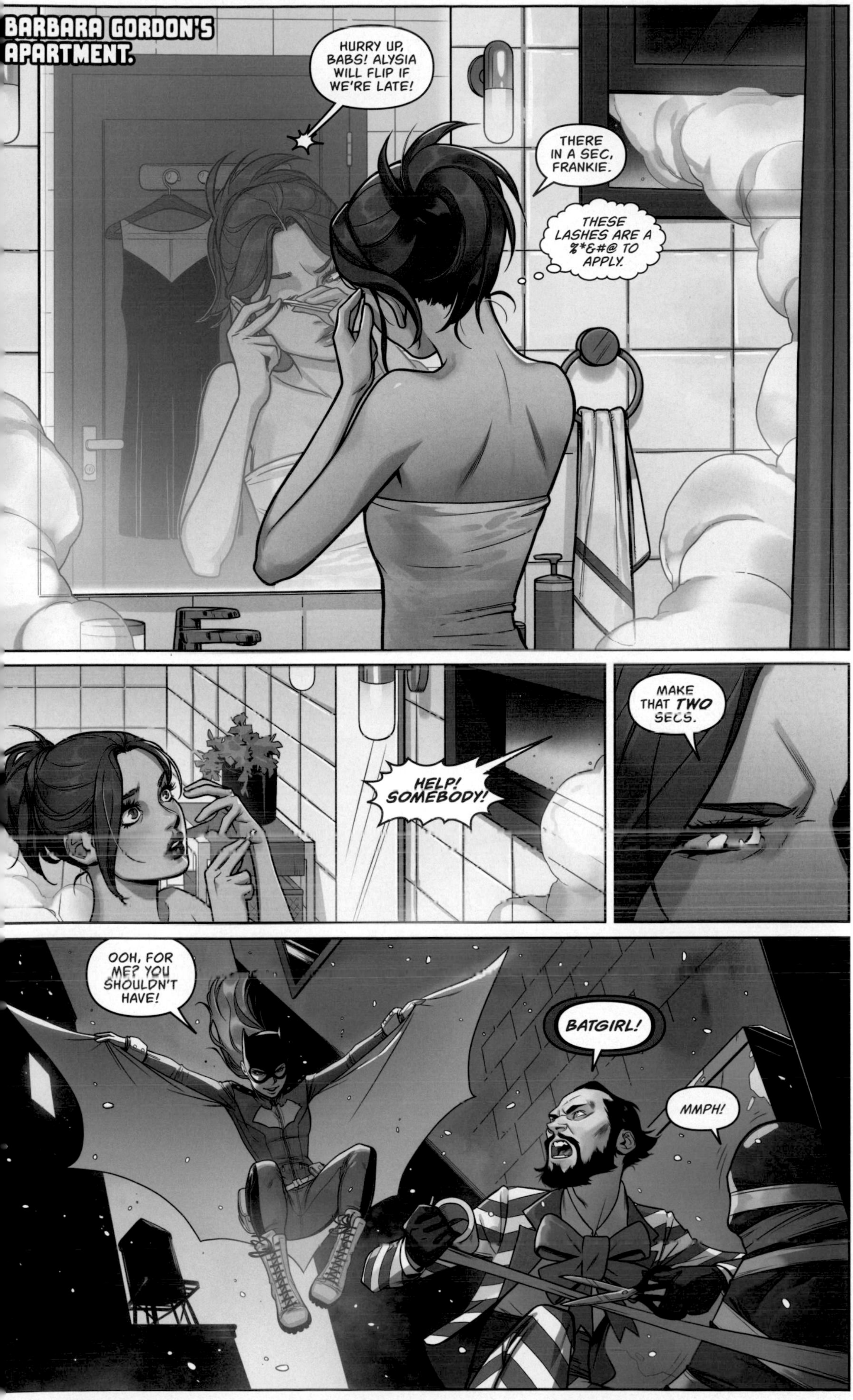
BARBARA GORDON'S APARTMENT.
HURRY UP, BABS! ALYSIA WILL FLIP IF WE'RE LATE!
THERE IN A SEC, FRANKIE.
THESE LASHES ARE A %*&#@ TO APPLY.
HELP! SOMEBODY!
MAKE THAT TWO SECS.
OOH, FOR ME? YOU SHOULDN'T HAVE!
BATGIRL!
MMPH!

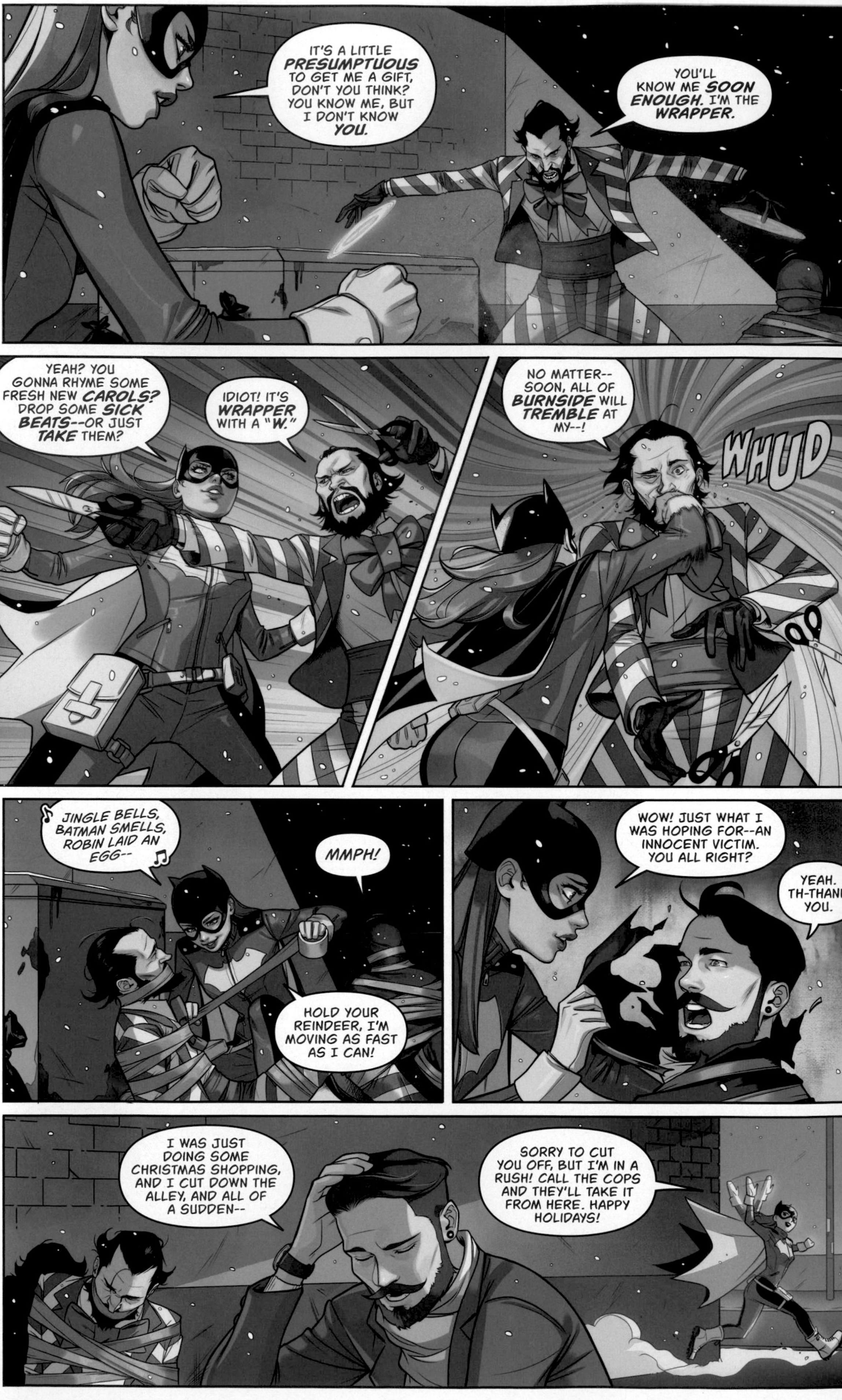
IT'S A LITTLE PRESUMPTUOUS TO GET ME A GIFT, DON'T YOU THINK? YOU KNOW ME, BUT I DON'T KNOW YOU.
YOU'LL KNOW ME SOON ENOUGH. I'M THE WRAPPER.
YEAH? YOU GONNA RHYME SOME FRESH NEW CAROLS? DROP SOME SICK BEATS--OR JUST TAKE THEM?
IDIOT! IT'S WRAPPER WITH A "W."
NO MATTER-- SOON, ALL OF BURNSIDE WILL TREMBLE AT MY--!
WHUD
JINGLE BELLS, BATMAN SMELLS, ROBIN LAID AN EGG--
MMPH!
HOLD YOUR REINDEER, I'M MOVING AS FAST AS I CAN!
WOW! JUST WHAT I WAS HOPING FOR--AN INNOCENT VICTIM. YOU ALL RIGHT?
YEAH. TH-THANK YOU.
I WAS JUST DOING SOME CHRISTMAS SHOPPING, AND I CUT DOWN THE ALLEY, AND ALL OF A SUDDEN--
SORRY TO CUT YOU OFF, BUT I'M IN A RUSH! CALL THE COPS AND THEY'LL TAKE IT FROM HERE. HAPPY HOLIDAYS!

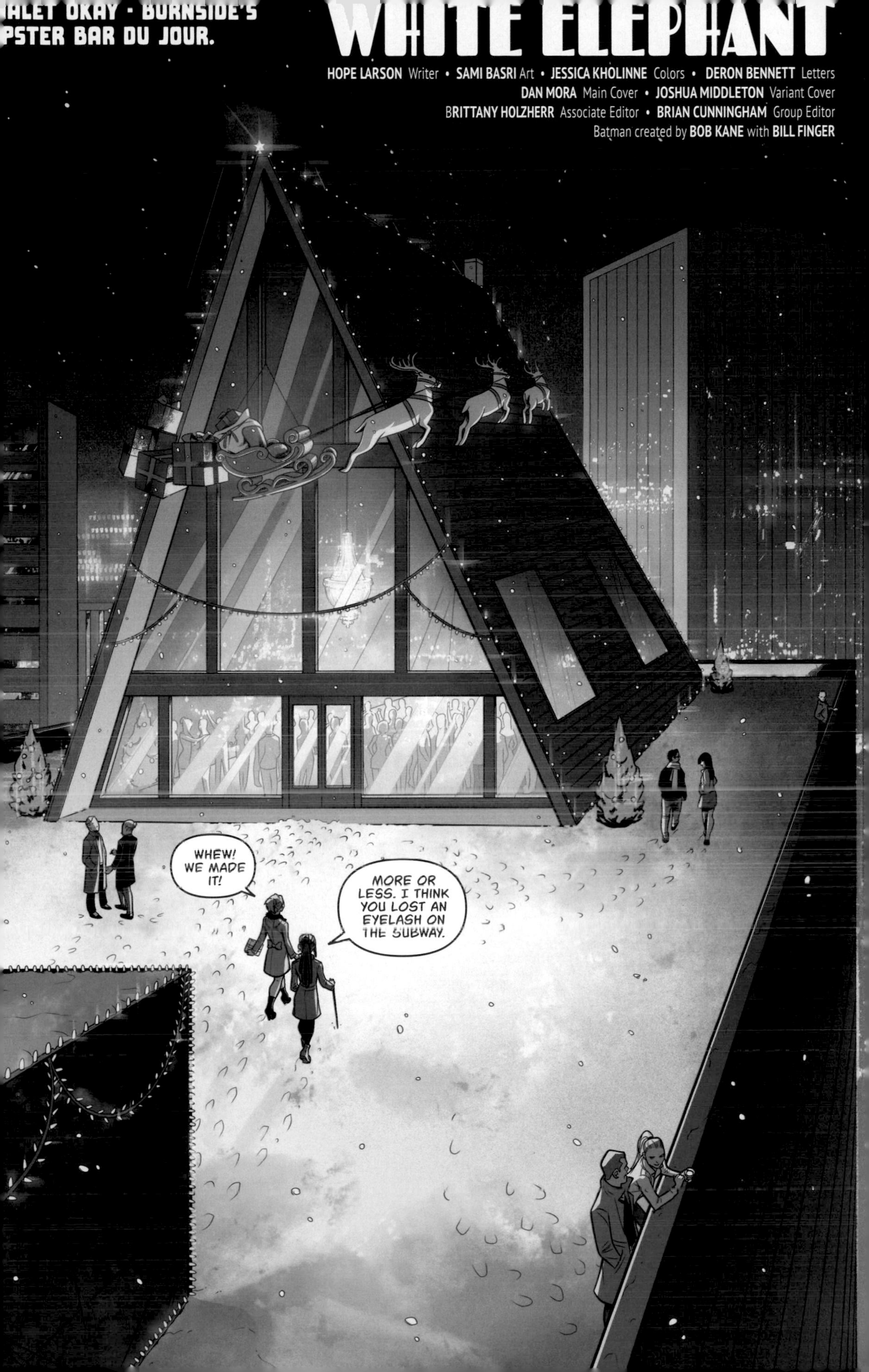

ALET OKAY - BURNSIDE'S
PSTER BAR DU JOUR.
WHITE ELEPHANT
HOPE LARSON Writer • SAMI BASRI Art • JESSICA KHOLINNE Colors • DERON BENNETT Letters
DAN MORA Main Cover • JOSHUA MIDDLETON Variant Cover
BRITTANY HOLZHERR Associate Editor • BRIAN CUNNINGHAM Group Editor
Batman created by BOB KANE with BILL FINGER
WHEW! WE MADE IT!
MORE OR LESS. I THINK YOU LOST AN EYELASH ON THE SUBWAY.

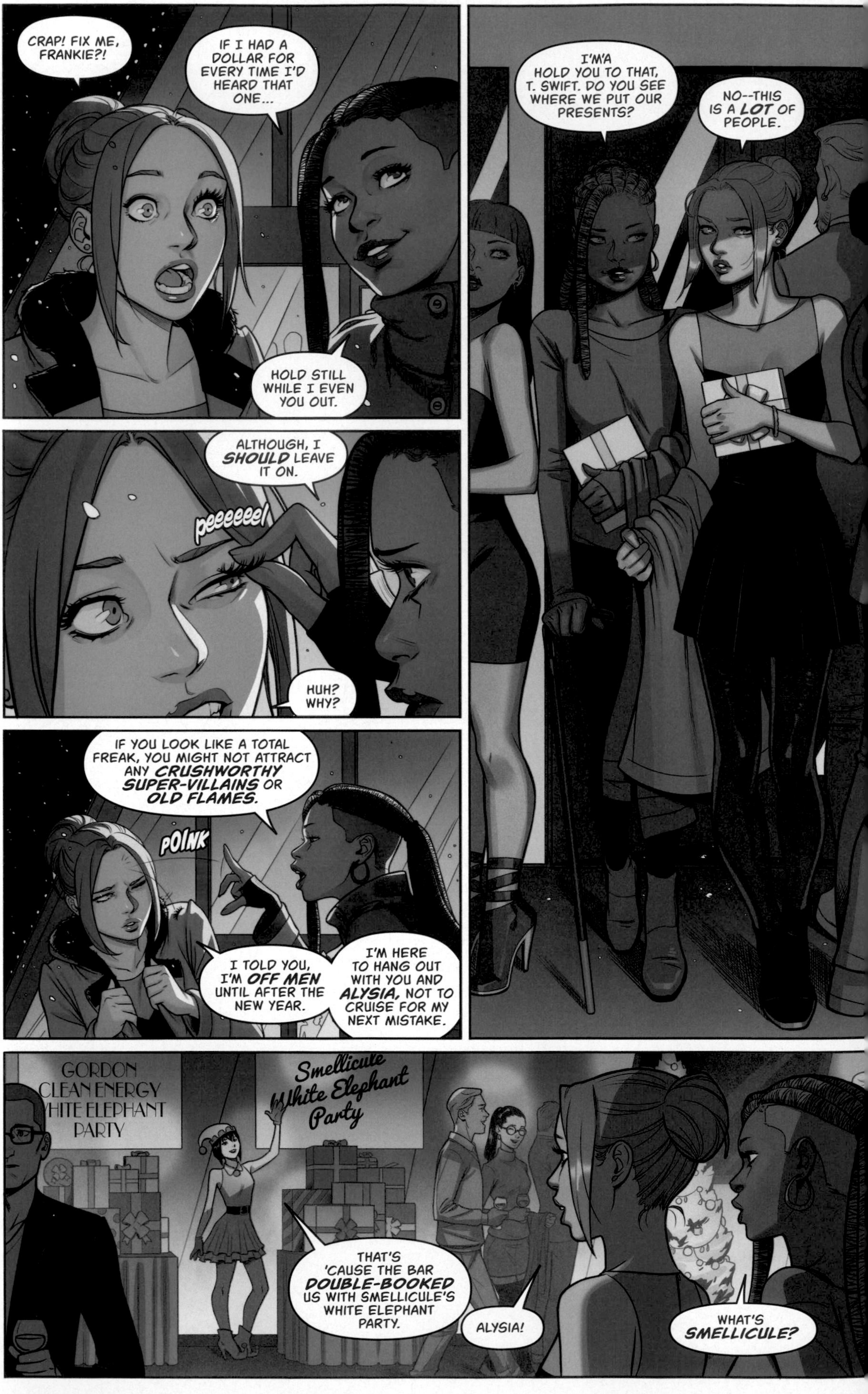

CRAP! FIX ME, FRANKIE?!
IF I HAD A DOLLAR FOR EVERY TIME I'D HEARD THAT ONE...
HOLD STILL WHILE I EVEN YOU OUT.
ALTHOUGH, I SHOULD LEAVE IT ON.
peeeeeel
HUH? WHY?
IF YOU LOOK LIKE A TOTAL FREAK, YOU MIGHT NOT ATTRACT ANY CRUSHWORTHY SUPER-VILLAINS OR OLD FLAMES.
POINK
I TOLD YOU, I'M OFF MEN UNTIL AFTER THE NEW YEAR.
I'M HERE TO HANG OUT WITH YOU AND ALYSIA, NOT TO CRUISE FOR MY NEXT MISTAKE.
I'M'A HOLD YOU TO THAT, T. SWIFT. DO YOU SEE WHERE WE PUT OUR PRESENTS?
NO--THIS IS A LOT OF PEOPLE.
GORDON CLEAN ENERGY WHITE ELEPHANT PARTY
Smellicule White Elephant Party
THAT'S 'CAUSE THE BAR DOUBLE-BOOKED US WITH SMELLICULE'S WHITE ELEPHANT PARTY.
ALYSIA!
WHAT'S SMELLICULE?

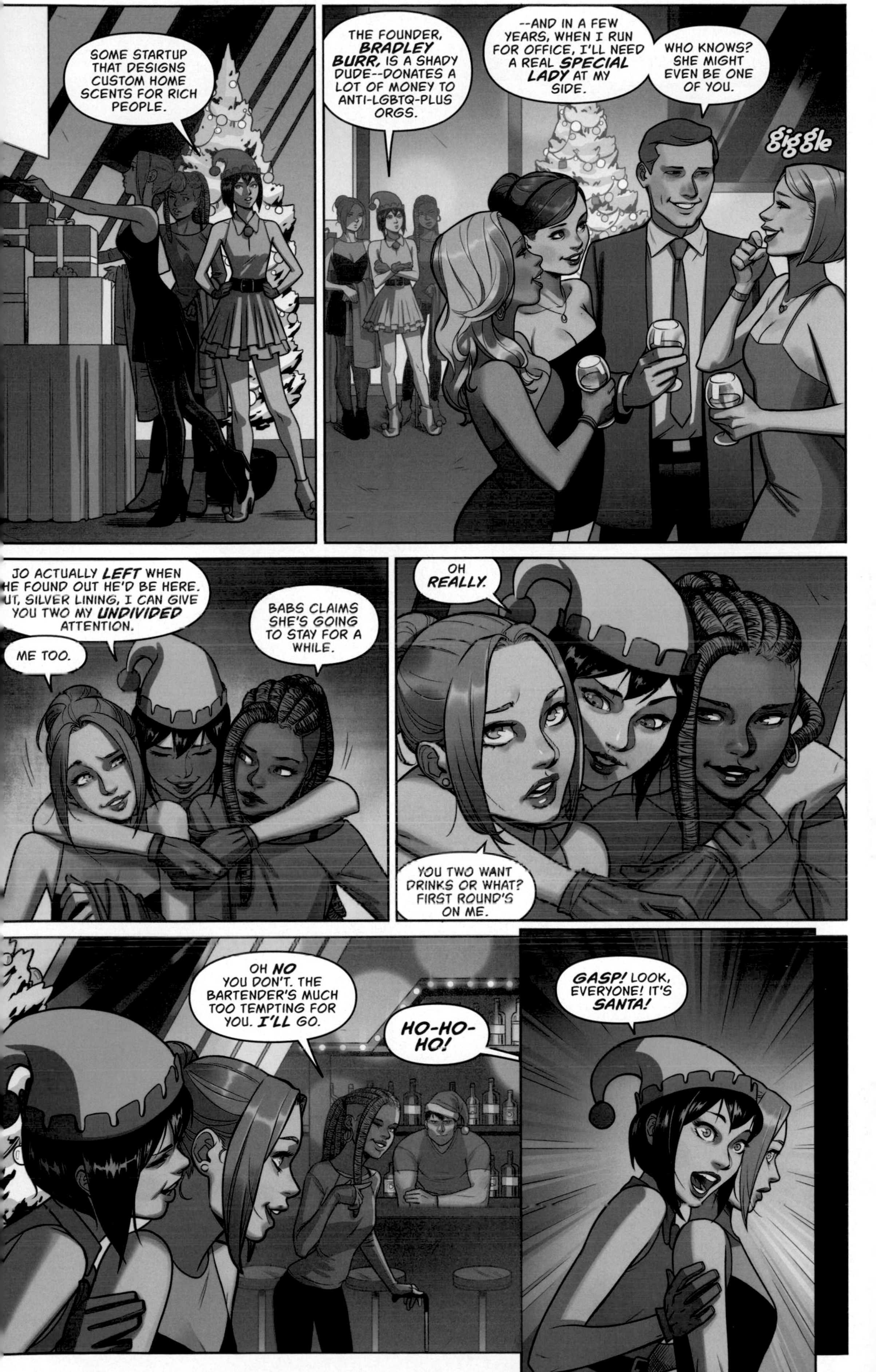
SOME STARTUP THAT DESIGNS CUSTOM HOME SCENTS FOR RICH PEOPLE.
THE FOUNDER, BRADLEY BURR, IS A SHADY DUDE--DONATES A LOT OF MONEY TO ANTI-LGBTQ-PLUS ORGS.
--AND IN A FEW YEARS, WHEN I RUN FOR OFFICE, I'LL NEED A REAL SPECIAL LADY AT MY SIDE.
WHO KNOWS? SHE MIGHT EVEN BE ONE OF YOU.
giggle
JO ACTUALLY LEFT WHEN HE FOUND OUT HE'D BE HERE. BUT, SILVER LINING, I CAN GIVE YOU TWO MY UNDIVIDED ATTENTION.
ME TOO.
BABS CLAIMS SHE'S GOING TO STAY FOR A WHILE.
OH REALLY.
YOU TWO WANT DRINKS OR WHAT? FIRST ROUND'S ON ME.
OH NO YOU DON'T. THE BARTENDER'S MUCH TOO TEMPTING FOR YOU. I'LL GO.
HO-HO-HO!
GASP! LOOK, EVERYONE! IT'S SANTA!

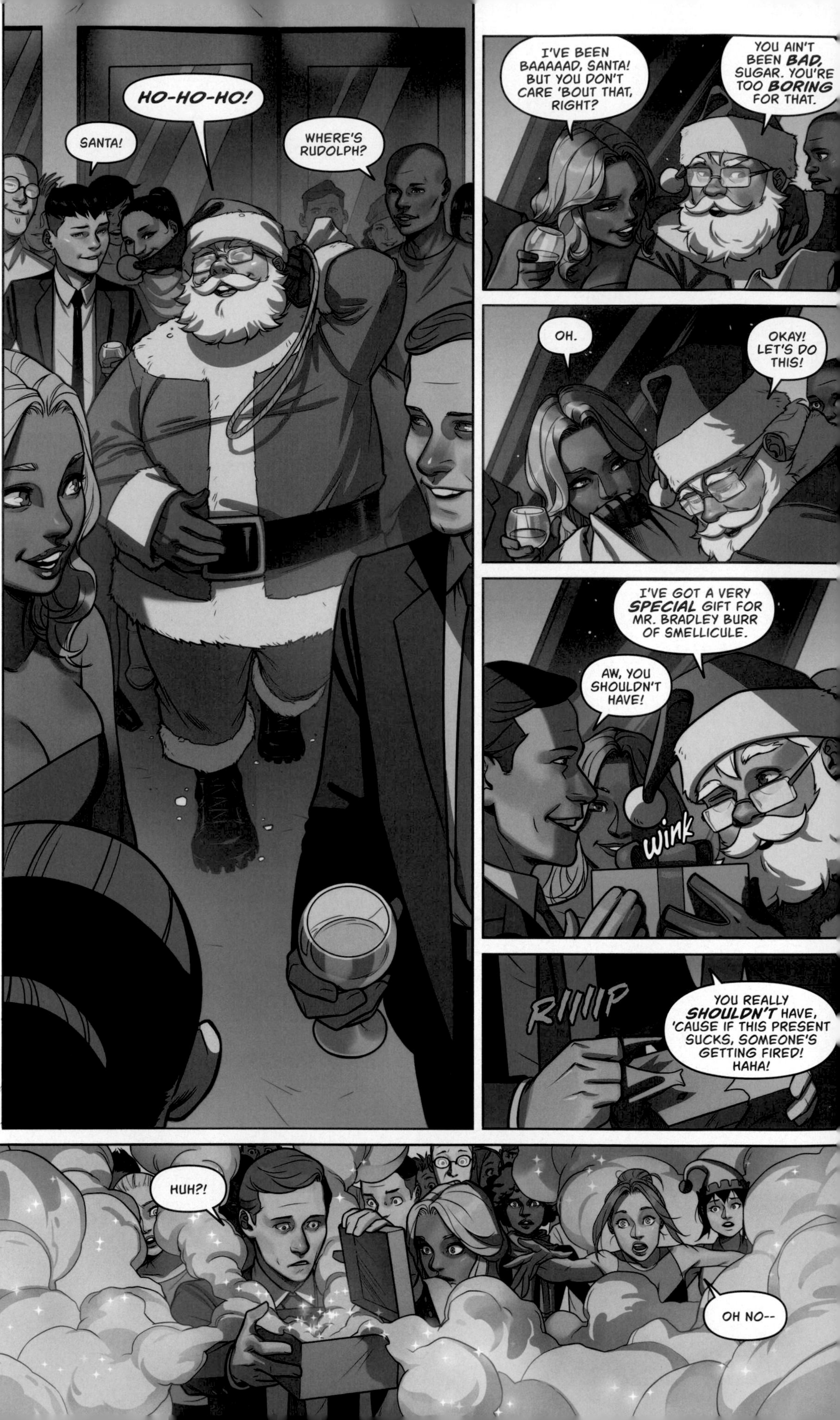
SANTA!
HO-HO-HO!
WHERE'S RUDOLPH?
I'VE BEEN BAAAAAD, SANTA! BUT YOU DON'T CARE 'BOUT THAT, RIGHT?
YOU AIN'T BEEN BAD, SUGAR. YOU'RE TOO BORING FOR THAT.
OH.
OKAY! LET'S DO THIS!
I'VE GOT A VERY SPECIAL GIFT FOR MR. BRADLEY BURR OF SMELLICULE.
AW, YOU SHOULDN'T HAVE!
WINK
RIIIIP
YOU REALLY SHOULDN'T HAVE, 'CAUSE IF THIS PRESENT SUCKS, SOMEONE'S GETTING FIRED! HAHA!
HUH?!
OH NO--

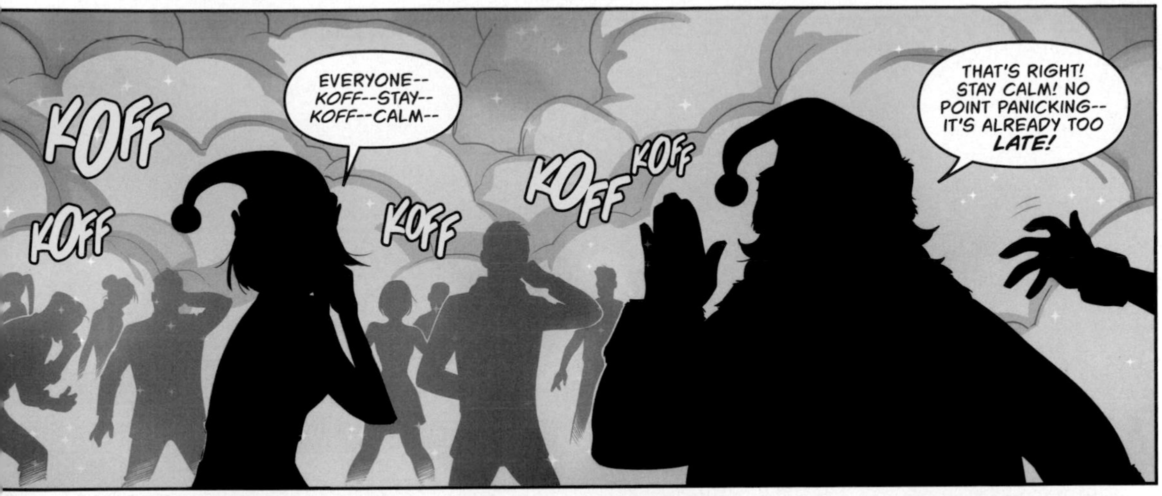
KOFF
KOFF
EVERYONE--KOFF--STAY--KOFF--CALM--
KOFF
KOFF KOFF
THAT'S RIGHT! STAY CALM! NO POINT PANICKING--IT'S ALREADY TOO LATE!

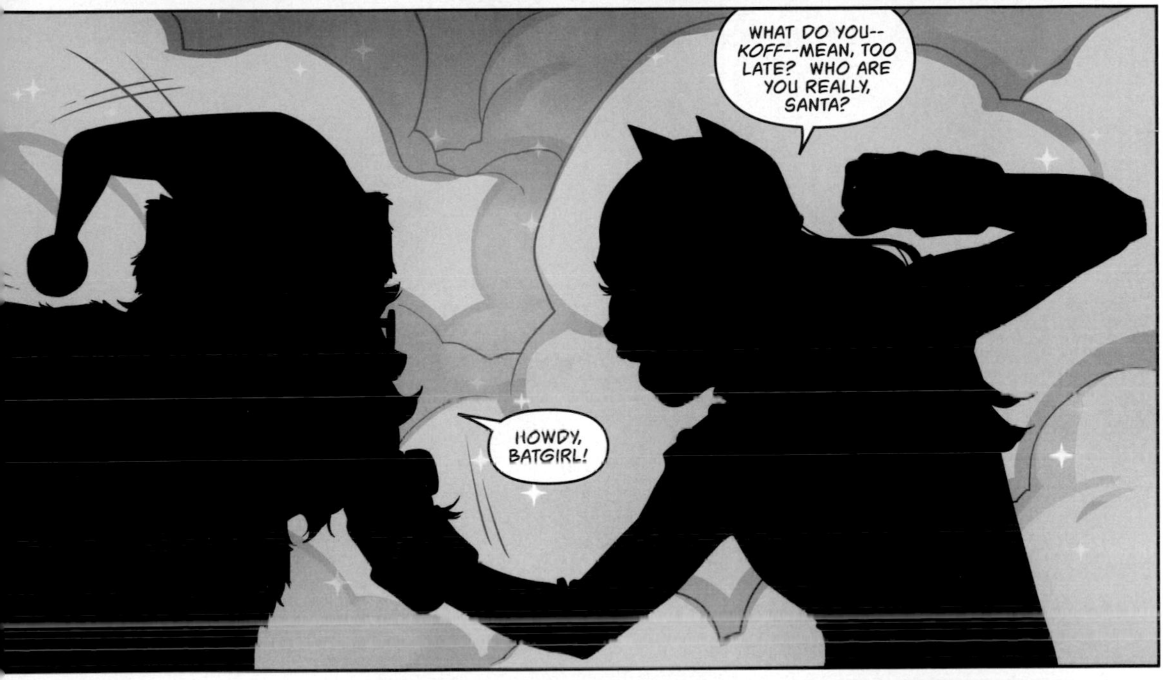
WHAT DO YOU--KOFF--MEAN, TOO LATE? WHO ARE YOU REALLY, SANTA?
HOWDY, BATGIRL!

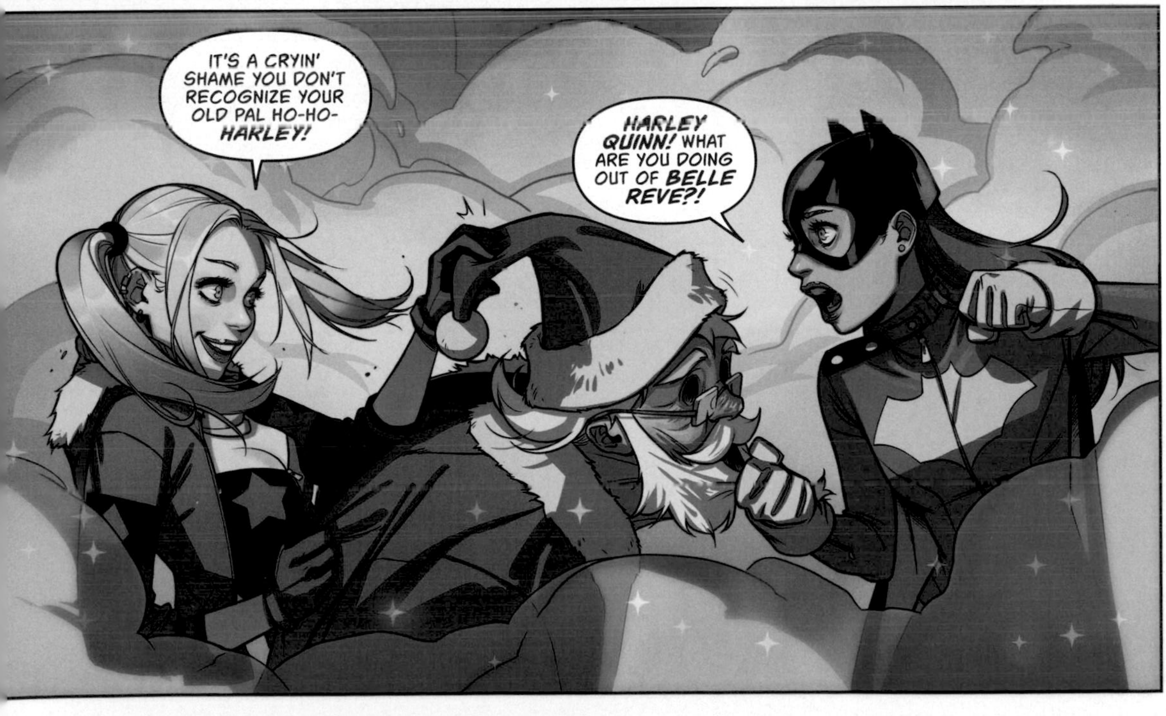
IT'S A CRYIN' SHAME YOU DON'T RECOGNIZE YOUR OLD PAL HO-HO-HARLEY!
HARLEY QUINN! WHAT ARE YOU DOING OUT OF BELLE REVE?!

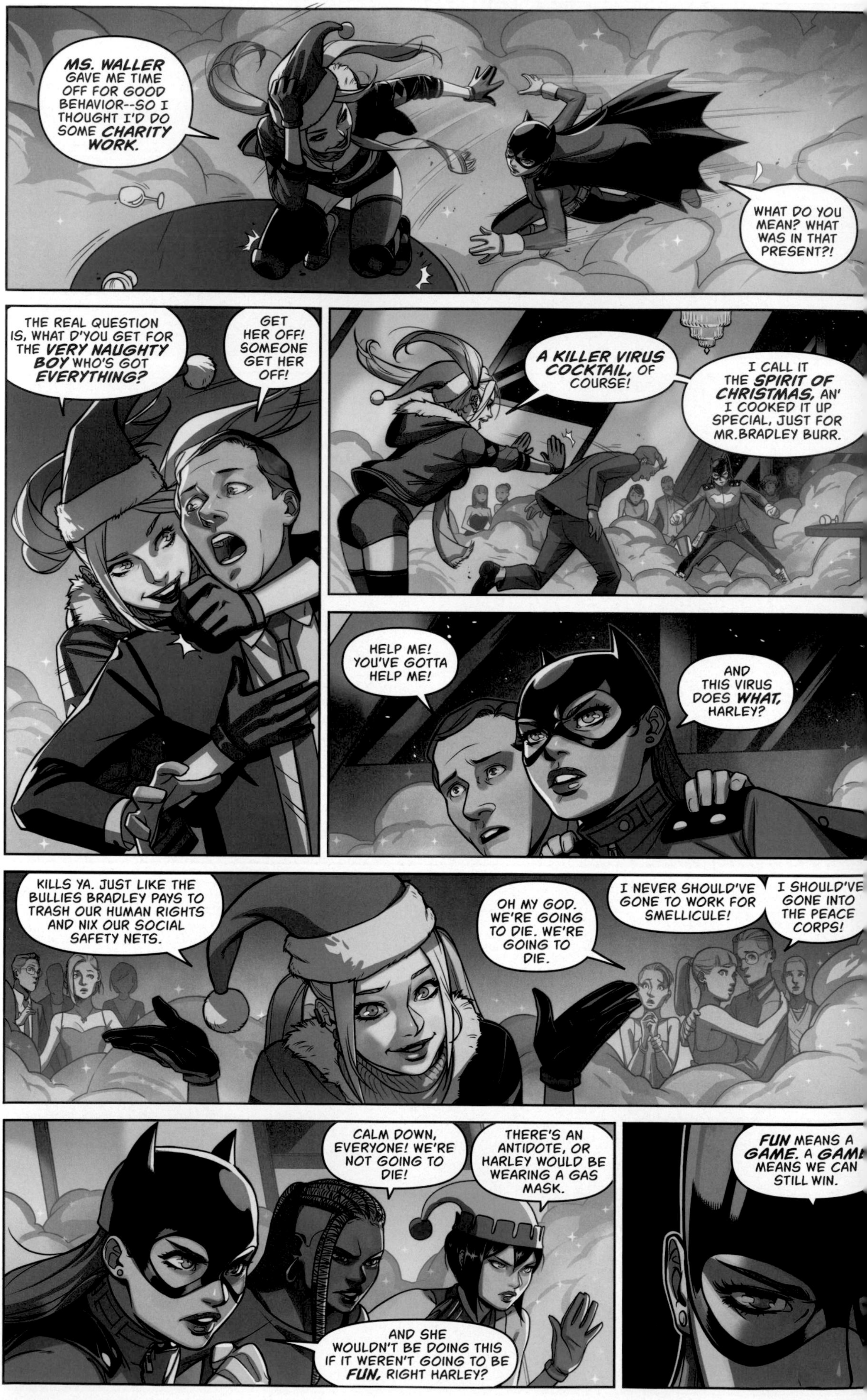

MS. WALLER GAVE ME TIME OFF FOR GOOD BEHAVIOR--SO I THOUGHT I'D DO SOME CHARITY WORK.
WHAT DO YOU MEAN? WHAT WAS IN THAT PRESENT?!
THE REAL QUESTION IS, WHAT D'YOU GET FOR THE VERY NAUGHTY BOY WHO'S GOT EVERYTHING?
GET HER OFF! SOMEONE GET HER OFF!
A KILLER VIRUS COCKTAIL, OF COURSE!
I CALL IT THE SPIRIT OF CHRISTMAS, AN' I COOKED IT UP SPECIAL, JUST FOR MR.BRADLEY BURR.
HELP ME! YOU'VE GOTTA HELP ME!
AND THIS VIRUS DOES WHAT, HARLEY?
KILLS YA. JUST LIKE THE BULLIES BRADLEY PAYS TO TRASH OUR HUMAN RIGHTS AND NIX OUR SOCIAL SAFETY NETS.
OH MY GOD. WE'RE GOING TO DIE. WE'RE GOING TO DIE.
I NEVER SHOULD'VE GONE TO WORK FOR SMELLICULE!
I SHOULD'VE GONE INTO THE PEACE CORPS!
CALM DOWN, EVERYONE! WE'RE NOT GOING TO DIE!
THERE'S AN ANTIDOTE, OR HARLEY WOULD BE WEARING A GAS MASK.
AND SHE WOULDN'T BE DOING THIS IF IT WEREN'T GOING TO BE FUN, RIGHT HARLEY?
FUN MEANS A GAME. A GAM
MEANS WE CAN STILL WIN.

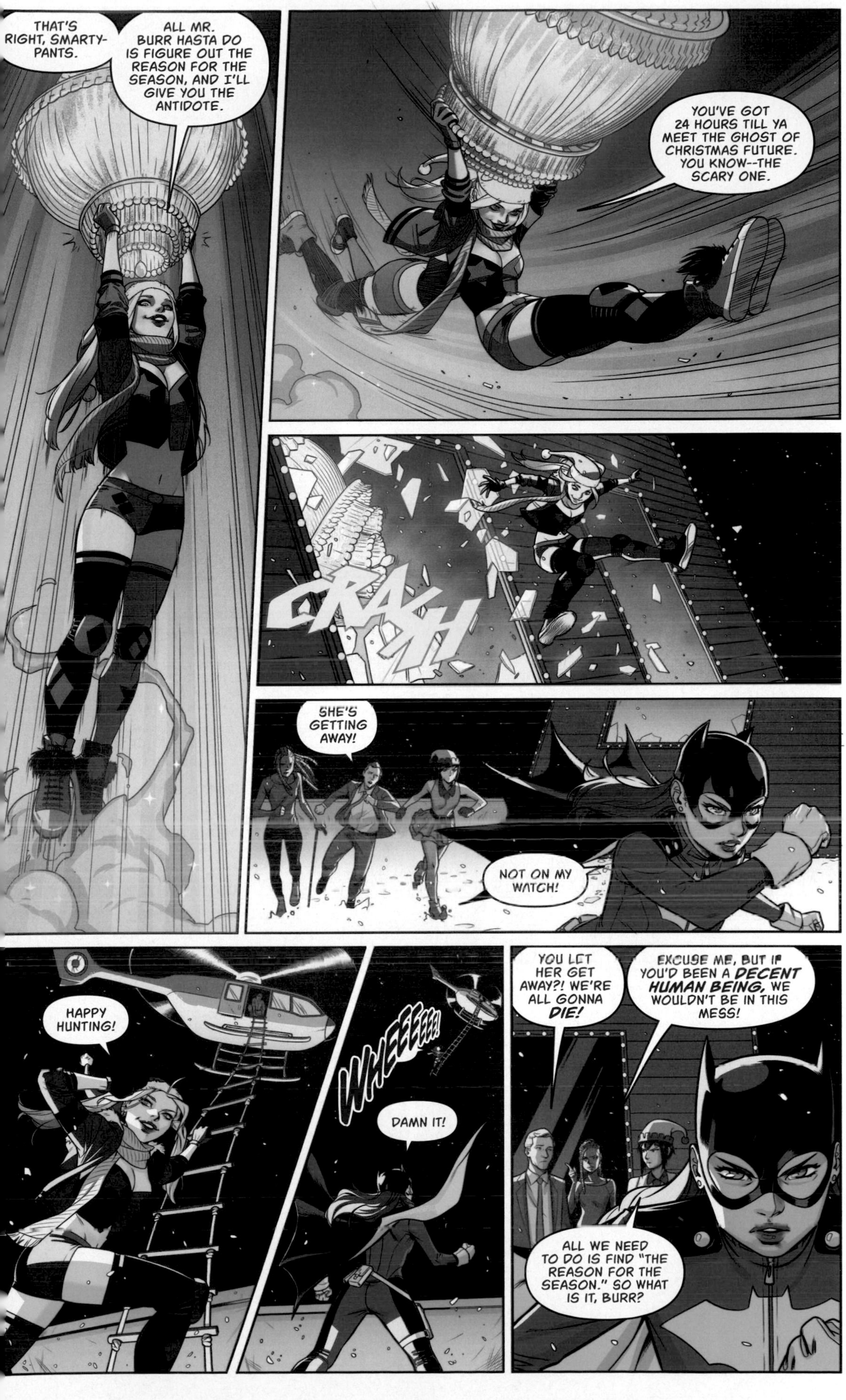
THAT'S RIGHT, SMARTY-PANTS.
ALL MR. BURR HASTA DO IS FIGURE OUT THE REASON FOR THE SEASON, AND I'LL GIVE YOU THE ANTIDOTE.
YOU'VE GOT 24 HOURS TILL YA MEET THE GHOST OF CHRISTMAS FUTURE. YOU KNOW--THE SCARY ONE.
CRASH
SHE'S GETTING AWAY!
NOT ON MY WATCH!
HAPPY HUNTING!
WHEEEEEE!
DAMN IT!
YOU LET HER GET AWAY?! WE'RE ALL GONNA DIE!
EXCUSE ME, BUT IF YOU'D BEEN A DECENT HUMAN BEING, WE WOULDN'T BE IN THIS MESS!
ALL WE NEED TO DO IS FIND "THE REASON FOR THE SEASON." SO WHAT IS IT, BURR?

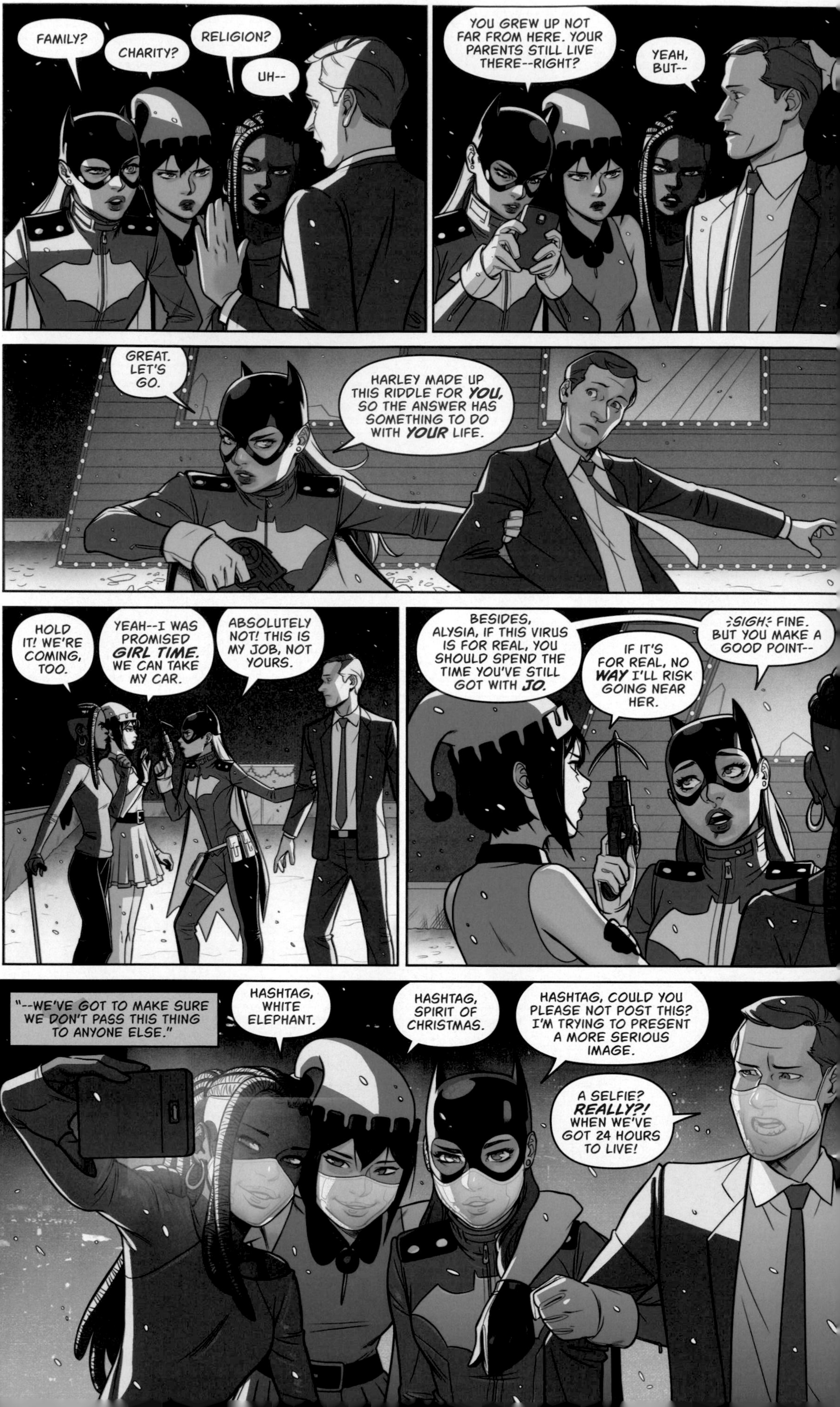

FAMILY?
CHARITY?
RELIGION?
UH--
YOU GREW UP NOT FAR FROM HERE. YOUR PARENTS STILL LIVE THERE--RIGHT?
YEAH, BUT--
GREAT. LET'S GO.
HARLEY MADE UP THIS RIDDLE FOR *YOU*, SO THE ANSWER HAS SOMETHING TO DO WITH *YOUR* LIFE.
HOLD IT! WE'RE COMING, TOO.
YEAH--I WAS PROMISED *GIRL TIME*. WE CAN TAKE MY CAR.
ABSOLUTELY NOT! THIS IS MY JOB, NOT YOURS.
BESIDES, ALYSIA, IF THIS VIRUS IS FOR REAL, YOU SHOULD SPEND THE TIME YOU'VE STILL GOT WITH *JO*.
IF IT'S FOR REAL, NO *WAY* I'LL RISK GOING NEAR HER.
SIGH FINE. BUT YOU MAKE A GOOD POINT--
"--WE'VE GOT TO MAKE SURE WE DON'T PASS THIS THING TO ANYONE ELSE."
HASHTAG, WHITE ELEPHANT.
HASHTAG, SPIRIT OF CHRISTMAS.
HASHTAG, COULD YOU PLEASE NOT POST THIS? I'M TRYING TO PRESENT A MORE SERIOUS IMAGE.
A SELFIE? *REALLY?!* WHEN WE'VE GOT 24 HOURS TO LIVE!

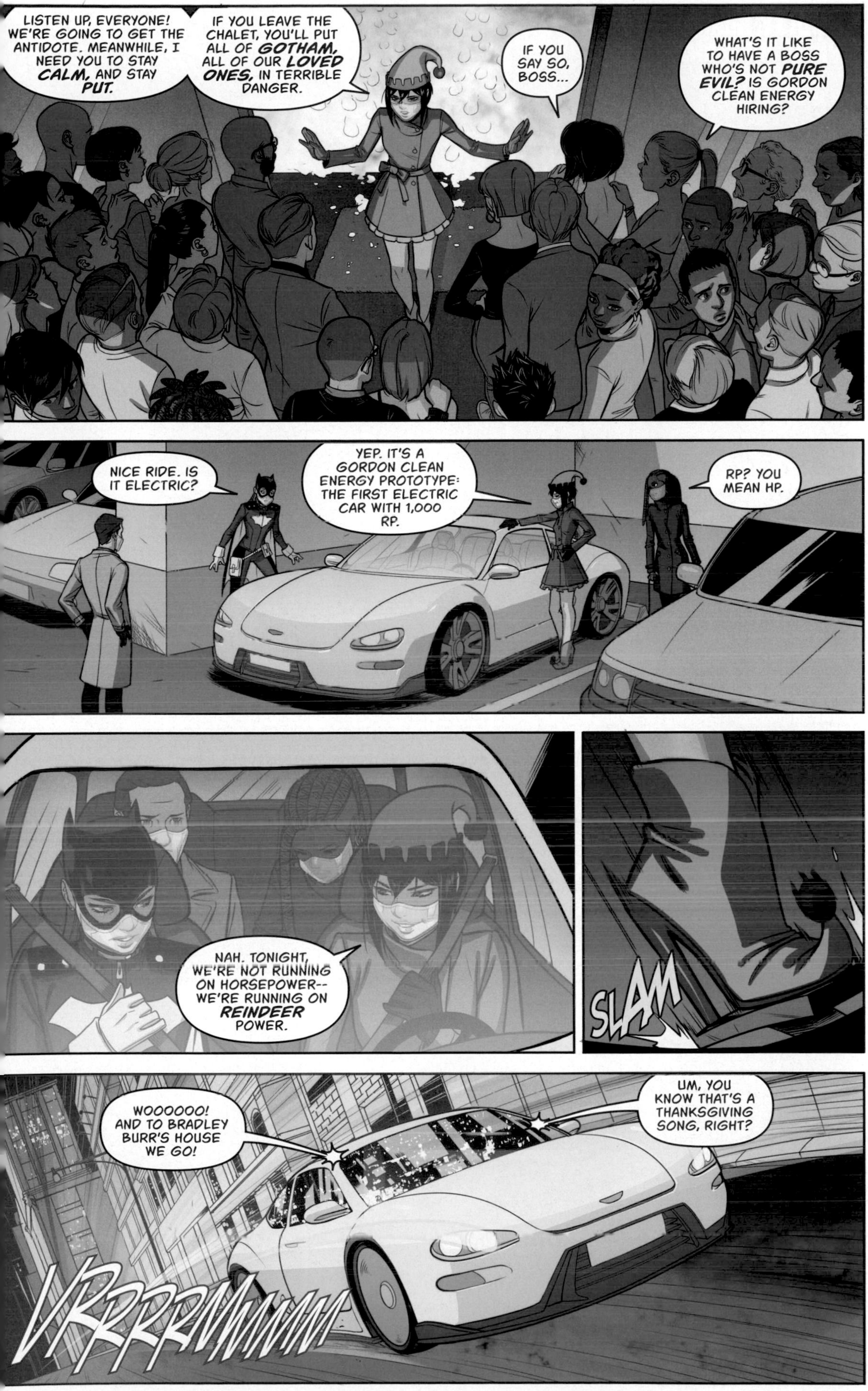
LISTEN UP, EVERYONE! WE'RE GOING TO GET THE ANTIDOTE. MEANWHILE, I NEED YOU TO STAY CALM, AND STAY PUT.
IF YOU LEAVE THE CHALET, YOU'LL PUT ALL OF GOTHAM, ALL OF OUR LOVED ONES, IN TERRIBLE DANGER.
IF YOU SAY SO, BOSS...
WHAT'S IT LIKE TO HAVE A BOSS WHO'S NOT PURE EVIL? IS GORDON CLEAN ENERGY HIRING?
NICE RIDE. IS IT ELECTRIC?
YEP. IT'S A GORDON CLEAN ENERGY PROTOTYPE: THE FIRST ELECTRIC CAR WITH 1,000 RP.
RP? YOU MEAN HP.
NAH. TONIGHT, WE'RE NOT RUNNING ON HORSEPOWER-- WE'RE RUNNING ON REINDEER POWER.
SLAM
WOOOOOO! AND TO BRADLEY BURR'S HOUSE WE GO!
UM, YOU KNOW THAT'S A THANKSGIVING SONG, RIGHT?
VRRRRMMMMM

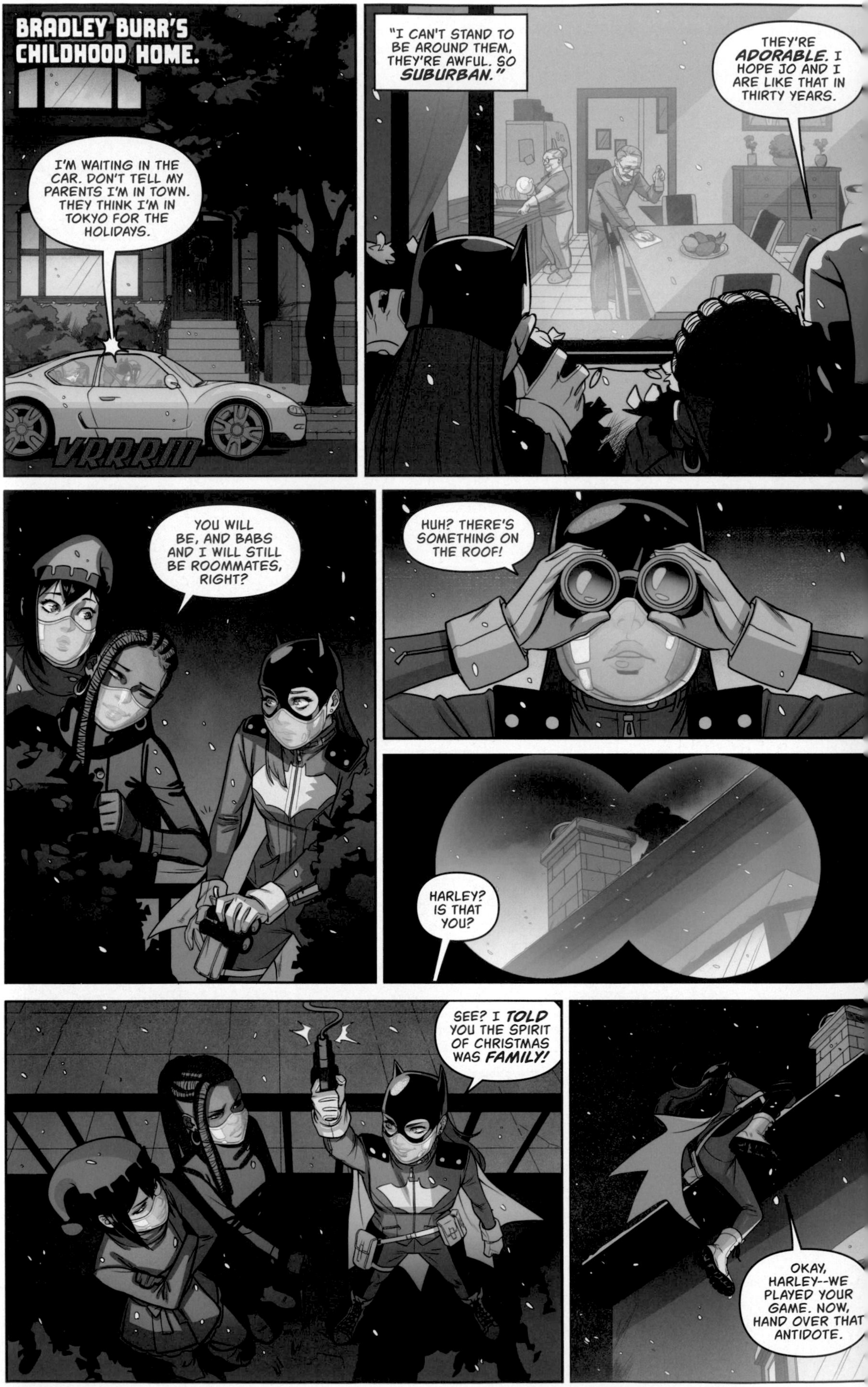
BRADLEY BURR'S CHILDHOOD HOME.
I'M WAITING IN THE CAR. DON'T TELL MY PARENTS I'M IN TOWN. THEY THINK I'M IN TOKYO FOR THE HOLIDAYS.
VRRRM
"I CAN'T STAND TO BE AROUND THEM, THEY'RE AWFUL. SO SUBURBAN."
THEY'RE ADORABLE. I HOPE JO AND I ARE LIKE THAT IN THIRTY YEARS.
YOU WILL BE, AND BABS AND I WILL STILL BE ROOMMATES, RIGHT?
HUH? THERE'S SOMETHING ON THE ROOF!
HARLEY? IS THAT YOU?
SEE? I TOLD YOU THE SPIRIT OF CHRISTMAS WAS FAMILY!
OKAY, HARLEY--WE PLAYED YOUR GAME. NOW, HAND OVER THAT ANTIDOTE.

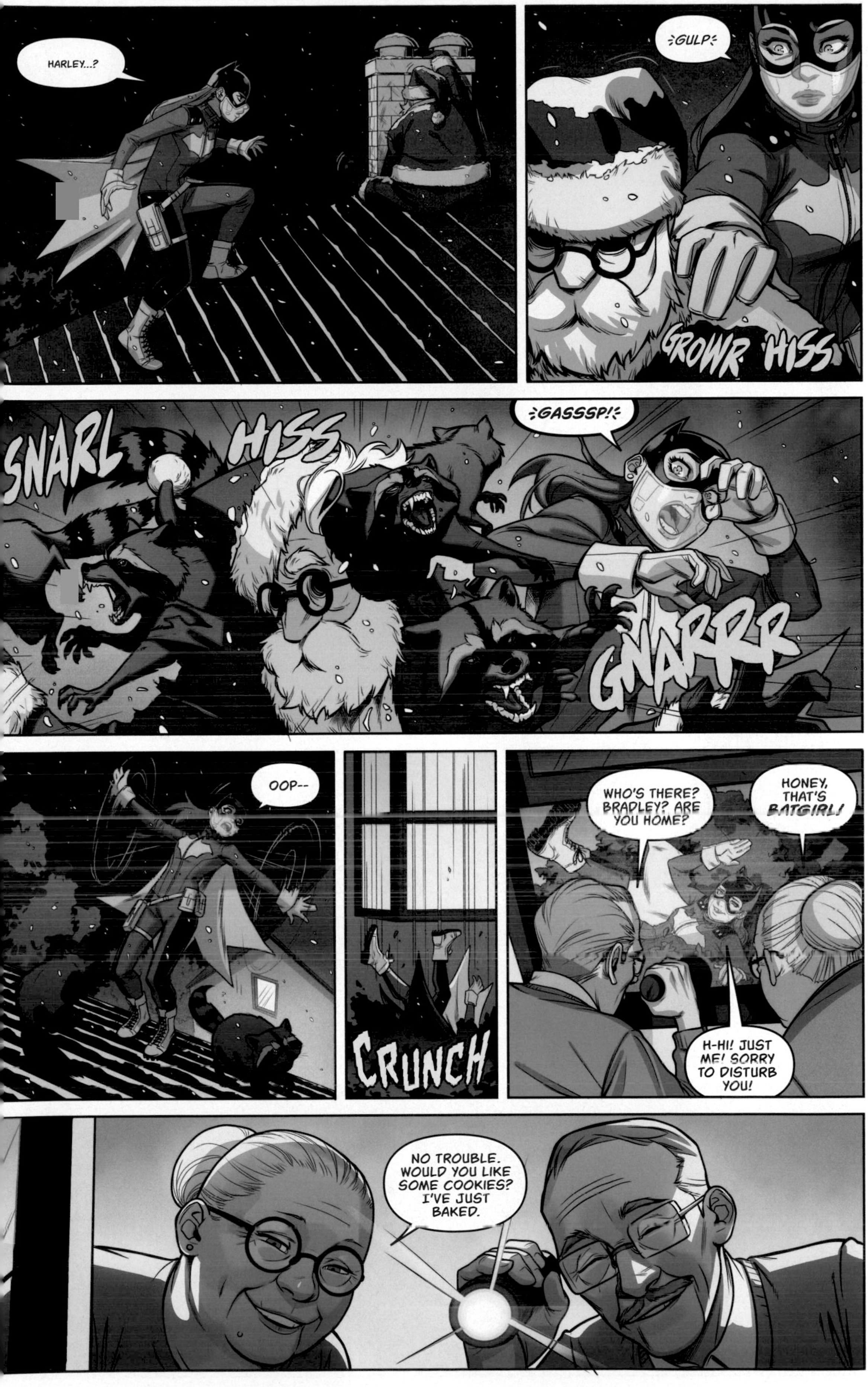
HARLEY...?
GULP
GROWR HISS
SNARL
HISS
GASSSP!
GNARRR
OOP--
CRUNCH
WHO'S THERE? BRADLEY? ARE YOU HOME?
HONEY, THAT'S BATGIRL!
H-HI! JUST ME! SORRY TO DISTURB YOU!
NO TROUBLE. WOULD YOU LIKE SOME COOKIES? I'VE JUST BAKED.

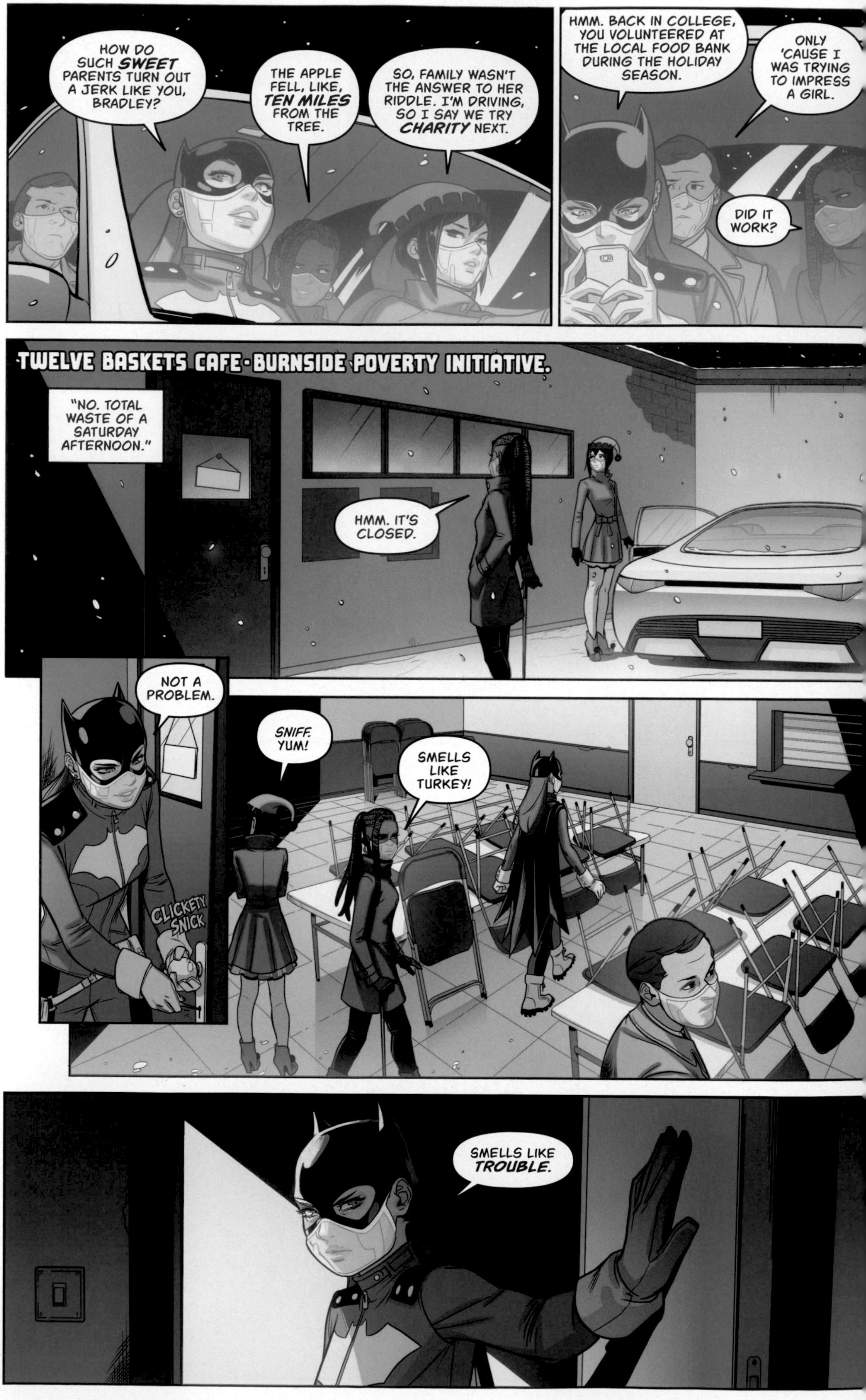
HOW DO SUCH SWEET PARENTS TURN OUT A JERK LIKE YOU, BRADLEY?
THE APPLE FELL, LIKE, TEN MILES FROM THE TREE.
SO, FAMILY WASN'T THE ANSWER TO HER RIDDLE. I'M DRIVING, SO I SAY WE TRY CHARITY NEXT.
HMM. BACK IN COLLEGE, YOU VOLUNTEERED AT THE LOCAL FOOD BANK DURING THE HOLIDAY SEASON.
ONLY 'CAUSE I WAS TRYING TO IMPRESS A GIRL.
DID IT WORK?
TWELVE BASKETS CAFE - BURNSIDE POVERTY INITIATIVE.
"NO. TOTAL WASTE OF A SATURDAY AFTERNOON."
HMM. IT'S CLOSED.
NOT A PROBLEM.
CLICKETY SNICK
SNIFF. YUM!
SMELLS LIKE TURKEY!
SMELLS LIKE TROUBLE.

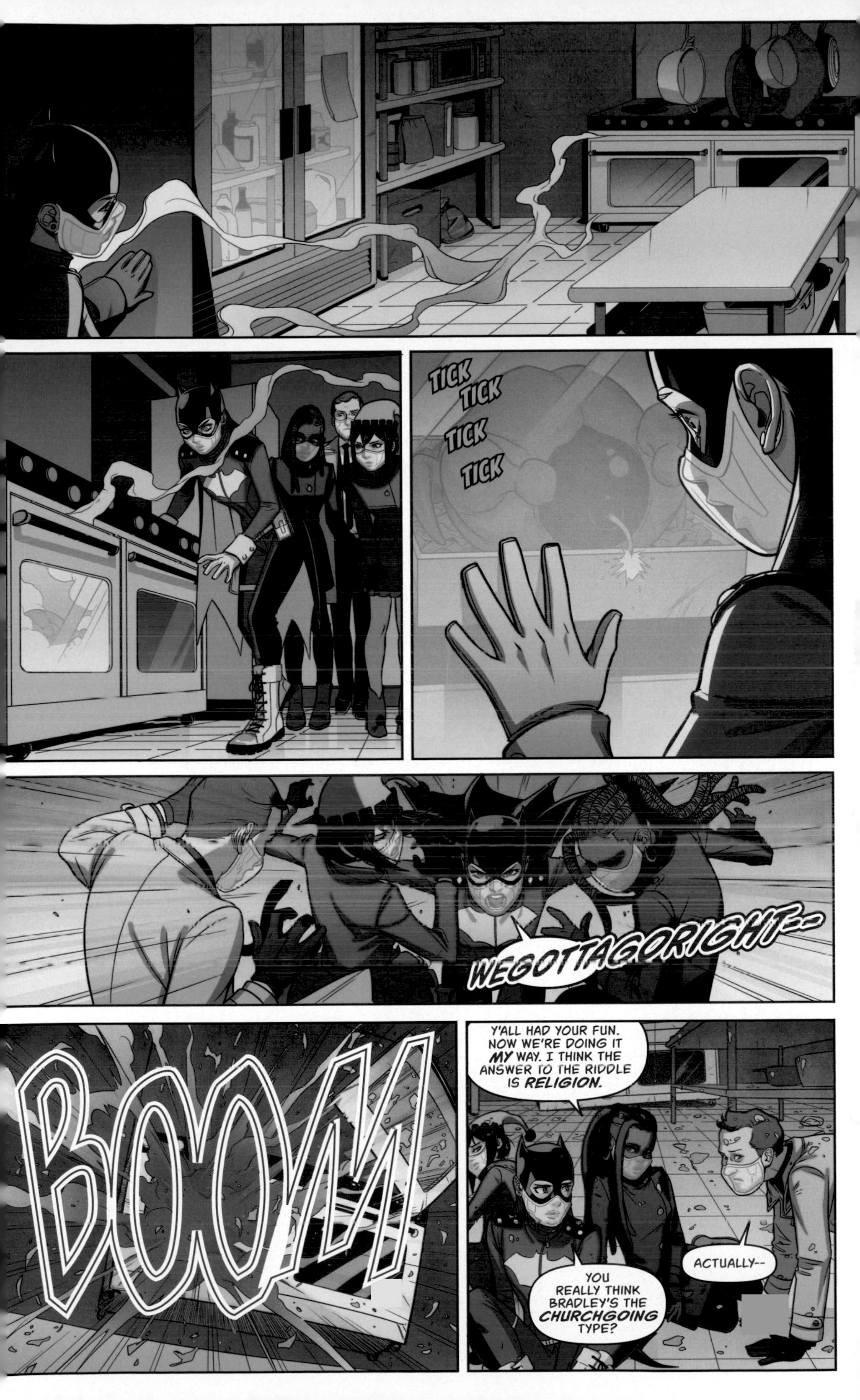
TICK
TICK
TICK
TICK
WEGOTTAGORIGHT--
BOOM
Y'ALL HAD YOUR FUN. NOW WE'RE DOING IT MY WAY. I THINK THE ANSWER TO THE RIDDLE IS RELIGION.
YOU REALLY THINK BRADLEY'S THE CHURCHGOING TYPE?
ACTUALLY--

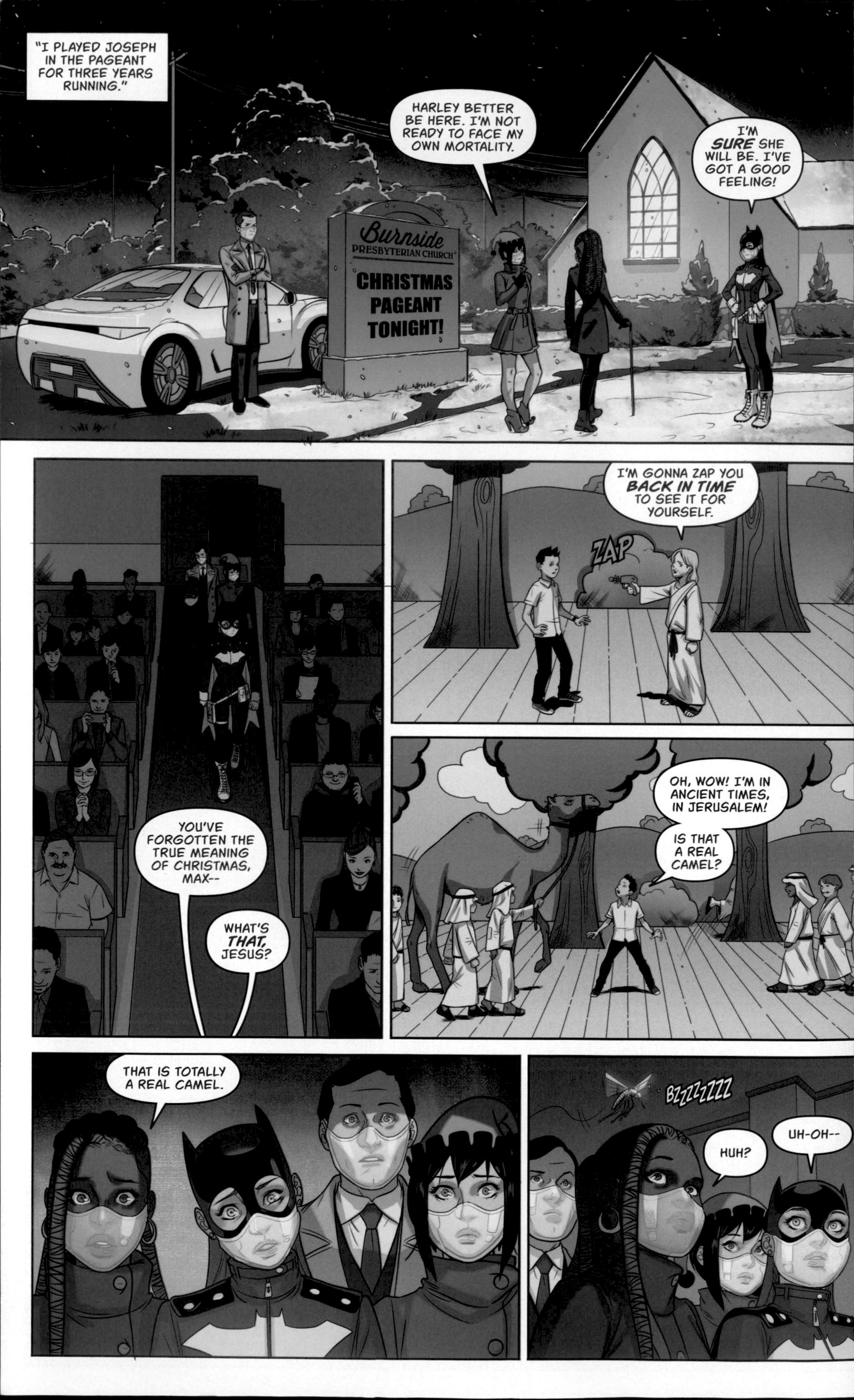
"I PLAYED JOSEPH IN THE PAGEANT FOR THREE YEARS RUNNING."
HARLEY BETTER BE HERE. I'M NOT READY TO FACE MY OWN MORTALITY.
I'M SURE SHE WILL BE. I'VE GOT A GOOD FEELING!
Burnside PRESBYTERIAN CHURCH
CHRISTMAS PAGEANT TONIGHT!
YOU'VE FORGOTTEN THE TRUE MEANING OF CHRISTMAS, MAX--
WHAT'S THAT, JESUS?
I'M GONNA ZAP YOU BACK IN TIME TO SEE IT FOR YOURSELF.
ZAP
OH, WOW! I'M IN ANCIENT TIMES, IN JERUSALEM!
IS THAT A REAL CAMEL?
THAT IS TOTALLY A REAL CAMEL.
BZZZZZZZ
HUH?
UH-OH--

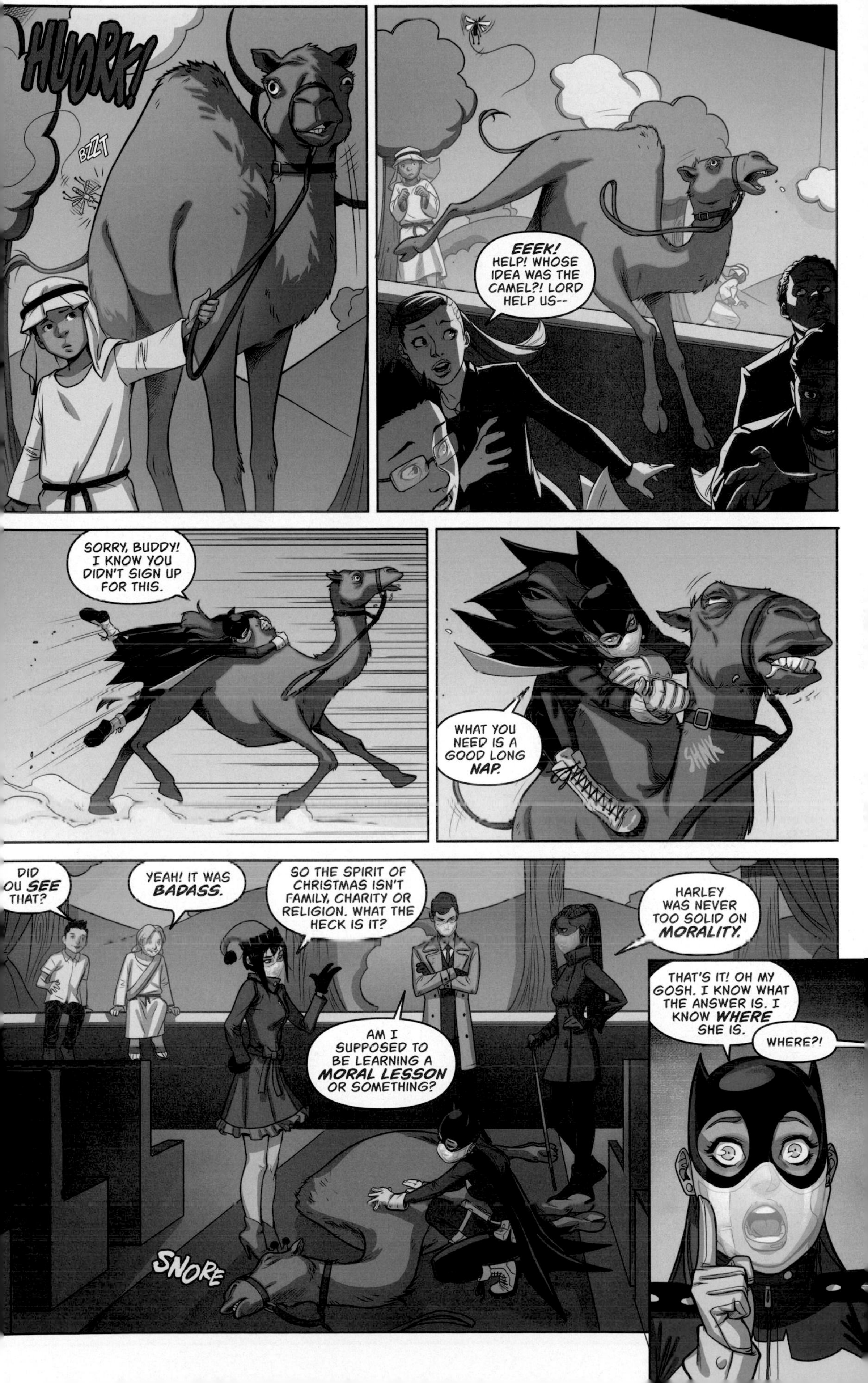
HUORK!
BZZT
EEEK! HELP! WHOSE IDEA WAS THE CAMEL?! LORD HELP US--
SORRY, BUDDY! I KNOW YOU DIDN'T SIGN UP FOR THIS.
WHAT YOU NEED IS A GOOD LONG NAP.
SHNK
DID OU SEE THAT?
YEAH! IT WAS BADASS.
SO THE SPIRIT OF CHRISTMAS ISN'T FAMILY, CHARITY OR RELIGION. WHAT THE HECK IS IT?
AM I SUPPOSED TO BE LEARNING A MORAL LESSON OR SOMETHING?
HARLEY WAS NEVER TOO SOLID ON MORALITY.
THAT'S IT! OH MY GOSH. I KNOW WHAT THE ANSWER IS. I KNOW WHERE SHE IS.
WHERE?!
SNORE

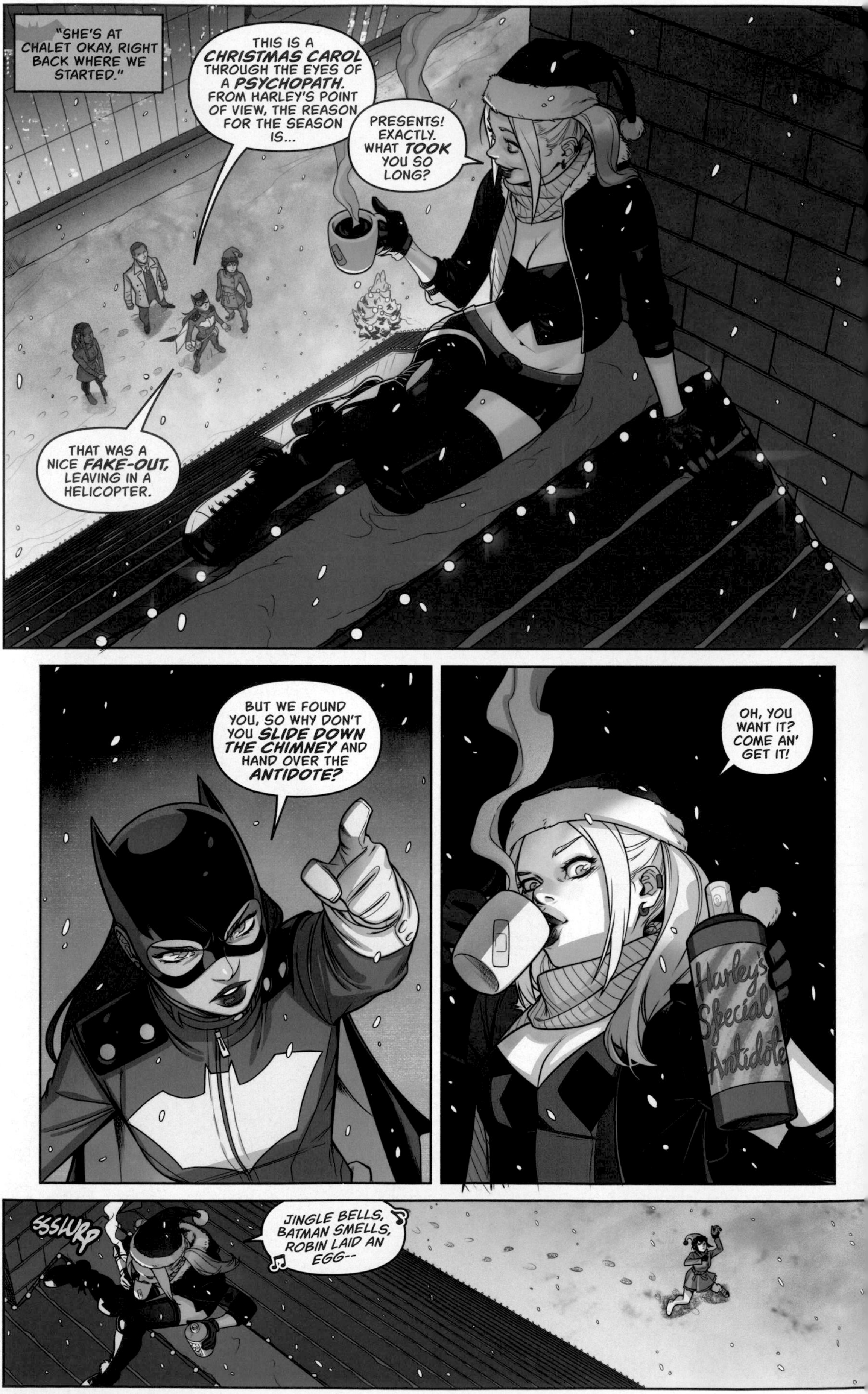
"SHE'S AT CHALET OKAY, RIGHT BACK WHERE WE STARTED."
THIS IS A CHRISTMAS CAROL THROUGH THE EYES OF A PSYCHOPATH. FROM HARLEY'S POINT OF VIEW, THE REASON FOR THE SEASON IS...
PRESENTS! EXACTLY. WHAT TOOK YOU SO LONG?
THAT WAS A NICE FAKE-OUT, LEAVING IN A HELICOPTER.
BUT WE FOUND YOU, SO WHY DON'T YOU SLIDE DOWN THE CHIMNEY AND HAND OVER THE ANTIDOTE?
OH, YOU WANT IT? COME AN' GET IT!
Harley's Special Antidote
SSSLURP
JINGLE BELLS, BATMAN SMELLS, ROBIN LAID AN EGG--

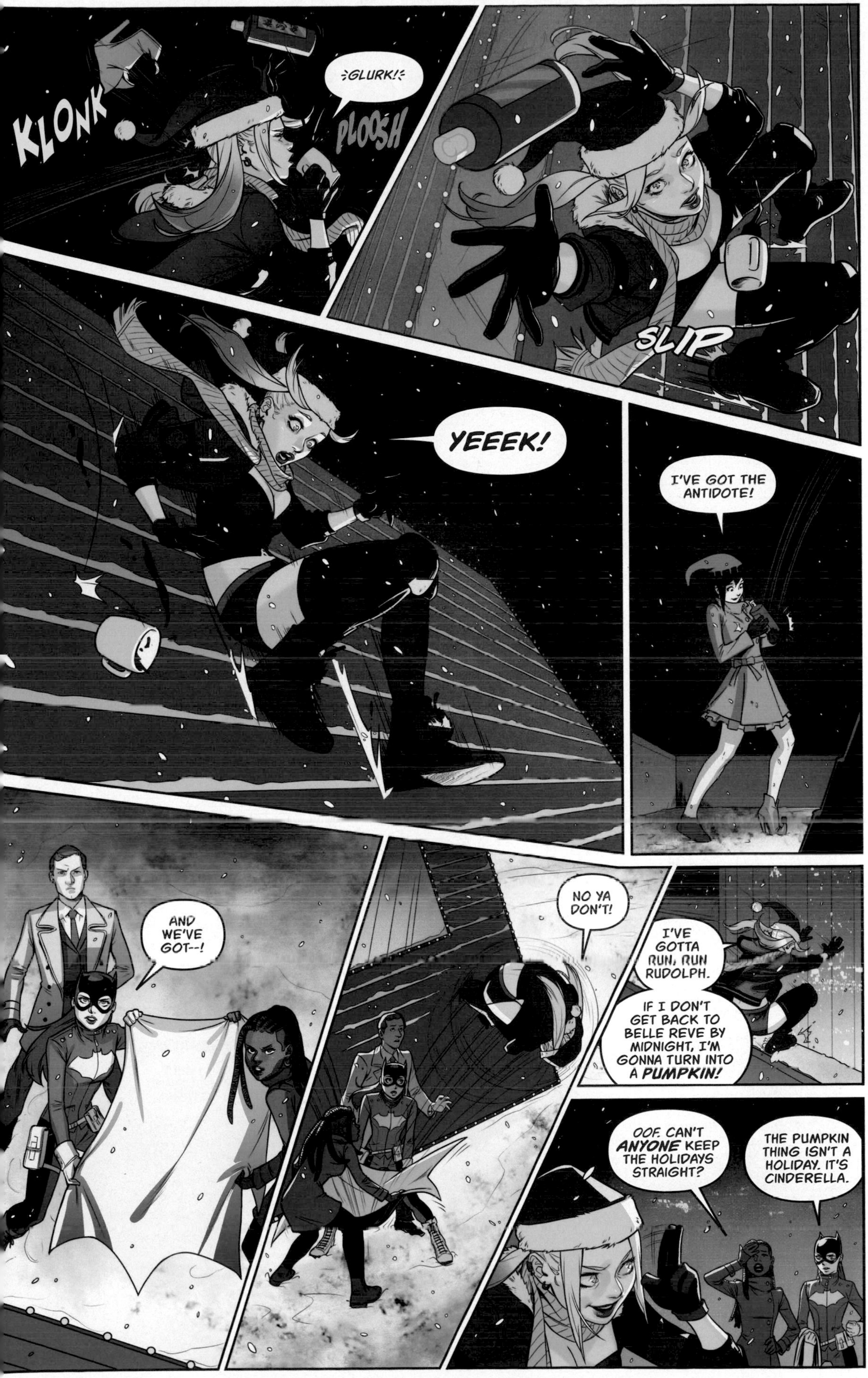
KLONK
GLURK!
PLOOSH
SLIP
YEEEK!
I'VE GOT THE ANTIDOTE!
AND WE'VE GOT--!
NO YA DON'T!
I'VE GOTTA RUN, RUN RUDOLPH.
IF I DON'T GET BACK TO BELLE REVE BY MIDNIGHT, I'M GONNA TURN INTO A PUMPKIN!
OOF. CAN'T ANYONE KEEP THE HOLIDAYS STRAIGHT?
THE PUMPKIN THING ISN'T A HOLIDAY. IT'S CINDERELLA.

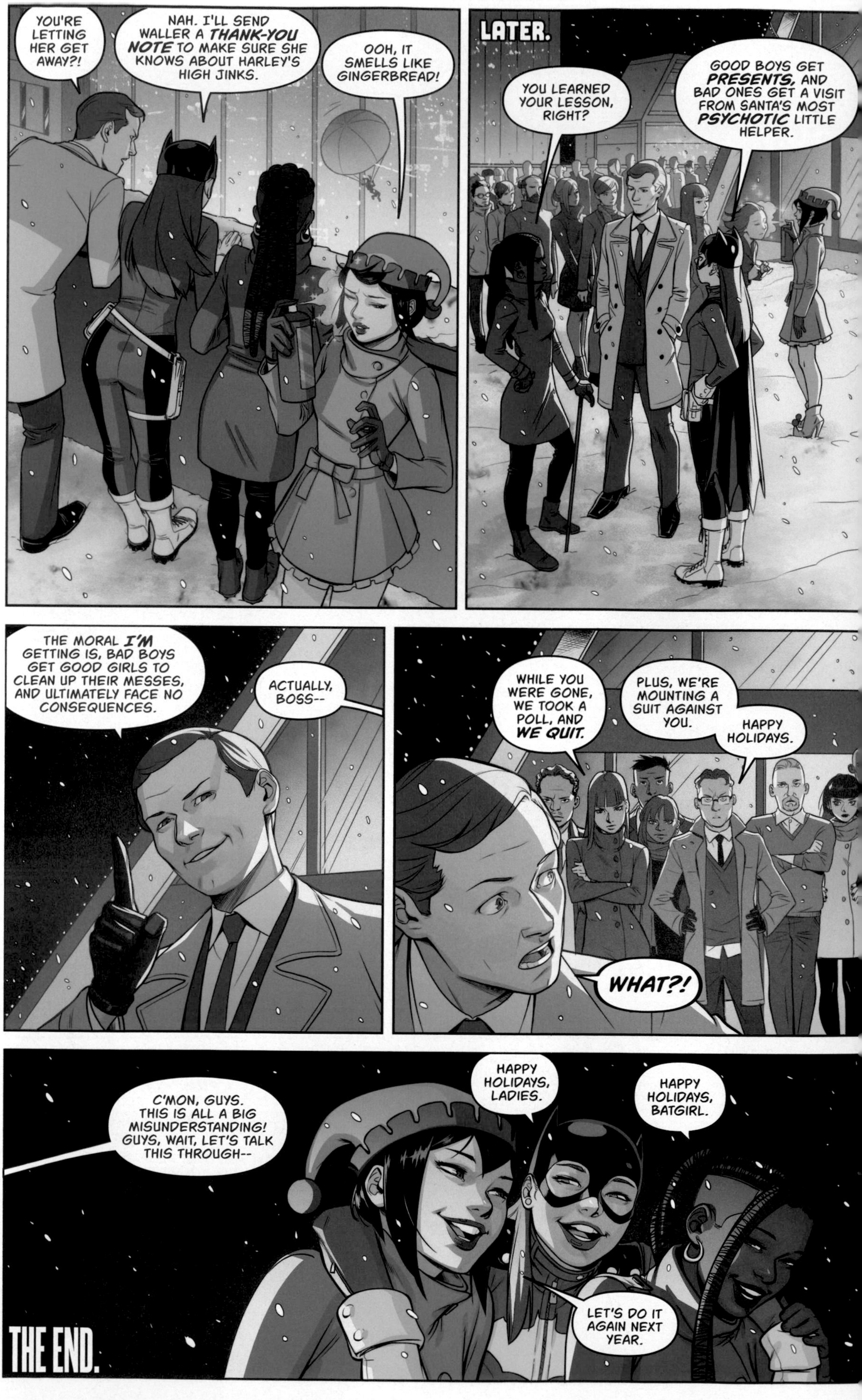
YOU'RE LETTING HER GET AWAY?!
NAH. I'LL SEND WALLER A THANK-YOU NOTE TO MAKE SURE SHE KNOWS ABOUT HARLEY'S HIGH JINKS.
OOH, IT SMELLS LIKE GINGERBREAD!
LATER.
YOU LEARNED YOUR LESSON, RIGHT?
GOOD BOYS GET PRESENTS, AND BAD ONES GET A VISIT FROM SANTA'S MOST PSYCHOTIC LITTLE HELPER.
THE MORAL I'M GETTING IS, BAD BOYS GET GOOD GIRLS TO CLEAN UP THEIR MESSES, AND ULTIMATELY FACE NO CONSEQUENCES.
ACTUALLY, BOSS--
WHILE YOU WERE GONE, WE TOOK A POLL, AND WE QUIT.
PLUS, WE'RE MOUNTING A SUIT AGAINST YOU.
HAPPY HOLIDAYS.
WHAT?!
C'MON, GUYS. THIS IS ALL A BIG MISUNDERSTANDING! GUYS, WAIT, LET'S TALK THIS THROUGH--
HAPPY HOLIDAYS, LADIES.
HAPPY HOLIDAYS, BATGIRL.
LET'S DO IT AGAIN NEXT YEAR.
THE END.

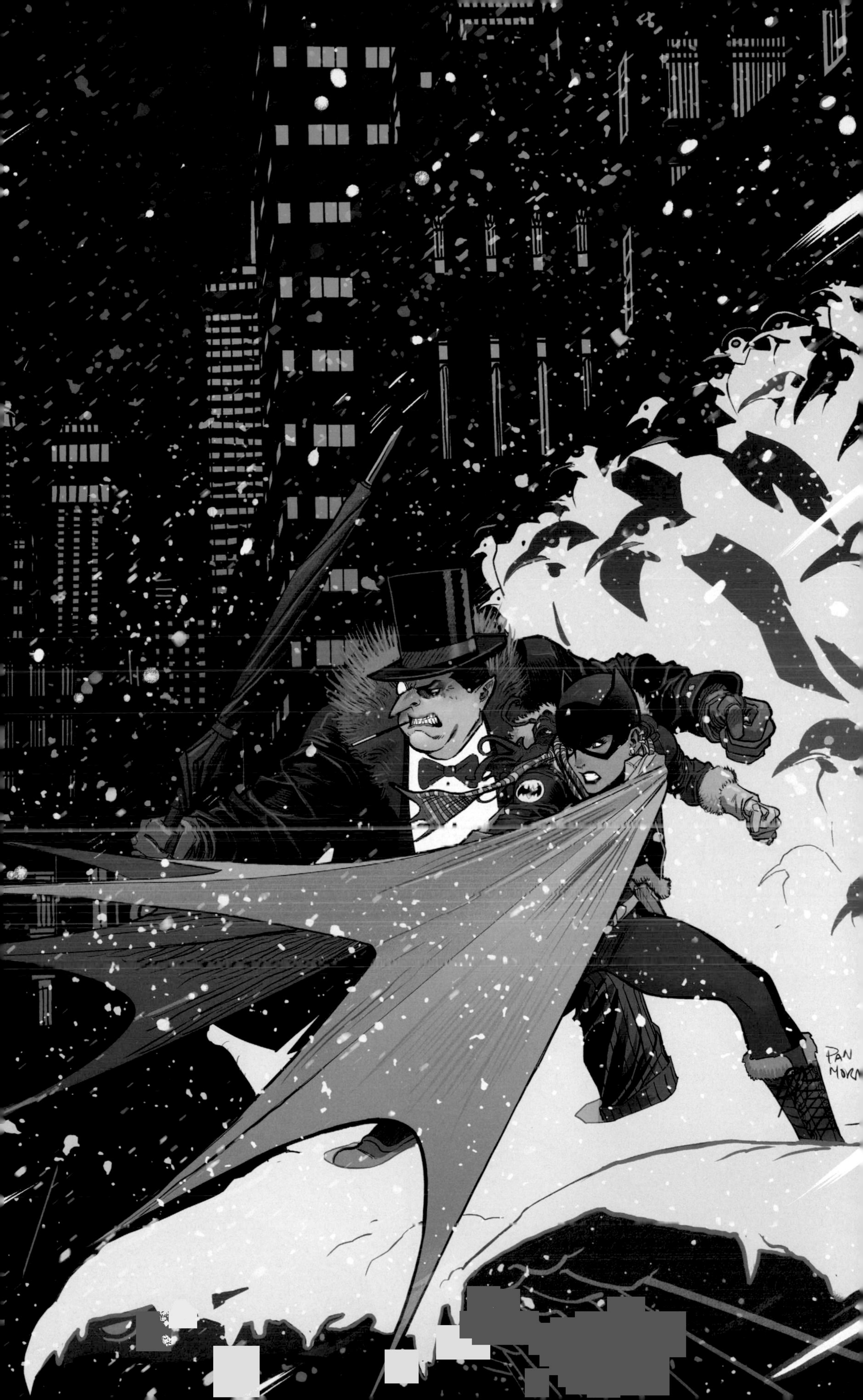

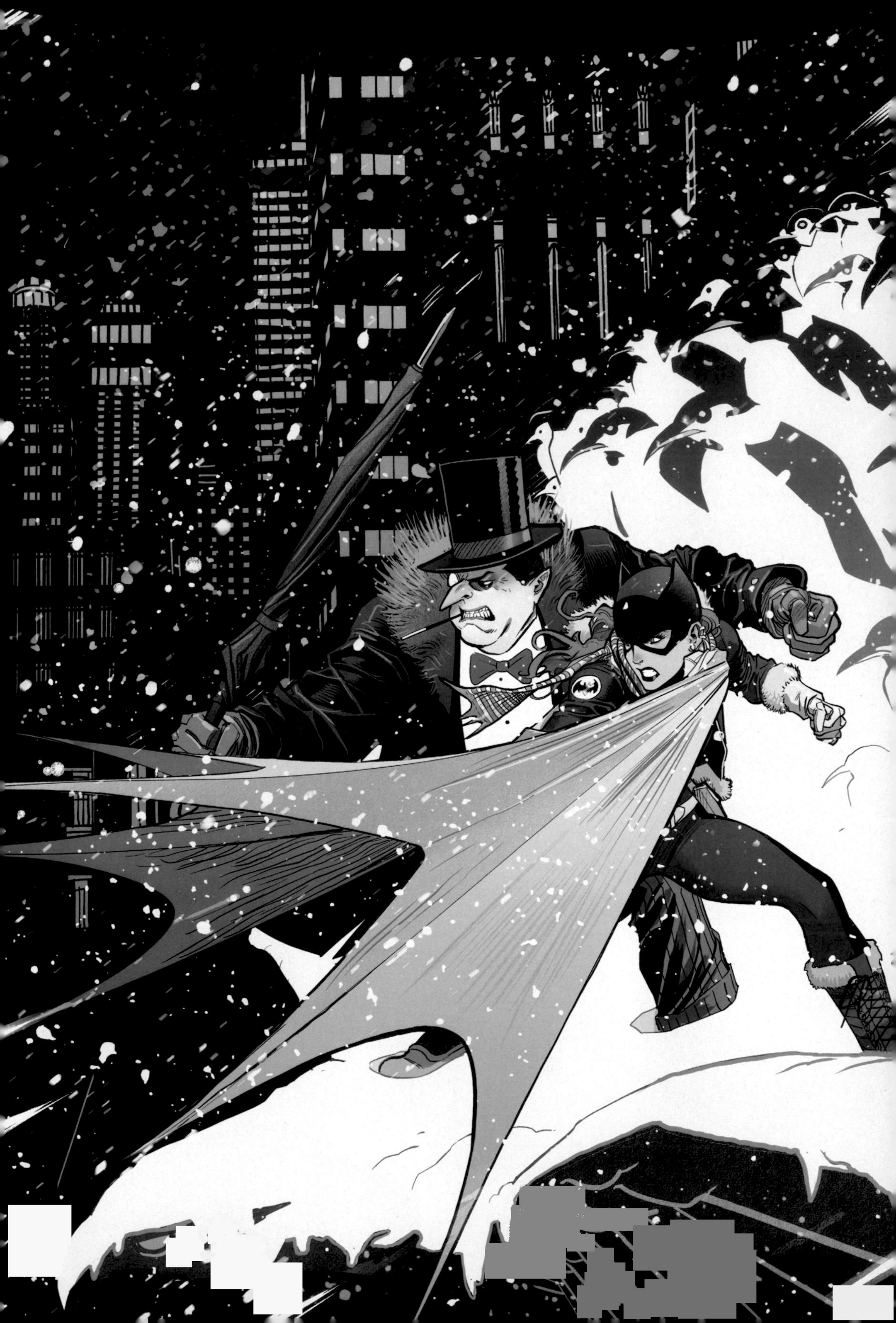

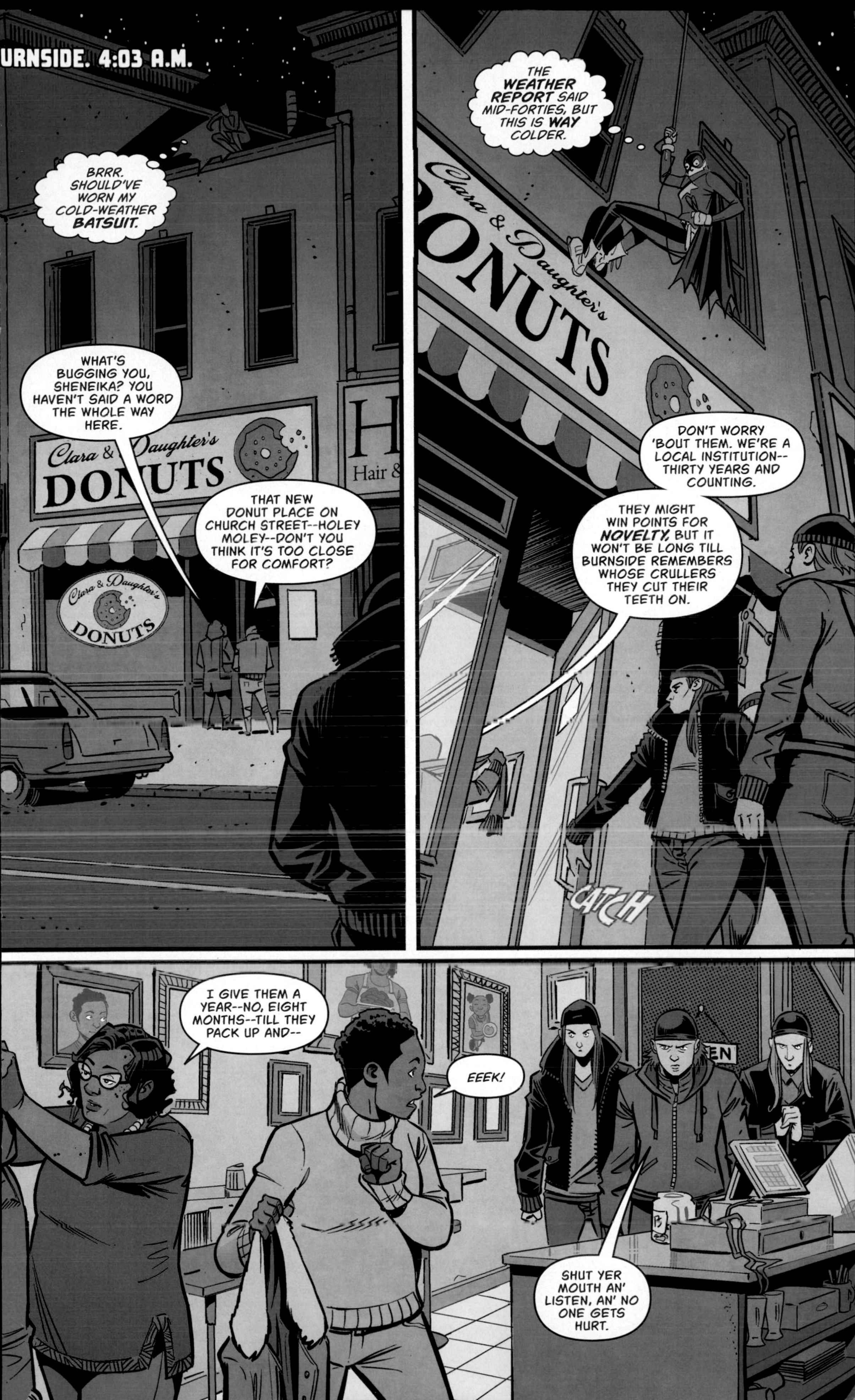
URNSIDE. 4:03 A.M.
BRRR. SHOULD'VE WORN MY COLD-WEATHER BATSUIT.
Clara & Daughter's DONUTS
Hair &
Clara & Daughter's DONUTS
WHAT'S BUGGING YOU, SHENEIKA? YOU HAVEN'T SAID A WORD THE WHOLE WAY HERE.
THAT NEW DONUT PLACE ON CHURCH STREET--HOLEY MOLEY--DON'T YOU THINK IT'S TOO CLOSE FOR COMFORT?
THE WEATHER REPORT SAID MID-FORTIES, BUT THIS IS WAY COLDER.
Clara & Daughter's DONUTS
DON'T WORRY 'BOUT THEM. WE'RE A LOCAL INSTITUTION--THIRTY YEARS AND COUNTING.
THEY MIGHT WIN POINTS FOR NOVELTY, BUT IT WON'T BE LONG TILL BURNSIDE REMEMBERS WHOSE CRULLERS THEY CUT THEIR TEETH ON.
CATCH
I GIVE THEM A YEAR--NO, EIGHT MONTHS--TILL THEY PACK UP AND--
EEEK!
SHUT YER MOUTH AN' LISTEN, AN' NO ONE GETS HURT.

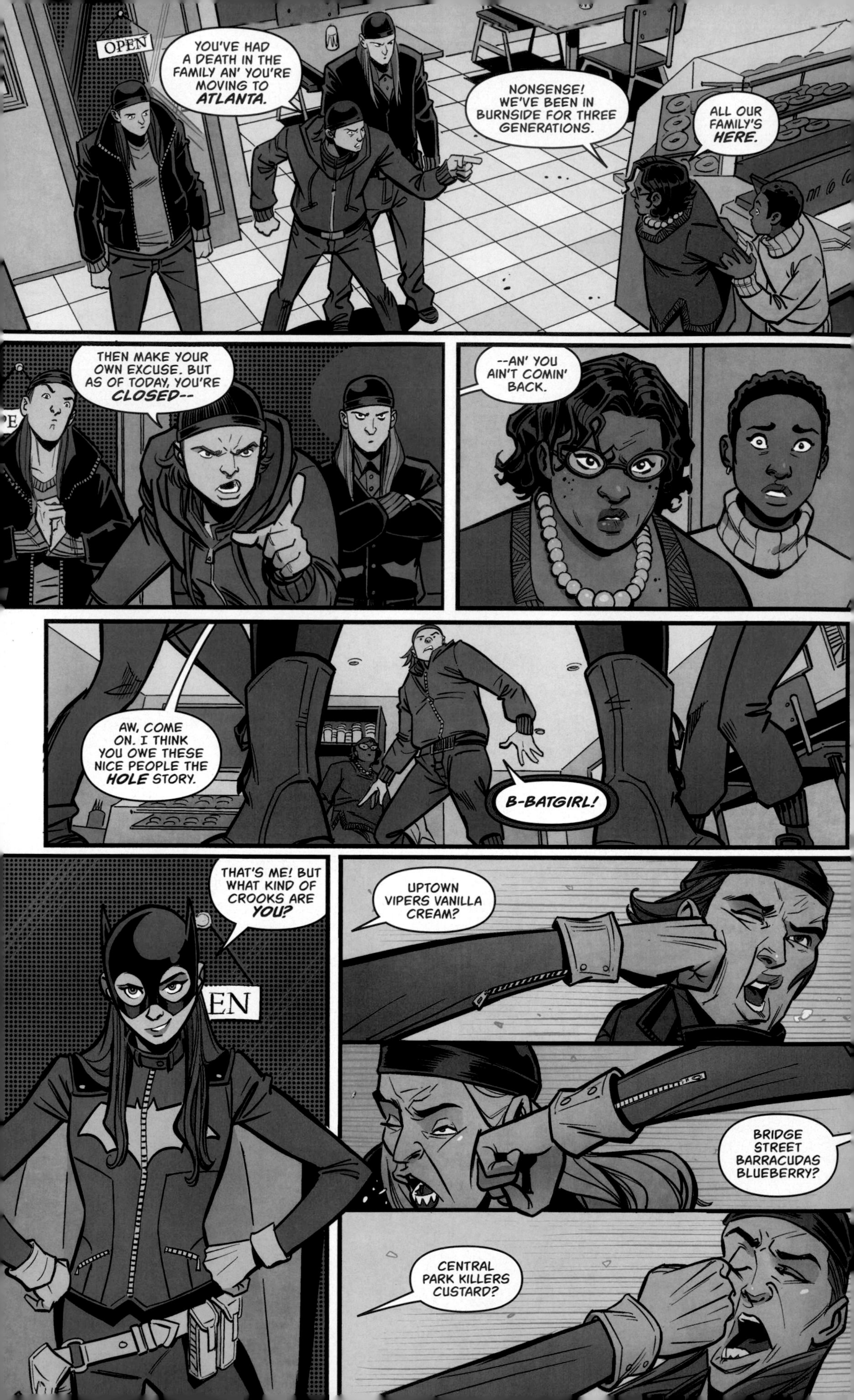
OPEN
YOU'VE HAD A DEATH IN THE FAMILY AN' YOU'RE MOVING TO ATLANTA.
NONSENSE! WE'VE BEEN IN BURNSIDE FOR THREE GENERATIONS.
ALL OUR FAMILY'S HERE.
THEN MAKE YOUR OWN EXCUSE. BUT AS OF TODAY, YOU'RE CLOSED--
--AN' YOU AIN'T COMIN' BACK.
AW, COME ON. I THINK YOU OWE THESE NICE PEOPLE THE HOLE STORY.
B-BATGIRL!
THAT'S ME! BUT WHAT KIND OF CROOKS ARE YOU?
EN
UPTOWN VIPERS VANILLA CREAM?
BRIDGE STREET BARRACUDAS BLUEBERRY?
CENTRAL PARK KILLERS CUSTARD?

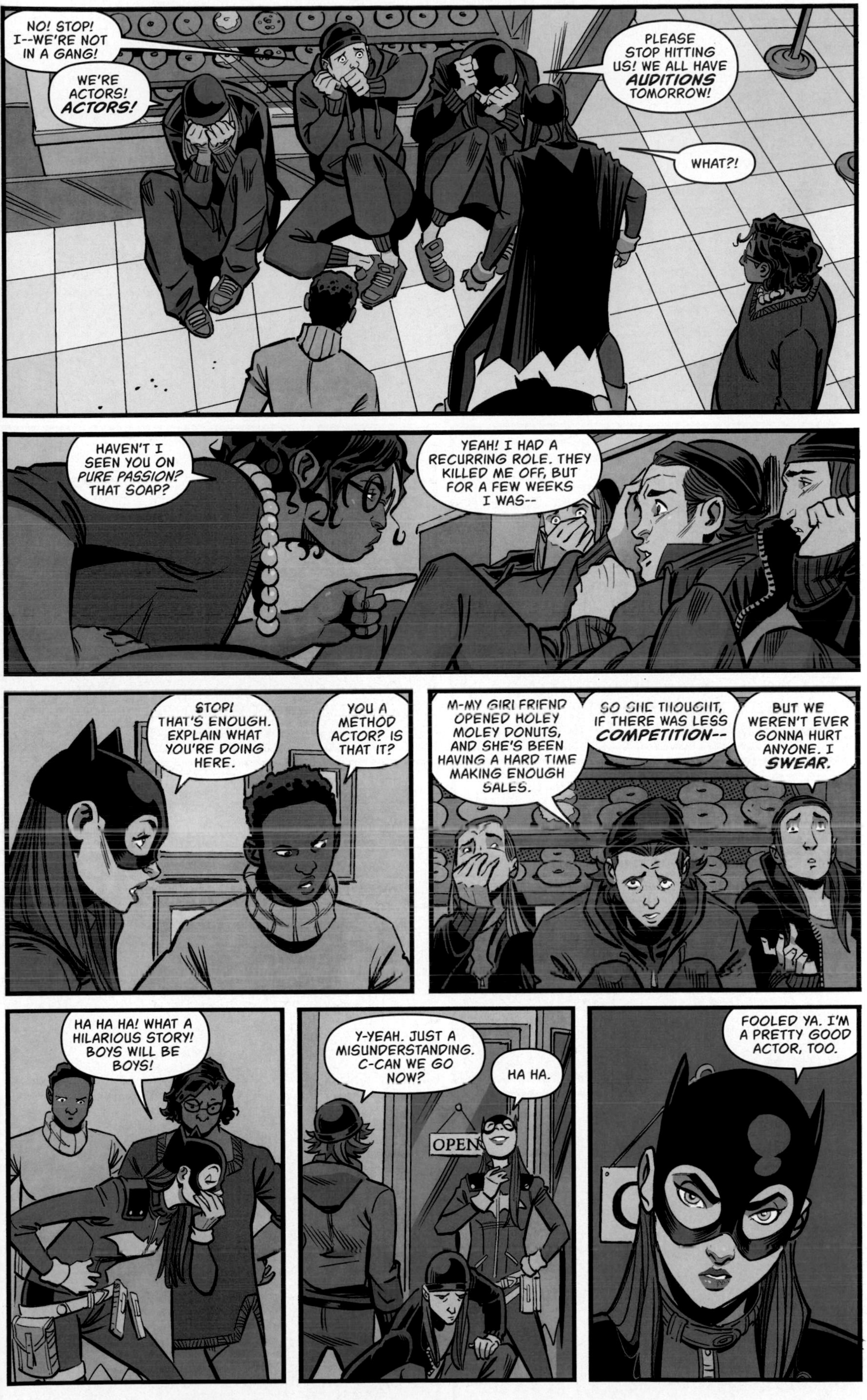
NO! STOP! I--WE'RE NOT IN A GANG!
WE'RE ACTORS! ACTORS!
PLEASE STOP HITTING US! WE ALL HAVE AUDITIONS TOMORROW!
WHAT?!
HAVEN'T I SEEN YOU ON PURE PASSION? THAT SOAP?
YEAH! I HAD A RECURRING ROLE. THEY KILLED ME OFF, BUT FOR A FEW WEEKS I WAS--
STOP! THAT'S ENOUGH. EXPLAIN WHAT YOU'RE DOING HERE.
YOU A METHOD ACTOR? IS THAT IT?
M-MY GIRLFRIEND OPENED HOLEY MOLEY DONUTS, AND SHE'S BEEN HAVING A HARD TIME MAKING ENOUGH SALES.
SO SHE THOUGHT, IF THERE WAS LESS COMPETITION--
BUT WE WEREN'T EVER GONNA HURT ANYONE. I SWEAR.
HA HA HA! WHAT A HILARIOUS STORY! BOYS WILL BE BOYS!
Y-YEAH. JUST A MISUNDERSTANDING. C-CAN WE GO NOW?
HA HA.
OPEN
FOOLED YA. I'M A PRETTY GOOD ACTOR, TOO.

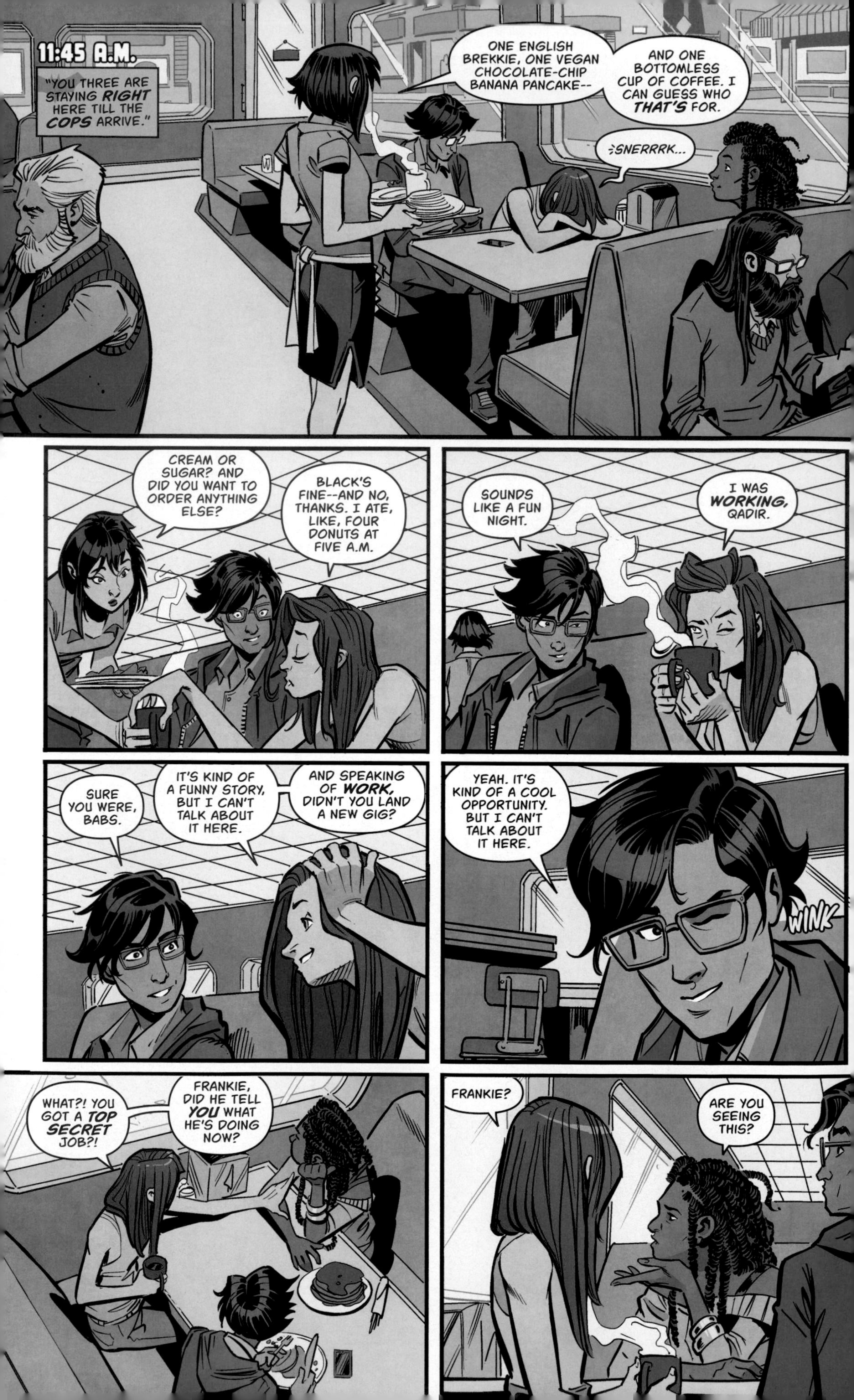

11:45 A.M.
"YOU THREE ARE STAYING RIGHT HERE TILL THE COPS ARRIVE."
ONE ENGLISH BREKKIE, ONE VEGAN CHOCOLATE-CHIP BANANA PANCAKE--
AND ONE BOTTOMLESS CUP OF COFFEE. I CAN GUESS WHO THAT'S FOR.
SNERRRK...
CREAM OR SUGAR? AND DID YOU WANT TO ORDER ANYTHING ELSE?
BLACK'S FINE--AND NO, THANKS. I ATE, LIKE, FOUR DONUTS AT FIVE A.M.
SOUNDS LIKE A FUN NIGHT.
I WAS WORKING, QADIR.
SURE YOU WERE, BABS.
IT'S KIND OF A FUNNY STORY, BUT I CAN'T TALK ABOUT IT HERE.
AND SPEAKING OF WORK, DIDN'T YOU LAND A NEW GIG?
YEAH. IT'S KIND OF A COOL OPPORTUNITY. BUT I CAN'T TALK ABOUT IT HERE.
WINK
WHAT?! YOU GOT A TOP SECRET JOB?!
FRANKIE, DID HE TELL YOU WHAT HE'S DOING NOW?
FRANKIE?
ARE YOU SEEING THIS?

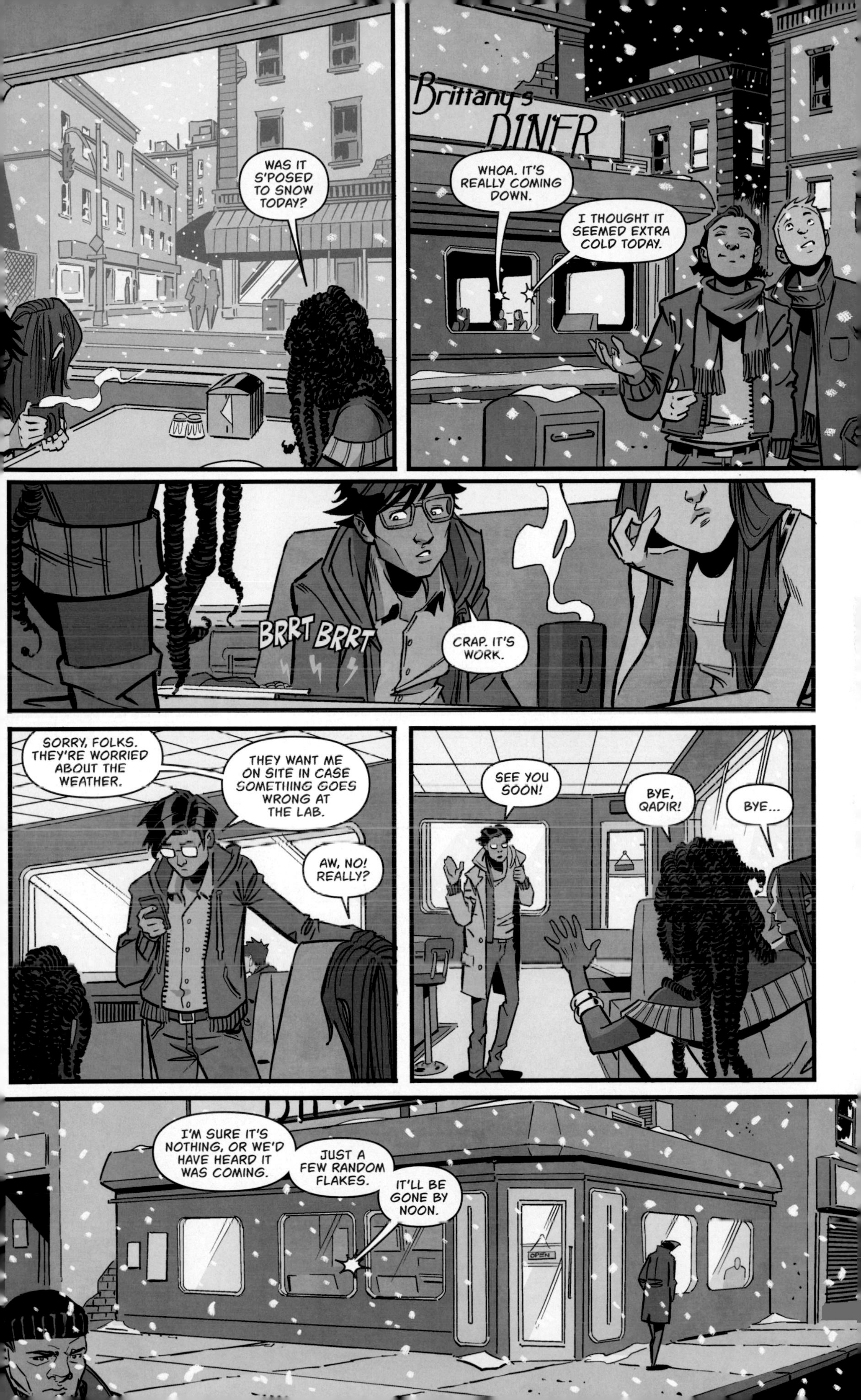
WAS IT S'POSED TO SNOW TODAY?
Brittany's DINER
WHOA. IT'S REALLY COMING DOWN.
I THOUGHT IT SEEMED EXTRA COLD TODAY.
BRRT BRRT
CRAP. IT'S WORK.
SORRY, FOLKS. THEY'RE WORRIED ABOUT THE WEATHER.
THEY WANT ME ON SITE IN CASE SOMETHING GOES WRONG AT THE LAB.
AW, NO! REALLY?
SEE YOU SOON!
BYE, QADIR!
BYE...
I'M SURE IT'S NOTHING, OR WE'D HAVE HEARD IT WAS COMING.
JUST A FEW RANDOM FLAKES.
IT'LL BE GONE BY NOON.
OPEN

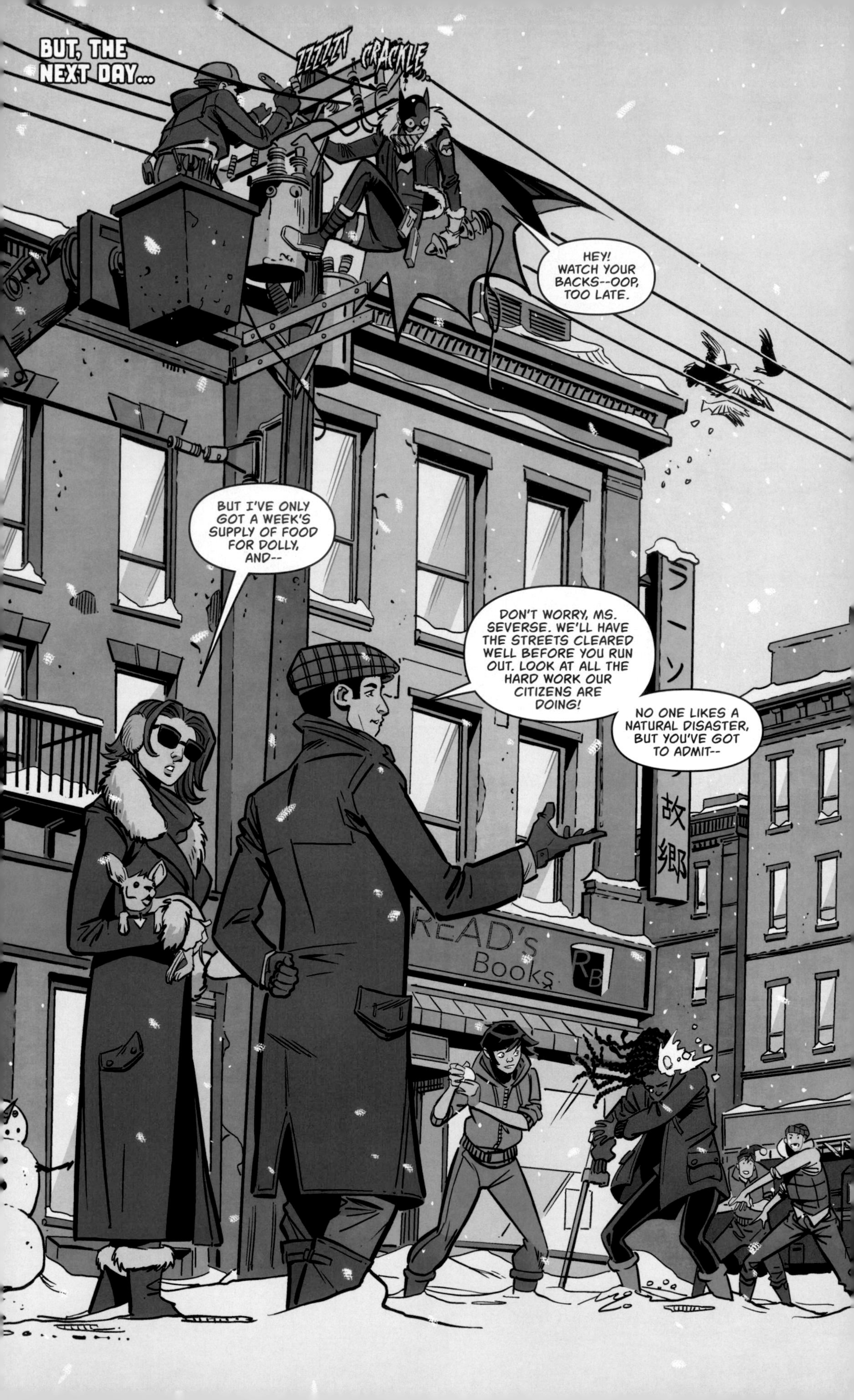
BUT, THE NEXT DAY...
ZZZZZZT
CRACKLE
HEY! WATCH YOUR BACKS--OOP, TOO LATE.
BUT I'VE ONLY GOT A WEEK'S SUPPLY OF FOOD FOR DOLLY, AND--
DON'T WORRY, MS. SEVERSE. WE'LL HAVE THE STREETS CLEARED WELL BEFORE YOU RUN OUT. LOOK AT ALL THE HARD WORK OUR CITIZENS ARE DOING!
NO ONE LIKES A NATURAL DISASTER, BUT YOU'VE GOT TO ADMIT--
故郷
READ's Books
RB

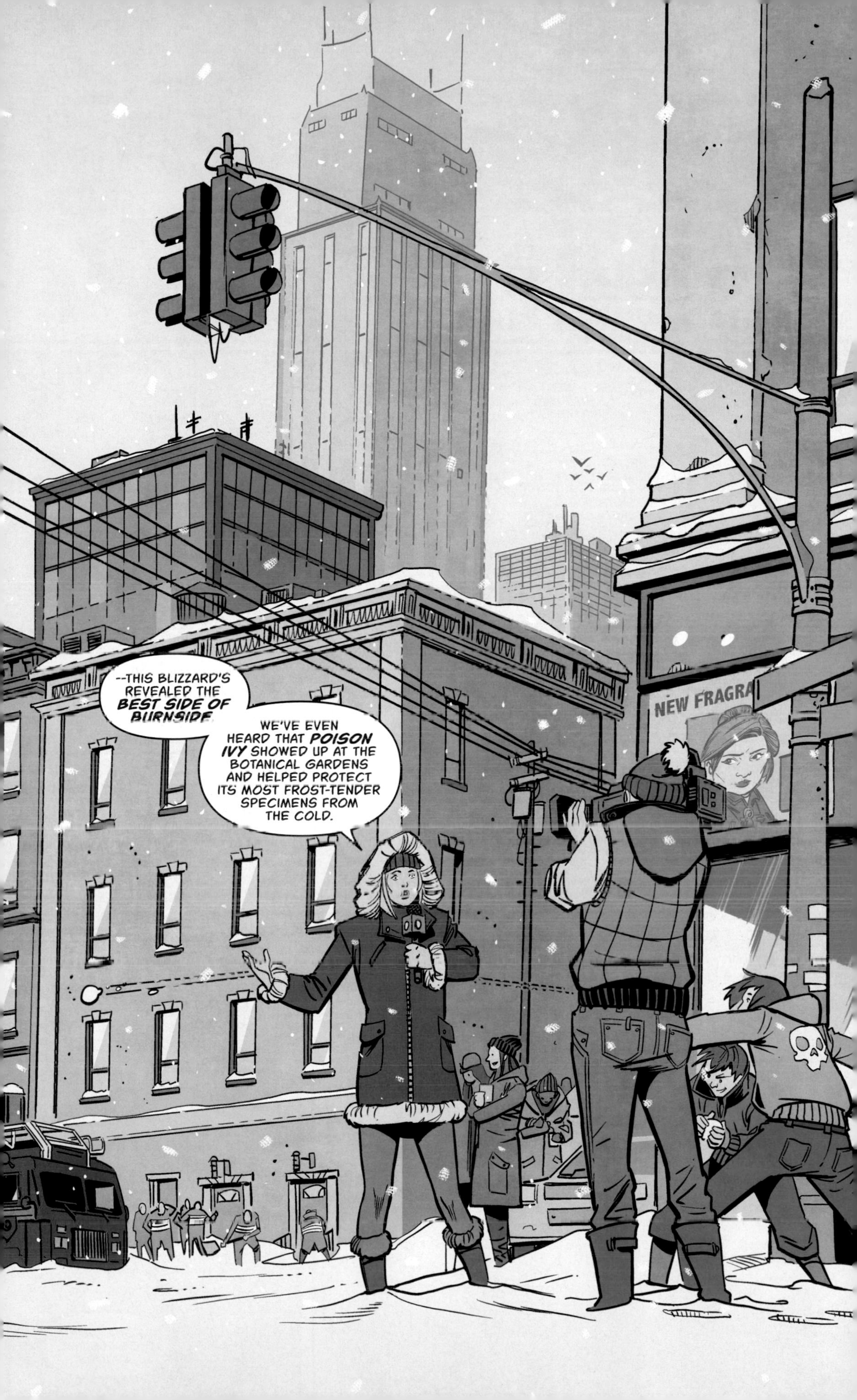
--THIS BLIZZARD'S REVEALED THE BEST SIDE OF BURNSIDE.
WE'VE EVEN HEARD THAT POISON IVY SHOWED UP AT THE BOTANICAL GARDENS AND HELPED PROTECT ITS MOST FROST-TENDER SPECIMENS FROM THE COLD.
NEW FRAGRA

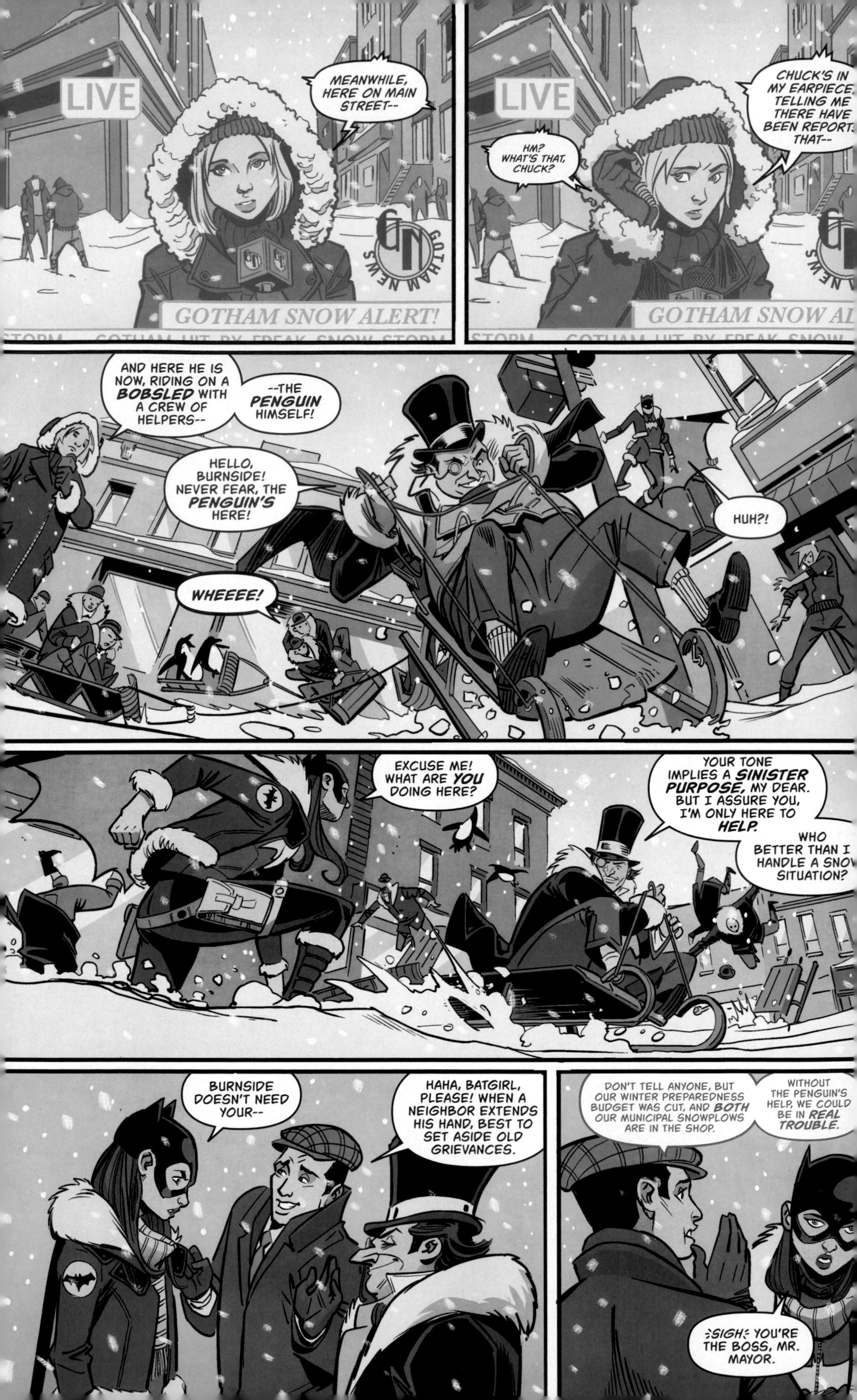
LIVE
MEANWHILE, HERE ON MAIN STREET--
GOTHAM SNOW ALERT!
GOTHAM NEWS
LIVE
HM? WHAT'S THAT, CHUCK?
CHUCK'S IN MY EARPIECE, TELLING ME THERE HAVE BEEN REPORT THAT--
GOTHAM SNOW AL
AND HERE HE IS NOW, RIDING ON A BOBSLED WITH A CREW OF HELPERS--
--THE PENGUIN HIMSELF!
HELLO, BURNSIDE! NEVER FEAR, THE PENGUIN'S HERE!
WHEEEE!
HUH?!
EXCUSE ME! WHAT ARE YOU DOING HERE?
YOUR TONE IMPLIES A SINISTER PURPOSE, MY DEAR. BUT I ASSURE YOU, I'M ONLY HERE TO HELP.
WHO BETTER THAN I HANDLE A SNO SITUATION?
BURNSIDE DOESN'T NEED YOUR--
HAHA, BATGIRL, PLEASE! WHEN A NEIGHBOR EXTENDS HIS HAND, BEST TO SET ASIDE OLD GRIEVANCES.
DON'T TELL ANYONE, BUT OUR WINTER PREPAREDNESS BUDGET WAS CUT, AND BOTH OUR MUNICIPAL SNOWPLOWS ARE IN THE SHOP.
WITHOUT THE PENGUIN'S HELP, WE COULD BE IN REAL TROUBLE.
SIGH YOU'RE THE BOSS, MR. MAYOR.

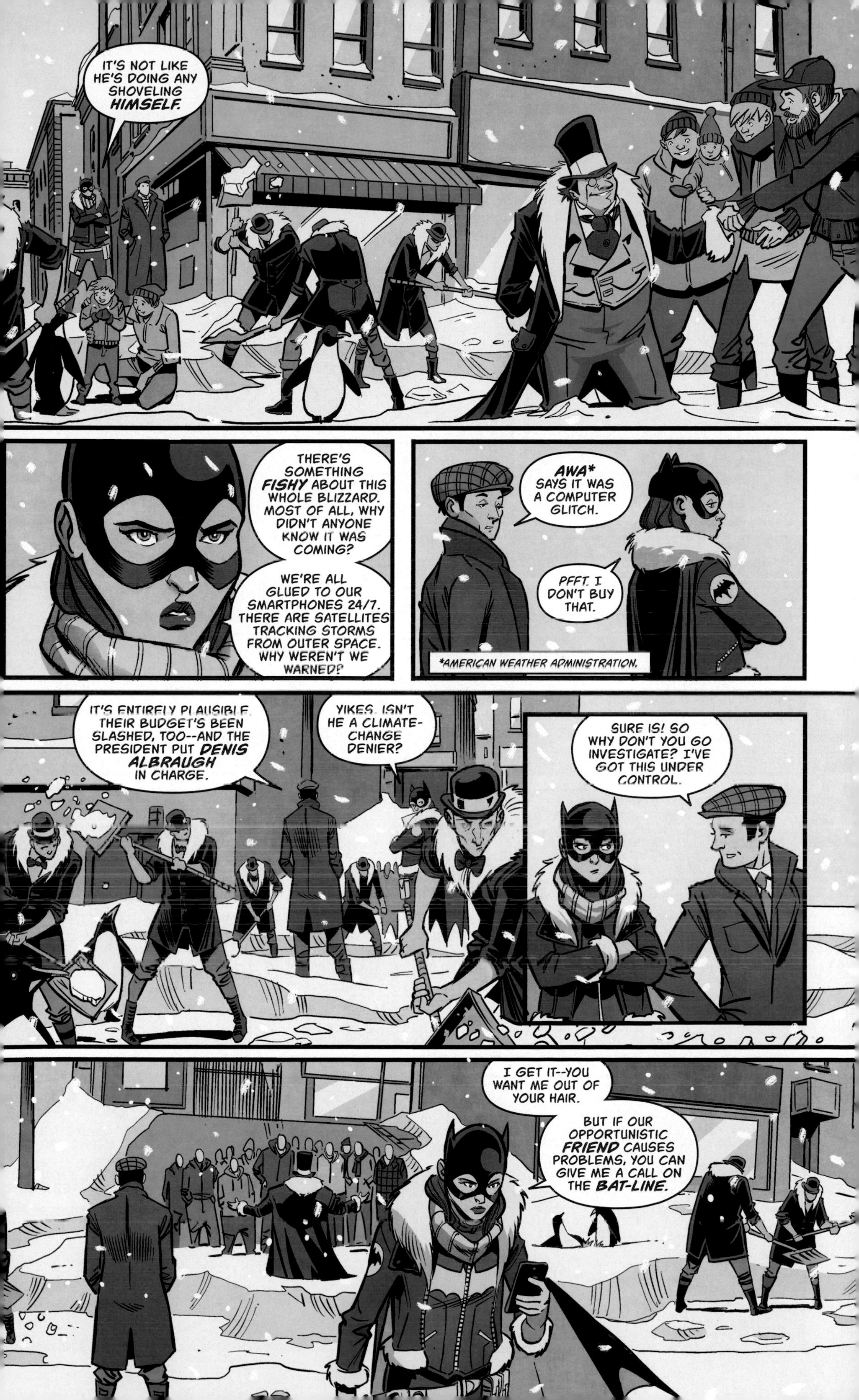

IT'S NOT LIKE HE'S DOING ANY SHOVELING HIMSELF.
THERE'S SOMETHING FISHY ABOUT THIS WHOLE BLIZZARD. MOST OF ALL, WHY DIDN'T ANYONE KNOW IT WAS COMING?
WE'RE ALL GLUED TO OUR SMARTPHONES 24/7. THERE ARE SATELLITES TRACKING STORMS FROM OUTER SPACE. WHY WEREN'T WE WARNED?
AWA* SAYS IT WAS A COMPUTER GLITCH.
PFFT. I DON'T BUY THAT.
*AMERICAN WEATHER ADMINISTRATION.
IT'S ENTIRELY PLAUSIBLE. THEIR BUDGET'S BEEN SLASHED, TOO--AND THE PRESIDENT PUT DENIS ALBRAUGH IN CHARGE.
YIKES. ISN'T HE A CLIMATE-CHANGE DENIER?
SURE IS! SO WHY DON'T YOU GO INVESTIGATE? I'VE GOT THIS UNDER CONTROL.
I GET IT--YOU WANT ME OUT OF YOUR HAIR.
BUT IF OUR OPPORTUNISTIC FRIEND CAUSES PROBLEMS, YOU CAN GIVE ME A CALL ON THE BAT-LINE.

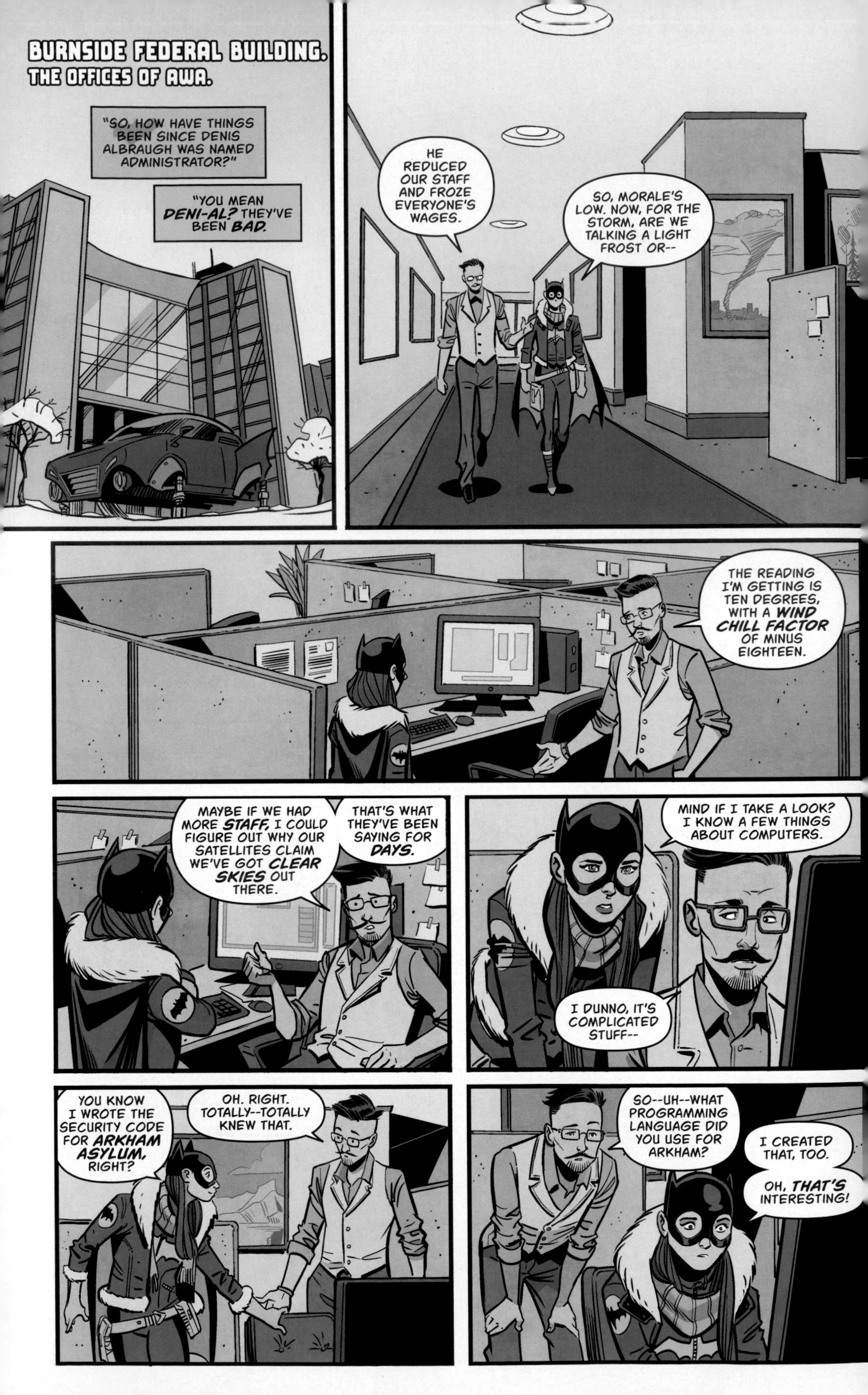
BURNSIDE FEDERAL BUILDING.
THE OFFICES OF AWA.
"SO, HOW HAVE THINGS BEEN SINCE DENIS ALBRAUGH WAS NAMED ADMINISTRATOR?"
"YOU MEAN DENI-AL? THEY'VE BEEN BAD.
HE REDUCED OUR STAFF AND FROZE EVERYONE'S WAGES.
SO, MORALE'S LOW. NOW, FOR THE STORM, ARE WE TALKING A LIGHT FROST OR--
THE READING I'M GETTING IS TEN DEGREES, WITH A WIND CHILL FACTOR OF MINUS EIGHTEEN.
MAYBE IF WE HAD MORE STAFF, I COULD FIGURE OUT WHY OUR SATELLITES CLAIM WE'VE GOT CLEAR SKIES OUT THERE.
THAT'S WHAT THEY'VE BEEN SAYING FOR DAYS.
MIND IF I TAKE A LOOK? I KNOW A FEW THINGS ABOUT COMPUTERS.
I DUNNO, IT'S COMPLICATED STUFF--
YOU KNOW I WROTE THE SECURITY CODE FOR ARKHAM ASYLUM, RIGHT?
OH. RIGHT. TOTALLY--TOTALLY KNEW THAT.
SO--UH--WHAT PROGRAMMING LANGUAGE DID YOU USE FOR ARKHAM?
I CREATED THAT, TOO.
OH, THAT'S INTERESTING!

DID YOU FIND THE PROBLEM?

HAVE YOU HEARD ABOUT STUXNET? THE SUPPOSED U.S.-ISRAELI HACK ON IRAN'S NUCLEAR PROGRAM?

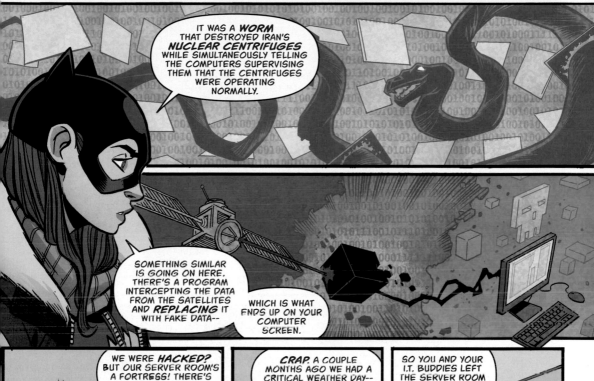

IT WAS A **WORM** THAT DESTROYED IRAN'S **NUCLEAR CENTRIFUGES** WHILE SIMULTANEOUSLY TELLING THE COMPUTERS SUPERVISING THEM THAT THE CENTRIFUGES WERE OPERATING NORMALLY.

SOMETHING SIMILAR IS GOING ON HERE. THERE'S A PROGRAM INTERCEPTING THE DATA FROM THE SATELLITES AND **REPLACING** IT WITH FAKE DATA--

WHICH IS WHAT ENDS UP ON YOUR COMPUTER SCREEN.

WE WERE **HACKED?** BUT OUR SERVER ROOM'S A FORTRESS! THERE'S ALWAYS SOMEONE IN THERE, EXCEPT--

CRAP. A COUPLE MONTHS AGO WE HAD A CRITICAL WEATHER DAY-- A BIG STORM SYSTEM MOVING THROUGH.

DAYS LIKE THAT, WE CAN'T TOUCH THE SERVERS AND RISK BRINGING THE SYSTEM DOWN, SO--

SO YOU AND YOUR I.T. BUDDIES LEFT THE SERVER ROOM UNATTENDED WHILE YOU WENT OUT TO LUNCH?

NOT EVEN. WE ORDERED A PIZZA AND CYBER-STALKED OUR COLLEGE GIRLFRIENDS.

MINE GOT TOGETHER WITH SOME **BIOLOGY** MAJOR, AND NOW THEY RUN A WOLF-DOG SANCTUARY IN UTAH.

IF ONLY I'D PLAYED MY CARDS RIGHT, THAT COULD BE **MY** LIFE, TOO.

UHHH, YOU **WANT** THAT LIFE?

HOW ABOUT YOU SHOW ME TO THE SERVER ROOM INSTEAD?

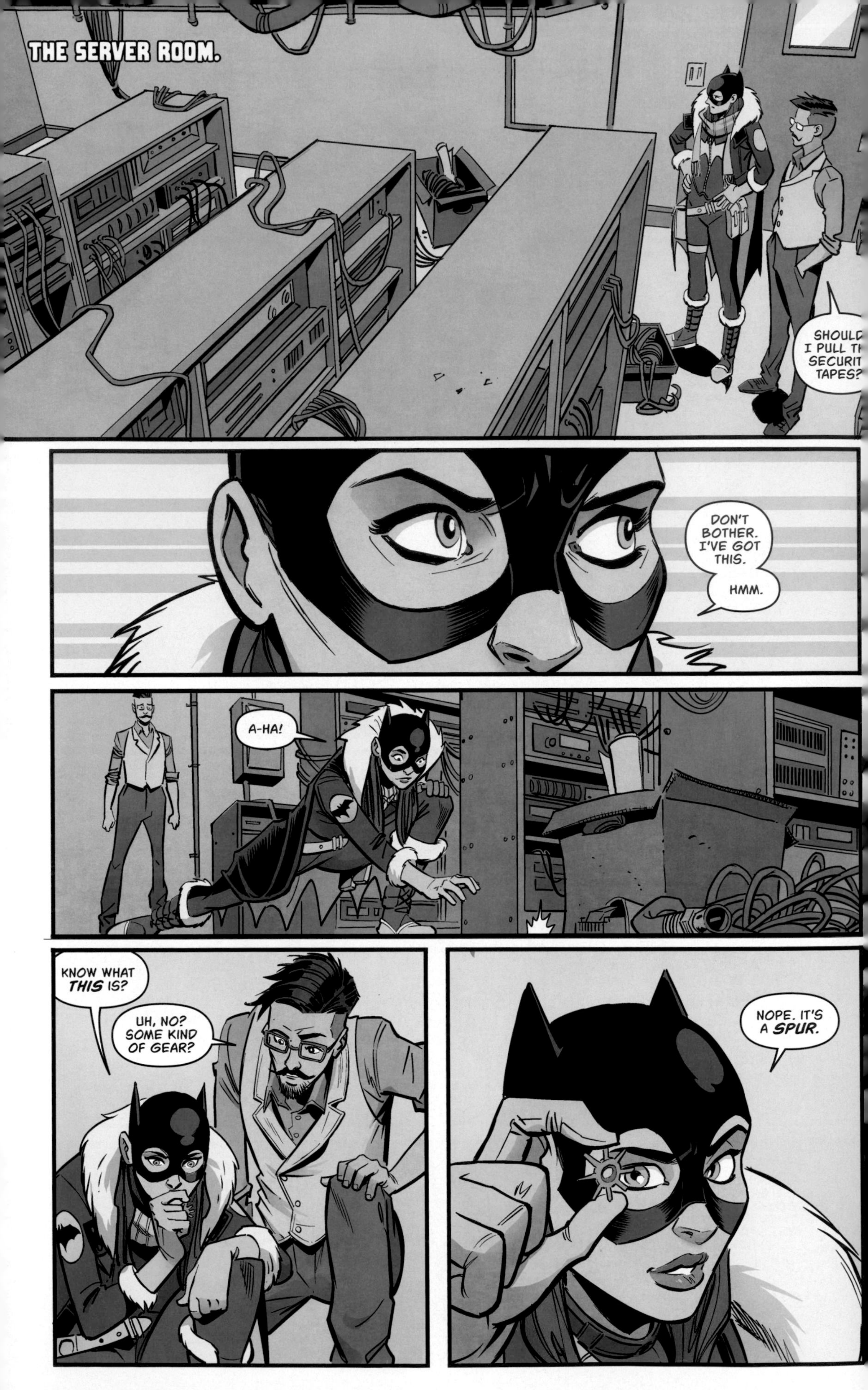

THE SERVER ROOM.
SHOULD I PULL THE SECURITY TAPES?
DON'T BOTHER. I'VE GOT THIS.
HMM.
A-HA!
KNOW WHAT *THIS* IS?
UH, NO? SOME KIND OF GEAR?
NOPE. IT'S A *SPUR*.

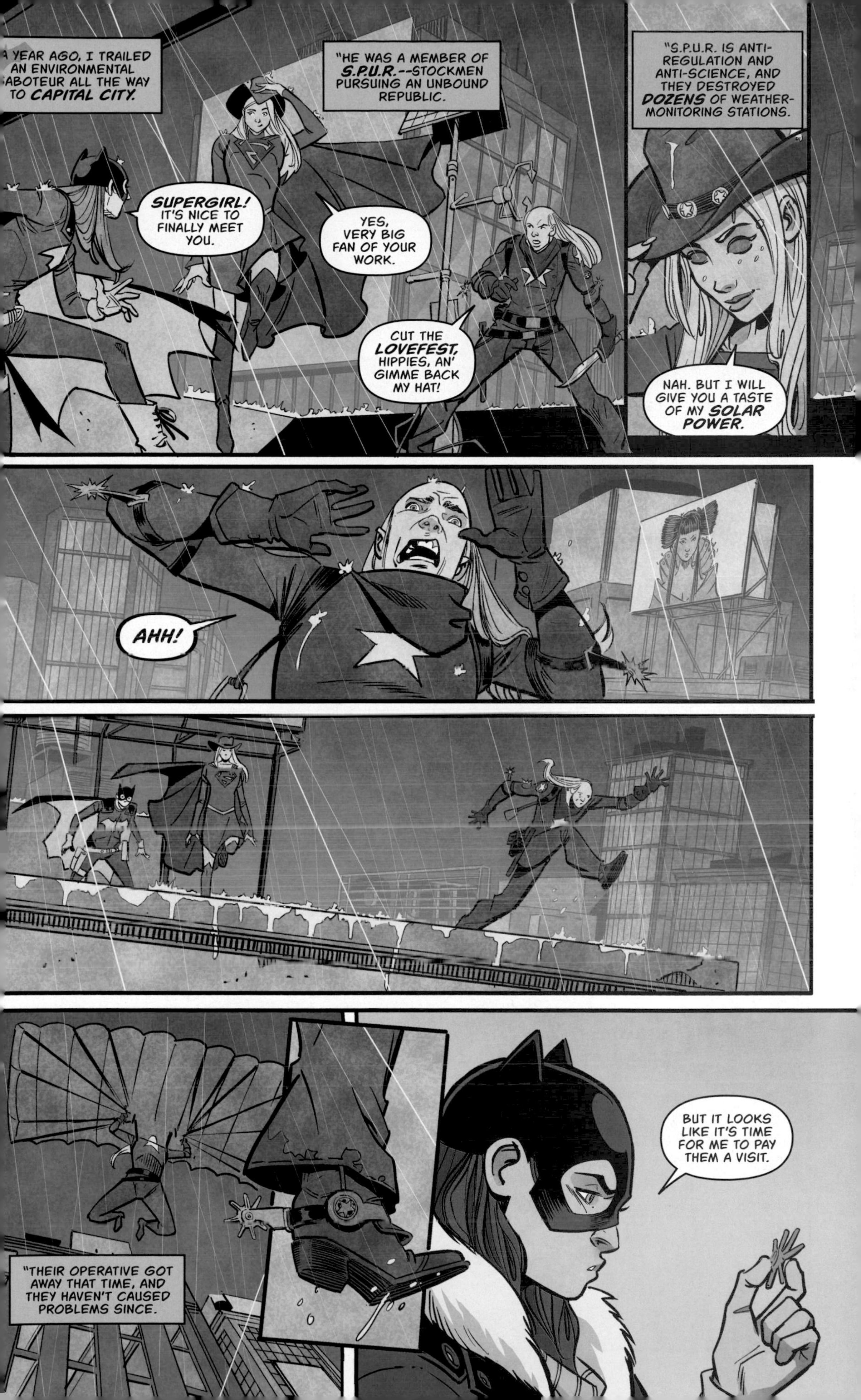
A YEAR AGO, I TRAILED AN ENVIRONMENTAL SABOTEUR ALL THE WAY TO CAPITAL CITY.
"HE WAS A MEMBER OF S.P.U.R.--STOCKMEN PURSUING AN UNBOUND REPUBLIC.
"S.P.U.R. IS ANTI-REGULATION AND ANTI-SCIENCE, AND THEY DESTROYED DOZENS OF WEATHER-MONITORING STATIONS.
SUPERGIRL! IT'S NICE TO FINALLY MEET YOU.
YES, VERY BIG FAN OF YOUR WORK.
CUT THE LOVEFEST, HIPPIES, AN' GIMME BACK MY HAT!
NAH. BUT I WILL GIVE YOU A TASTE OF MY SOLAR POWER.
AHH!
"THEIR OPERATIVE GOT AWAY THAT TIME, AND THEY HAVEN'T CAUSED PROBLEMS SINCE.
BUT IT LOOKS LIKE IT'S TIME FOR ME TO PAY THEM A VISIT.

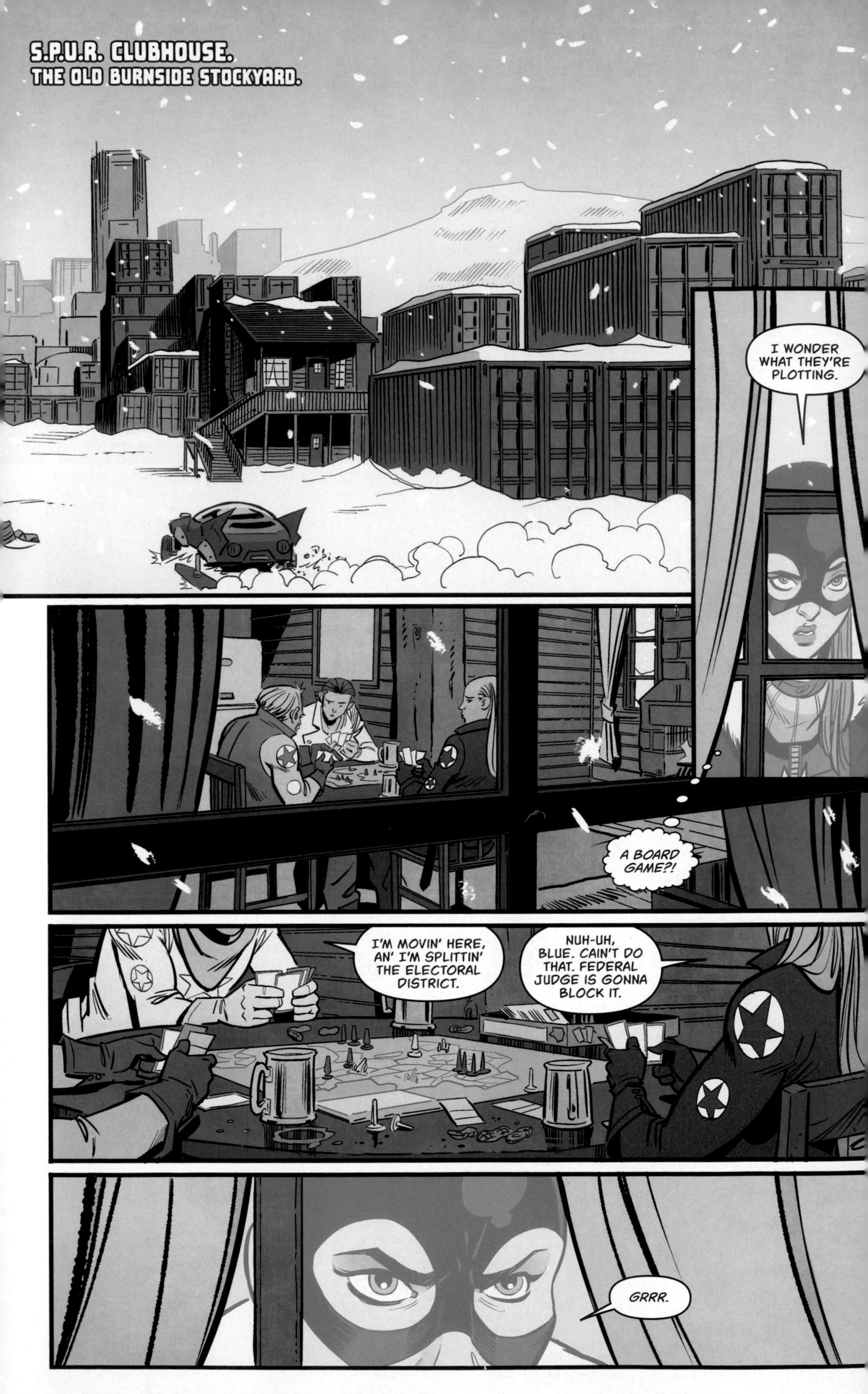
S.P.U.R. CLUBHOUSE.
THE OLD BURNSIDE STOCKYARD.
I WONDER WHAT THEY'RE PLOTTING.
A BOARD GAME?!
I'M MOVIN' HERE, AN' I'M SPLITTIN' THE ELECTORAL DISTRICT.
NUH-UH, BLUE. CAIN'T DO THAT. FEDERAL JUDGE IS GONNA BLOCK IT.
GRRR.

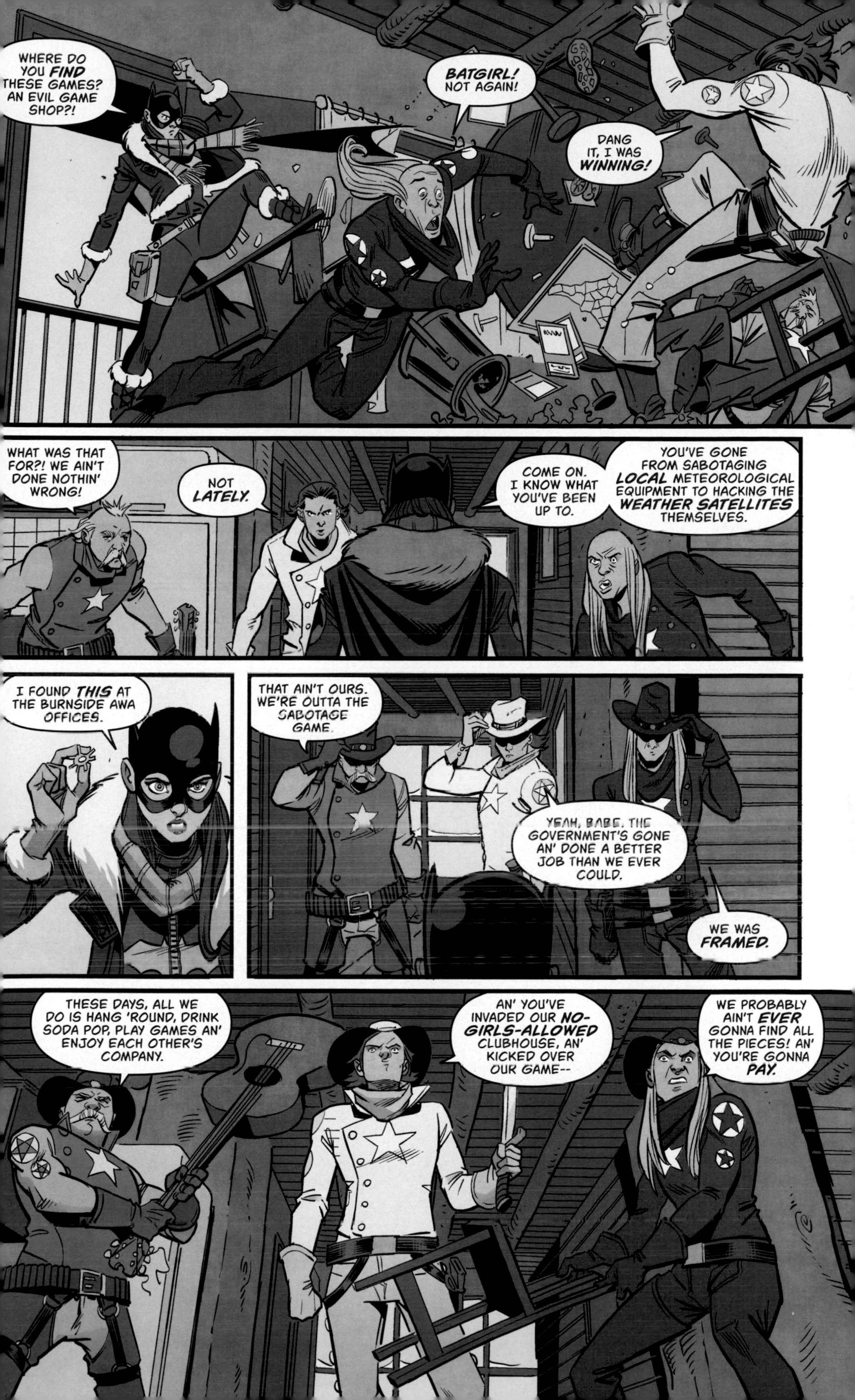

WHERE DO YOU FIND THESE GAMES? AN EVIL GAME SHOP?!
BATGIRL! NOT AGAIN!
DANG IT, I WAS WINNING!
WHAT WAS THAT FOR?! WE AIN'T DONE NOTHIN' WRONG!
NOT LATELY.
COME ON. I KNOW WHAT YOU'VE BEEN UP TO.
YOU'VE GONE FROM SABOTAGING LOCAL METEOROLOGICAL EQUIPMENT TO HACKING THE WEATHER SATELLITES THEMSELVES.
I FOUND THIS AT THE BURNSIDE AWA OFFICES.
THAT AIN'T OURS. WE'RE OUTTA THE SABOTAGE GAME.
YEAH, BABE. THE GOVERNMENT'S GONE AN' DONE A BETTER JOB THAN WE EVER COULD.
WE WAS FRAMED.
THESE DAYS, ALL WE DO IS HANG 'ROUND, DRINK SODA POP, PLAY GAMES AN' ENJOY EACH OTHER'S COMPANY.
AN' YOU'VE INVADED OUR NO-GIRLS-ALLOWED CLUBHOUSE, AN' KICKED OVER OUR GAME--
WE PROBABLY AIN'T EVER GONNA FIND ALL THE PIECES! AN' YOU'RE GONNA PAY.

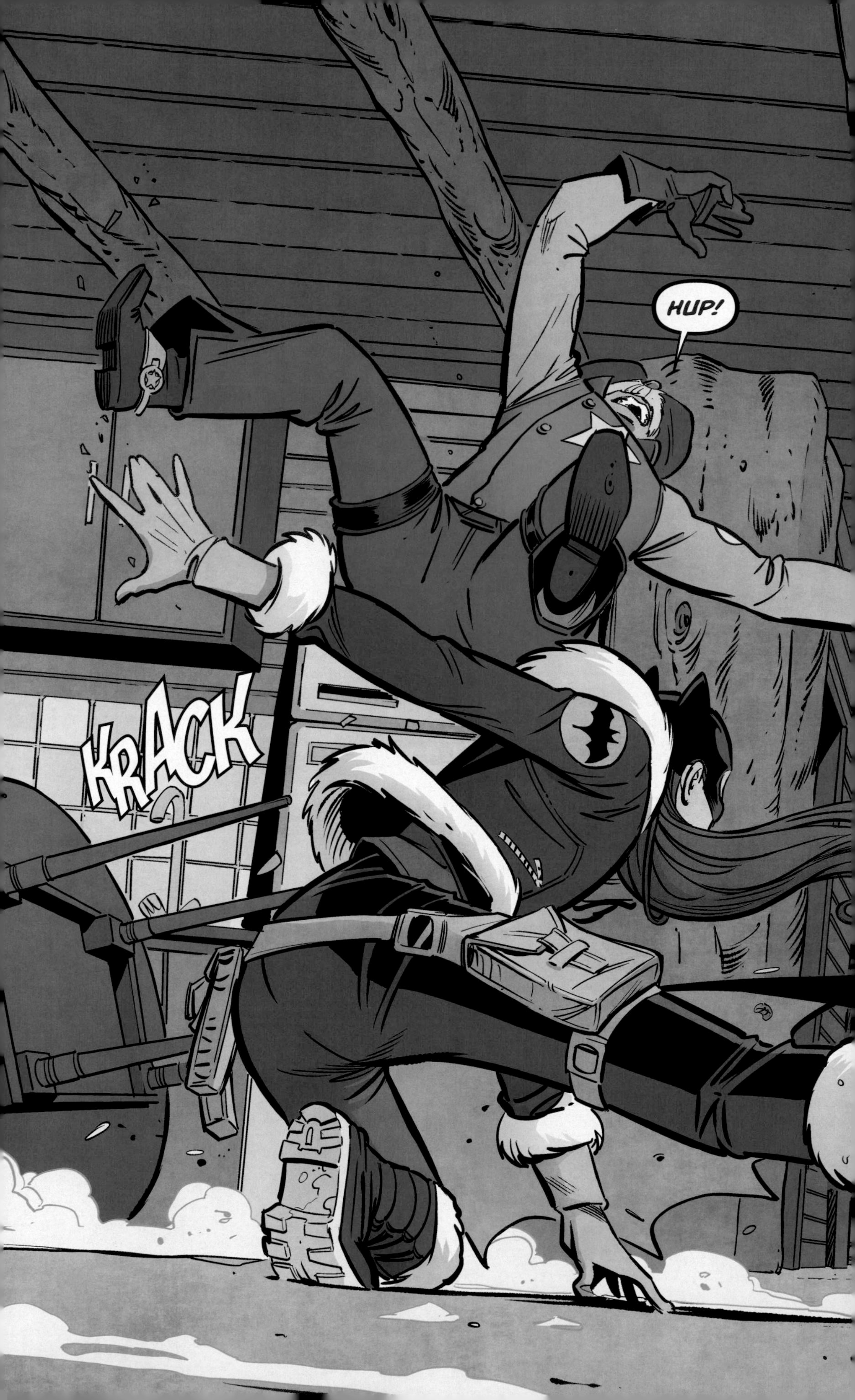
HUP!
KRACK

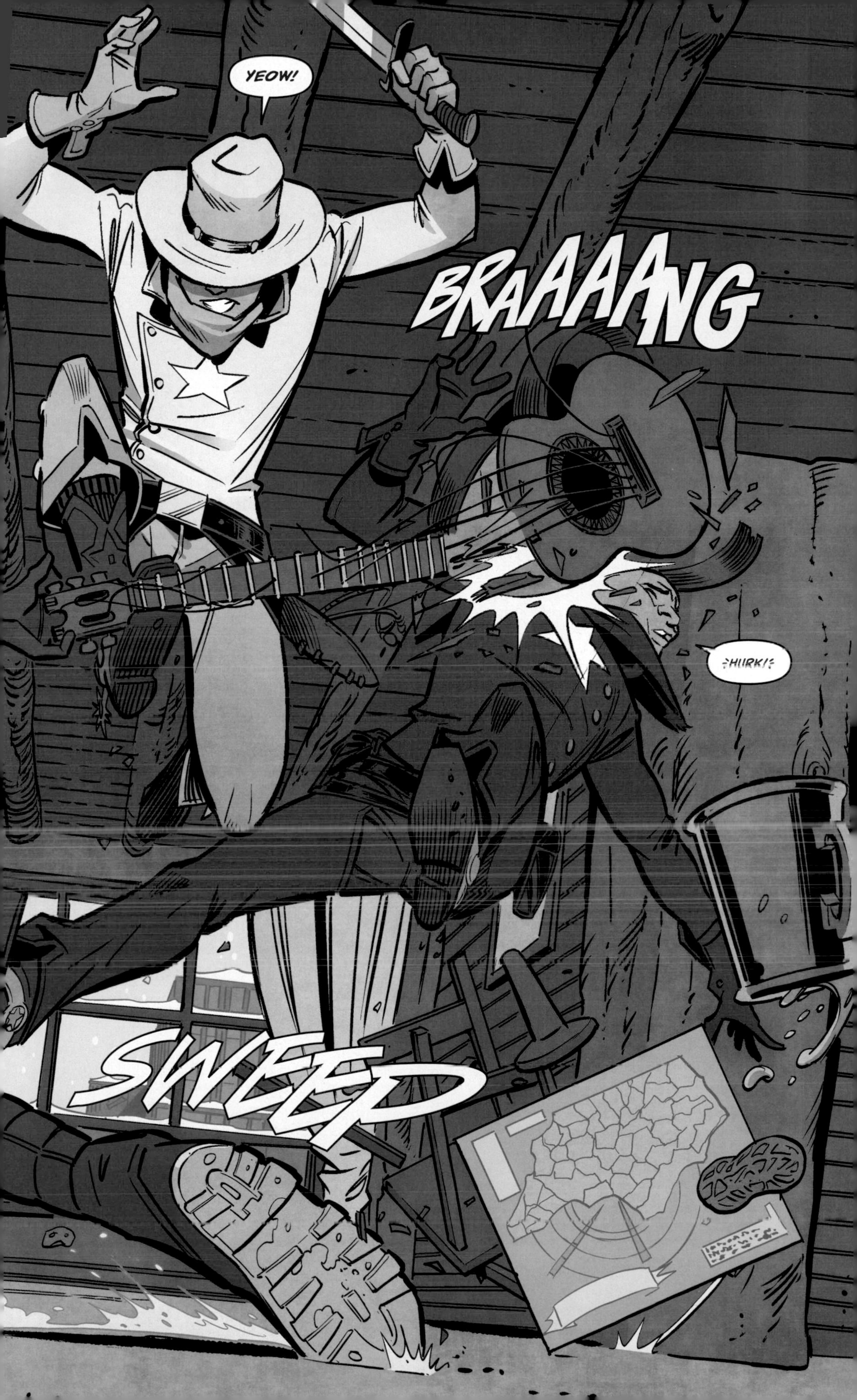
YEOW!
BRAAAANG
HURK!
SWEEP

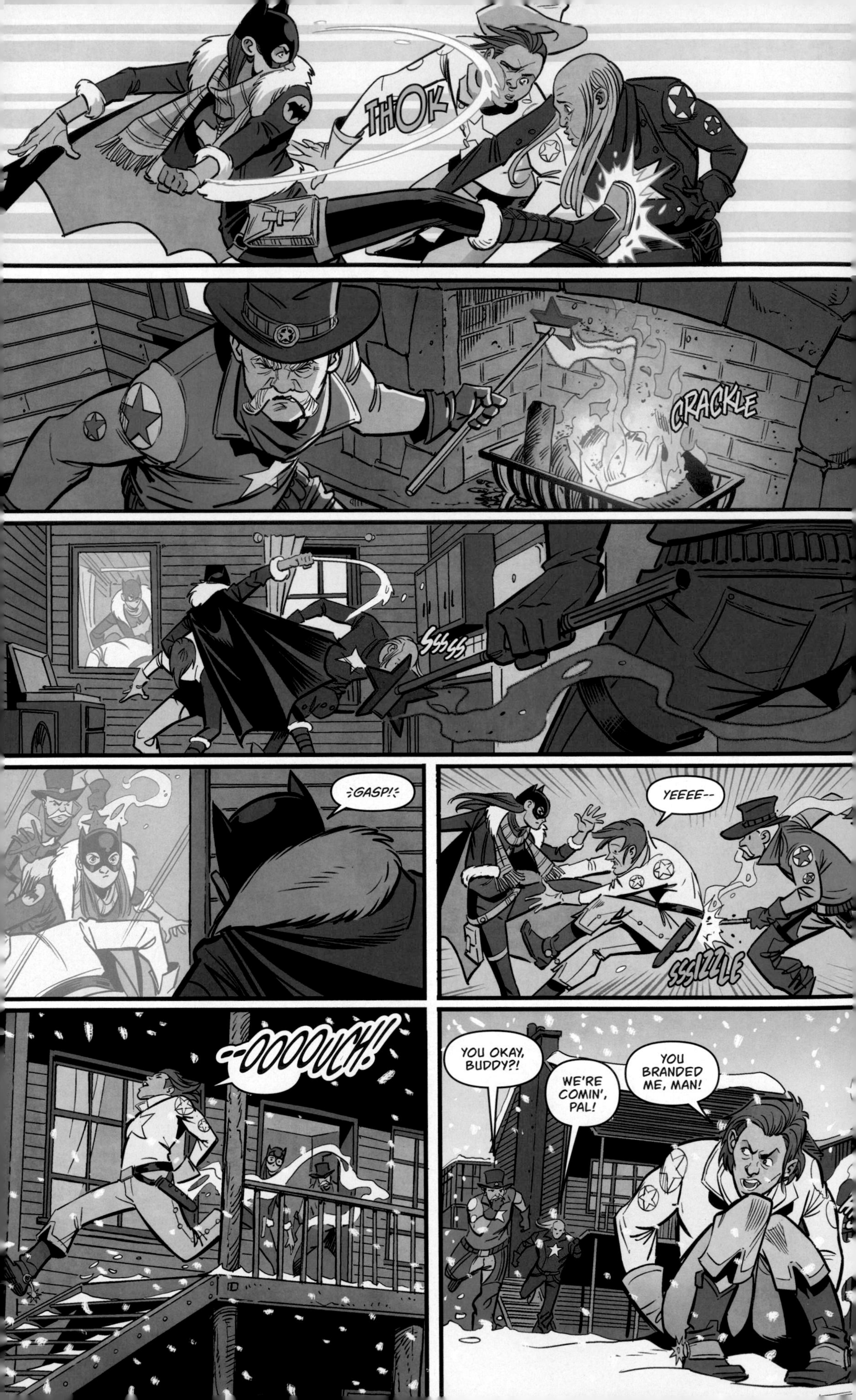
THOK
CRACKLE
SSSSS
-GASP!-
YEEEE--
SSSIZZLE
--OOOOUCH!
YOU OKAY, BUDDY?!
WE'RE COMIN', PAL!
YOU BRANDED ME, MAN!

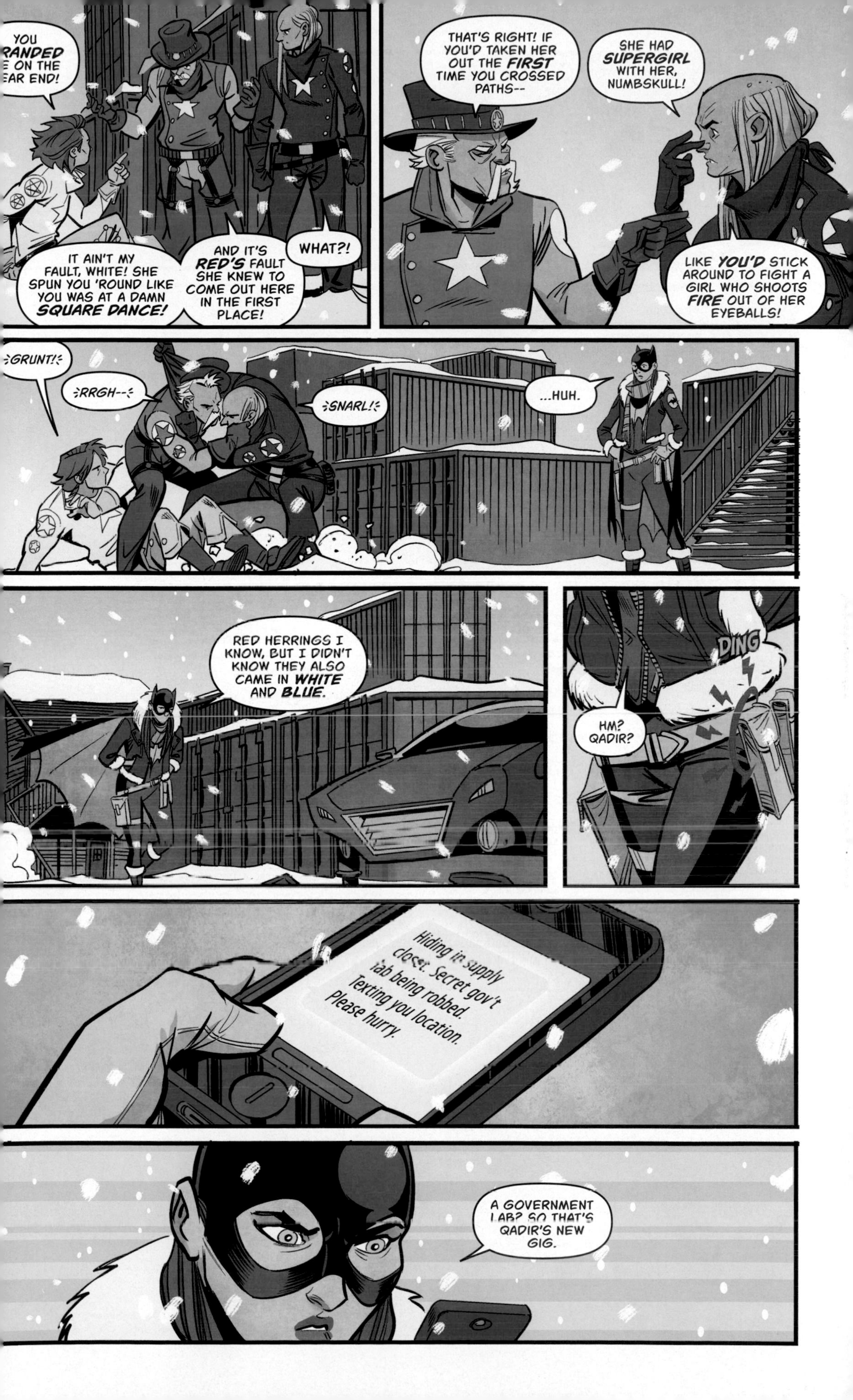
YOU BRANDED ME ON THE REAR END!
IT AIN'T MY FAULT, WHITE! SHE SPUN YOU 'ROUND LIKE YOU WAS AT A DAMN SQUARE DANCE!
AND IT'S RED'S FAULT SHE KNEW TO COME OUT HERE IN THE FIRST PLACE!
WHAT?!
THAT'S RIGHT! IF YOU'D TAKEN HER OUT THE FIRST TIME YOU CROSSED PATHS--
SHE HAD SUPERGIRL WITH HER, NUMBSKULL!
LIKE YOU'D STICK AROUND TO FIGHT A GIRL WHO SHOOTS FIRE OUT OF HER EYEBALLS!
GRUNT!
RRGH--
SNARL!
...HUH.
RED HERRINGS I KNOW, BUT I DIDN'T KNOW THEY ALSO CAME IN WHITE AND BLUE.
DING
HM? QADIR?
Hiding in supply closet. Secret gov't lab being robbed. Texting you location. Please hurry.
A GOVERNMENT LAB? SO THAT'S QADIR'S NEW GIG.

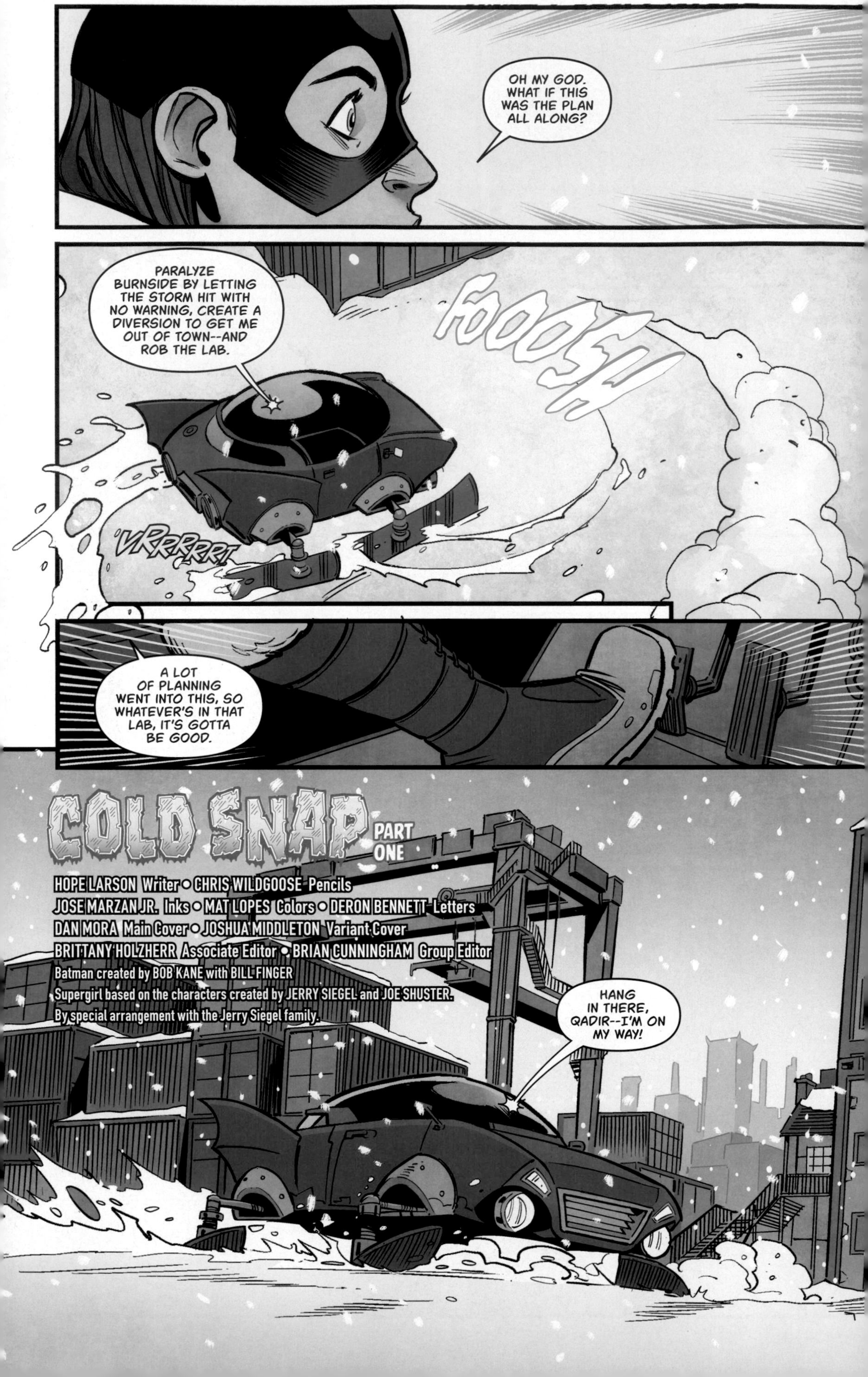
OH MY GOD. WHAT IF THIS WAS THE PLAN ALL ALONG?
PARALYZE BURNSIDE BY LETTING THE STORM HIT WITH NO WARNING, CREATE A DIVERSION TO GET ME OUT OF TOWN--AND ROB THE LAB.
FOOOSH
VRRRRRT
A LOT OF PLANNING WENT INTO THIS, SO WHATEVER'S IN THAT LAB, IT'S GOTTA BE GOOD.
COLD SNAP PART ONE
HOPE LARSON Writer • CHRIS WILDGOOSE Pencils
JOSE MARZAN JR. Inks • MAT LOPES Colors • DERON BENNETT Letters
DAN MORA Main Cover • JOSHUA MIDDLETON Variant Cover
BRITTANY HOLZHERR Associate Editor • BRIAN CUNNINGHAM Group Editor
Batman created by BOB KANE with BILL FINGER
Supergirl based on the characters created by JERRY SIEGEL and JOE SHUSTER.
By special arrangement with the Jerry Siegel family.
HANG IN THERE, QADIR--I'M ON MY WAY!

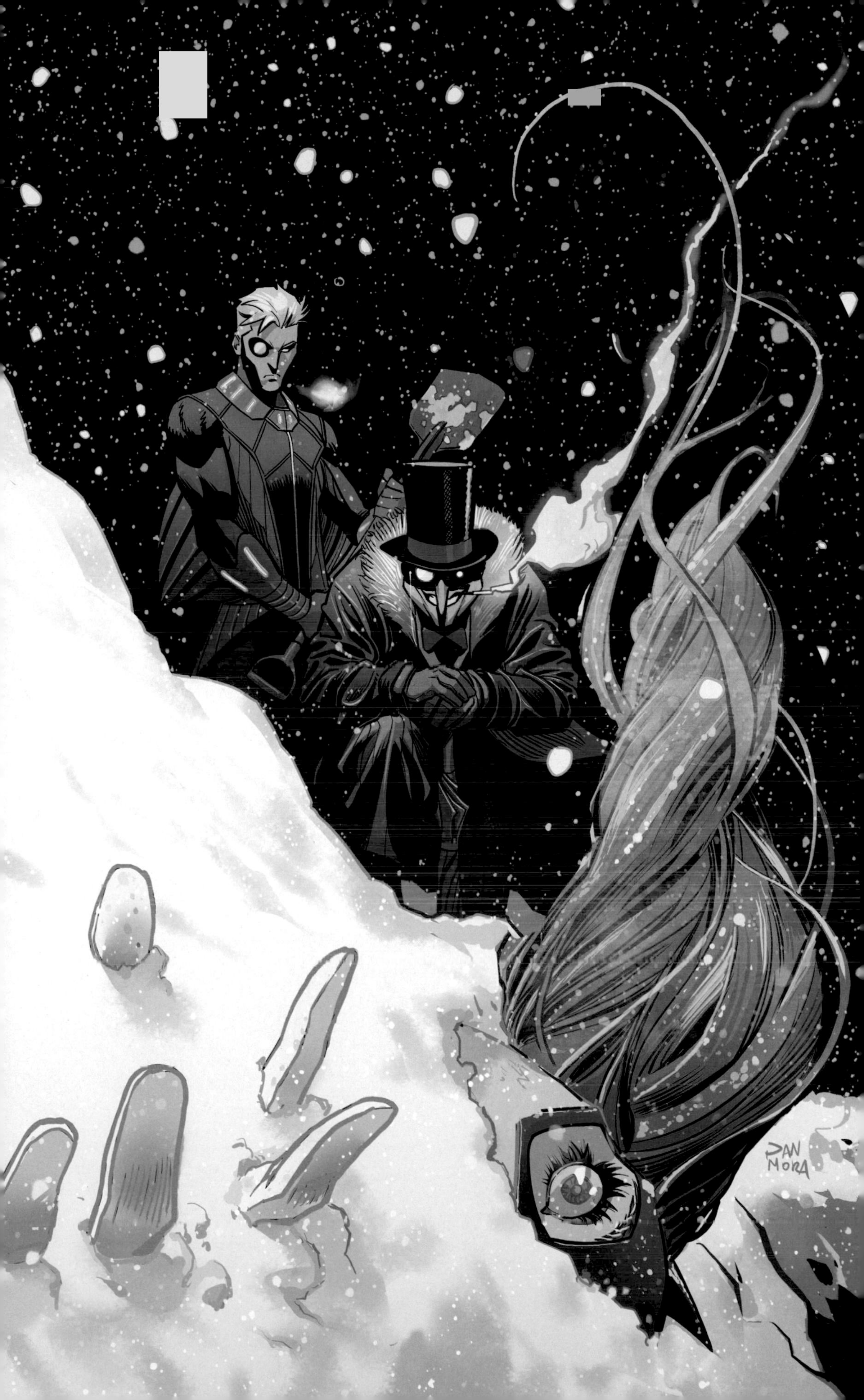
DAN
MORA

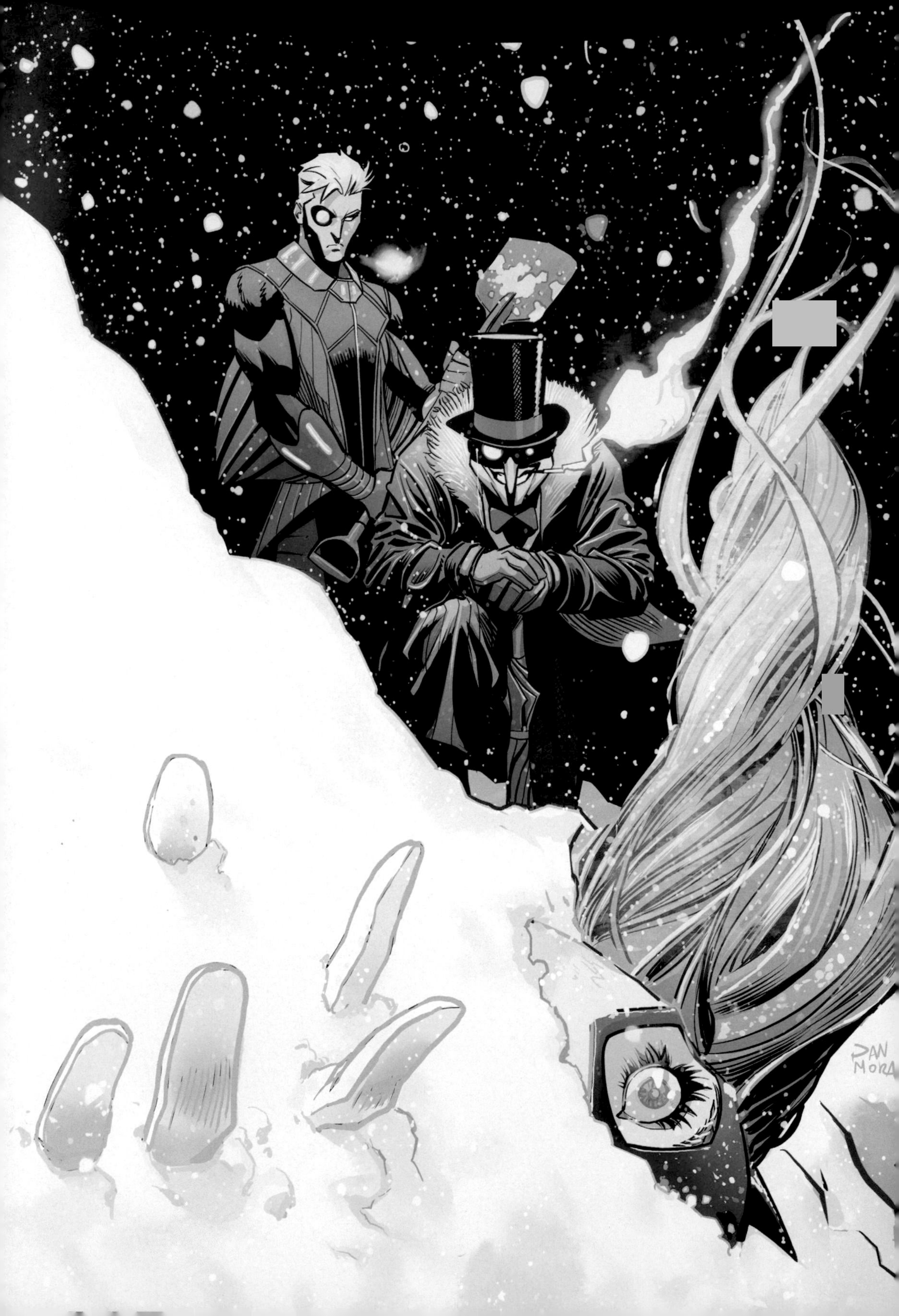
DAN MORA

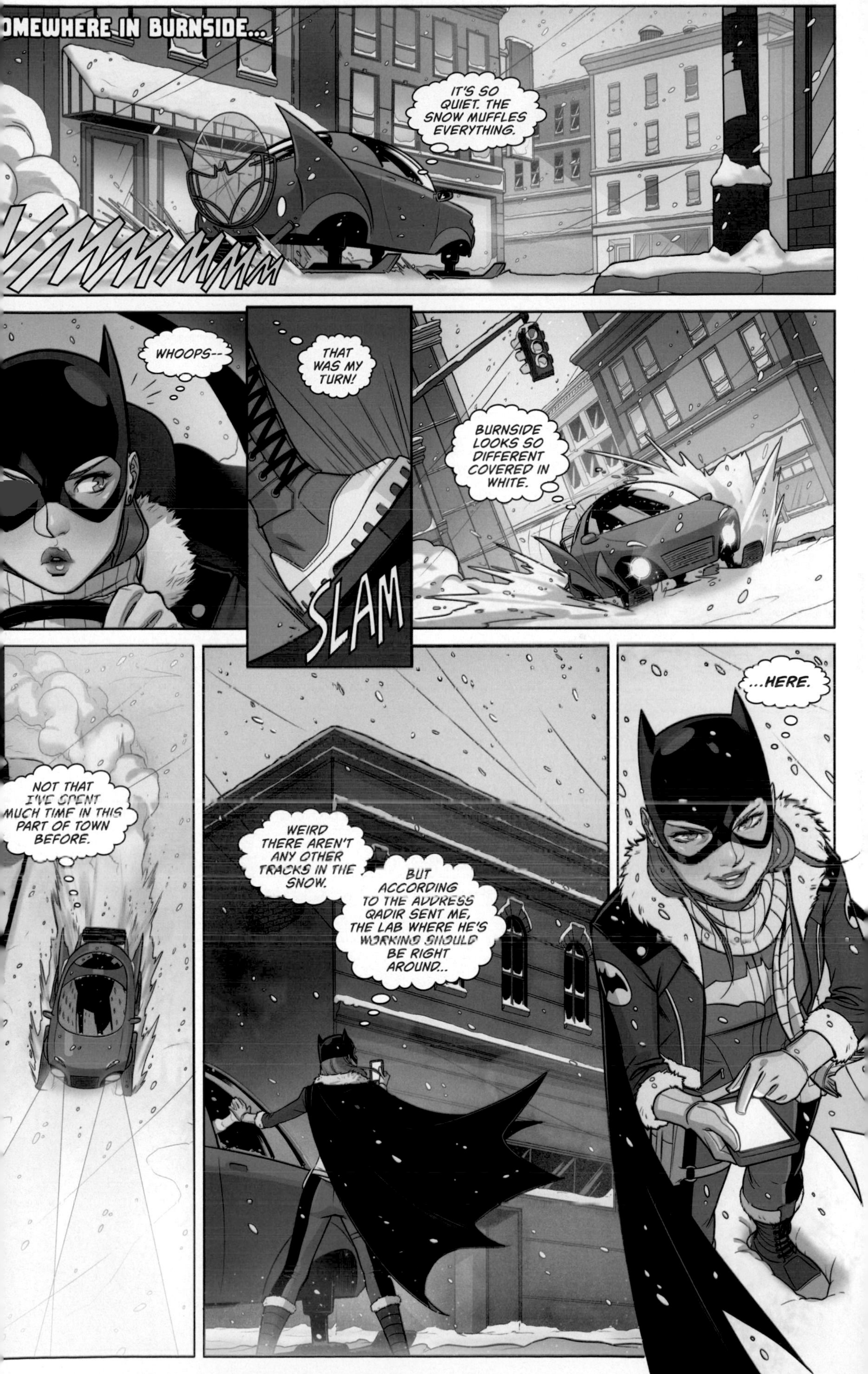
OMEWHERE IN BURNSIDE...
IT'S SO QUIET. THE SNOW MUFFLES EVERYTHING.
WHOOPS--
THAT WAS MY TURN!
SLAM
BURNSIDE LOOKS SO DIFFERENT COVERED IN WHITE.
NOT THAT I'VE SPENT MUCH TIME IN THIS PART OF TOWN BEFORE.
WEIRD THERE AREN'T ANY OTHER TRACKS IN THE SNOW.
BUT ACCORDING TO THE ADDRESS QADIR SENT ME, THE LAB WHERE HE'S WORKING SHOULD BE RIGHT AROUND...
...HERE.

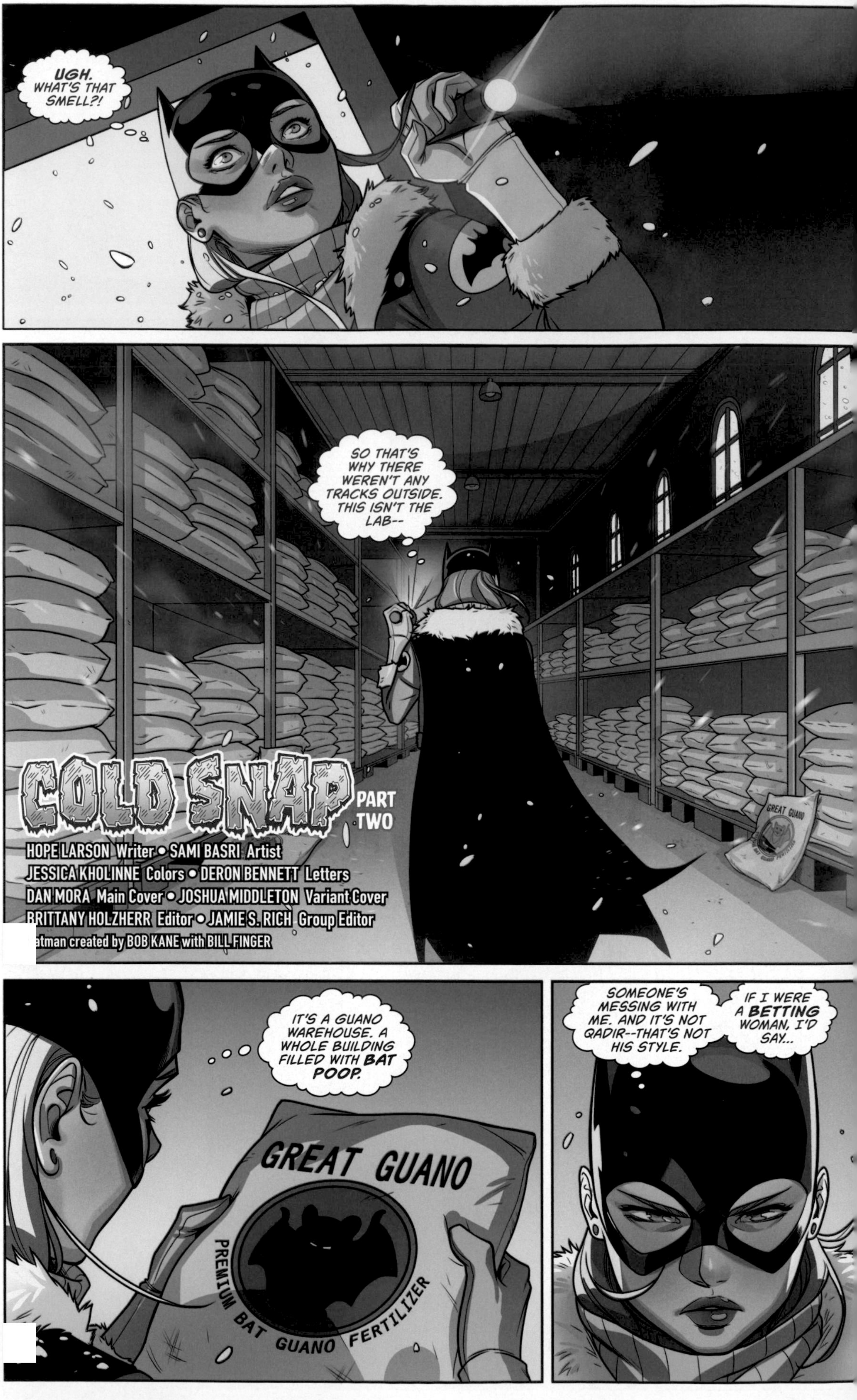
UGH. WHAT'S THAT SMELL?!
SO THAT'S WHY THERE WEREN'T ANY TRACKS OUTSIDE. THIS ISN'T THE LAB--
COLD SNAP PART TWO
HOPE LARSON Writer • SAMI BASRI Artist
JESSICA KHOLINNE Colors • DERON BENNETT Letters
DAN MORA Main Cover • JOSHUA MIDDLETON Variant Cover
BRITTANY HOLZHERR Editor • JAMIE S. RICH Group Editor
atman created by BOB KANE with BILL FINGER
GREAT GUANO
IT'S A GUANO WAREHOUSE. A WHOLE BUILDING FILLED WITH BAT POOP.
GREAT GUANO
PREMIUM BAT GUANO FERTILIZER
SOMEONE'S MESSING WITH ME. AND IT'S NOT QADIR--THAT'S NOT HIS STYLE.
IF I WERE A BETTING WOMAN, I'D SAY...

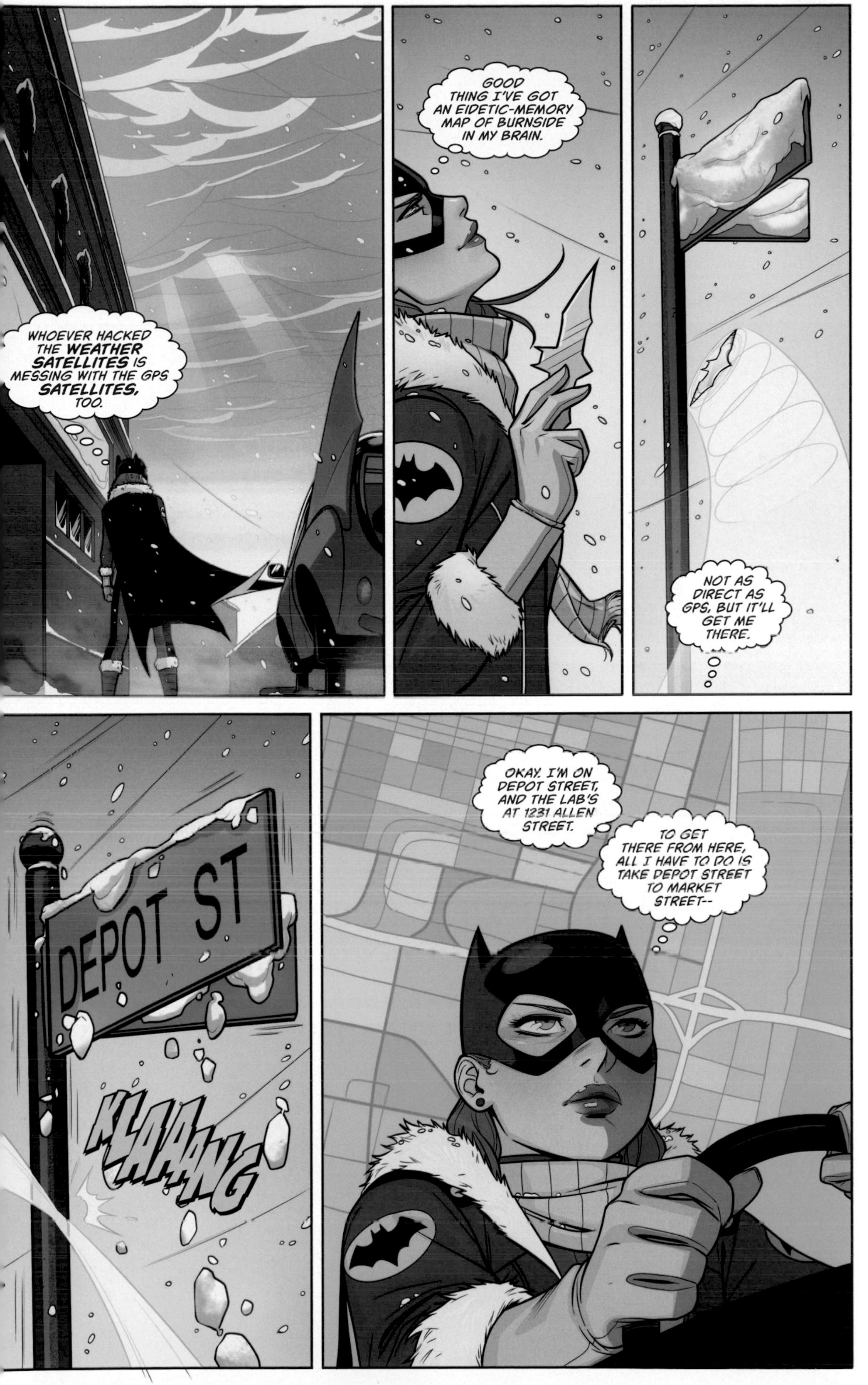
WHOEVER HACKED THE WEATHER SATELLITES IS MESSING WITH THE GPS SATELLITES, TOO.
GOOD THING I'VE GOT AN EIDETIC-MEMORY MAP OF BURNSIDE IN MY BRAIN.
NOT AS DIRECT AS GPS, BUT IT'LL GET ME THERE.
DEPOT ST
KLAANG
OKAY. I'M ON DEPOT STREET, AND THE LAB'S AT 1231 ALLEN STREET.
TO GET THERE FROM HERE, ALL I HAVE TO DO IS TAKE DEPOT STREET TO MARKET STREET--

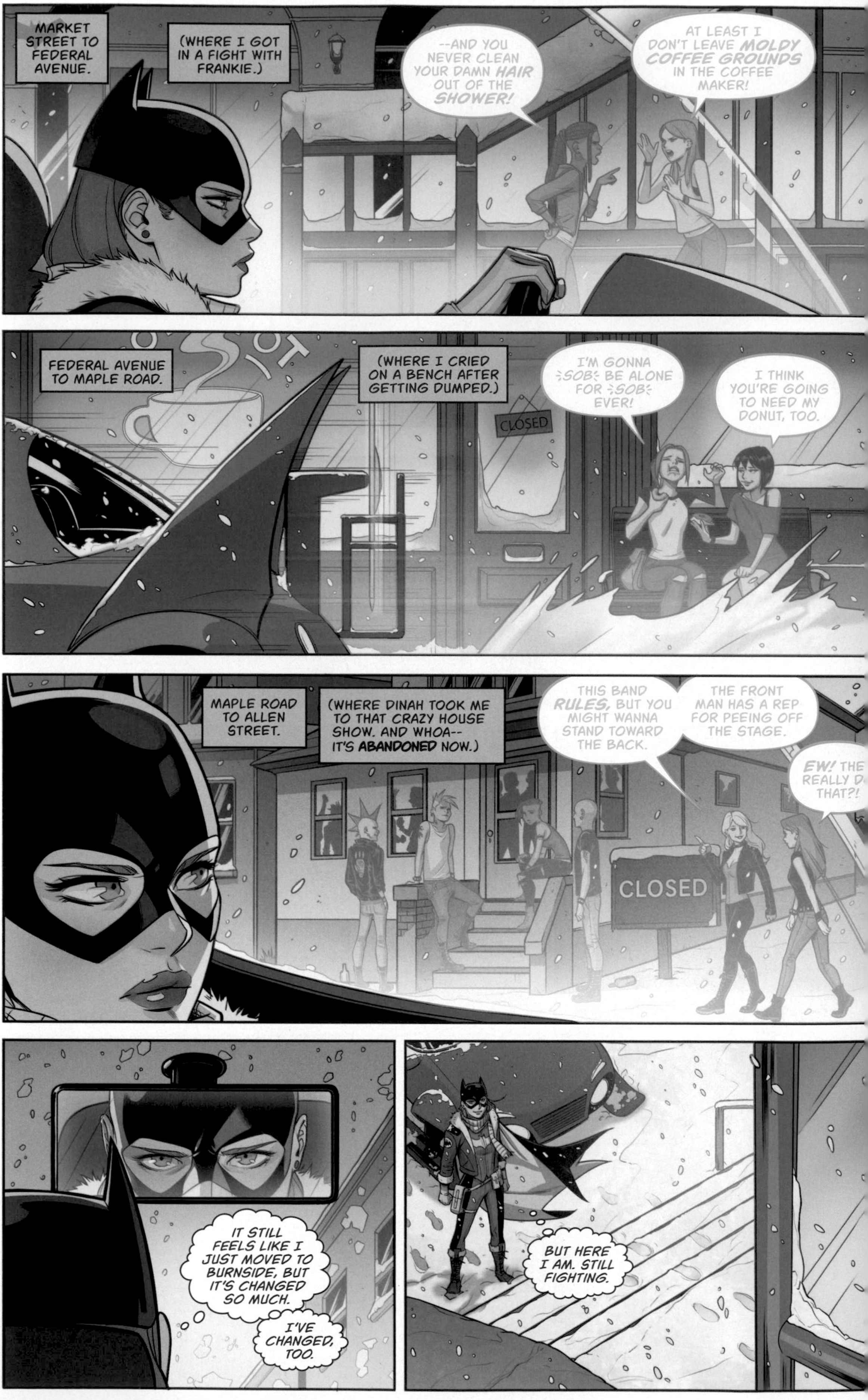
MARKET STREET TO FEDERAL AVENUE.
(WHERE I GOT IN A FIGHT WITH FRANKIE.)
--AND YOU NEVER CLEAN YOUR DAMN HAIR OUT OF THE SHOWER!
AT LEAST I DON'T LEAVE MOLDY COFFEE GROUNDS IN THE COFFEE MAKER!
FEDERAL AVENUE TO MAPLE ROAD.
(WHERE I CRIED ON A BENCH AFTER GETTING DUMPED.)
CLOSED
I'M GONNA *SOB* BE ALONE FOR *SOB* EVER!
I THINK YOU'RE GOING TO NEED MY DONUT, TOO.
MAPLE ROAD TO ALLEN STREET.
(WHERE DINAH TOOK ME TO THAT CRAZY HOUSE SHOW. AND WHOA-- IT'S ABANDONED NOW.)
THIS BAND RULES, BUT YOU MIGHT WANNA STAND TOWARD THE BACK.
THE FRONT MAN HAS A REP FOR PEEING OFF THE STAGE.
CLOSED
IT STILL FEELS LIKE I JUST MOVED TO BURNSIDE, BUT IT'S CHANGED SO MUCH.
I'VE CHANGED, TOO.
BUT HERE I AM. STILL FIGHTING.

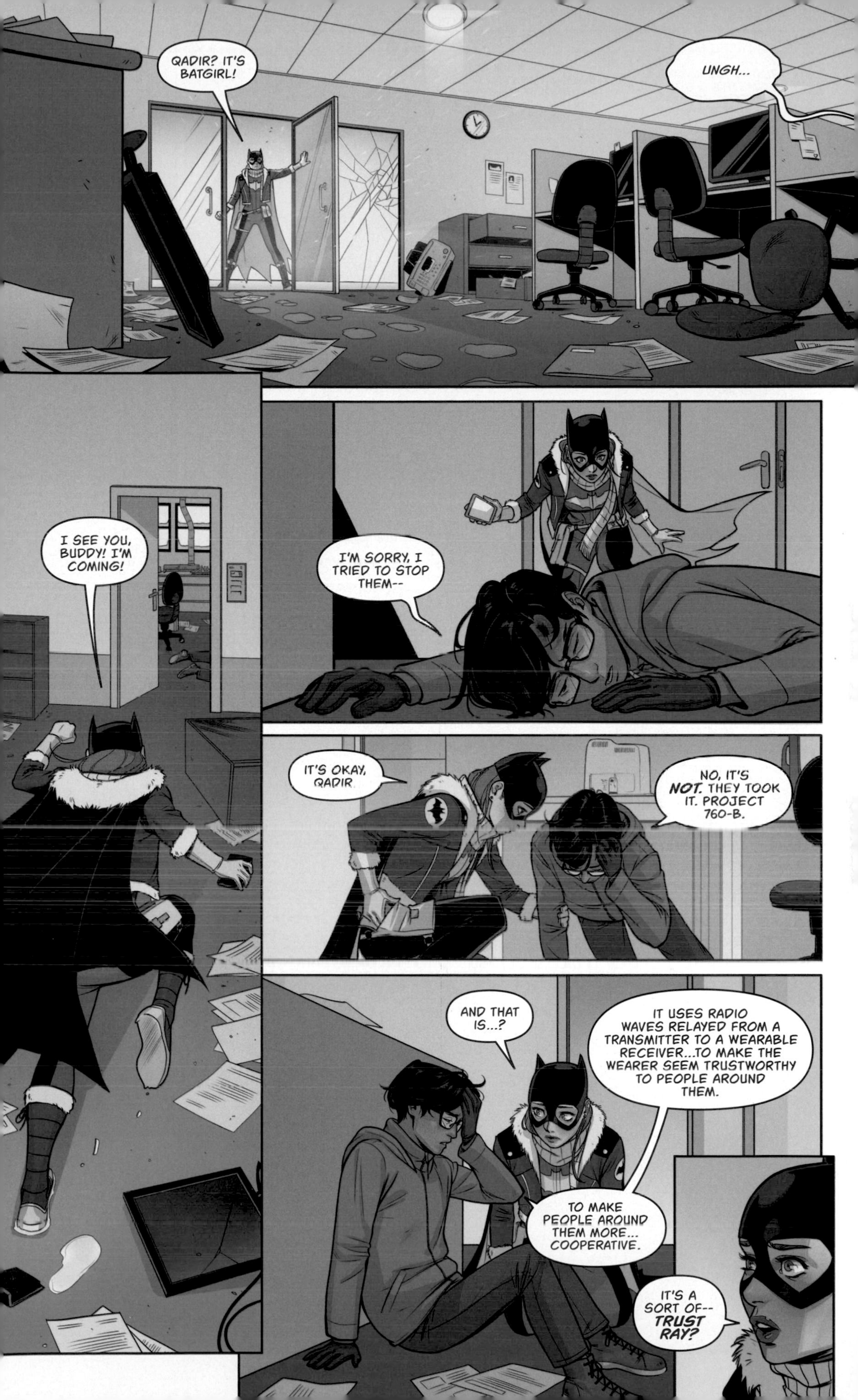
QADIR? IT'S BATGIRL!
UNGH...
I SEE YOU, BUDDY! I'M COMING!
I'M SORRY, I TRIED TO STOP THEM--
IT'S OKAY, QADIR.
NO, IT'S NOT. THEY TOOK IT. PROJECT 760-B.
AND THAT IS...?
IT USES RADIO WAVES RELAYED FROM A TRANSMITTER TO A WEARABLE RECEIVER...TO MAKE THE WEARER SEEM TRUSTWORTHY TO PEOPLE AROUND THEM.
TO MAKE PEOPLE AROUND THEM MORE... COOPERATIVE.
IT'S A SORT OF-- TRUST RAY?

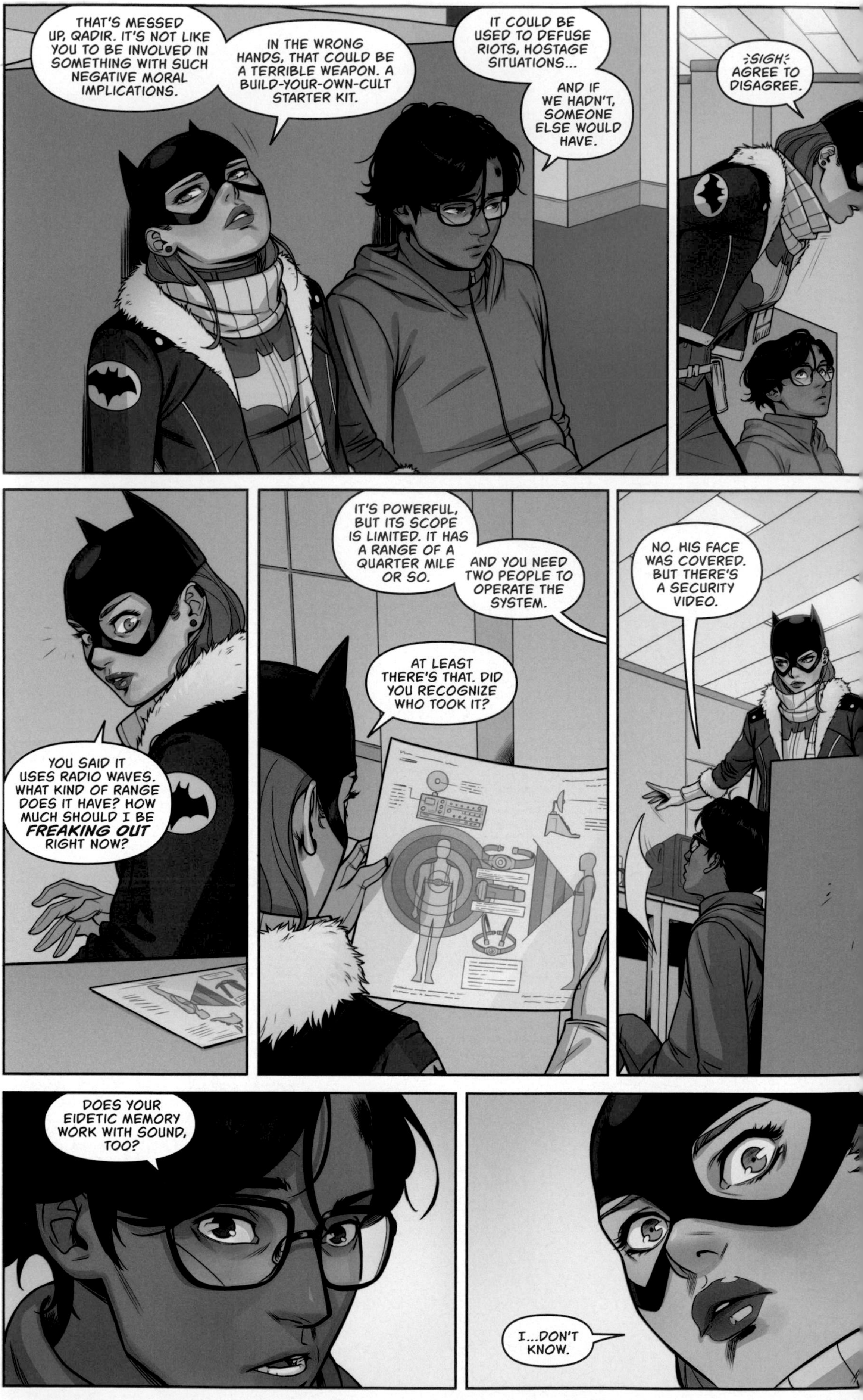
THAT'S MESSED UP, QADIR. IT'S NOT LIKE YOU TO BE INVOLVED IN SOMETHING WITH SUCH NEGATIVE MORAL IMPLICATIONS.
IN THE WRONG HANDS, THAT COULD BE A TERRIBLE WEAPON. A BUILD-YOUR-OWN-CULT STARTER KIT.
IT COULD BE USED TO DEFUSE RIOTS, HOSTAGE SITUATIONS...
AND IF WE HADN'T, SOMEONE ELSE WOULD HAVE.
SIGH AGREE TO DISAGREE.
YOU SAID IT USES RADIO WAVES. WHAT KIND OF RANGE DOES IT HAVE? HOW MUCH SHOULD I BE FREAKING OUT RIGHT NOW?
IT'S POWERFUL, BUT ITS SCOPE IS LIMITED. IT HAS A RANGE OF A QUARTER MILE OR SO.
AND YOU NEED TWO PEOPLE TO OPERATE THE SYSTEM.
AT LEAST THERE'S THAT. DID YOU RECOGNIZE WHO TOOK IT?
NO. HIS FACE WAS COVERED. BUT THERE'S A SECURITY VIDEO.
DOES YOUR EIDETIC MEMORY WORK WITH SOUND, TOO?
I...DON'T KNOW.

"I'VE NEVER TRIED IT. BUT LET'S FIND OUT."

THERE HE IS.

HERE.

READY?

ANY TIME.

SLAK

CRASH

THUD

WHERE IS IT? THE DEVICE?!

I--I DON'T KNOW WHAT YOU'RE TALKING ABOUT.

DON'T BE STUPID. I HACKED YOUR NETWORK. I KNOW WHAT YOU'RE BUILDING IN HERE!

YOU'RE MISTAKEN. WE DON'T HAVE ANYTHING THAT--

WHUD UNGH--

AHA! THIS IS IT! I'VE GOT IT.

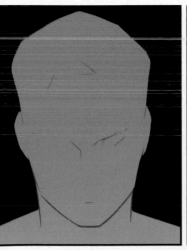

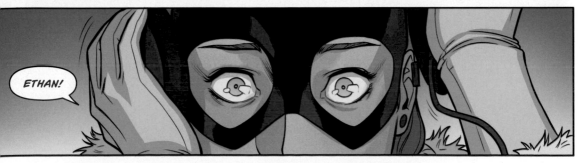

ETHAN!

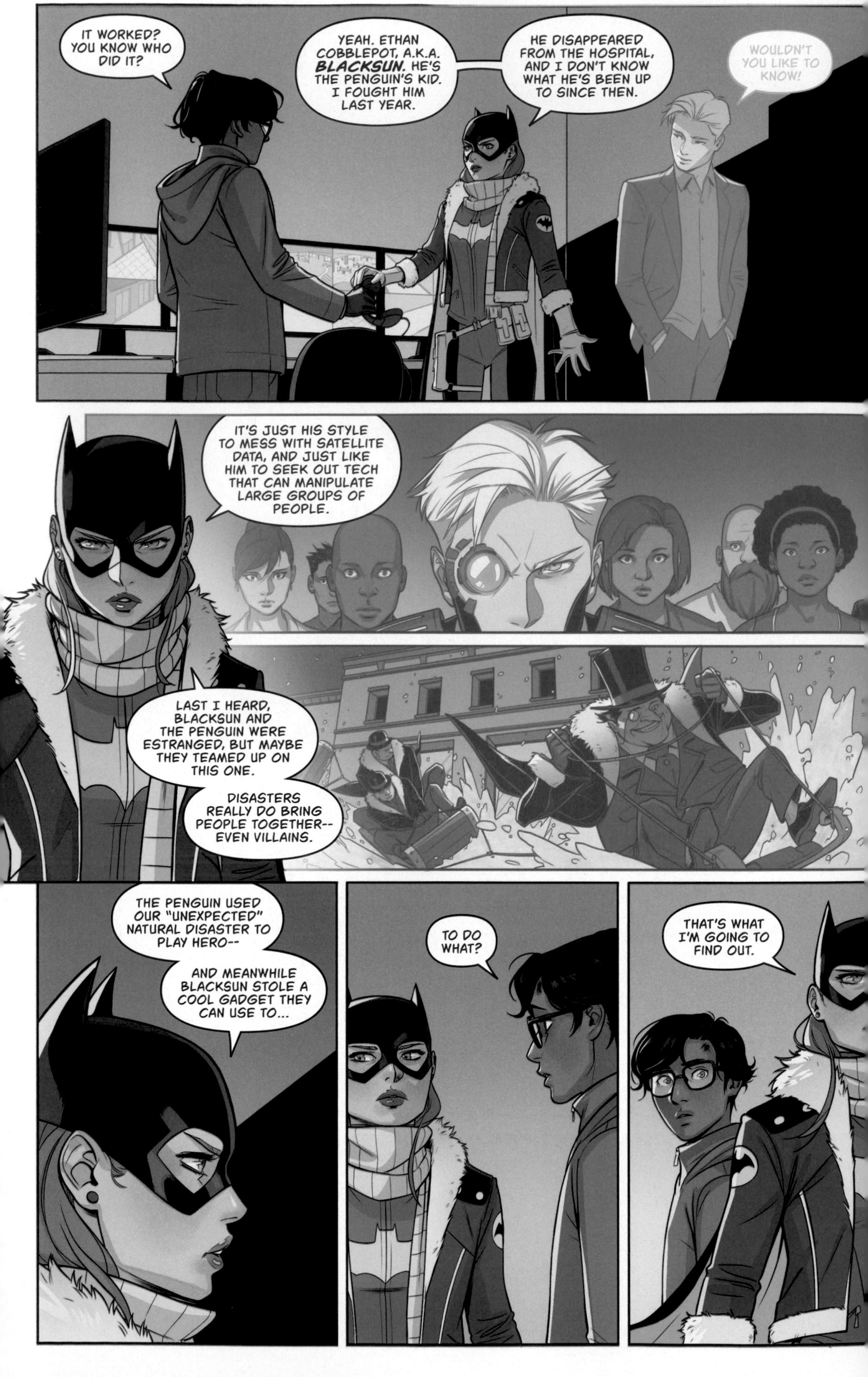
IT WORKED? YOU KNOW WHO DID IT?
YEAH. ETHAN COBBLEPOT, A.K.A. BLACKSUN. HE'S THE PENGUIN'S KID. I FOUGHT HIM LAST YEAR.
HE DISAPPEARED FROM THE HOSPITAL, AND I DON'T KNOW WHAT HE'S BEEN UP TO SINCE THEN.
WOULDN'T YOU LIKE TO KNOW!
IT'S JUST HIS STYLE TO MESS WITH SATELLITE DATA, AND JUST LIKE HIM TO SEEK OUT TECH THAT CAN MANIPULATE LARGE GROUPS OF PEOPLE.
LAST I HEARD, BLACKSUN AND THE PENGUIN WERE ESTRANGED, BUT MAYBE THEY TEAMED UP ON THIS ONE.
DISASTERS REALLY DO BRING PEOPLE TOGETHER-- EVEN VILLAINS.
THE PENGUIN USED OUR "UNEXPECTED" NATURAL DISASTER TO PLAY HERO--
AND MEANWHILE BLACKSUN STOLE A COOL GADGET THEY CAN USE TO...
TO DO WHAT?
THAT'S WHAT I'M GOING TO FIND OUT.

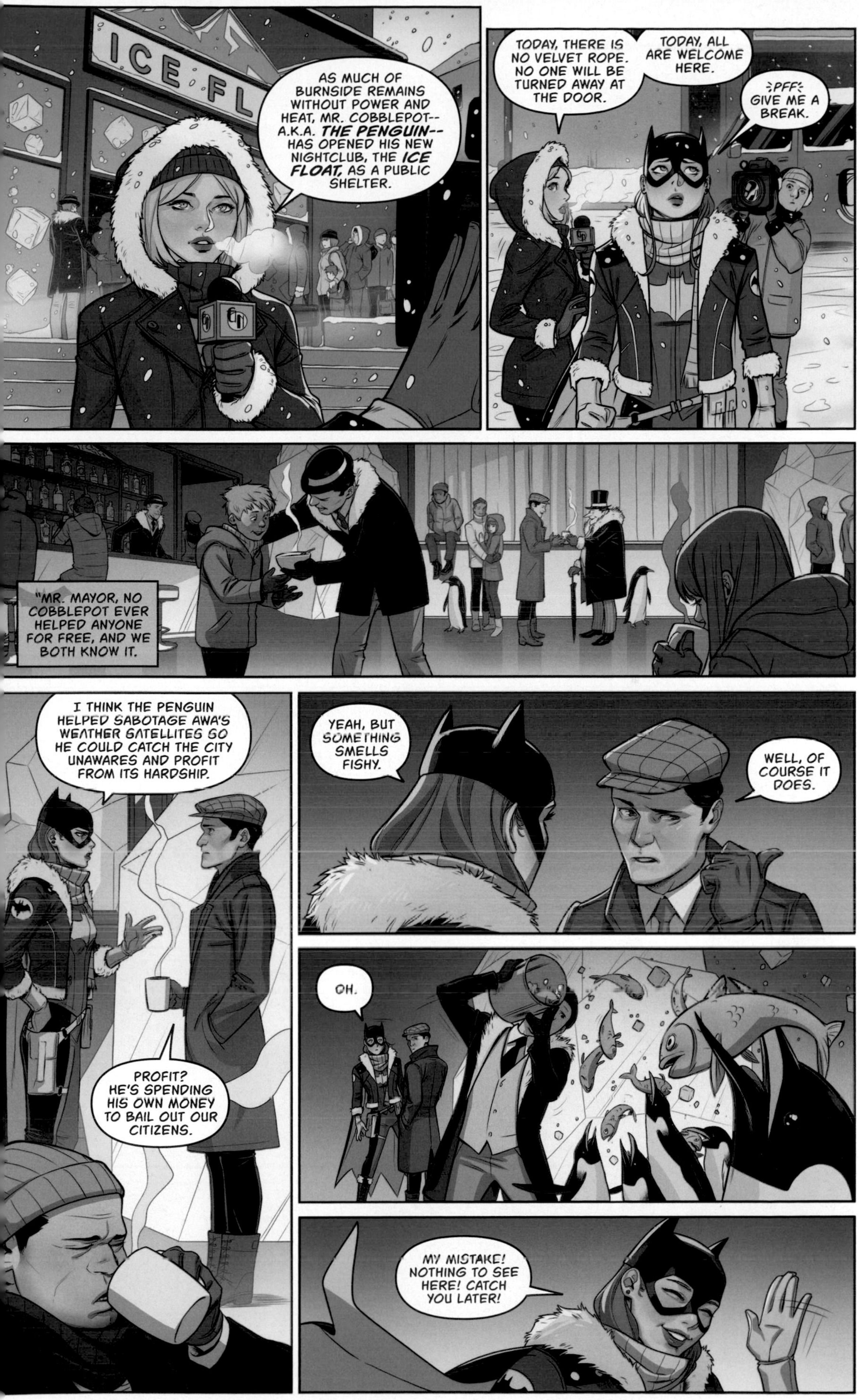
ICE FL
AS MUCH OF BURNSIDE REMAINS WITHOUT POWER AND HEAT, MR. COBBLEPOT-- A.K.A. THE PENGUIN-- HAS OPENED HIS NEW NIGHTCLUB, THE ICE FLOAT, AS A PUBLIC SHELTER.
TODAY, THERE IS NO VELVET ROPE. NO ONE WILL BE TURNED AWAY AT THE DOOR.
TODAY, ALL ARE WELCOME HERE.
PFF GIVE ME A BREAK.
"MR. MAYOR, NO COBBLEPOT EVER HELPED ANYONE FOR FREE, AND WE BOTH KNOW IT.
I THINK THE PENGUIN HELPED SABOTAGE AWA'S WEATHER SATELLITES SO HE COULD CATCH THE CITY UNAWARES AND PROFIT FROM ITS HARDSHIP.
PROFIT? HE'S SPENDING HIS OWN MONEY TO BAIL OUT OUR CITIZENS.
YEAH, BUT SOMETHING SMELLS FISHY.
WELL, OF COURSE IT DOES.
OH.
MY MISTAKE! NOTHING TO SEE HERE! CATCH YOU LATER!

♫♪♪♫

HUH?
WHY DID I
JUST--?

THE *TRUST RAY.*
IT GOT THE MAYOR,
AND IT GOT ME, TOO.
WHICH MEANS THE
PENGUIN'S ALREADY
WEARING IT.

I CAN'T
GO AFTER THE
PENGUIN DIRECTLY,
WHICH MEANS I NEED
TO FIND BLACKSUN
AND SHUT THE DEVICE
DOWN FROM THE
TRANSMITTER
END.

IF THE SYSTEM
HAS A RANGE OF
A QUARTER MILE,
LIKE QADIR SAID, THEN
BLACKSUN ISN'T FAR
FROM HERE.

ALL I
HAVE TO DO
IS LOCATE THE
SIGNAL...

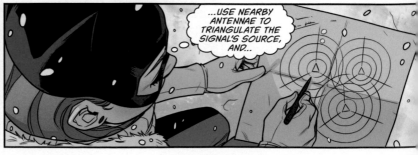

...USE NEARBY
ANTENNAE TO
TRIANGULATE THE
SIGNAL'S SOURCE,
AND...

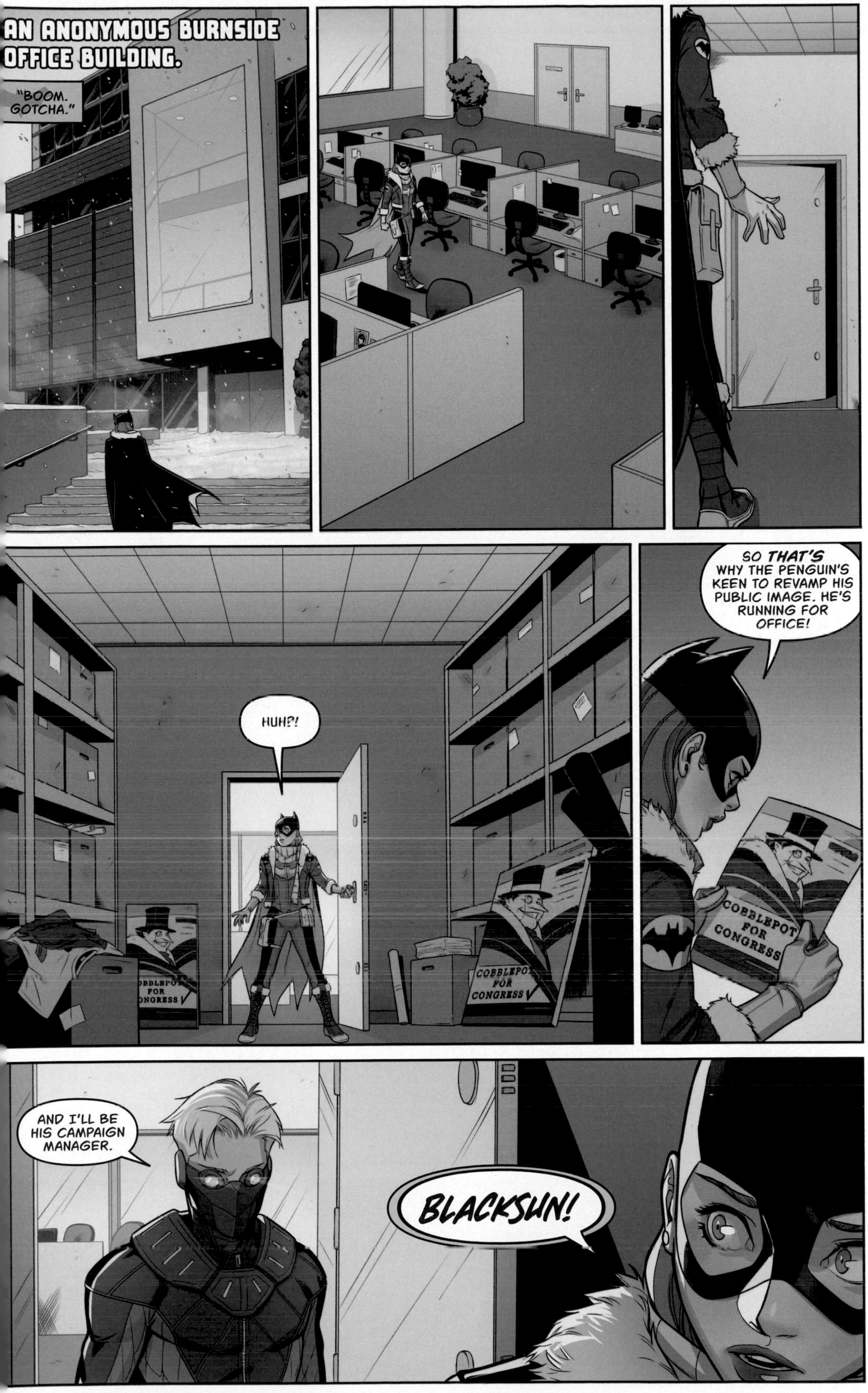
AN ANONYMOUS BURNSIDE OFFICE BUILDING.
"BOOM. GOTCHA."
HUH?!
SO THAT'S WHY THE PENGUIN'S KEEN TO REVAMP HIS PUBLIC IMAGE. HE'S RUNNING FOR OFFICE!
COBBLEPOT FOR CONGRESS
AND I'LL BE HIS CAMPAIGN MANAGER.
BLACKSUN!

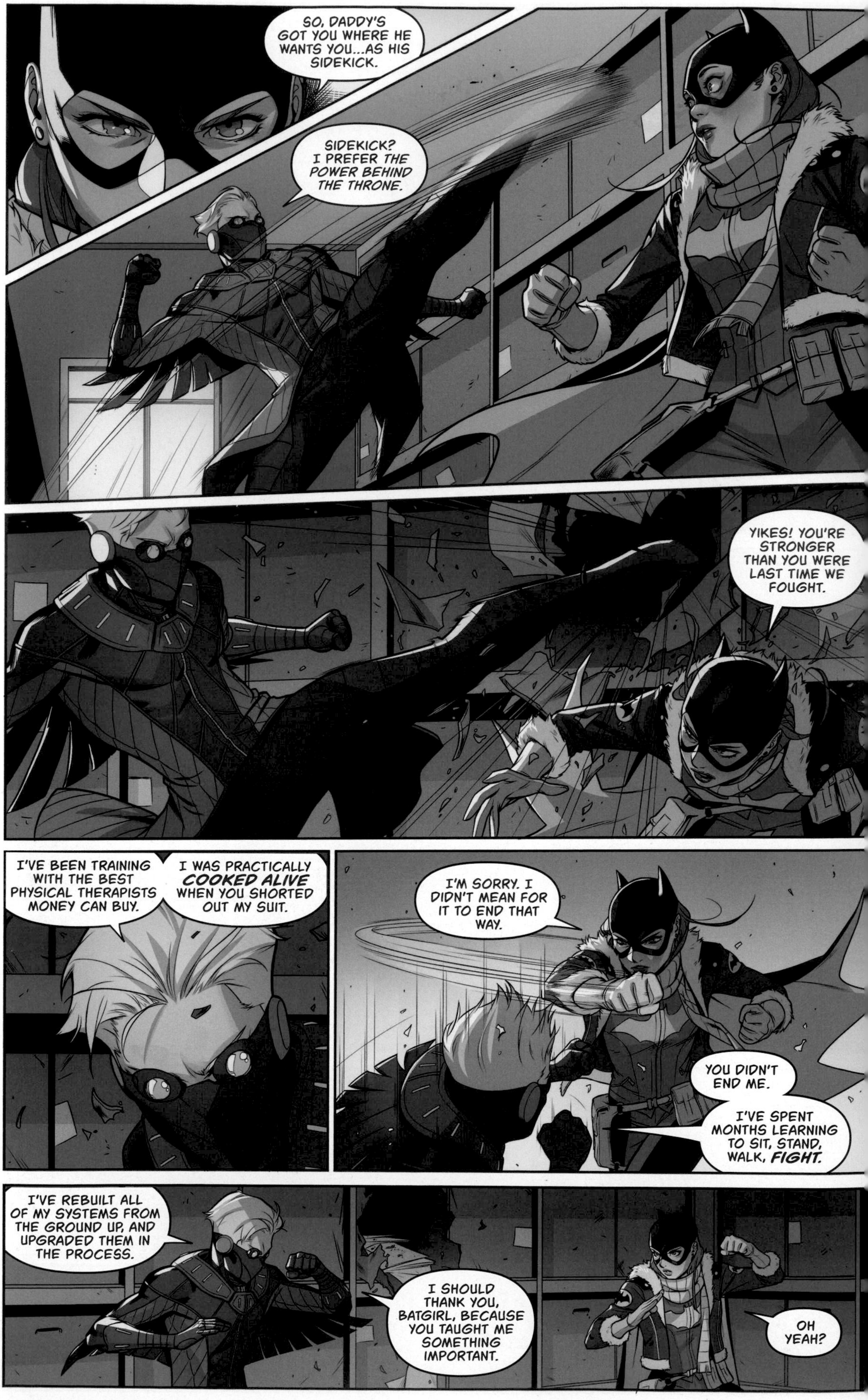
SO, DADDY'S GOT YOU WHERE HE WANTS YOU...AS HIS SIDEKICK.
SIDEKICK? I PREFER *THE POWER BEHIND THE THRONE.*
YIKES! YOU'RE STRONGER THAN YOU WERE LAST TIME WE FOUGHT.
I'VE BEEN TRAINING WITH THE BEST PHYSICAL THERAPISTS MONEY CAN BUY.
I WAS PRACTICALLY **COOKED ALIVE** WHEN YOU SHORTED OUT MY SUIT.
I'M SORRY. I DIDN'T MEAN FOR IT TO END THAT WAY.
YOU DIDN'T END ME.
I'VE SPENT MONTHS LEARNING TO SIT, STAND, WALK, ***FIGHT.***
I'VE REBUILT ALL OF MY SYSTEMS FROM THE GROUND UP, AND UPGRADED THEM IN THE PROCESS.
I SHOULD THANK YOU, BATGIRL, BECAUSE YOU TAUGHT ME SOMETHING IMPORTANT.
OH YEAH?

YOU MADE ME REALIZE I WAS THINKING ABOUT TECH IN THE WRONG WAY.

I SPENT SO MUCH TIME BUILDING BEAUTIFUL, COMPLEX SYSTEMS OF CODE, *MICROMANAGING* PEOPLE SO THEY'D DO JUST WHAT I WANTED...

≥HRK!≤

BUT WHY MESS AROUND WITH DETAILS WHEN I CAN GET WHAT I WANT WITH A FEW *BOLD STROKES?*

≥GASP!≤

SHNK

YOU MEAN THE SATELLITES. CONTROL WHAT THE SATELLITES SAY, AND YOU CONTROL EVERYTHING ON EARTH.

IT'S ALL ABOUT PERCEPTION. WE TRUST WHAT OUR PHONES TELL US MORE THAN WE TRUST OUR OWN EYES.

PLINK PLINK PLINK

DARK CLOUDS ON THE HORIZON? IF YOUR POCKET COMPUTER SAYS YOU DON'T NEED TO WORRY, YOU WON'T.

AND WHILE YOU'RE AT IT, WHY NOT HEDGE YOUR BETS WITH A LITTLE *LIGHT BRAINWASHING?*

SMOOTH AWAY ANY MISGIVINGS FOLKS MAY HAVE ABOUT CEDING CONTROL OF BURNSIDE TO *KNOWN CRIMINALS.*

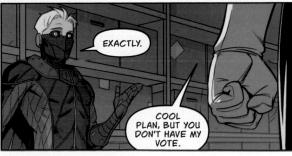

EXACTLY.

COOL PLAN, BUT YOU DON'T HAVE MY VOTE.

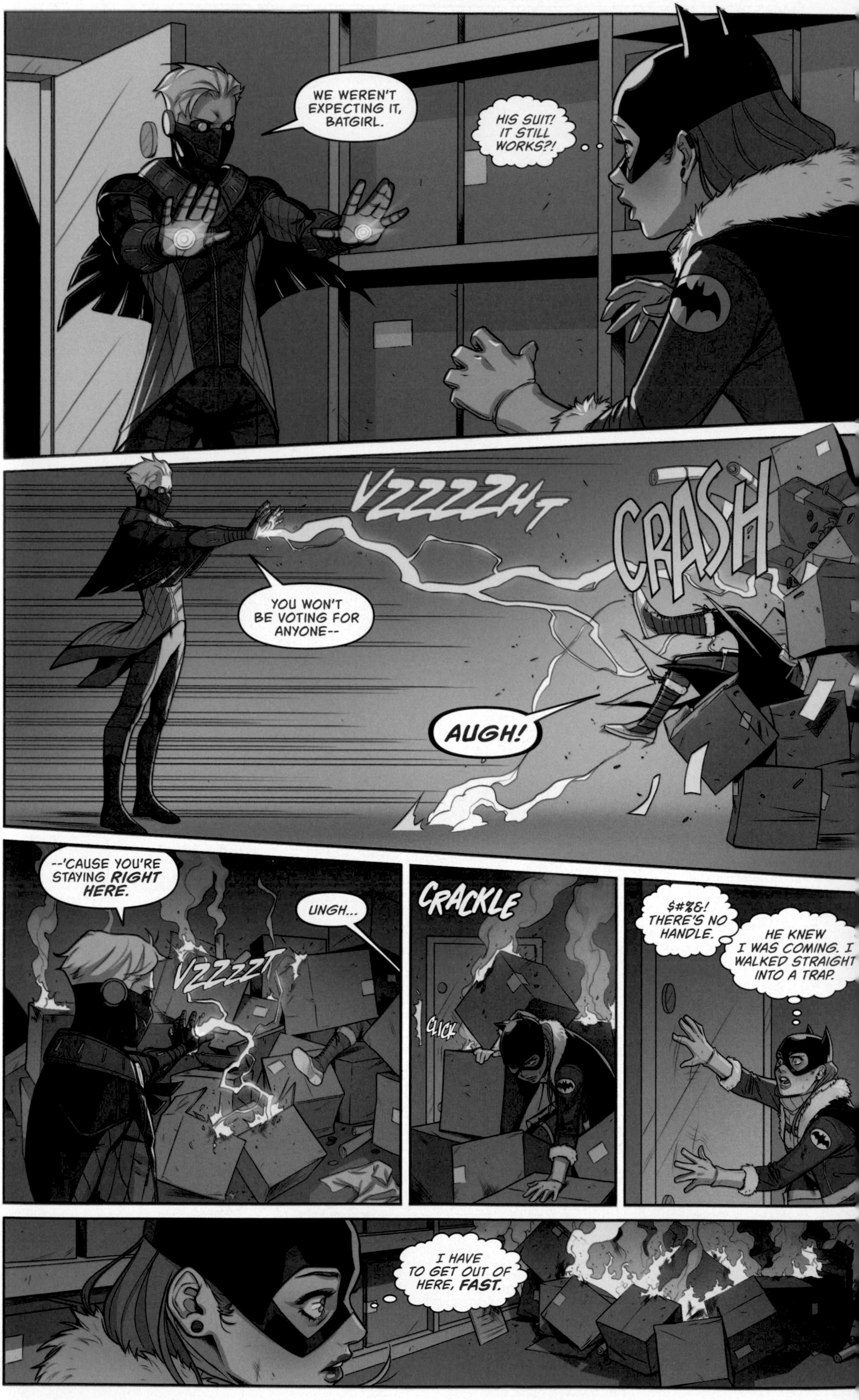
WE WEREN'T EXPECTING IT, BATGIRL.
HIS SUIT! IT STILL WORKS?!
VZZZZZHT
CRASH
YOU WON'T BE VOTING FOR ANYONE--
AUGH!
--'CAUSE YOU'RE STAYING RIGHT HERE.
UNGH...
VZZZZT
CRACKLE
CLICK
$#%&! THERE'S NO HANDLE.
HE KNEW I WAS COMING. I WALKED STRAIGHT INTO A TRAP.
I HAVE TO GET OUT OF HERE, FAST.

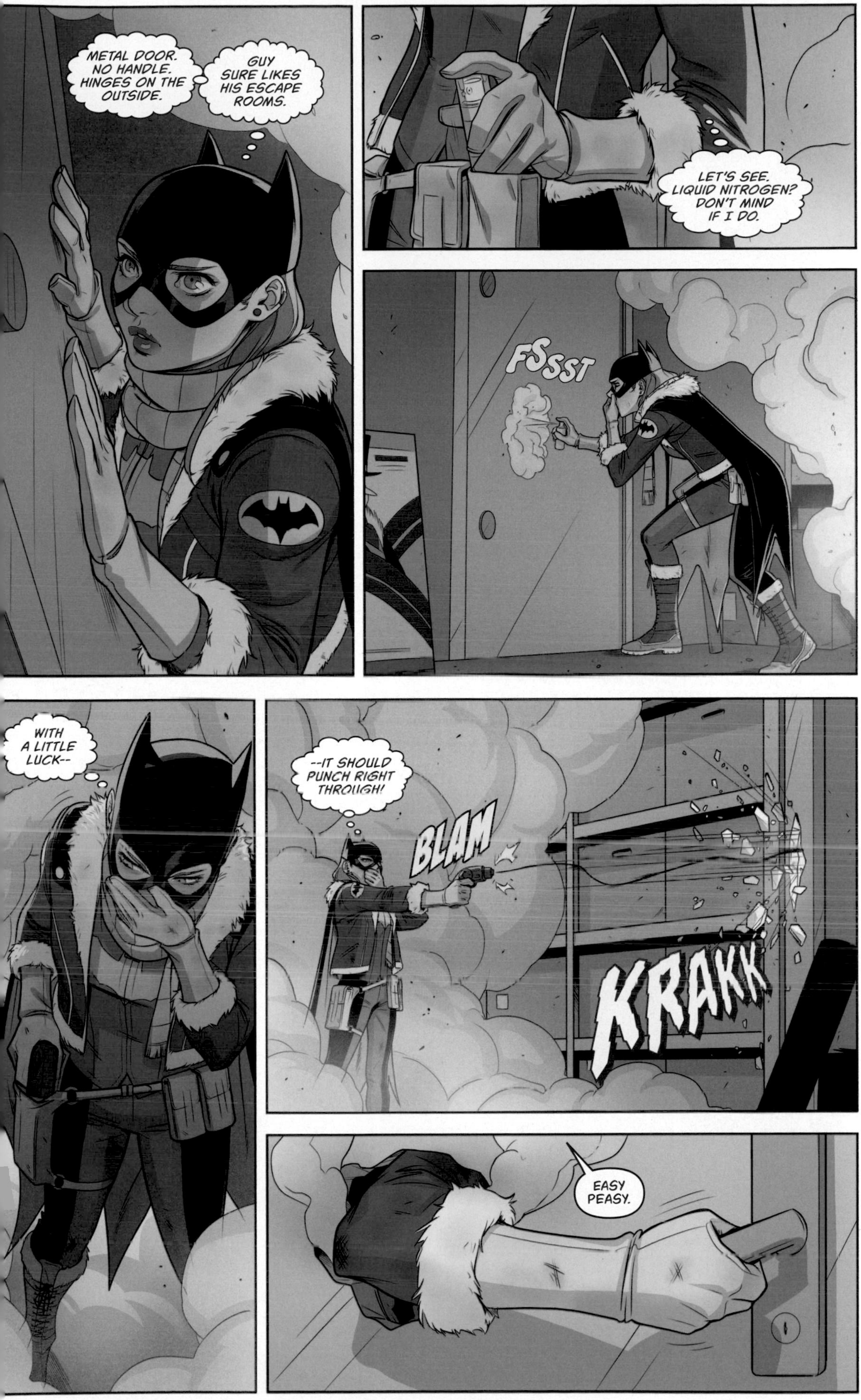
METAL DOOR. NO HANDLE. HINGES ON THE OUTSIDE.
GUY SURE LIKES HIS ESCAPE ROOMS.
LET'S SEE. LIQUID NITROGEN? DON'T MIND IF I DO.
FSSST
WITH A LITTLE LUCK--
--IT SHOULD PUNCH RIGHT THROUGH!
BLAM
KRAKK
EASY PEASY.

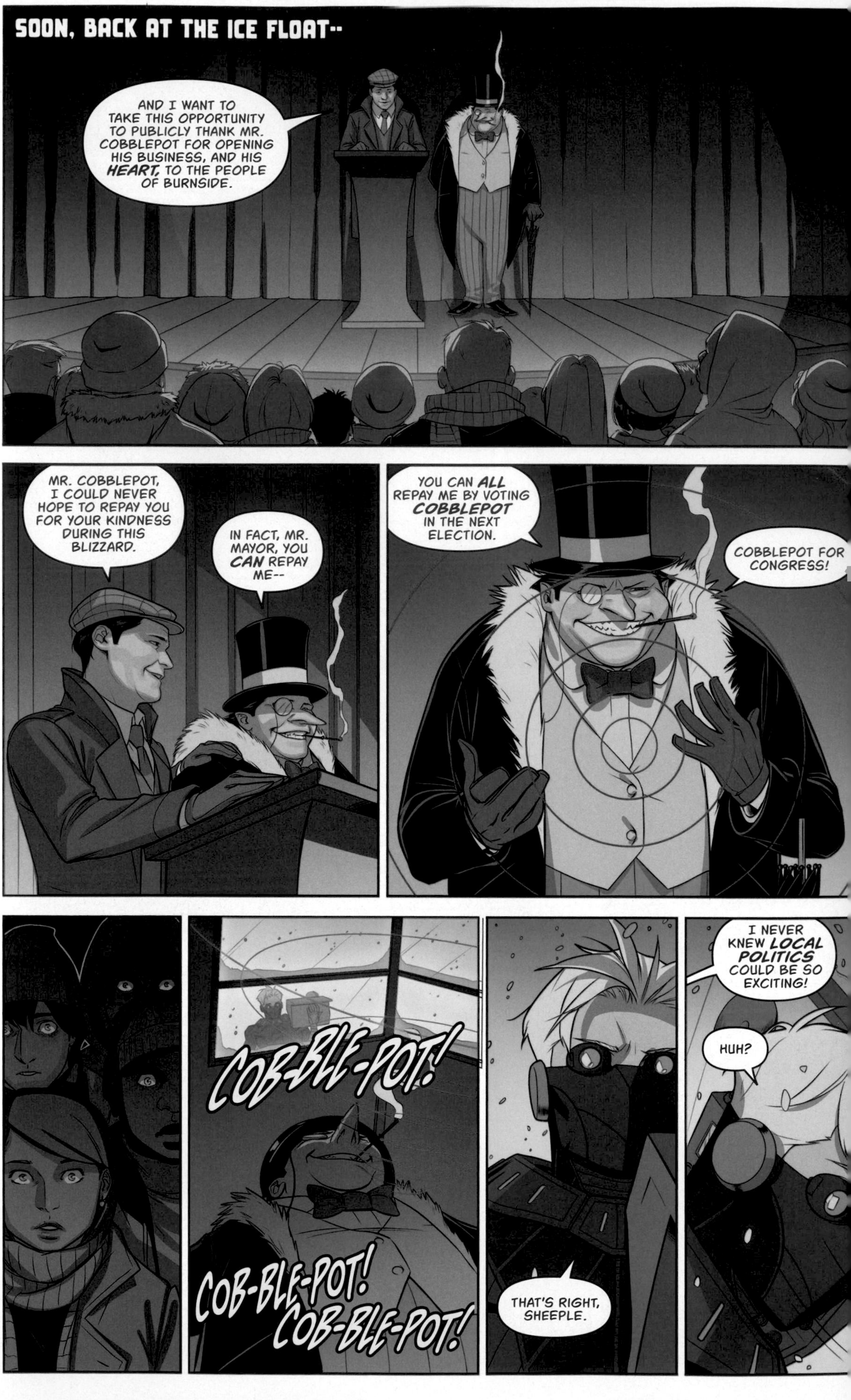
SOON, BACK AT THE ICE FLOAT--
AND I WANT TO TAKE THIS OPPORTUNITY TO PUBLICLY THANK MR. COBBLEPOT FOR OPENING HIS BUSINESS, AND HIS HEART, TO THE PEOPLE OF BURNSIDE.
MR. COBBLEPOT, I COULD NEVER HOPE TO REPAY YOU FOR YOUR KINDNESS DURING THIS BLIZZARD.
IN FACT, MR. MAYOR, YOU CAN REPAY ME--
YOU CAN ALL REPAY ME BY VOTING COBBLEPOT IN THE NEXT ELECTION.
COBBLEPOT FOR CONGRESS!
COB-BLE-POT!
COB-BLE-POT!
COB-BLE-POT!
THAT'S RIGHT, SHEEPLE.
I NEVER KNEW LOCAL POLITICS COULD BE SO EXCITING!
HUH?

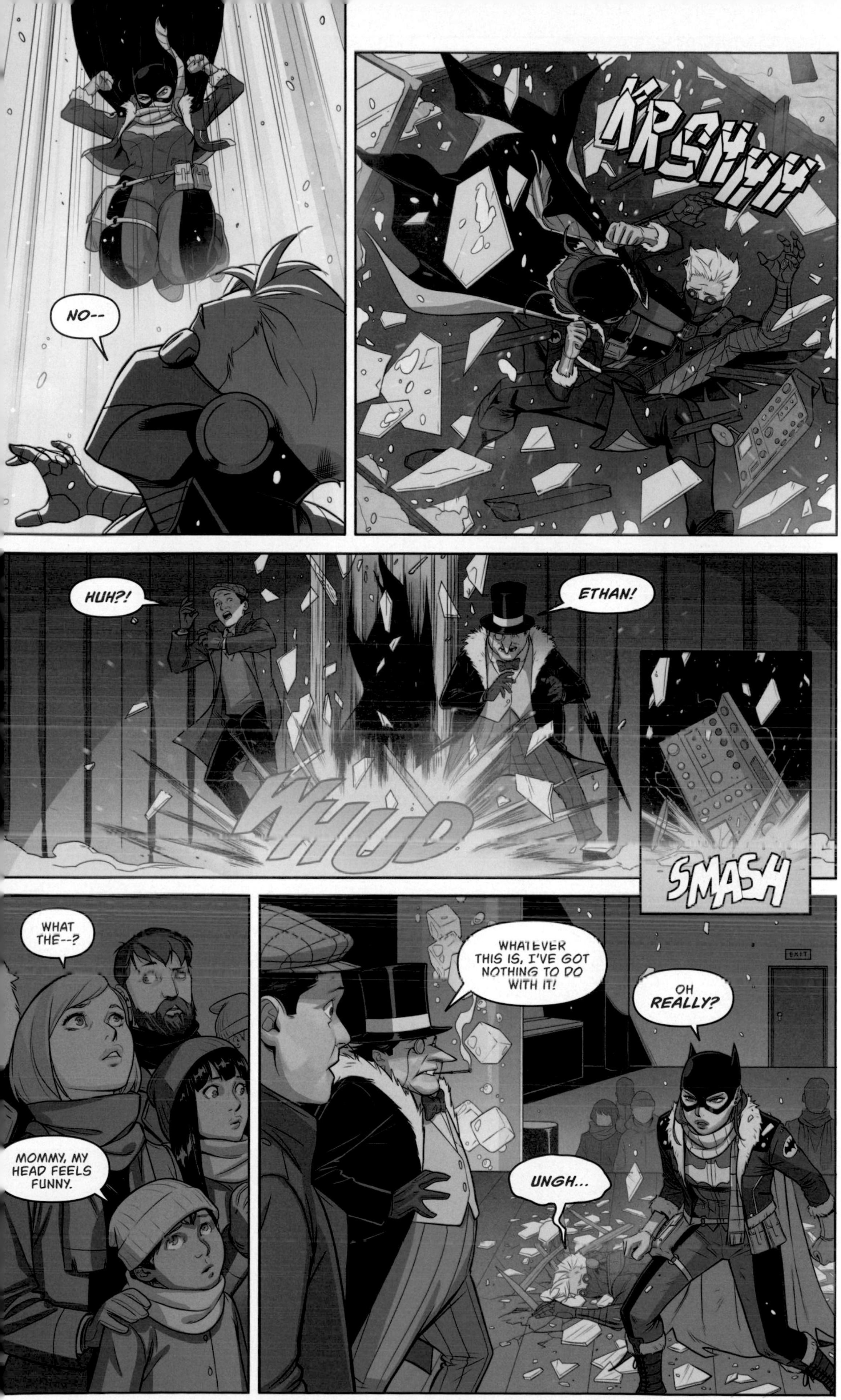
NO--
KRSHHH
HUH?!
ETHAN!
WHUD
SMASH
WHAT THE--?
MOMMY, MY HEAD FEELS FUNNY.
WHATEVER THIS IS, I'VE GOT NOTHING TO DO WITH IT!
OH REALLY?
UNGH...
EXIT

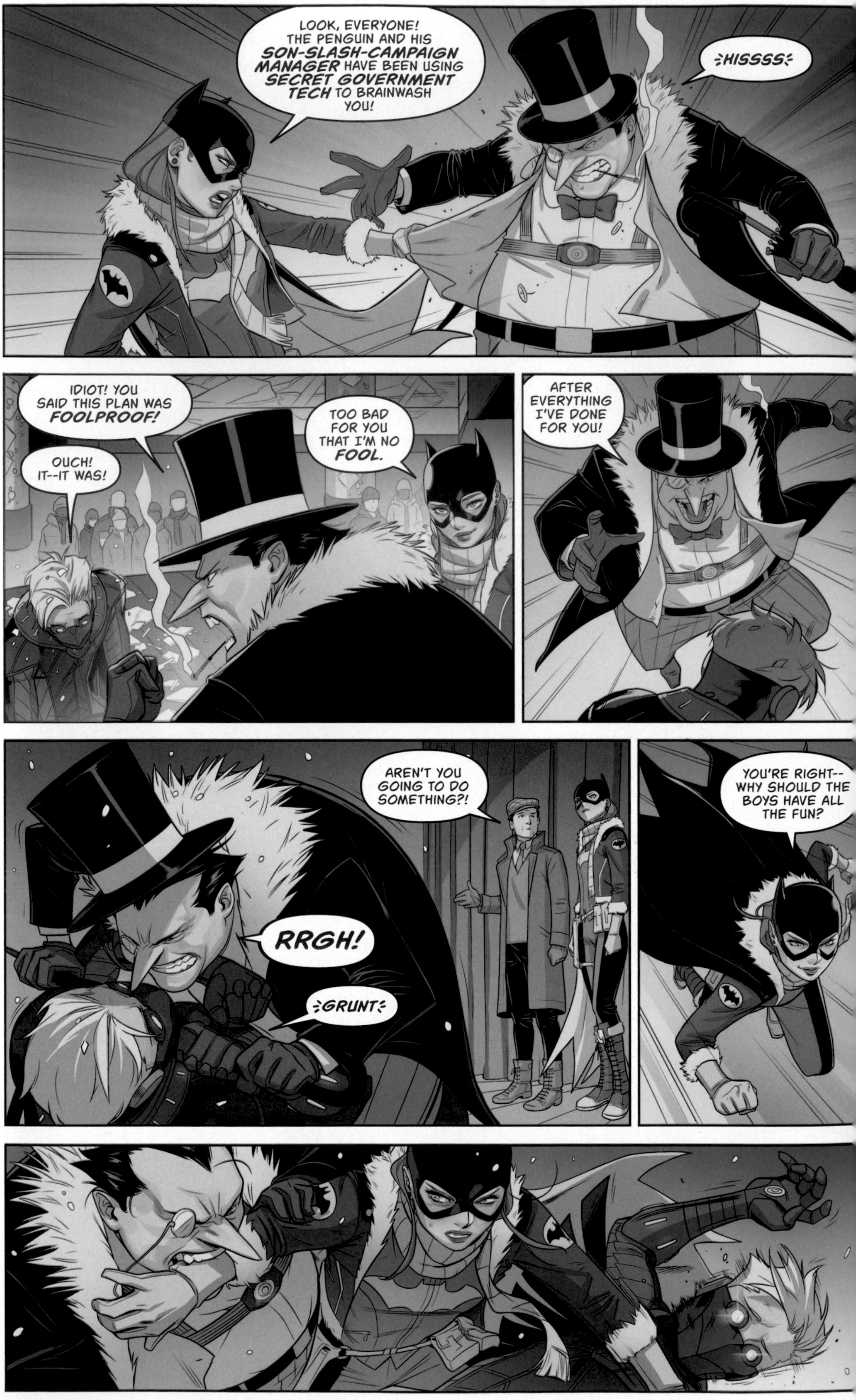
LOOK, EVERYONE! THE PENGUIN AND HIS SON-SLASH-CAMPAIGN MANAGER HAVE BEEN USING SECRET GOVERNMENT TECH TO BRAINWASH YOU!
HISSSS
IDIOT! YOU SAID THIS PLAN WAS FOOLPROOF!
OUCH! IT--IT WAS!
TOO BAD FOR YOU THAT I'M NO FOOL.
AFTER EVERYTHING I'VE DONE FOR YOU!
RRGH!
GRUNT
AREN'T YOU GOING TO DO SOMETHING?!
YOU'RE RIGHT-- WHY SHOULD THE BOYS HAVE ALL THE FUN?

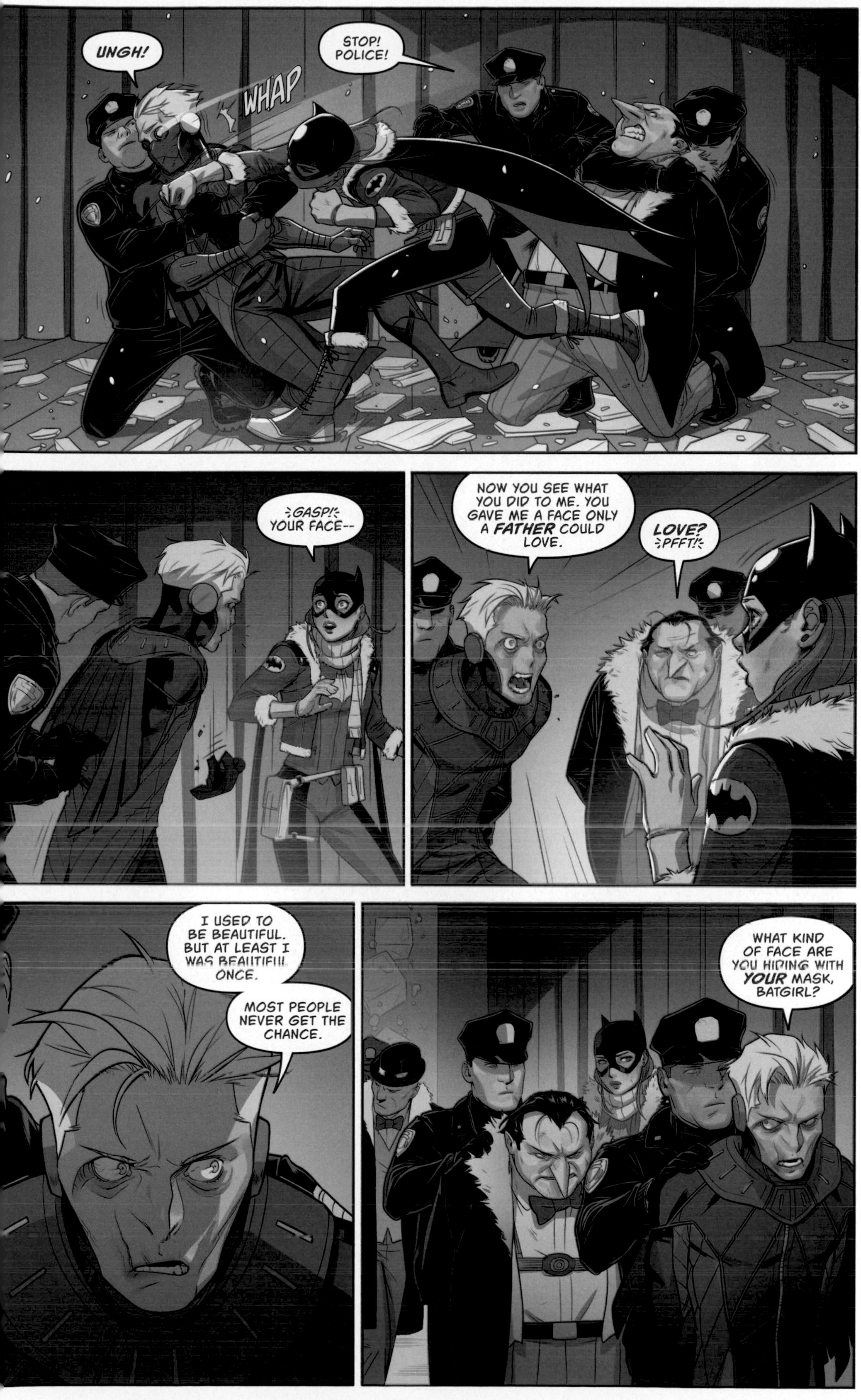
UNGH!
STOP! POLICE!
WHAP
GASP! YOUR FACE--
NOW YOU SEE WHAT YOU DID TO ME. YOU GAVE ME A FACE ONLY A FATHER COULD LOVE.
LOVE? PFFT!
I USED TO BE BEAUTIFUL. BUT AT LEAST I WAS BEAUTIFUL ONCE.
MOST PEOPLE NEVER GET THE CHANCE.
WHAT KIND OF FACE ARE YOU HIDING WITH YOUR MASK, BATGIRL?

LATER.

"I BET *YOU'VE* GOT SCARS, TOO."

HE'S RIGHT. I HAVE SCARS.

I WAS SO YOUNG WHEN I CAME TO BURNSIDE. THE LAST FEW YEARS HAVE LEFT THEIR MARK.

THE DECISIONS I'VE MADE, THE LATE NIGHTS AND EARLY MORNINGS, THE NARROW ESCAPES...

THEY'RE ALL THERE.

I'M NOT A KID ANYMORE.

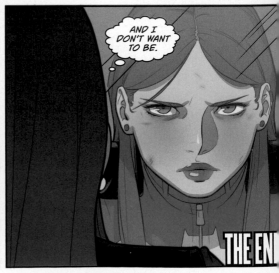

AND I DON'T WANT TO BE.

THE EN

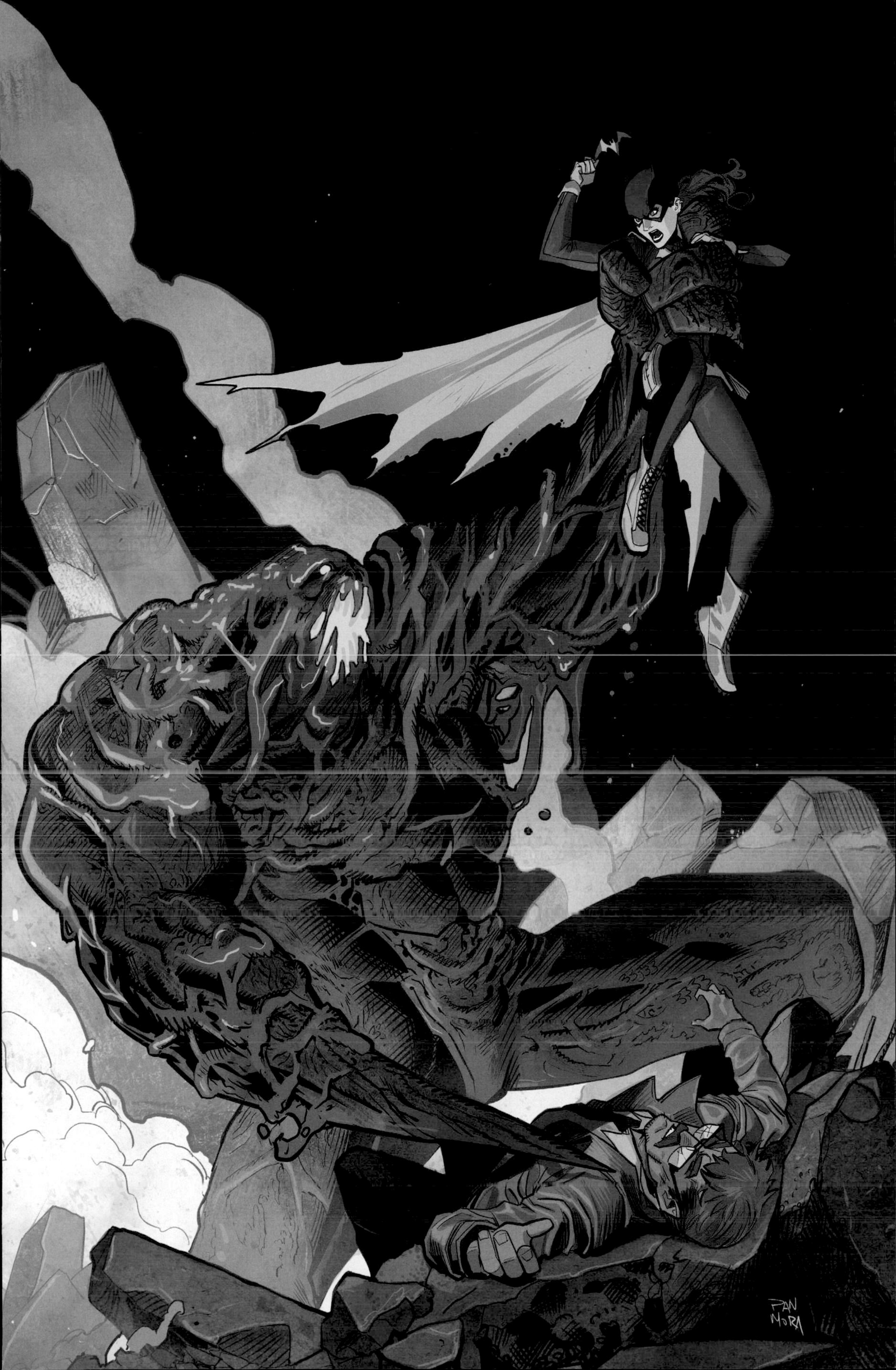
DAN MORA

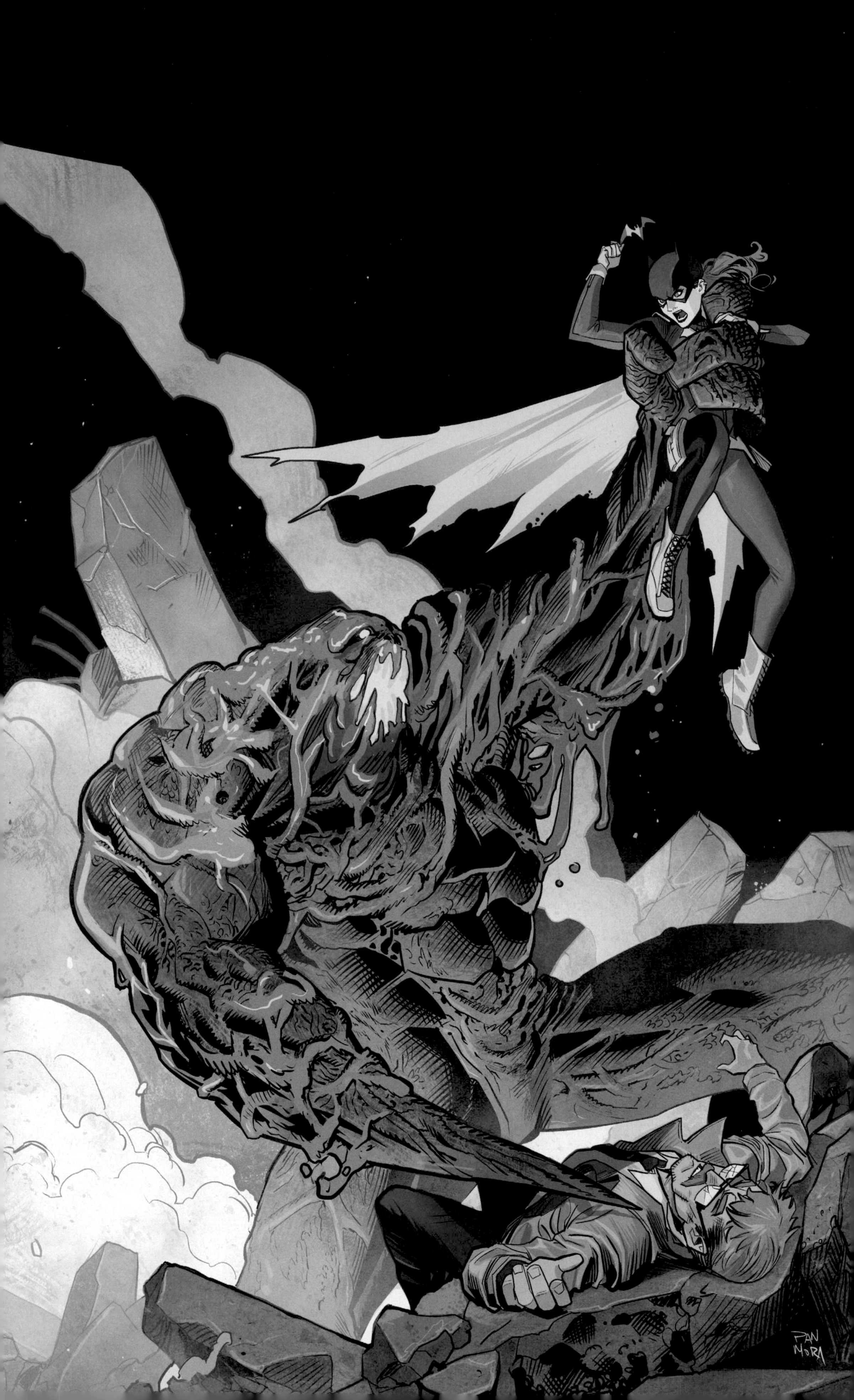
PAN
MORA

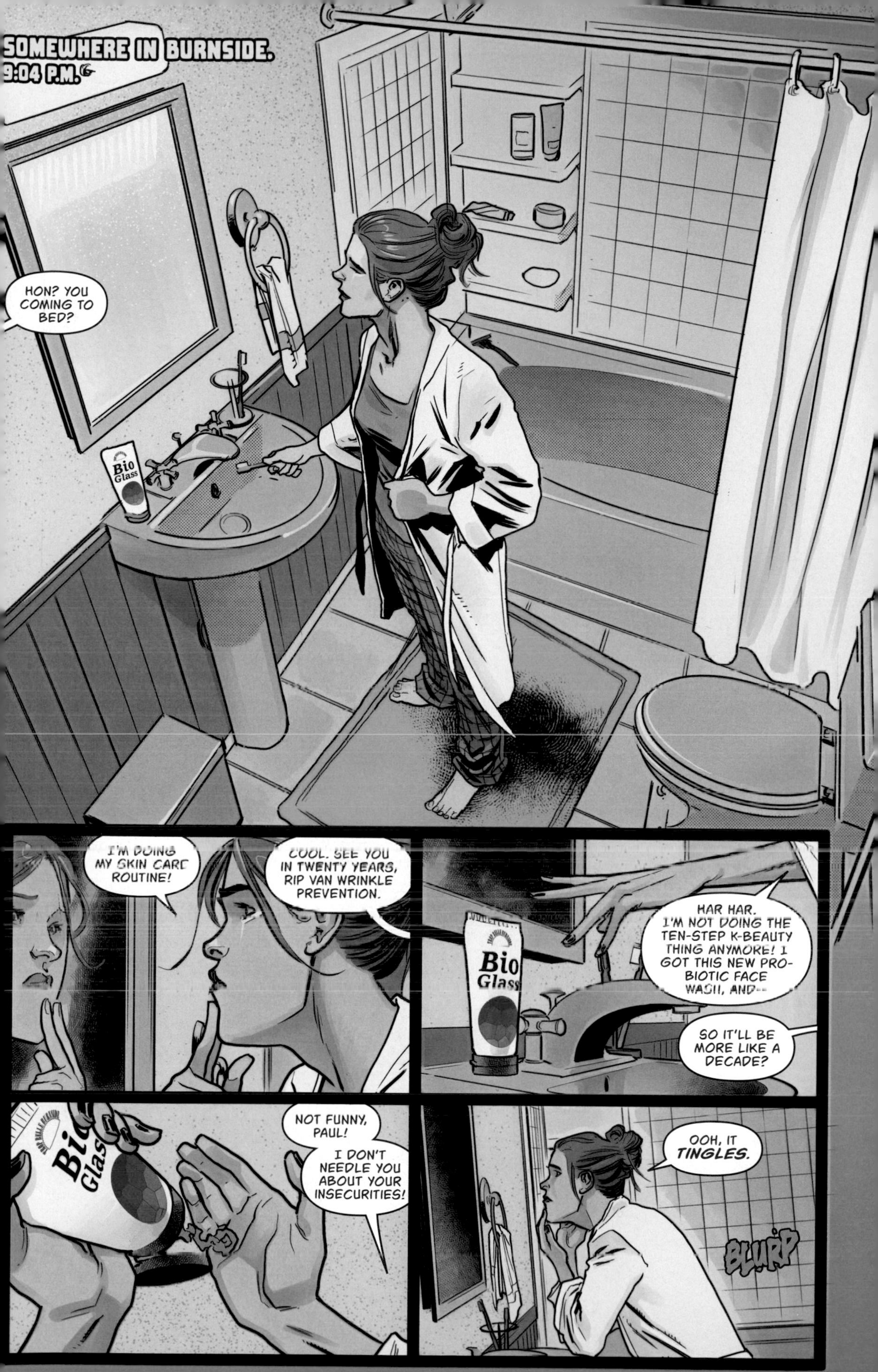
SOMEWHERE IN BURNSIDE.
9:04 P.M.
HON? YOU COMING TO BED?
Bio Glass
I'M DOING MY SKIN CARE ROUTINE!
COOL. SEE YOU IN TWENTY YEARS, RIP VAN WRINKLE PREVENTION.
Bio Glass
HAR HAR. I'M NOT DOING THE TEN-STEP K-BEAUTY THING ANYMORE! I GOT THIS NEW PRO-BIOTIC FACE WASH, AND--
SO IT'LL BE MORE LIKE A DECADE?
NOT FUNNY, PAUL!
I DON'T NEEDLE YOU ABOUT YOUR INSECURITIES!
OOH, IT *TINGLES.*
BLURP

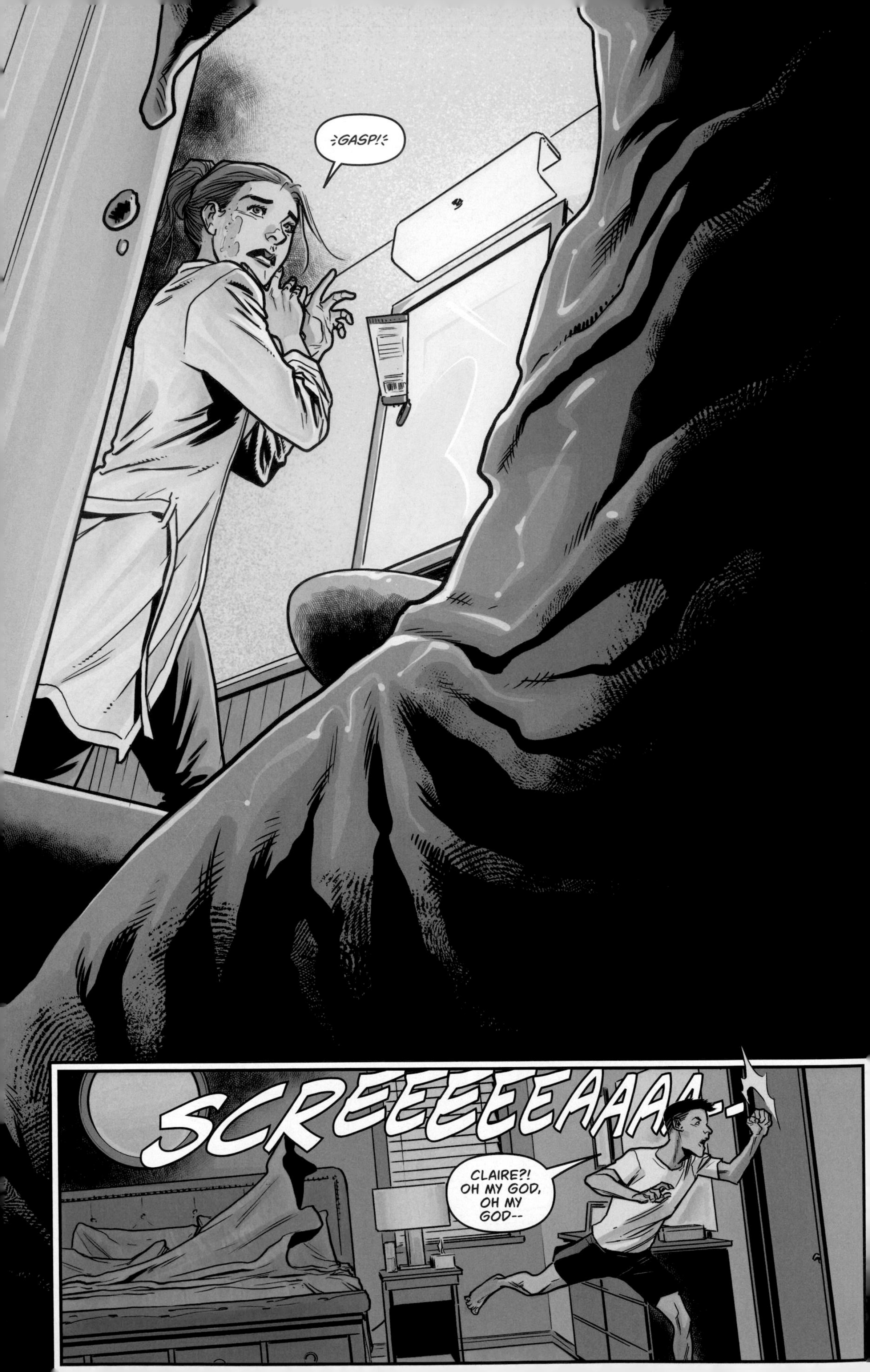
GASP!
SCREEEEEEAAAA--
CLAIRE?! OH MY GOD, OH MY GOD--

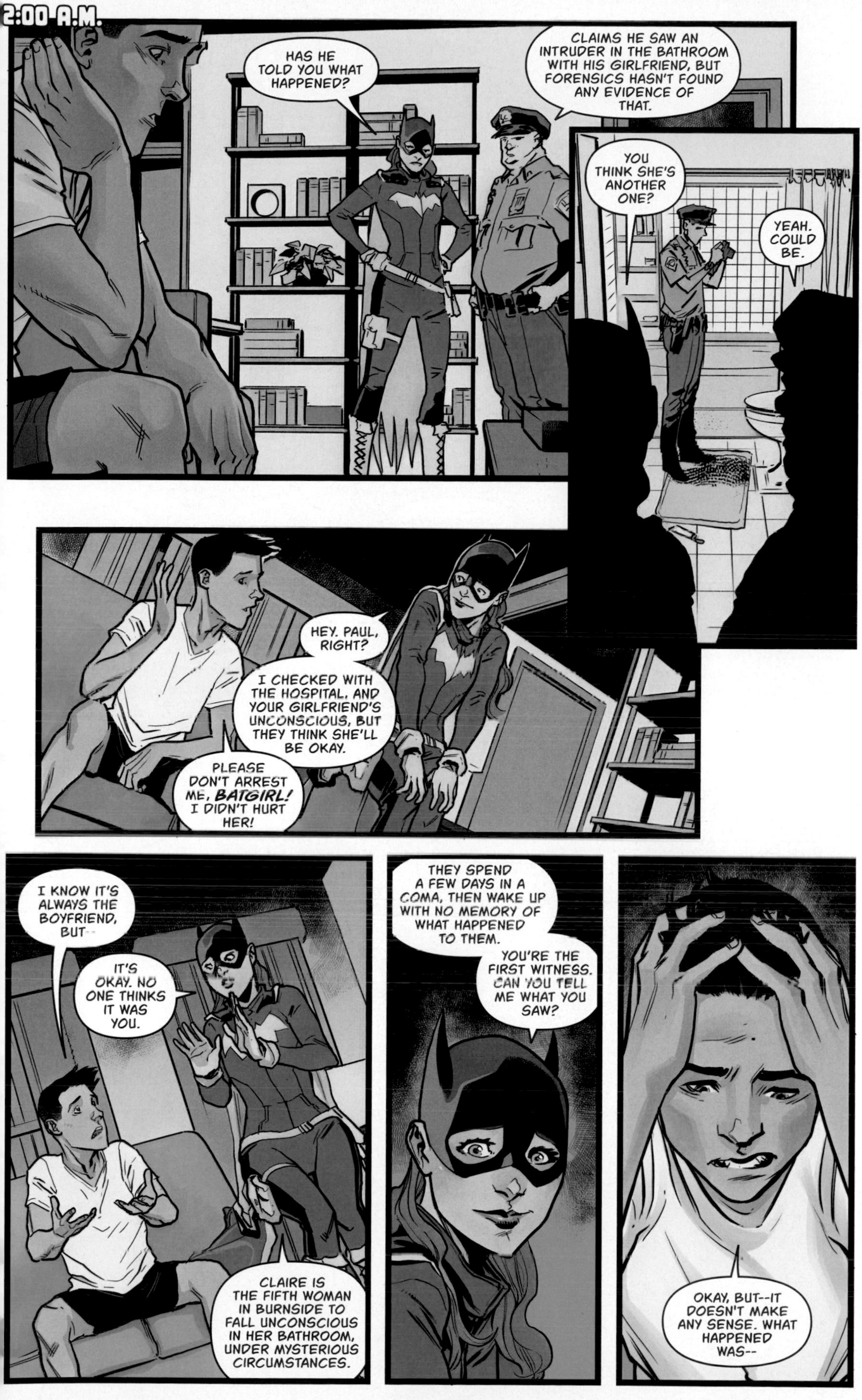
2:00 A.M.
HAS HE TOLD YOU WHAT HAPPENED?
CLAIMS HE SAW AN INTRUDER IN THE BATHROOM WITH HIS GIRLFRIEND, BUT FORENSICS HASN'T FOUND ANY EVIDENCE OF THAT.
YOU THINK SHE'S ANOTHER ONE?
YEAH. COULD BE.
HEY. PAUL, RIGHT?
I CHECKED WITH THE HOSPITAL, AND YOUR GIRLFRIEND'S UNCONSCIOUS, BUT THEY THINK SHE'LL BE OKAY.
PLEASE DON'T ARREST ME, BATGIRL! I DIDN'T HURT HER!
I KNOW IT'S ALWAYS THE BOYFRIEND, BUT--
IT'S OKAY. NO ONE THINKS IT WAS YOU.
CLAIRE IS THE FIFTH WOMAN IN BURNSIDE TO FALL UNCONSCIOUS IN HER BATHROOM, UNDER MYSTERIOUS CIRCUMSTANCES.
THEY SPEND A FEW DAYS IN A COMA, THEN WAKE UP WITH NO MEMORY OF WHAT HAPPENED TO THEM.
YOU'RE THE FIRST WITNESS. CAN YOU TELL ME WHAT YOU SAW?
OKAY, BUT--IT DOESN'T MAKE ANY SENSE. WHAT HAPPENED WAS--

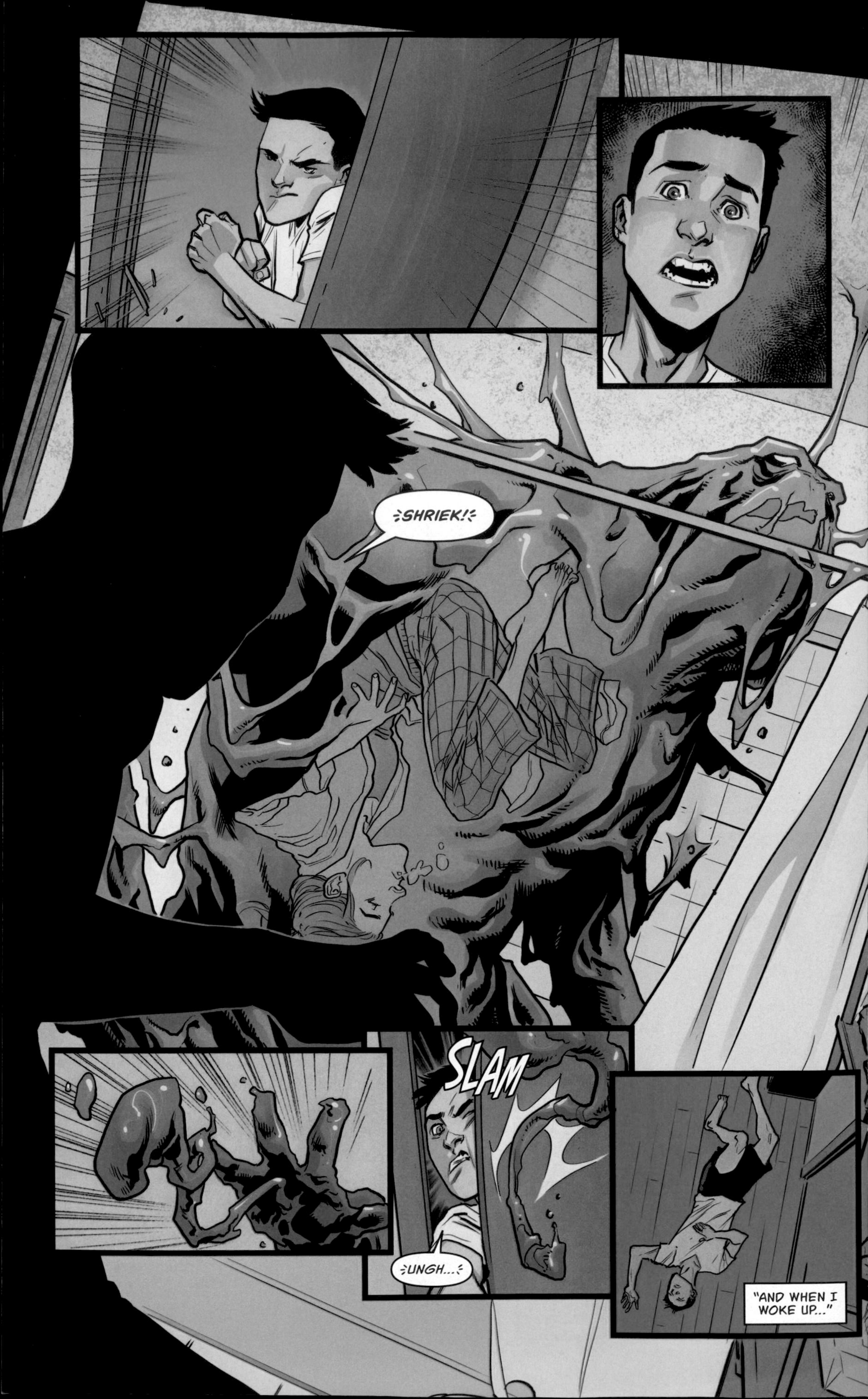
SHRIEK!
SLAM
UNGH...
"AND WHEN I WOKE UP..."

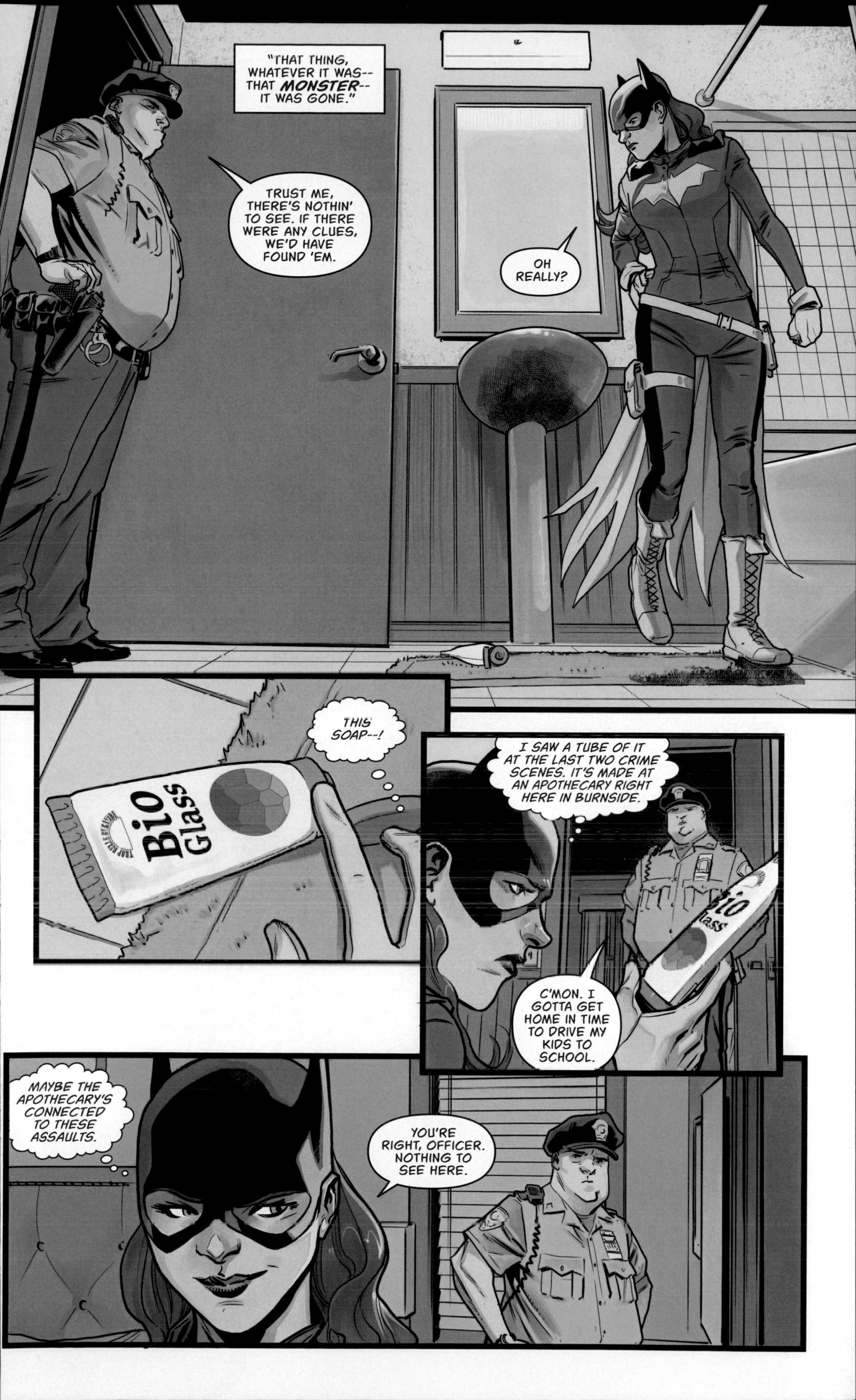
"THAT THING, WHATEVER IT WAS-- THAT MONSTER-- IT WAS GONE."
TRUST ME, THERE'S NOTHIN' TO SEE. IF THERE WERE ANY CLUES, WE'D HAVE FOUND 'EM.
OH REALLY?
THIS SOAP--!
Bio Glass
I SAW A TUBE OF IT AT THE LAST TWO CRIME SCENES. IT'S MADE AT AN APOTHECARY RIGHT HERE IN BURNSIDE.
C'MON. I GOTTA GET HOME IN TIME TO DRIVE MY KIDS TO SCHOOL.
MAYBE THE APOTHECARY'S CONNECTED TO THESE ASSAULTS.
YOU'RE RIGHT, OFFICER. NOTHING TO SEE HERE.

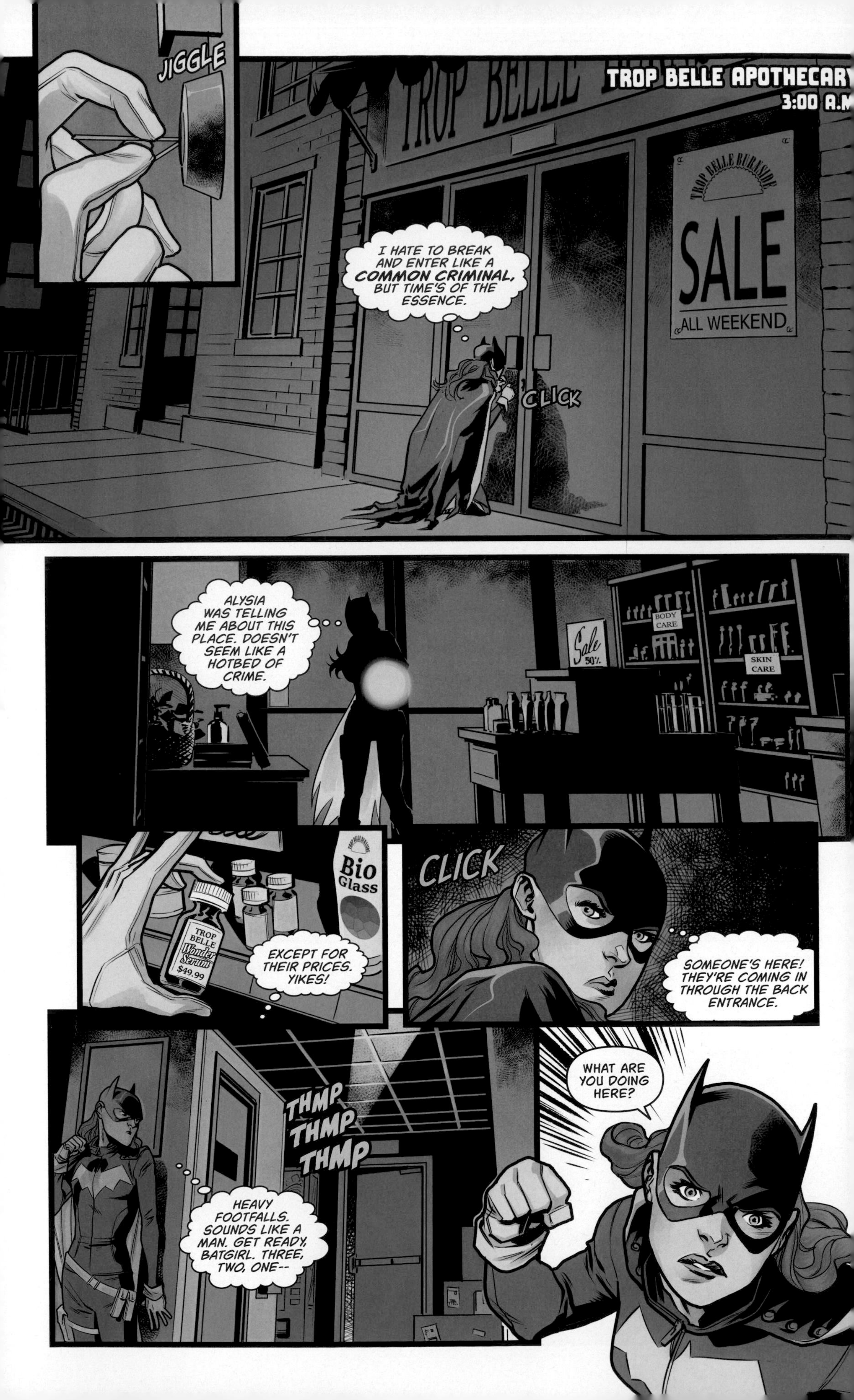

JIGGLE
TROP BELLE APOTHECARY
3:00 A.M.
TROP BELLE
TROP BELLE BURNSIDE
SALE
ALL WEEKEND
I HATE TO BREAK AND ENTER LIKE A COMMON CRIMINAL, BUT TIME'S OF THE ESSENCE.
CLICK
ALYSIA WAS TELLING ME ABOUT THIS PLACE. DOESN'T SEEM LIKE A HOTBED OF CRIME.
BODY CARE
Sale 50%
SKIN CARE
Bio Glass
TROP BELLE Wonder Serum $49.99
EXCEPT FOR THEIR PRICES. YIKES!
CLICK
SOMEONE'S HERE! THEY'RE COMING IN THROUGH THE BACK ENTRANCE.
THMP THMP THMP
HEAVY FOOTFALLS. SOUNDS LIKE A MAN. GET READY, BATGIRL. THREE, TWO, ONE--
WHAT ARE YOU DOING HERE?

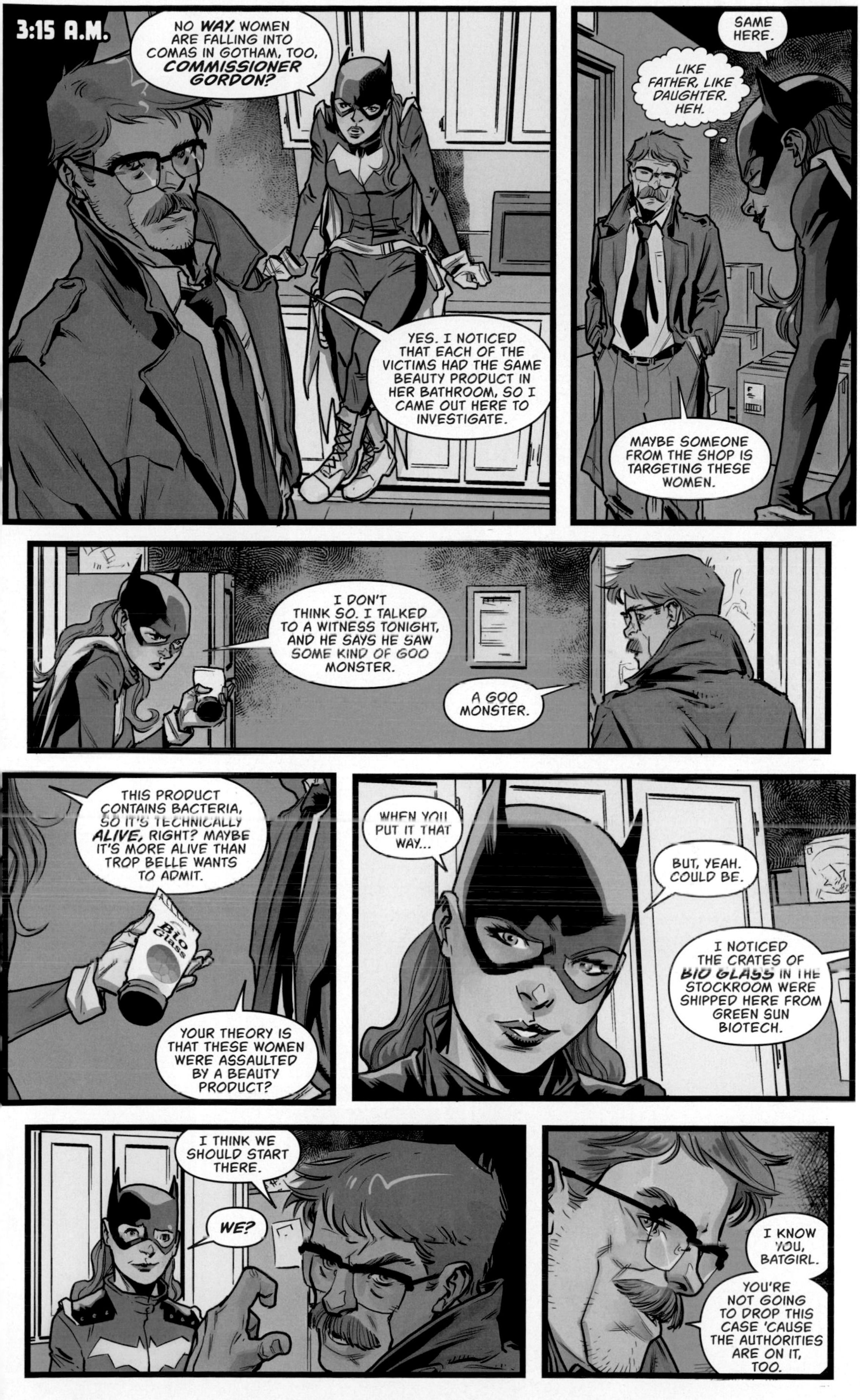
3:15 A.M.
NO WAY. WOMEN ARE FALLING INTO COMAS IN GOTHAM, TOO, COMMISSIONER GORDON?
YES. I NOTICED THAT EACH OF THE VICTIMS HAD THE SAME BEAUTY PRODUCT IN HER BATHROOM, SO I CAME OUT HERE TO INVESTIGATE.
SAME HERE.
LIKE FATHER, LIKE DAUGHTER. HEH.
MAYBE SOMEONE FROM THE SHOP IS TARGETING THESE WOMEN.
I DON'T THINK SO. I TALKED TO A WITNESS TONIGHT, AND HE SAYS HE SAW SOME KIND OF GOO MONSTER.
A GOO MONSTER.
THIS PRODUCT CONTAINS BACTERIA, SO IT'S TECHNICALLY ALIVE, RIGHT? MAYBE IT'S MORE ALIVE THAN TROP BELLE WANTS TO ADMIT.
Bio Glass
YOUR THEORY IS THAT THESE WOMEN WERE ASSAULTED BY A BEAUTY PRODUCT?
WHEN YOU PUT IT THAT WAY...
BUT, YEAH. COULD BE.
I NOTICED THE CRATES OF BIO GLASS IN THE STOCKROOM WERE SHIPPED HERE FROM GREEN SUN BIOTECH.
I THINK WE SHOULD START THERE.
WE?
I KNOW YOU, BATGIRL.
YOU'RE NOT GOING TO DROP THIS CASE 'CAUSE THE AUTHORITIES ARE ON IT, TOO.

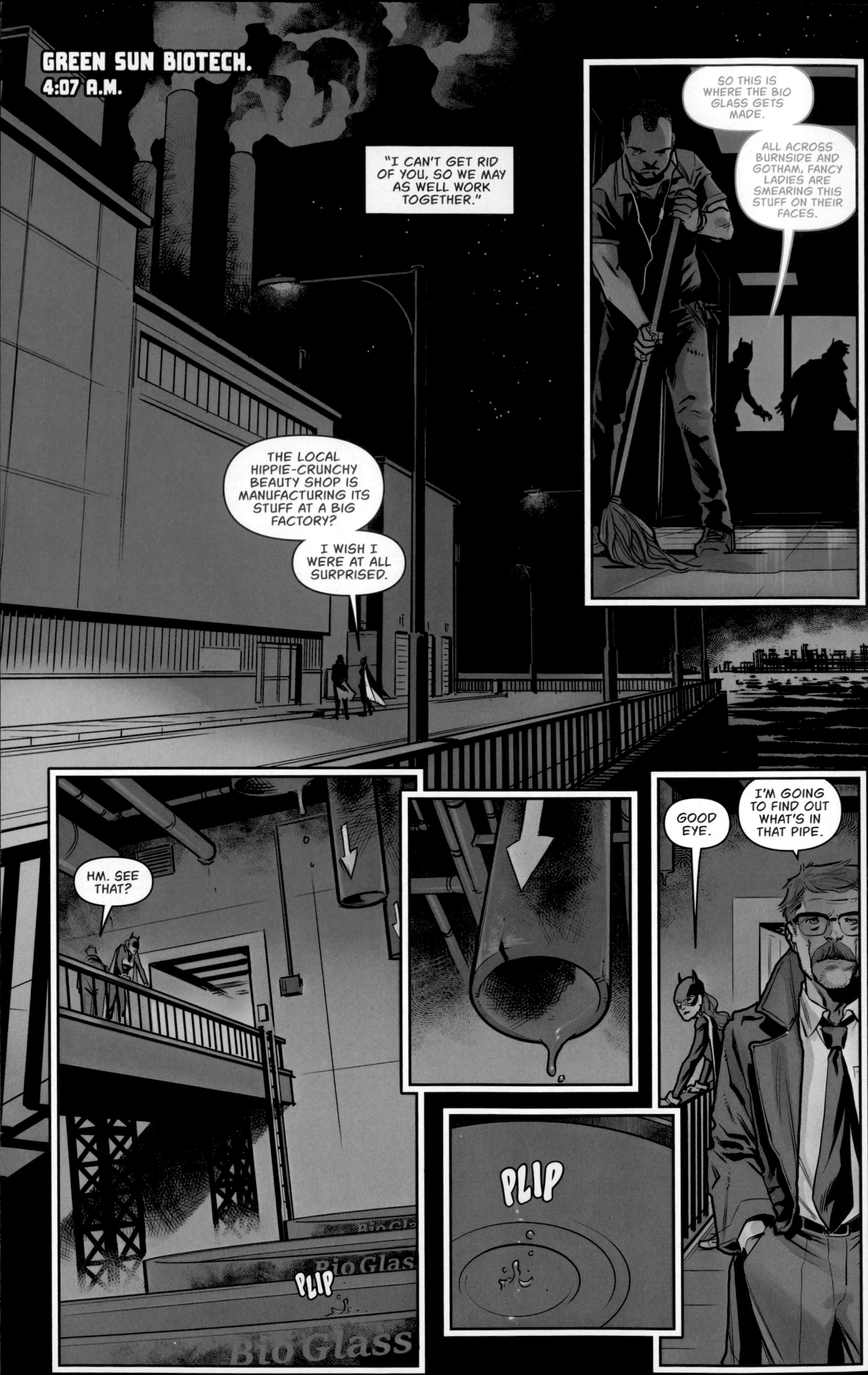

GREEN SUN BIOTECH.
4:07 A.M.
"I CAN'T GET RID OF YOU, SO WE MAY AS WELL WORK TOGETHER."
SO THIS IS WHERE THE BIO GLASS GETS MADE.
ALL ACROSS BURNSIDE AND GOTHAM, FANCY LADIES ARE SMEARING THIS STUFF ON THEIR FACES.
THE LOCAL HIPPIE-CRUNCHY BEAUTY SHOP IS MANUFACTURING ITS STUFF AT A BIG FACTORY?
I WISH I WERE AT ALL SURPRISED.
HM. SEE THAT?
Bio Glass
PLIP
Bio Glass
PLIP
GOOD EYE.
I'M GOING TO FIND OUT WHAT'S IN THAT PIPE.

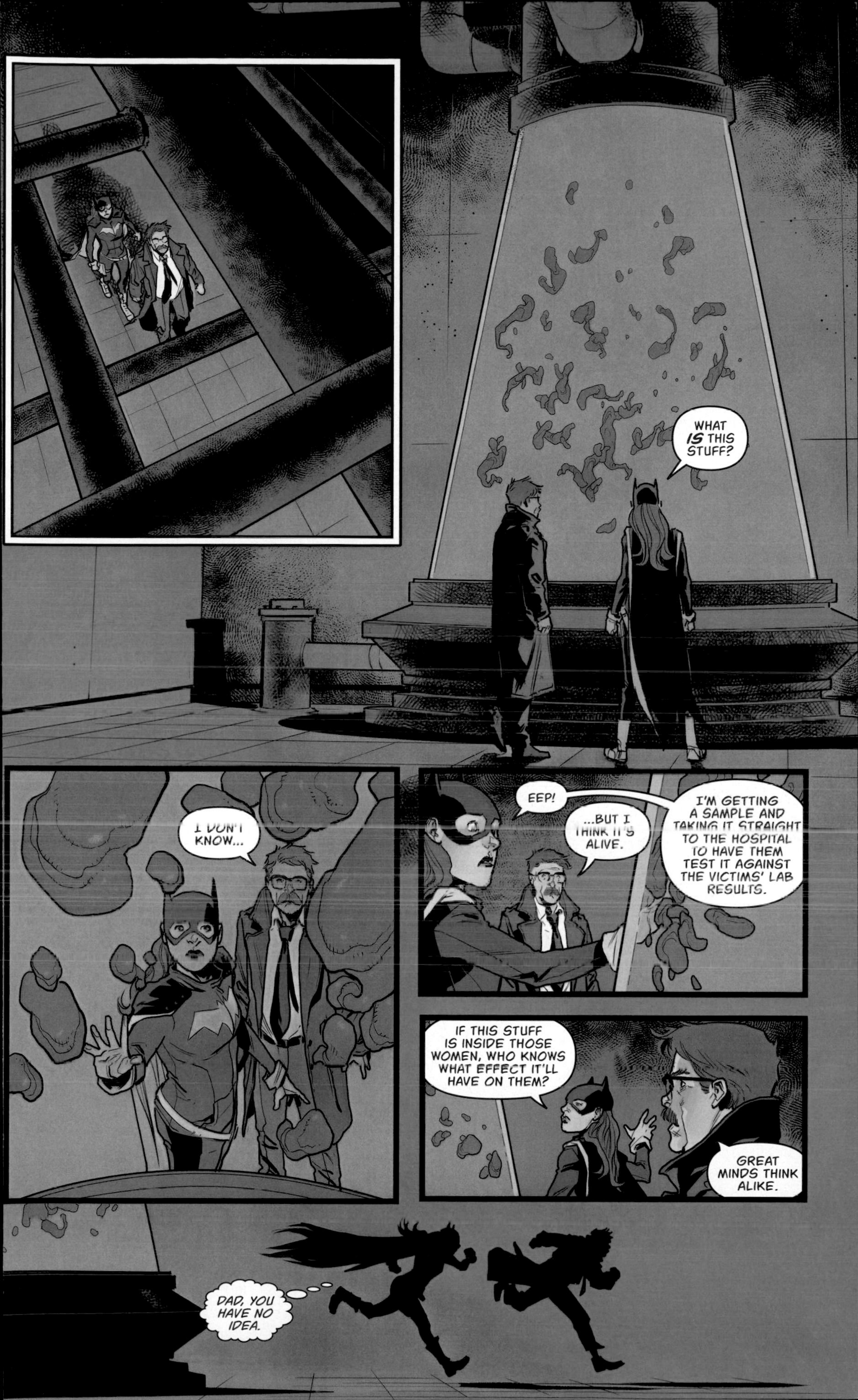
WHAT IS THIS STUFF?
I DON'T KNOW...
EEP!
...BUT I THINK IT'S ALIVE.
I'M GETTING A SAMPLE AND TAKING IT STRAIGHT TO THE HOSPITAL TO HAVE THEM TEST IT AGAINST THE VICTIMS' LAB RESULTS.
IF THIS STUFF IS INSIDE THOSE WOMEN, WHO KNOWS WHAT EFFECT IT'LL HAVE ON THEM?
GREAT MINDS THINK ALIKE.
DAD, YOU HAVE NO IDEA.

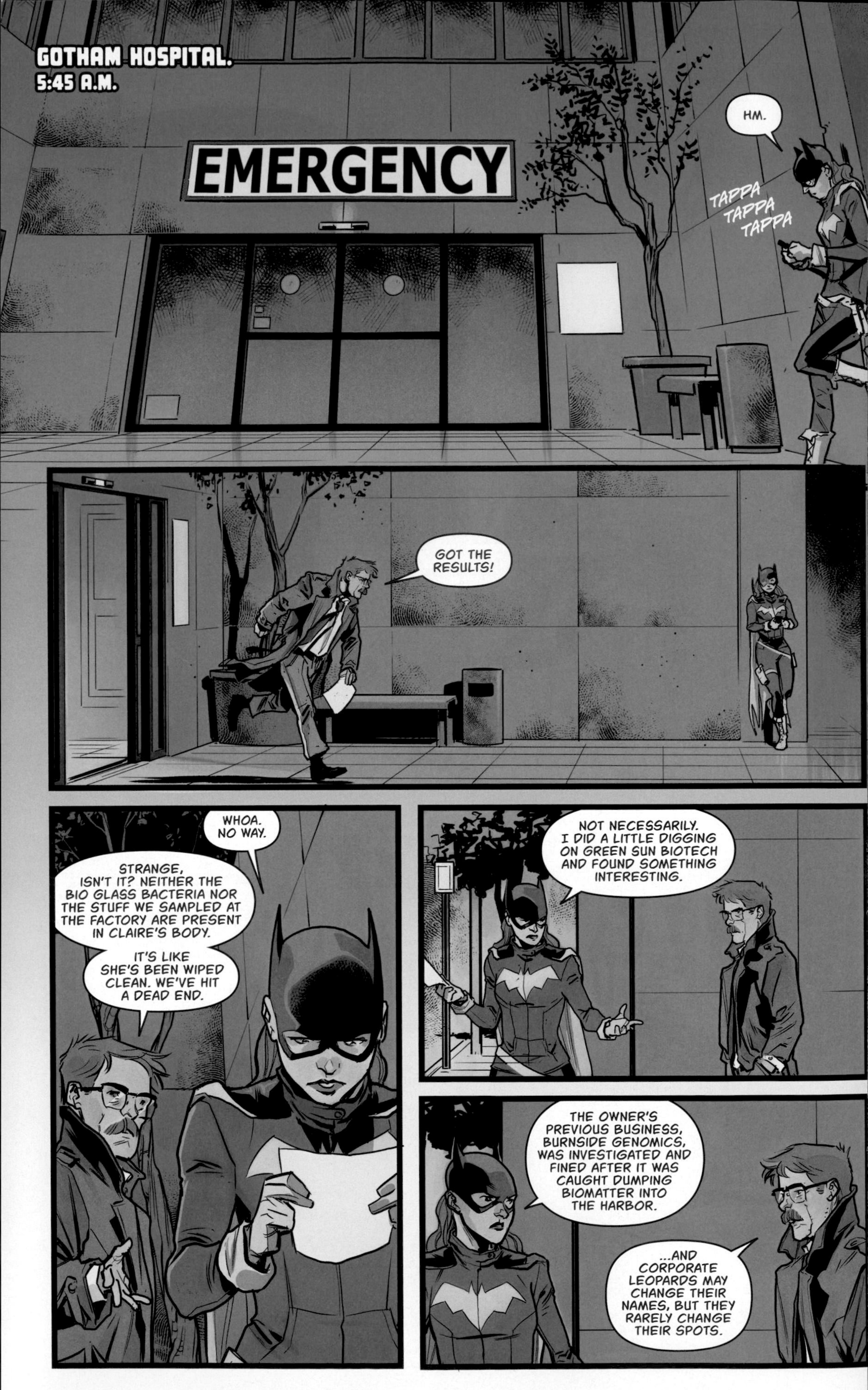
GOTHAM HOSPITAL.
5:45 A.M.
EMERGENCY
HM.
TAPPA TAPPA TAPPA
GOT THE RESULTS!
WHOA. NO WAY.
STRANGE, ISN'T IT? NEITHER THE BIO GLASS BACTERIA NOR THE STUFF WE SAMPLED AT THE FACTORY ARE PRESENT IN CLAIRE'S BODY.
IT'S LIKE SHE'S BEEN WIPED CLEAN. WE'VE HIT A DEAD END.
NOT NECESSARILY. I DID A LITTLE DIGGING ON GREEN SUN BIOTECH AND FOUND SOMETHING INTERESTING.
THE OWNER'S PREVIOUS BUSINESS, BURNSIDE GENOMICS, WAS INVESTIGATED AND FINED AFTER IT WAS CAUGHT DUMPING BIOMATTER INTO THE HARBOR.
...AND CORPORATE LEOPARDS MAY CHANGE THEIR NAMES, BUT THEY RARELY CHANGE THEIR SPOTS.

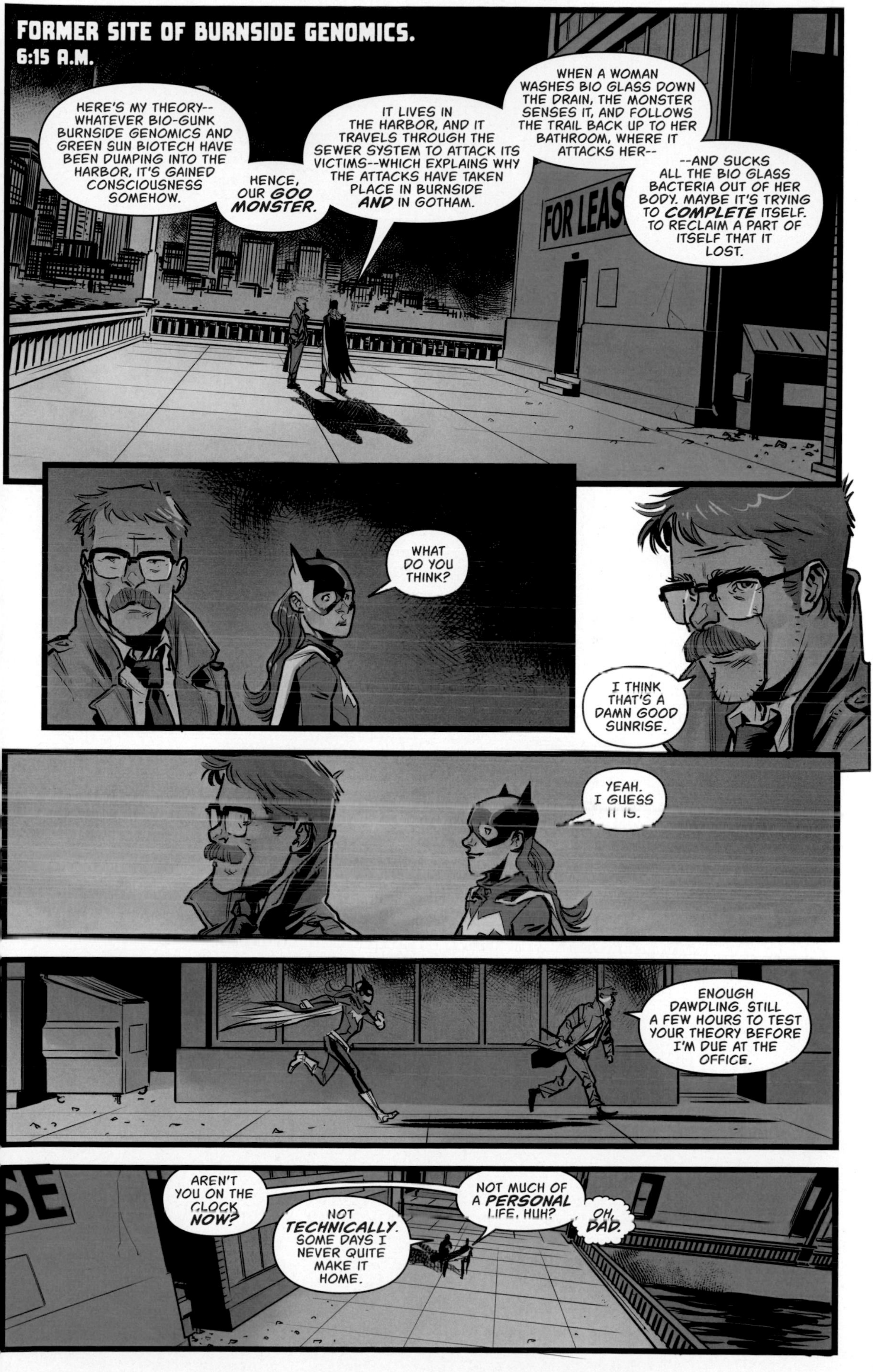
FORMER SITE OF BURNSIDE GENOMICS.
6:15 A.M.
HERE'S MY THEORY-- WHATEVER BIO-GUNK BURNSIDE GENOMICS AND GREEN SUN BIOTECH HAVE BEEN DUMPING INTO THE HARBOR, IT'S GAINED CONSCIOUSNESS SOMEHOW.
HENCE, OUR GOO MONSTER.
IT LIVES IN THE HARBOR, AND IT TRAVELS THROUGH THE SEWER SYSTEM TO ATTACK ITS VICTIMS--WHICH EXPLAINS WHY THE ATTACKS HAVE TAKEN PLACE IN BURNSIDE AND IN GOTHAM.
WHEN A WOMAN WASHES BIO GLASS DOWN THE DRAIN, THE MONSTER SENSES IT, AND FOLLOWS THE TRAIL BACK UP TO HER BATHROOM, WHERE IT ATTACKS HER--
--AND SUCKS ALL THE BIO GLASS BACTERIA OUT OF HER BODY. MAYBE IT'S TRYING TO COMPLETE ITSELF. TO RECLAIM A PART OF ITSELF THAT IT LOST.
FOR LEAS
WHAT DO YOU THINK?
I THINK THAT'S A DAMN GOOD SUNRISE.
YEAH. I GUESS IT IS.
ENOUGH DAWDLING. STILL A FEW HOURS TO TEST YOUR THEORY BEFORE I'M DUE AT THE OFFICE.
SE
AREN'T YOU ON THE CLOCK NOW?
NOT TECHNICALLY. SOME DAYS I NEVER QUITE MAKE IT HOME.
NOT MUCH OF A PERSONAL LIFE, HUH?
OH, DAD.

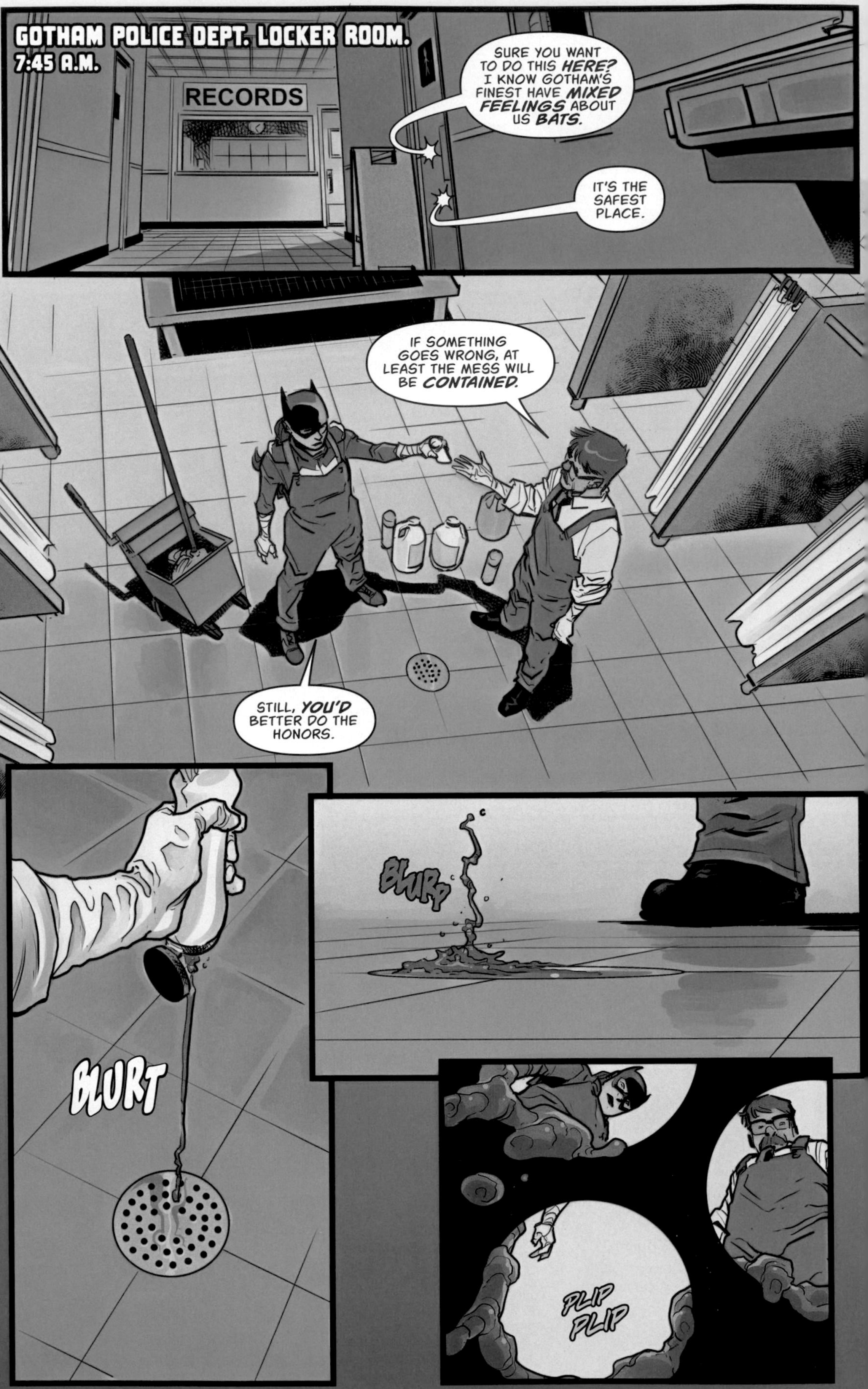
GOTHAM POLICE DEPT. LOCKER ROOM.
7:45 A.M.
RECORDS
SURE YOU WANT TO DO THIS HERE? I KNOW GOTHAM'S FINEST HAVE MIXED FEELINGS ABOUT US BATS.
IT'S THE SAFEST PLACE.
IF SOMETHING GOES WRONG, AT LEAST THE MESS WILL BE CONTAINED.
STILL, YOU'D BETTER DO THE HONORS.
BLURT
BLURP
PLIP
PLIP

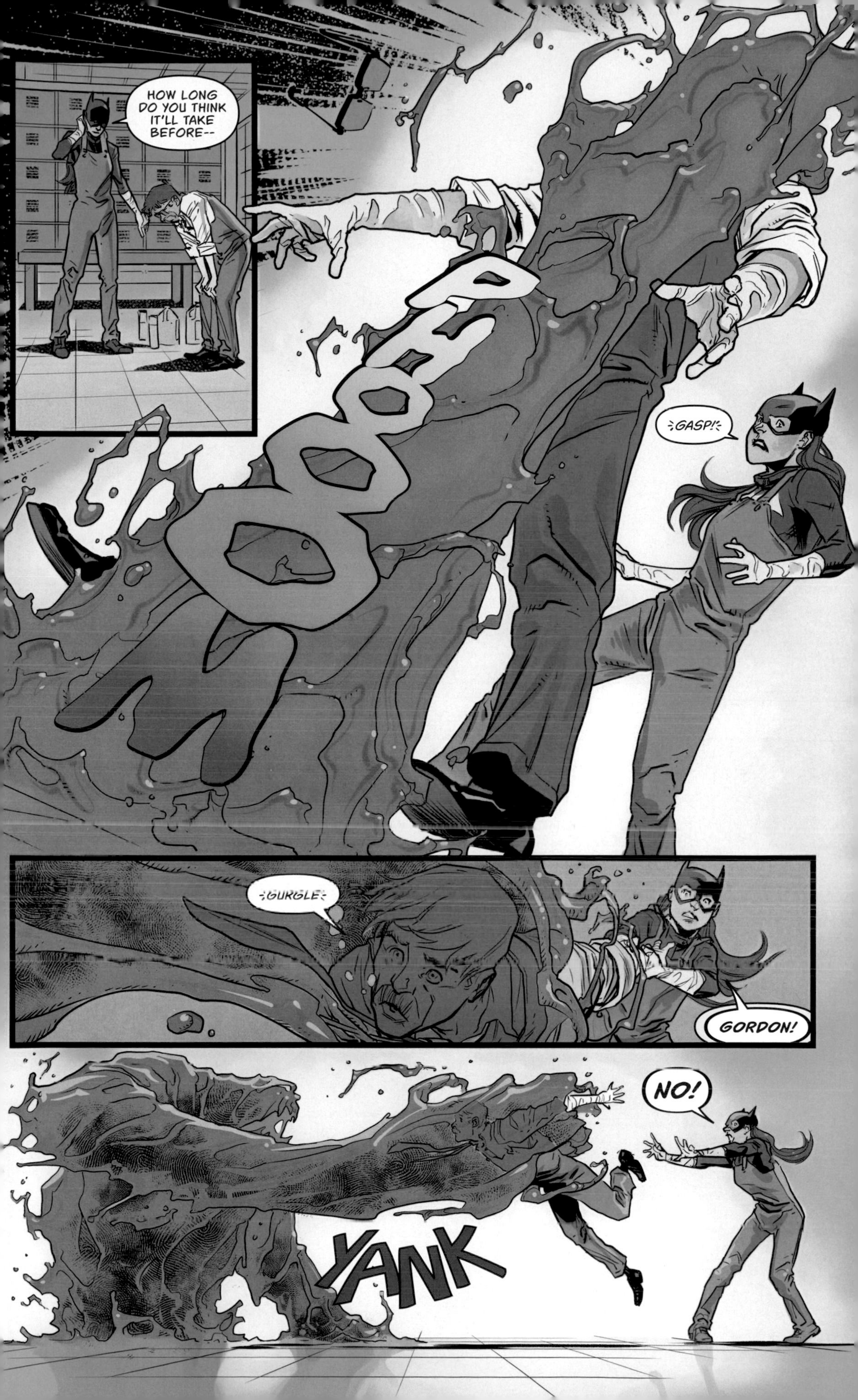
HOW LONG DO YOU THINK IT'LL TAKE BEFORE--
WOOOP
GASP!
GURGLE
GORDON!
NO!
YANK

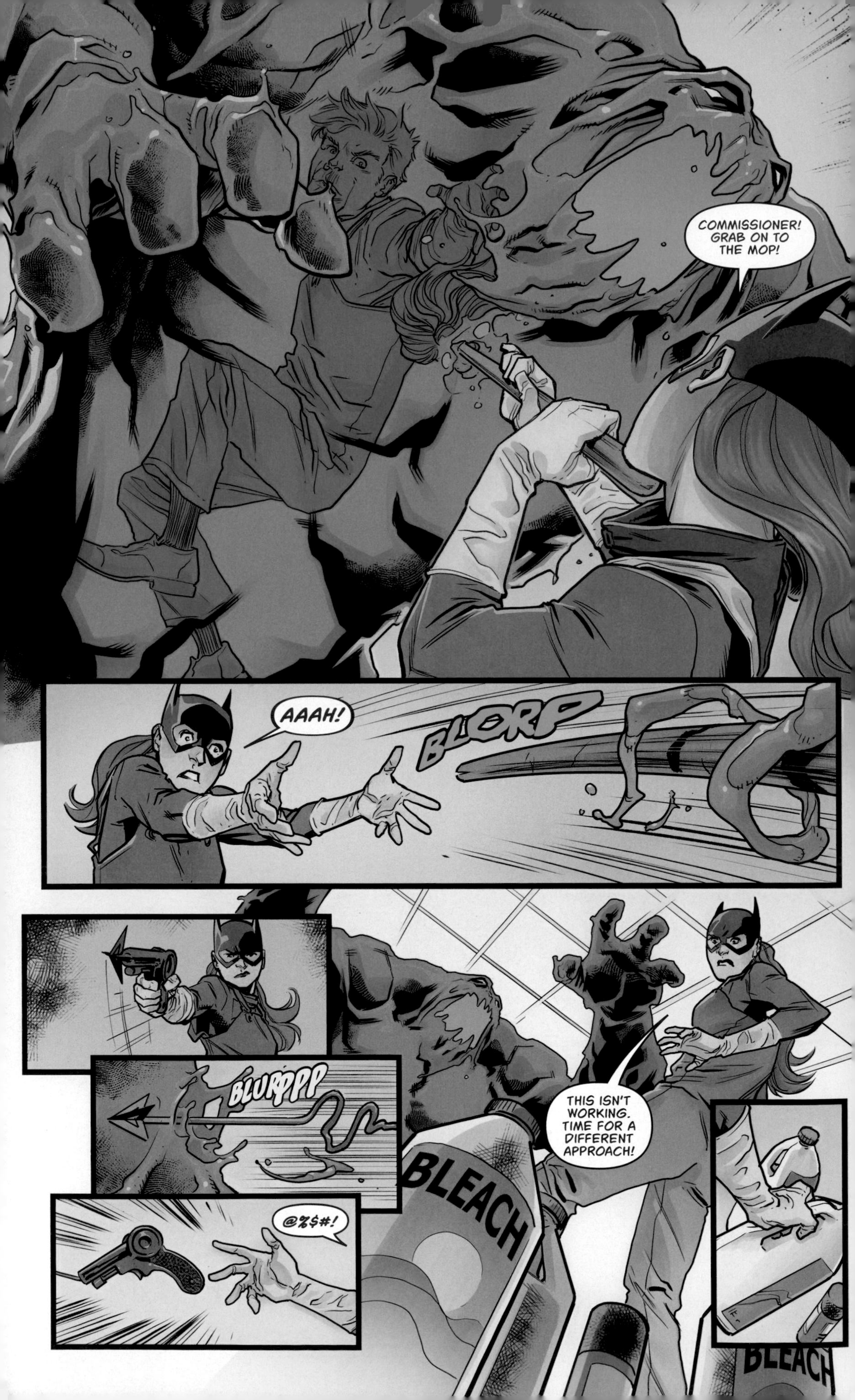
COMMISSIONER! GRAB ON TO THE MOP!
AAAH!
BLORP
BLURPPP
@%$#!
THIS ISN'T WORKING. TIME FOR A DIFFERENT APPROACH!
BLEACH
BLEACH

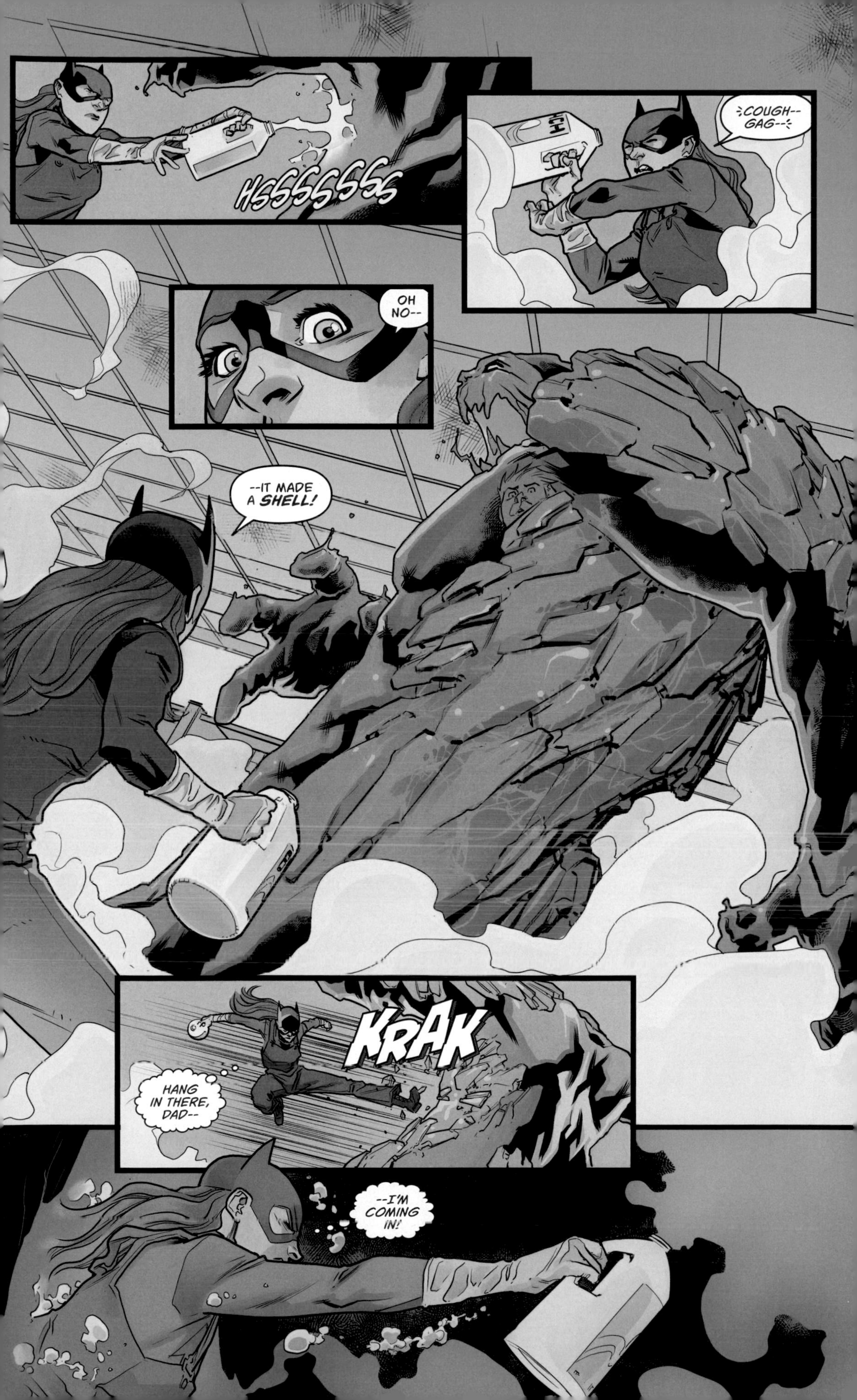
HSSSSSSSS
COUGH-- GAG--
OH NO--
--IT MADE A SHELL!
KRAK
HANG IN THERE, DAD--
--I'M COMING IN!

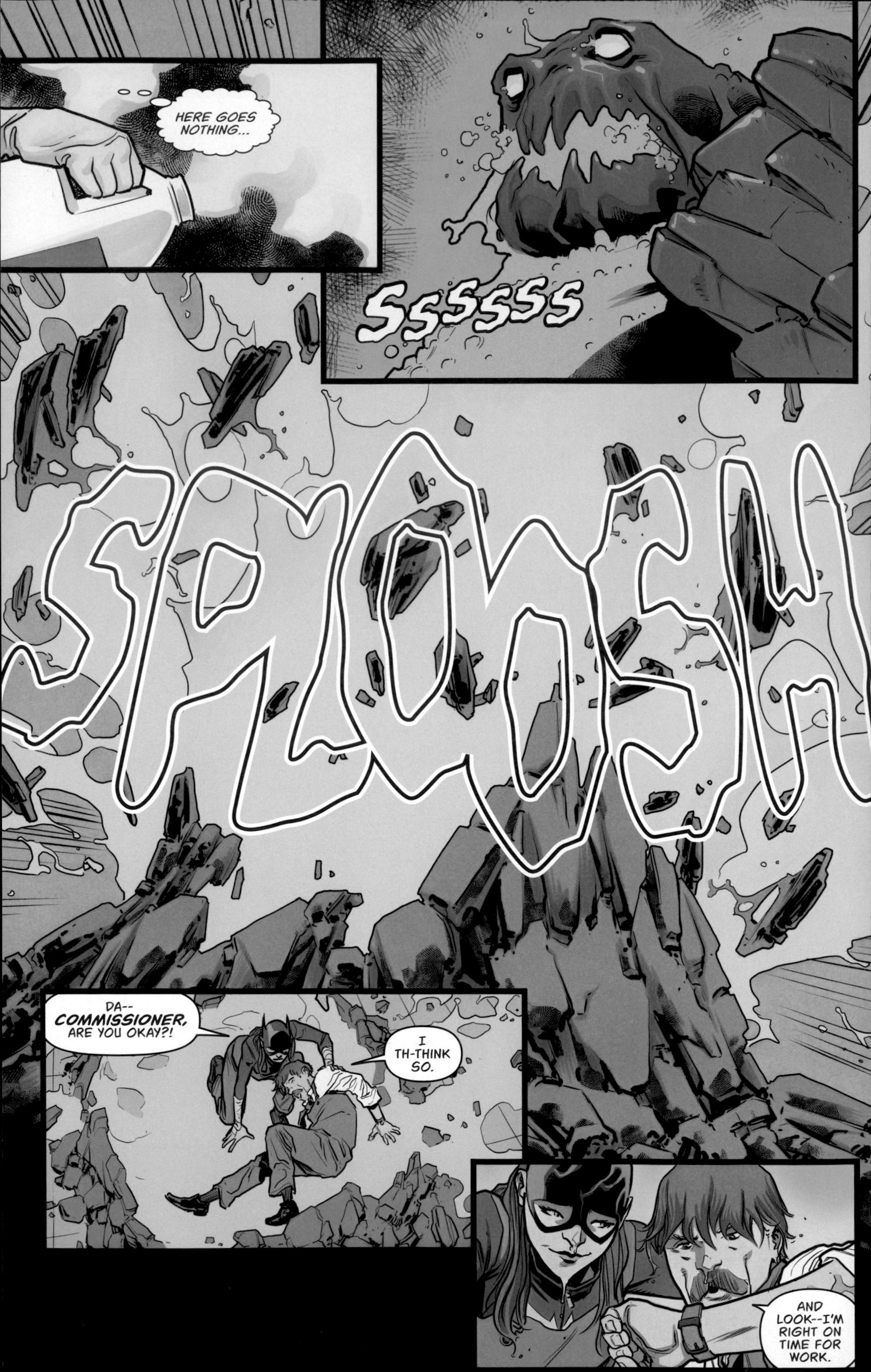
HERE GOES NOTHING...
SSSSSS
SPLOOSH
DA-- COMMISSIONER, ARE YOU OKAY?!
I TH-THINK SO.
AND LOOK--I'M RIGHT ON TIME FOR WORK.

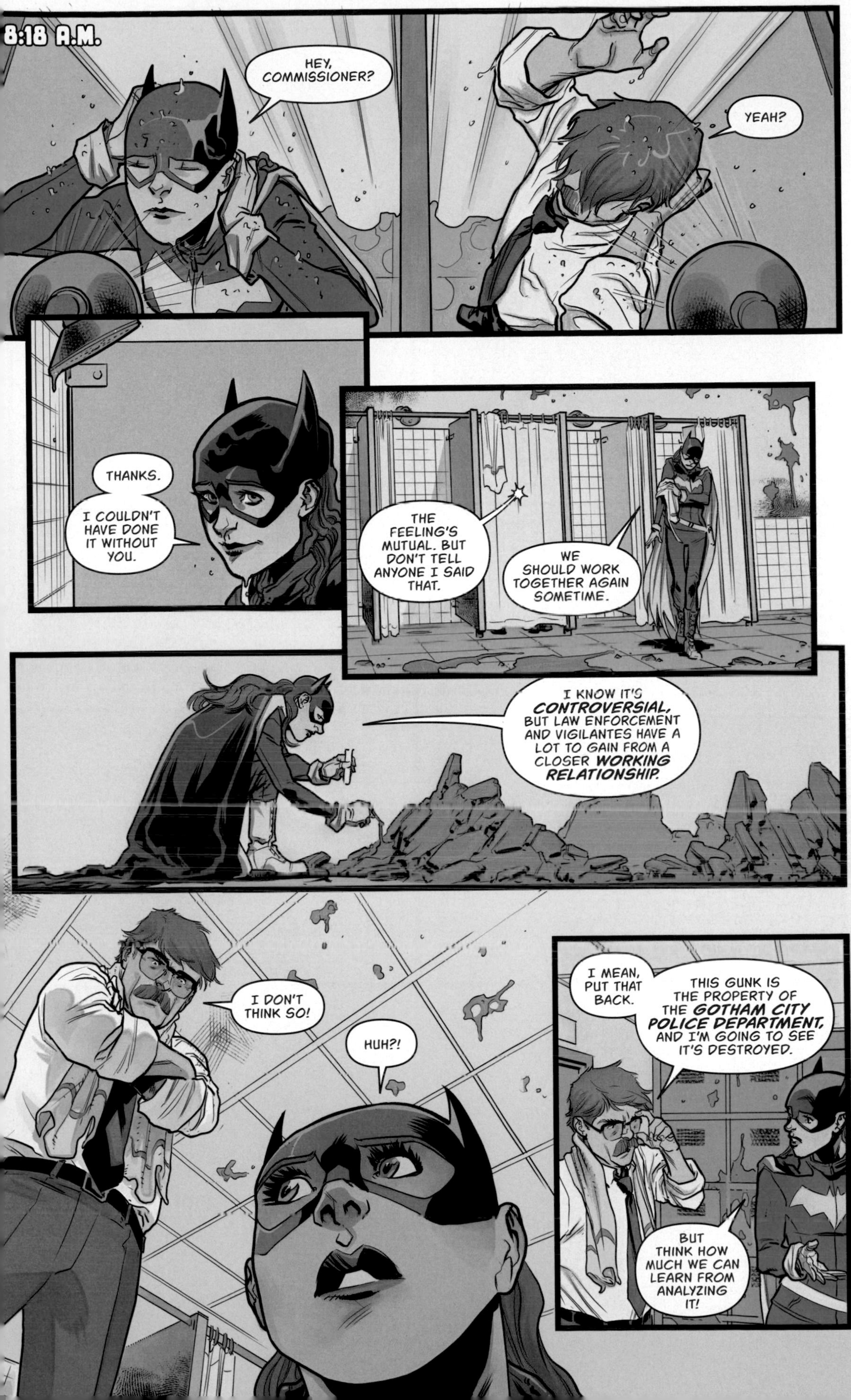
8:18 A.M.
HEY, COMMISSIONER?
YEAH?
THANKS.
I COULDN'T HAVE DONE IT WITHOUT YOU.
THE FEELING'S MUTUAL. BUT DON'T TELL ANYONE I SAID THAT.
WE SHOULD WORK TOGETHER AGAIN SOMETIME.
I KNOW IT'S CONTROVERSIAL, BUT LAW ENFORCEMENT AND VIGILANTES HAVE A LOT TO GAIN FROM A CLOSER WORKING RELATIONSHIP.
I DON'T THINK SO!
HUH?!
I MEAN, PUT THAT BACK.
THIS GUNK IS THE PROPERTY OF THE GOTHAM CITY POLICE DEPARTMENT, AND I'M GOING TO SEE IT'S DESTROYED.
BUT THINK HOW MUCH WE CAN LEARN FROM ANALYZING IT!

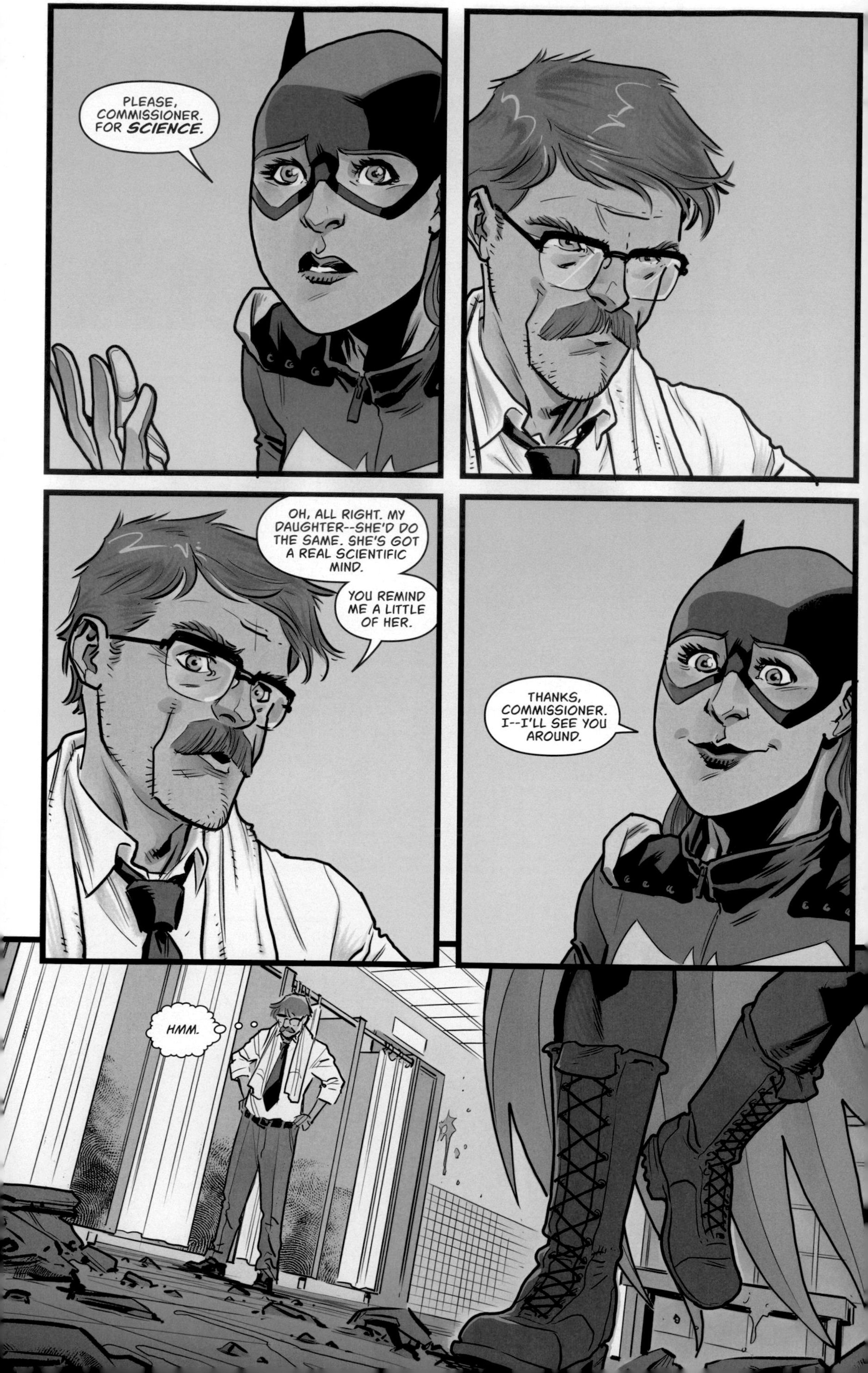
PLEASE, COMMISSIONER. FOR SCIENCE.
OH, ALL RIGHT. MY DAUGHTER--SHE'D DO THE SAME. SHE'S GOT A REAL SCIENTIFIC MIND.
YOU REMIND ME A LITTLE OF HER.
THANKS, COMMISSIONER. I--I'LL SEE YOU AROUND.
HMM.

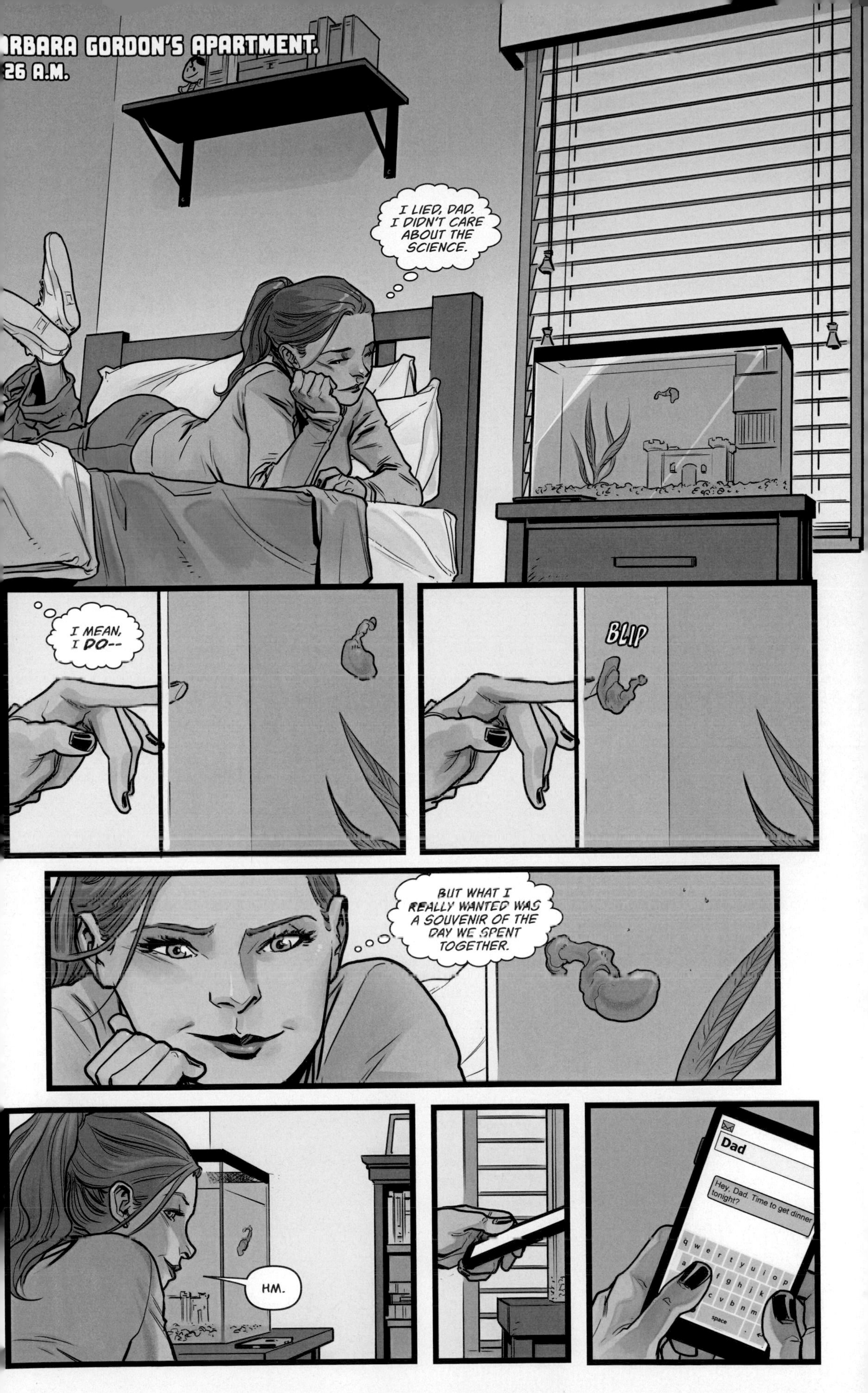
RBARA GORDON'S APARTMENT.
26 A.M.
I LIED, DAD. I DIDN'T CARE ABOUT THE SCIENCE.
I MEAN, I DO--
BLIP
BUT WHAT I REALLY WANTED WAS A SOUVENIR OF THE DAY WE SPENT TOGETHER.
HM.
Dad
Hey, Dad. Time to get dinner tonight?

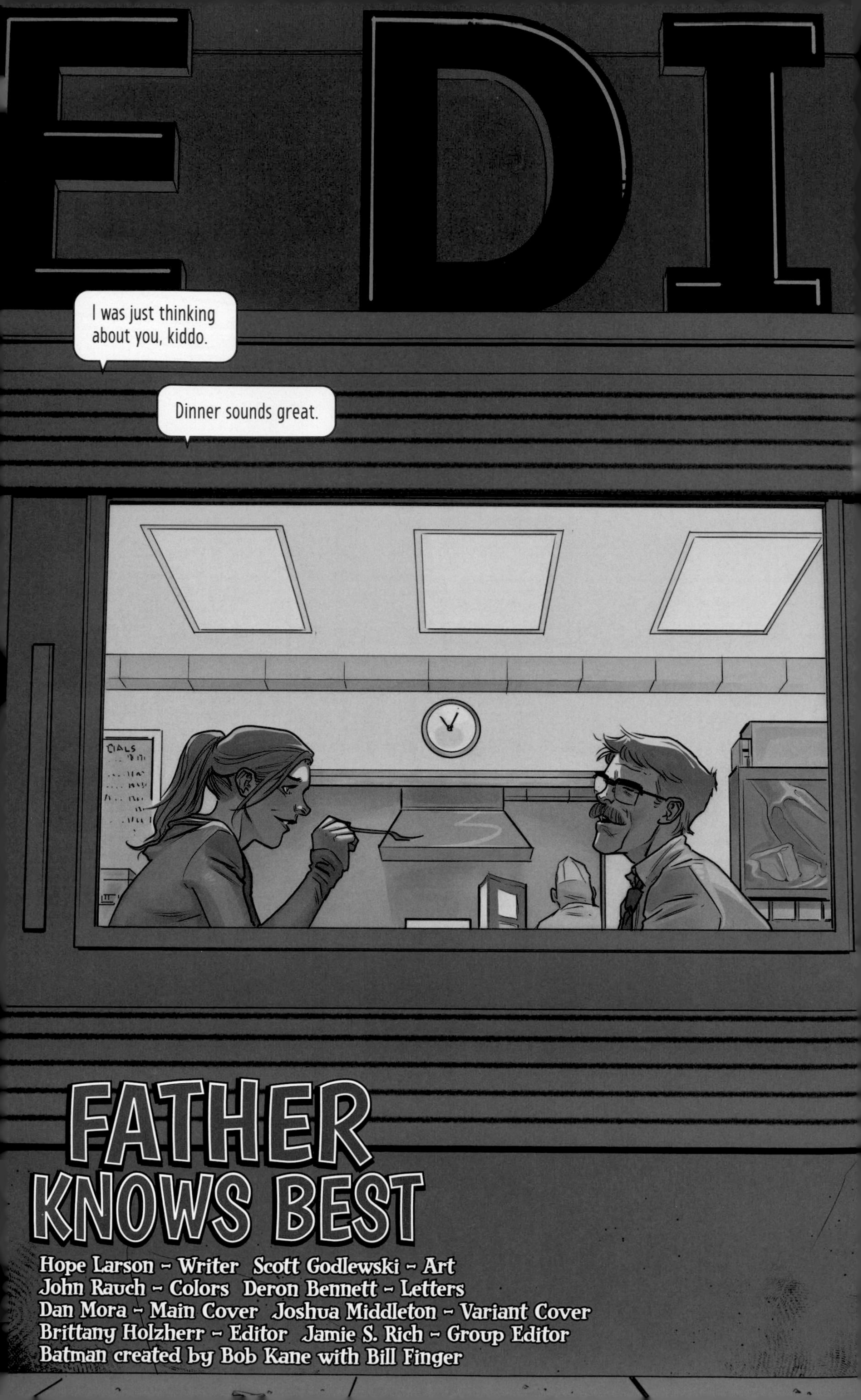
I was just thinking about you, kiddo.
Dinner sounds great.
FATHER KNOWS BEST
Hope Larson ~ Writer Scott Godlewski ~ Art
John Rauch ~ Colors Deron Bennett ~ Letters
Dan Mora ~ Main Cover Joshua Middleton ~ Variant Cover
Brittany Holzherr ~ Editor Jamie S. Rich ~ Group Editor
Batman created by Bob Kane with Bill Finger

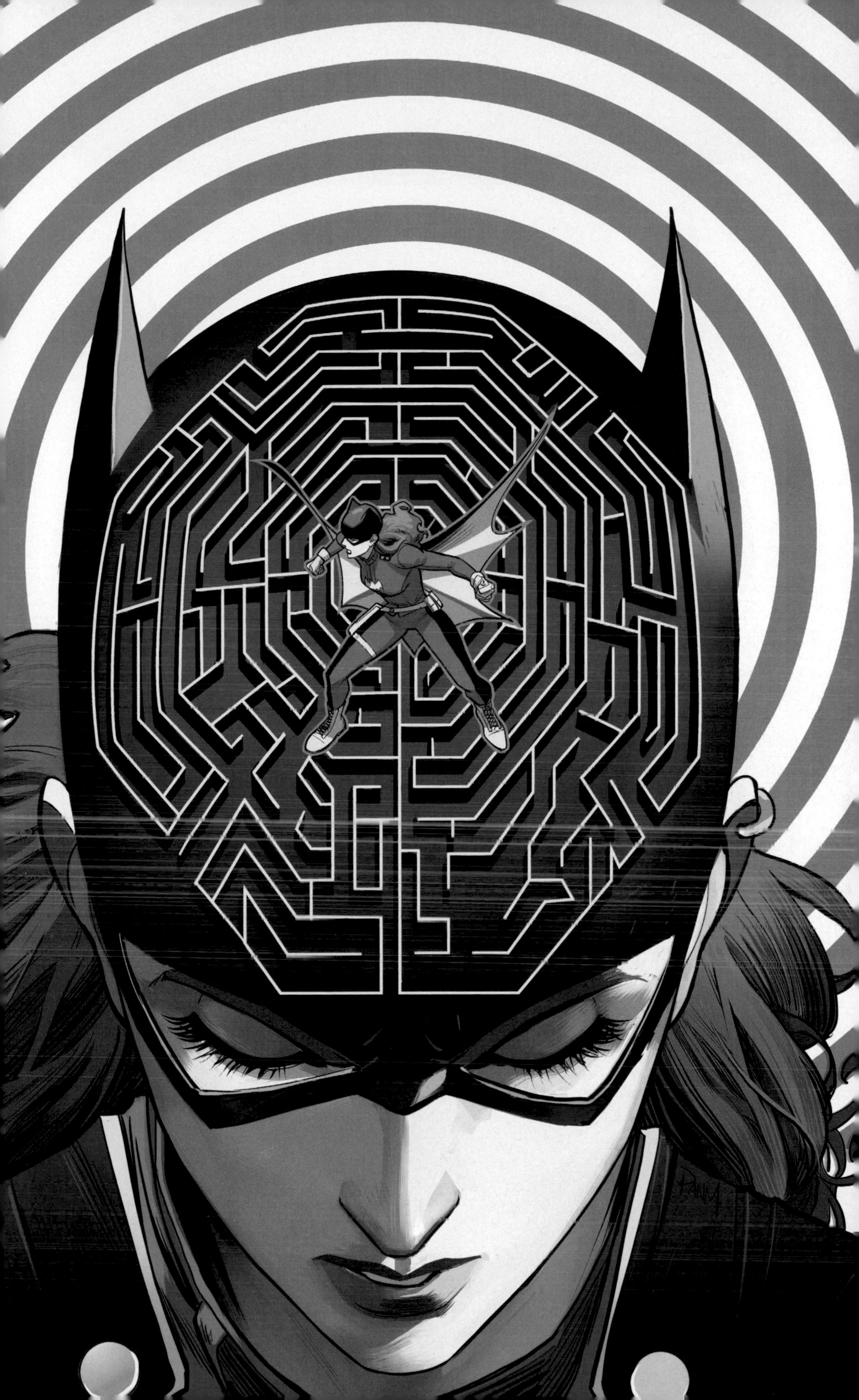

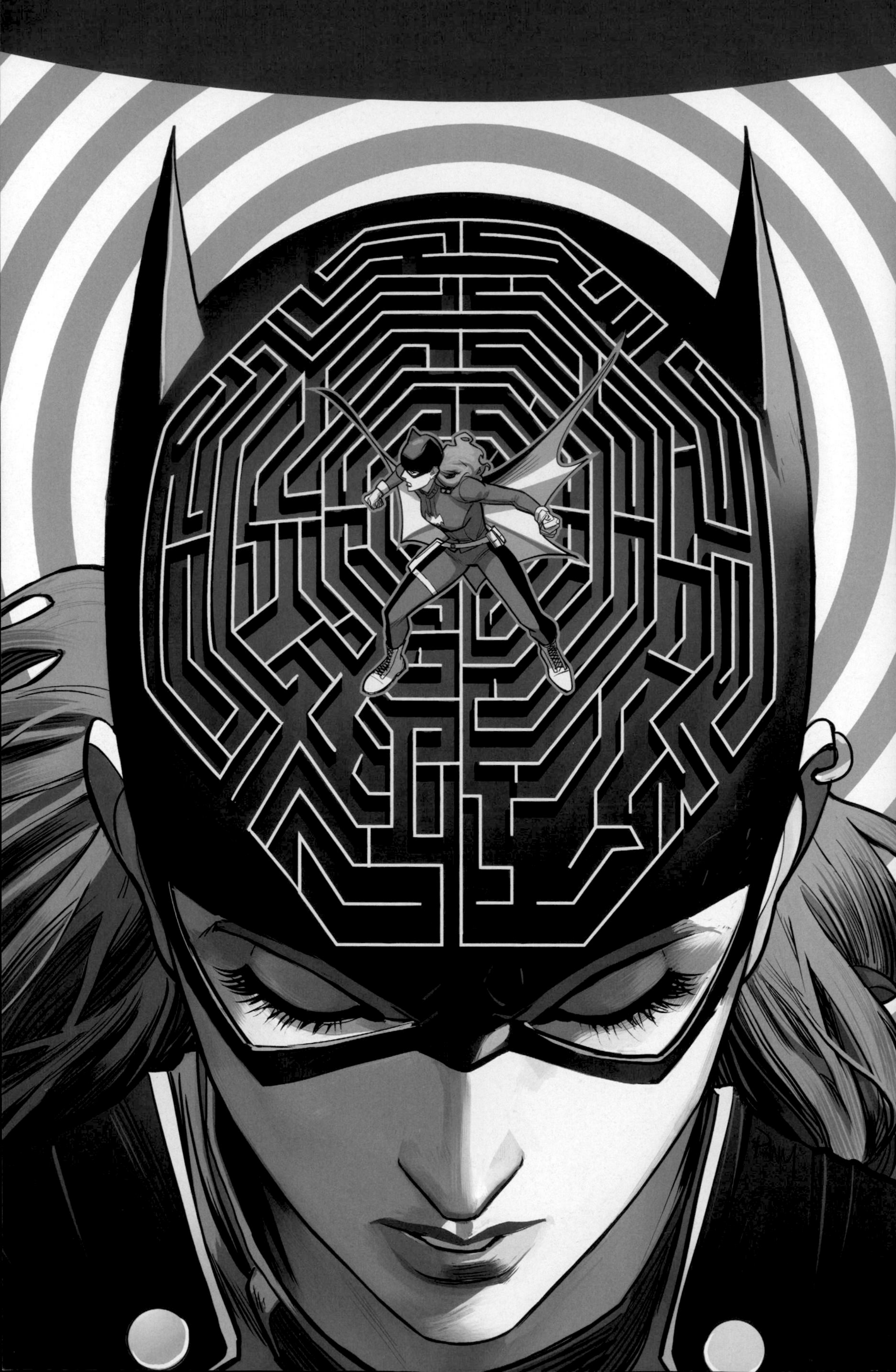

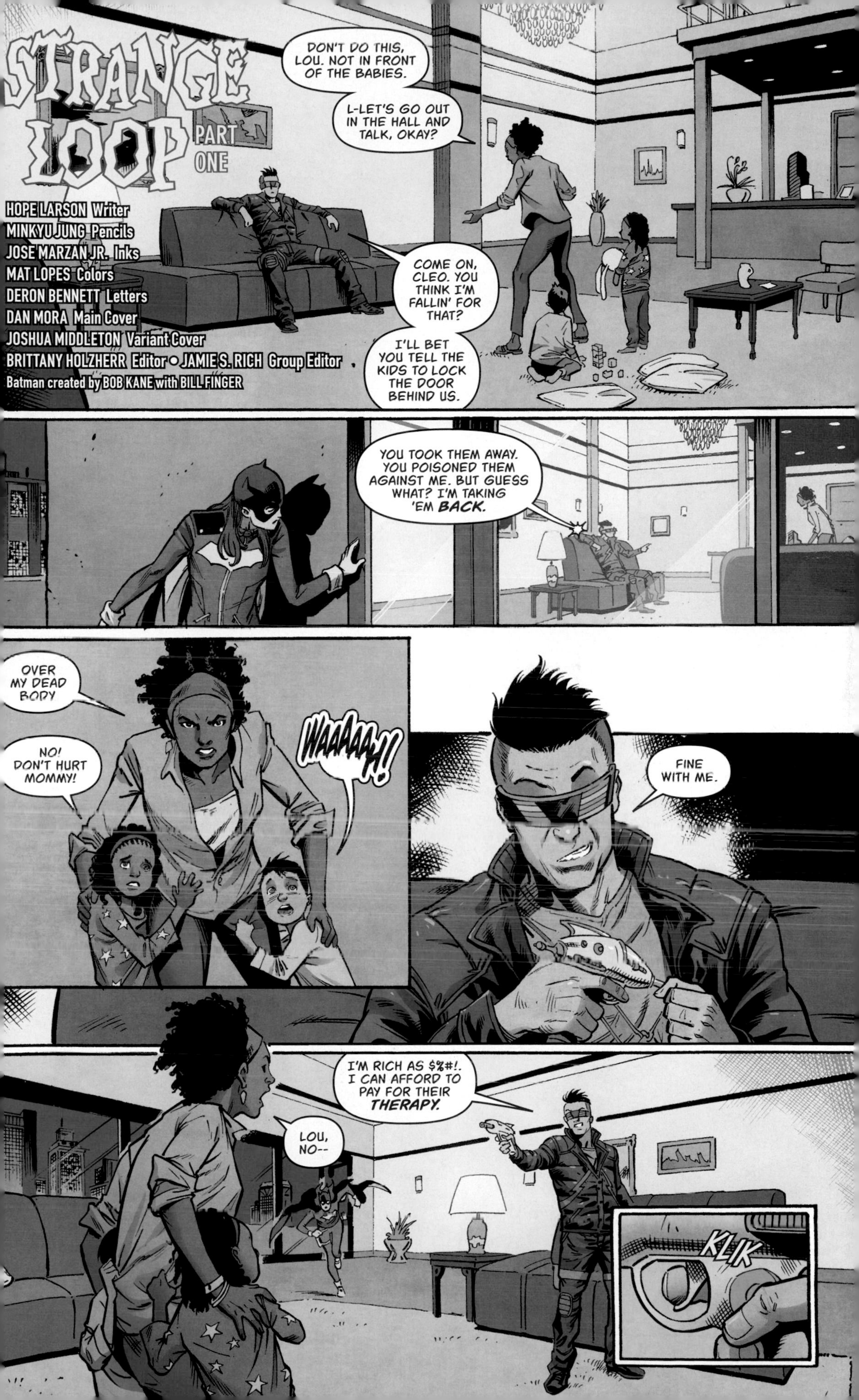
STRANGE LOOP PART ONE
HOPE LARSON Writer
MINKYU JUNG Pencils
JOSE MARZAN JR. Inks
MAT LOPES Colors
DERON BENNETT Letters
DAN MORA Main Cover
JOSHUA MIDDLETON Variant Cover
BRITTANY HOLZHERR Editor • JAMIE S. RICH Group Editor
Batman created by BOB KANE with BILL FINGER
DON'T DO THIS, LOU. NOT IN FRONT OF THE BABIES.
L-LET'S GO OUT IN THE HALL AND TALK, OKAY?
COME ON, CLEO. YOU THINK I'M FALLIN' FOR THAT?
I'LL BET YOU TELL THE KIDS TO LOCK THE DOOR BEHIND US.
YOU TOOK THEM AWAY. YOU POISONED THEM AGAINST ME. BUT GUESS WHAT? I'M TAKING 'EM BACK.
OVER MY DEAD BODY
NO! DON'T HURT MOMMY!
WAAAAAH!
FINE WITH ME.
I'M RICH AS $%#!. I CAN AFFORD TO PAY FOR THEIR THERAPY.
LOU, NO--
KLIK

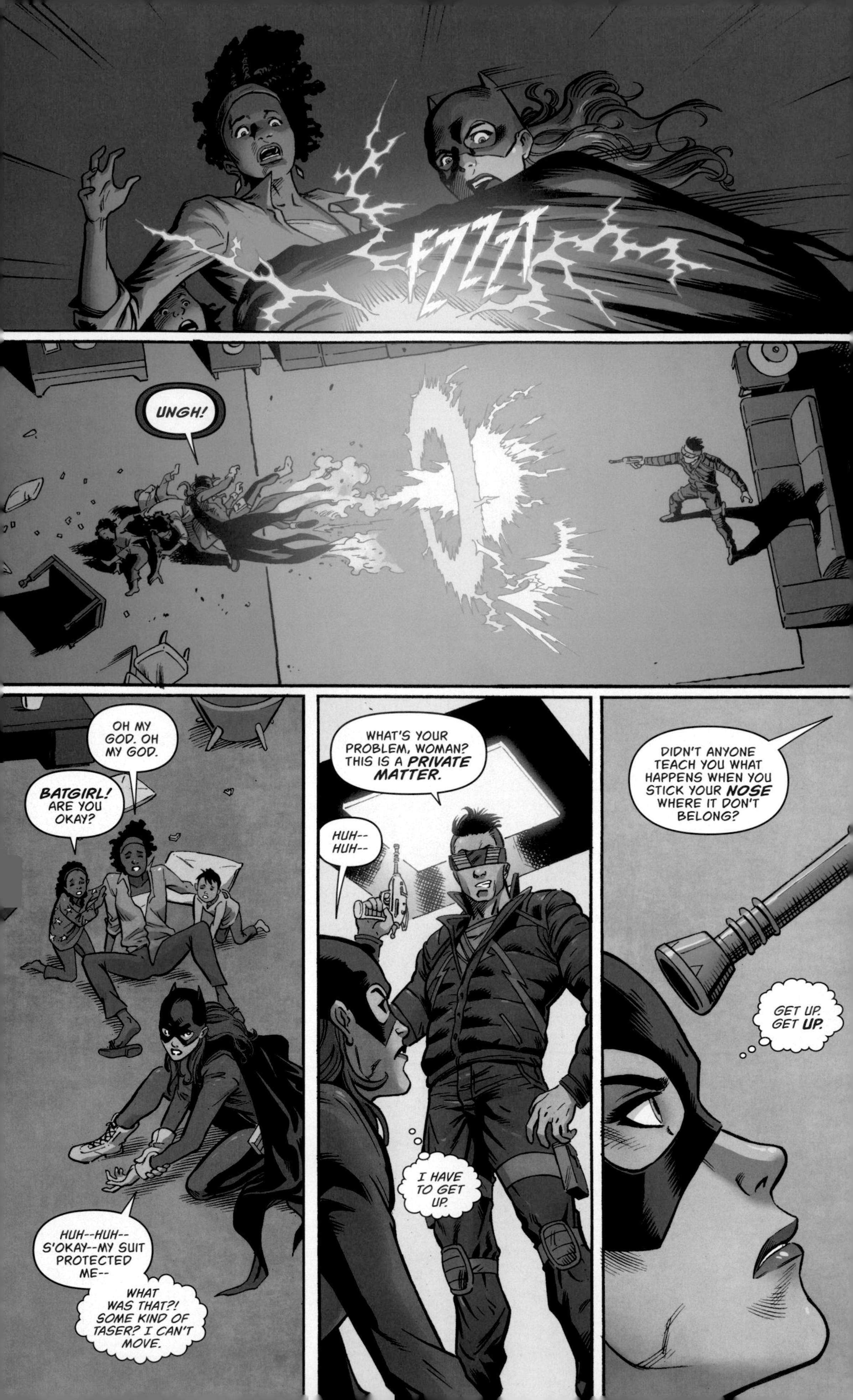
FZZZT
UNGH!
OH MY GOD. OH MY GOD.
BATGIRL! ARE YOU OKAY?
HUH--HUH-- S'OKAY--MY SUIT PROTECTED ME--
WHAT WAS THAT?! SOME KIND OF TASER? I CAN'T MOVE.
WHAT'S YOUR PROBLEM, WOMAN? THIS IS A PRIVATE MATTER.
HUH-- HUH--
I HAVE TO GET UP.
DIDN'T ANYONE TEACH YOU WHAT HAPPENS WHEN YOU STICK YOUR NOSE WHERE IT DON'T BELONG?
GET UP. GET UP.

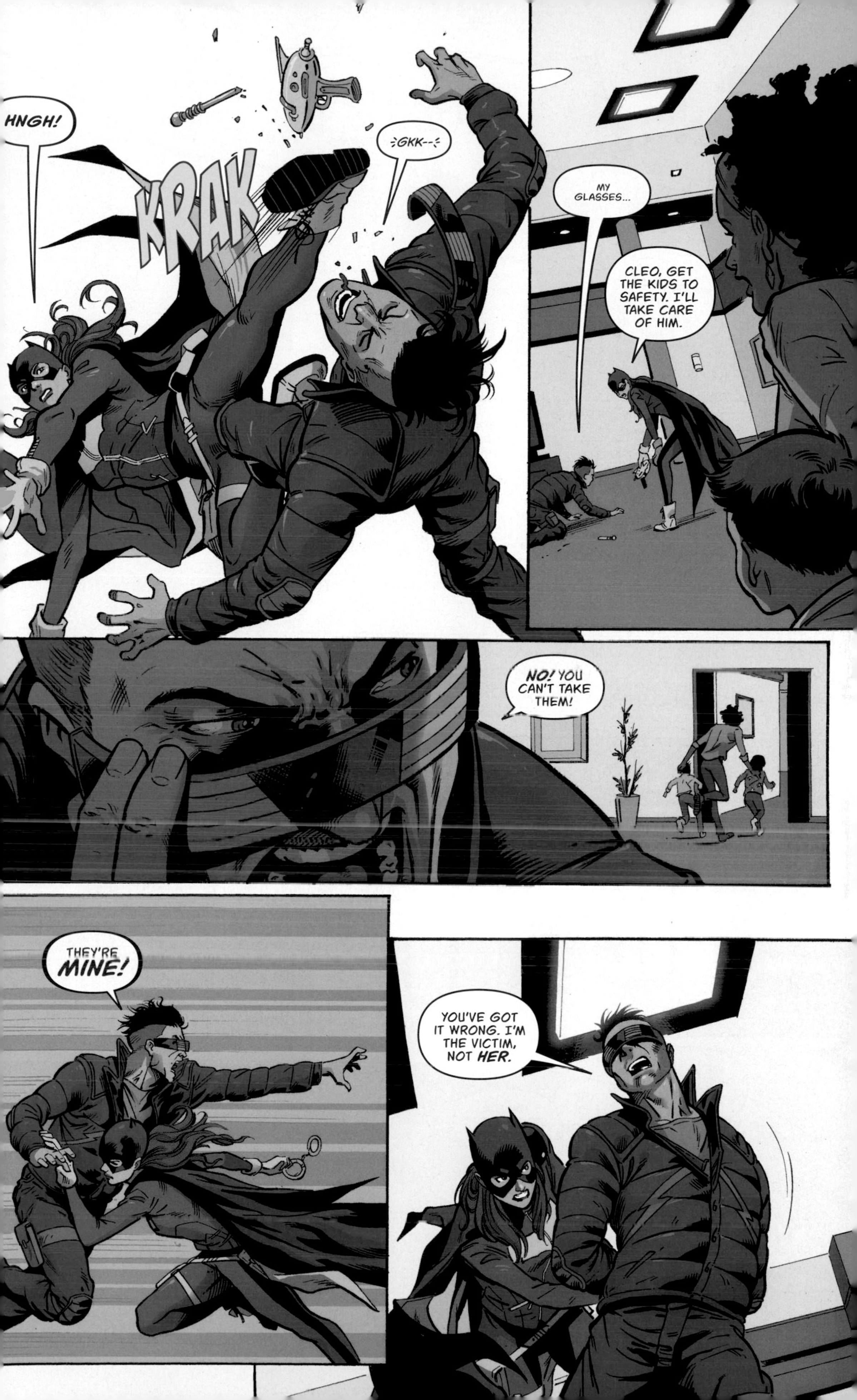
HNGH!
KRAK
GKK--
MY GLASSES...
CLEO, GET THE KIDS TO SAFETY. I'LL TAKE CARE OF HIM.
NO! YOU CAN'T TAKE THEM!
THEY'RE MINE!
YOU'VE GOT IT WRONG. I'M THE VICTIM, NOT HER.

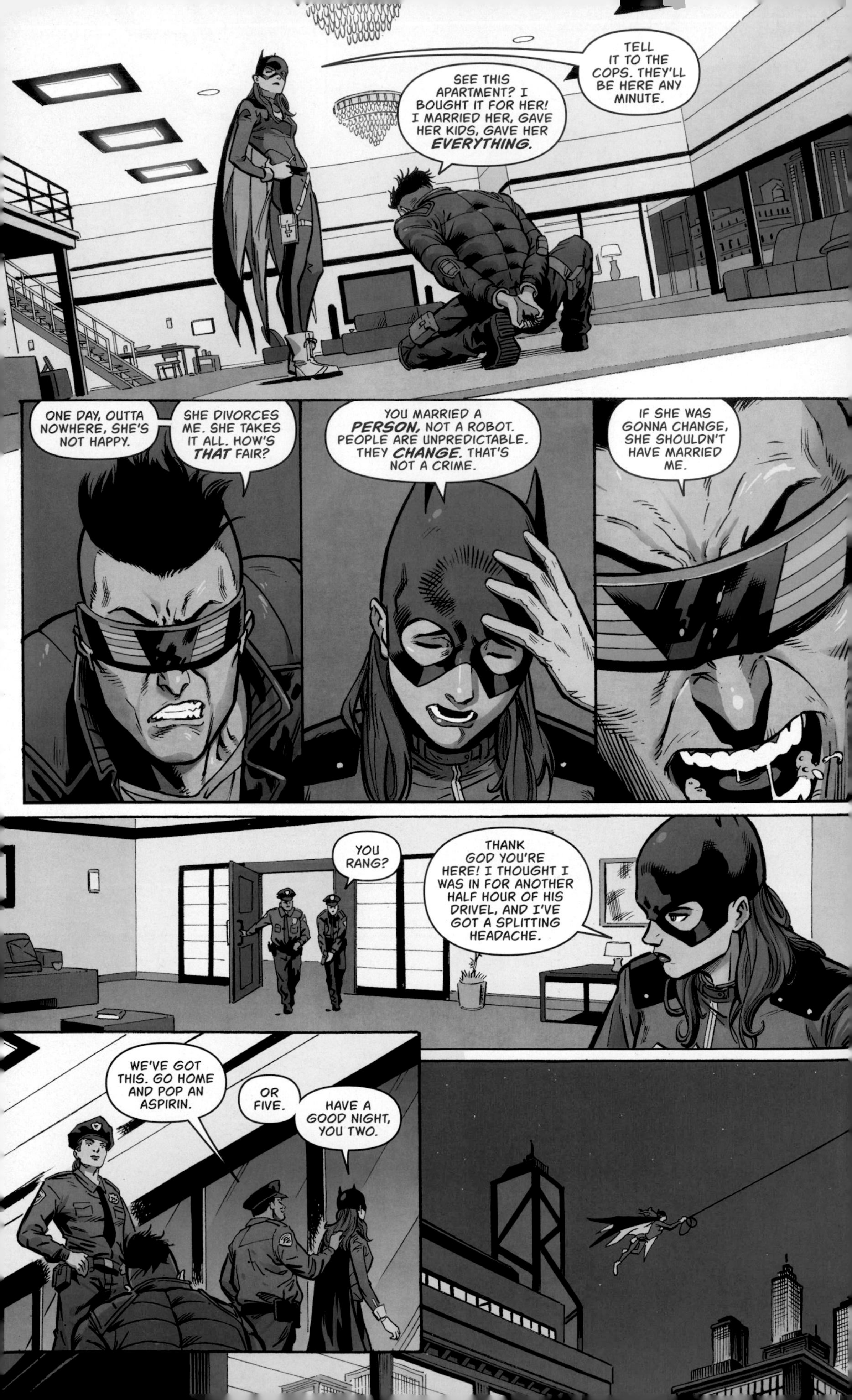
SEE THIS APARTMENT? I BOUGHT IT FOR HER! I MARRIED HER, GAVE HER KIDS, GAVE HER EVERYTHING.
TELL IT TO THE COPS. THEY'LL BE HERE ANY MINUTE.
ONE DAY, OUTTA NOWHERE, SHE'S NOT HAPPY.
SHE DIVORCES ME. SHE TAKES IT ALL. HOW'S THAT FAIR?
YOU MARRIED A PERSON, NOT A ROBOT. PEOPLE ARE UNPREDICTABLE. THEY CHANGE. THAT'S NOT A CRIME.
IF SHE WAS GONNA CHANGE, SHE SHOULDN'T HAVE MARRIED ME.
YOU RANG?
THANK GOD YOU'RE HERE! I THOUGHT I WAS IN FOR ANOTHER HALF HOUR OF HIS DRIVEL, AND I'VE GOT A SPLITTING HEADACHE.
WE'VE GOT THIS. GO HOME AND POP AN ASPIRIN.
OR FIVE.
HAVE A GOOD NIGHT, YOU TWO.

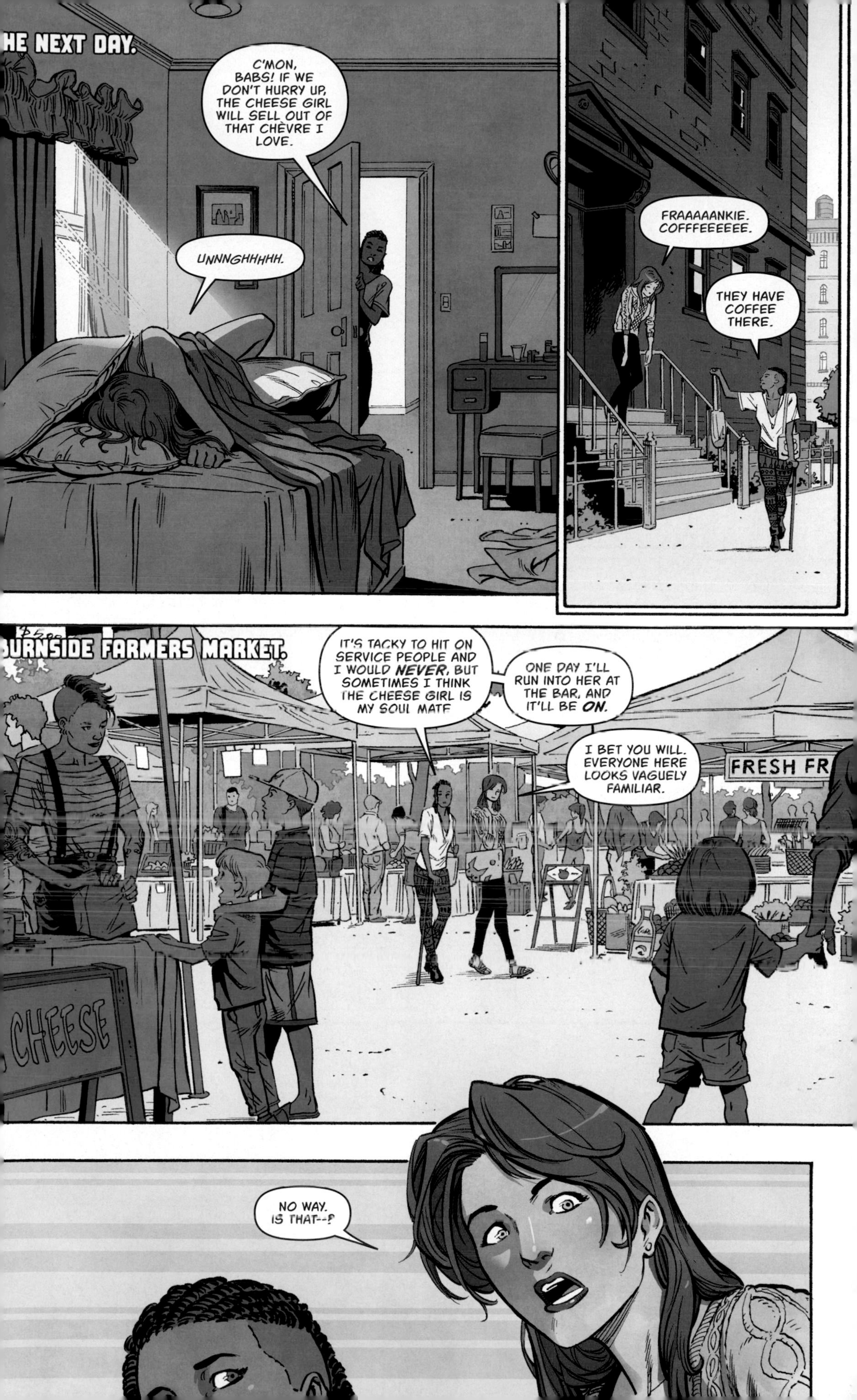
THE NEXT DAY.
C'MON, BABS! IF WE DON'T HURRY UP, THE CHEESE GIRL WILL SELL OUT OF THAT CHÈVRE I LOVE.
UNNNGHHHHH.
FRAAAAAANKIE. COFFFEEEEEE.
THEY HAVE COFFEE THERE.
URNSIDE FARMERS MARKET.
IT'S TACKY TO HIT ON SERVICE PEOPLE AND I WOULD NEVER, BUT SOMETIMES I THINK THE CHEESE GIRL IS MY SOUL MATE.
ONE DAY I'LL RUN INTO HER AT THE BAR, AND IT'LL BE ON.
I BET YOU WILL. EVERYONE HERE LOOKS VAGUELY FAMILIAR.
FRESH FR
CHEESE
NO WAY. IS THAT--?

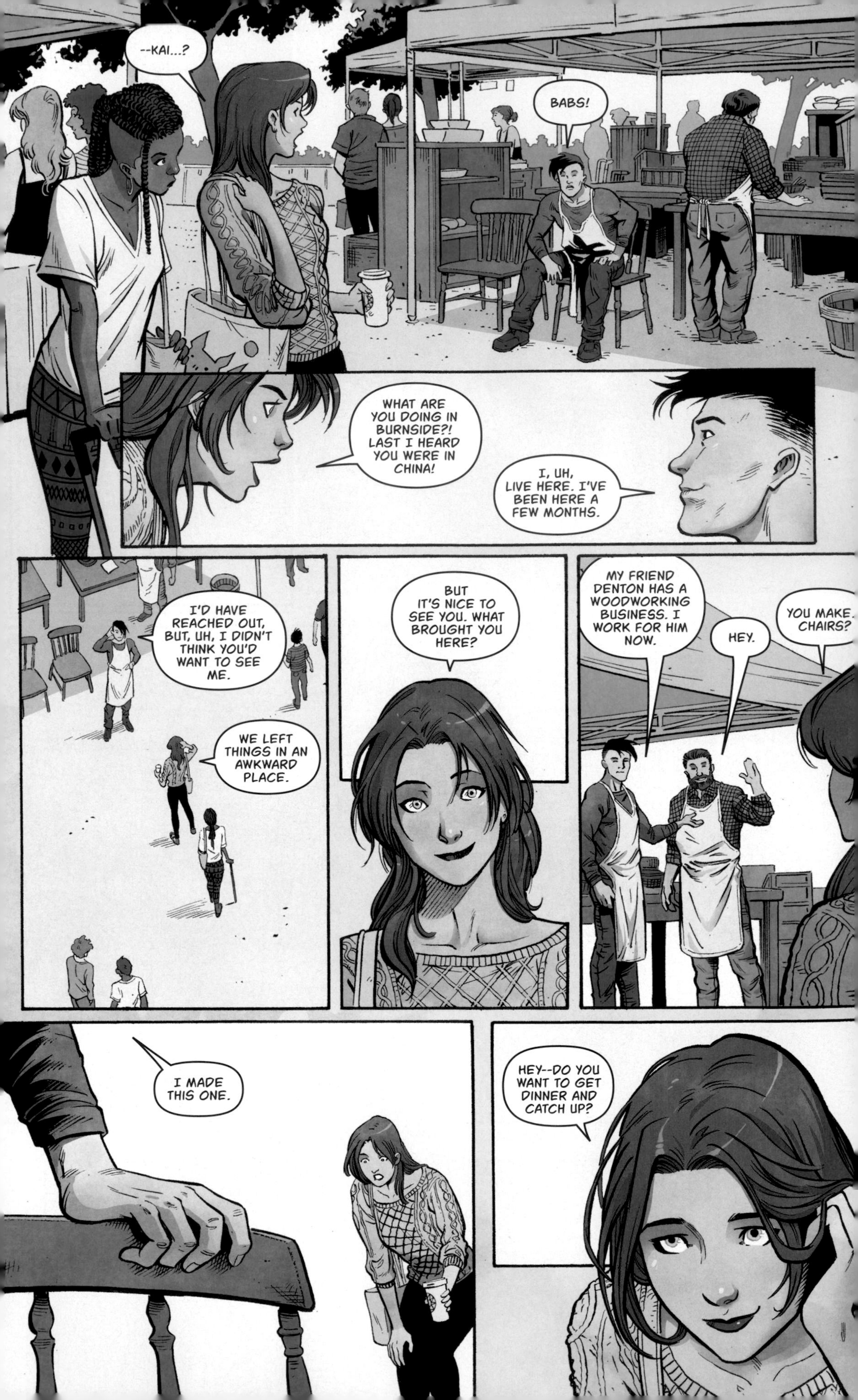
--KAI...?
BABS!
WHAT ARE YOU DOING IN BURNSIDE?! LAST I HEARD YOU WERE IN CHINA!
I, UH, LIVE HERE. I'VE BEEN HERE A FEW MONTHS.
I'D HAVE REACHED OUT, BUT, UH, I DIDN'T THINK YOU'D WANT TO SEE ME.
WE LEFT THINGS IN AN AWKWARD PLACE.
BUT IT'S NICE TO SEE YOU. WHAT BROUGHT YOU HERE?
MY FRIEND DENTON HAS A WOODWORKING BUSINESS. I WORK FOR HIM NOW.
HEY.
YOU MAKE CHAIRS?
I MADE THIS ONE.
HEY--DO YOU WANT TO GET DINNER AND CATCH UP?

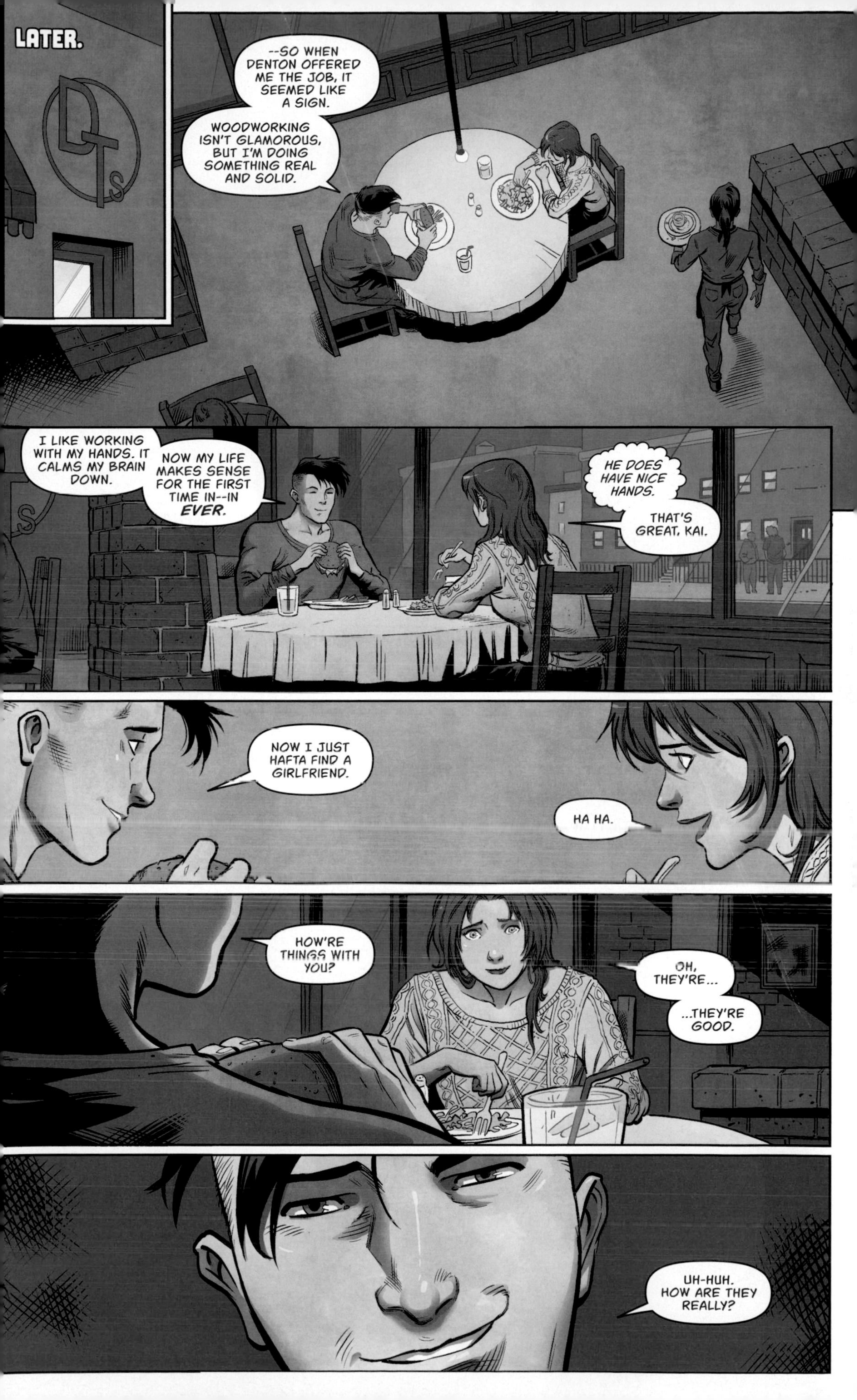
LATER.
--SO WHEN DENTON OFFERED ME THE JOB, IT SEEMED LIKE A SIGN.
WOODWORKING ISN'T GLAMOROUS, BUT I'M DOING SOMETHING REAL AND SOLID.
I LIKE WORKING WITH MY HANDS. IT CALMS MY BRAIN DOWN.
NOW MY LIFE MAKES SENSE FOR THE FIRST TIME IN--IN *EVER.*
HE DOES HAVE NICE HANDS.
THAT'S GREAT, KAI.
NOW I JUST HAFTA FIND A GIRLFRIEND.
HA HA.
HOW'RE THINGS WITH YOU?
OH, THEY'RE...
...THEY'RE GOOD.
UH-HUH. HOW ARE THEY REALLY?

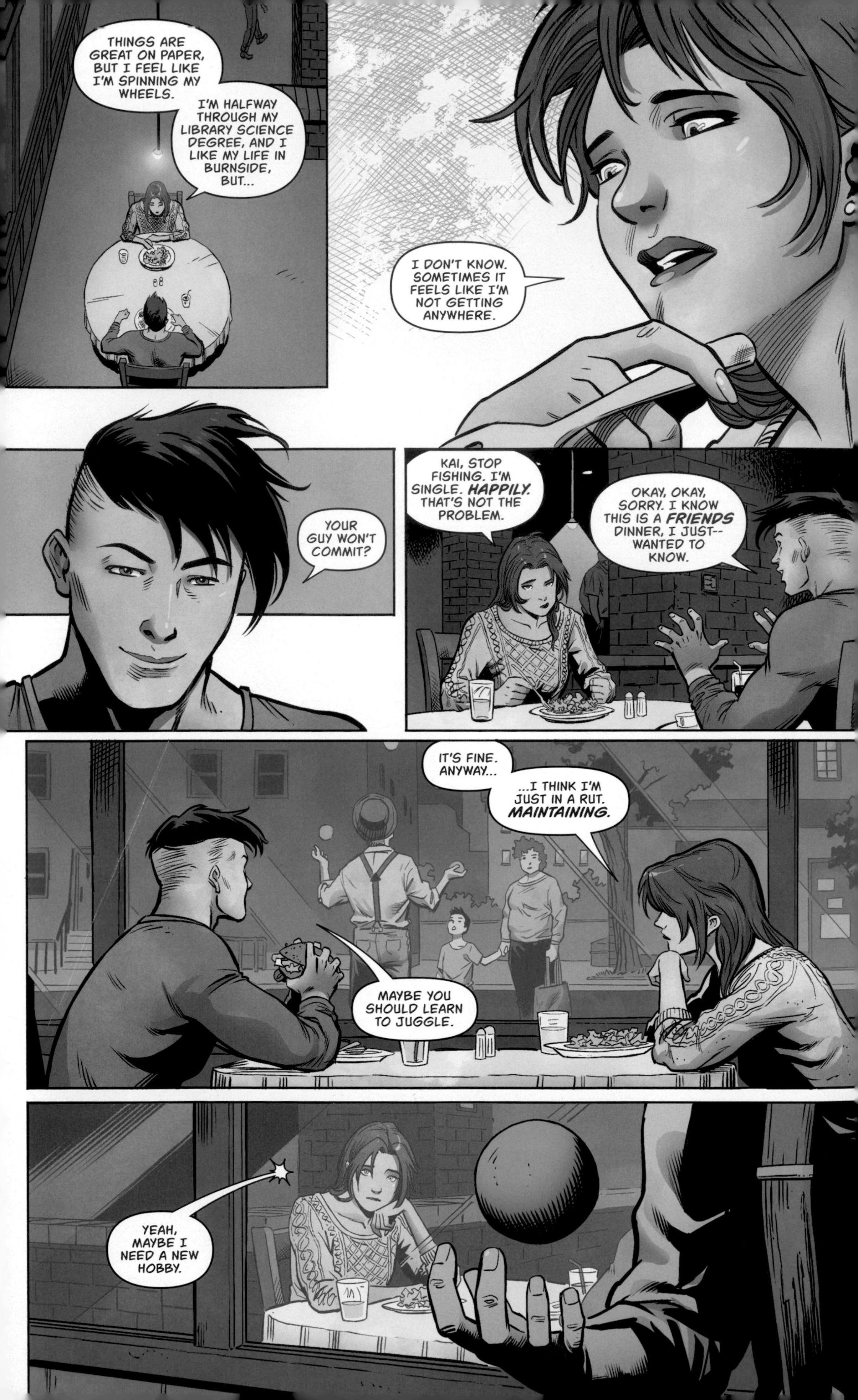
THINGS ARE GREAT ON PAPER, BUT I FEEL LIKE I'M SPINNING MY WHEELS.
I'M HALFWAY THROUGH MY LIBRARY SCIENCE DEGREE, AND I LIKE MY LIFE IN BURNSIDE, BUT...
I DON'T KNOW. SOMETIMES IT FEELS LIKE I'M NOT GETTING ANYWHERE.
YOUR GUY WON'T COMMIT?
KAI, STOP FISHING. I'M SINGLE. **HAPPILY.** THAT'S NOT THE PROBLEM.
OKAY, OKAY, SORRY. I KNOW THIS IS A **FRIENDS** DINNER, I JUST--WANTED TO KNOW.
IT'S FINE. ANYWAY...
...I THINK I'M JUST IN A RUT. **MAINTAINING.**
MAYBE YOU SHOULD LEARN TO JUGGLE.
YEAH, MAYBE I NEED A NEW HOBBY.

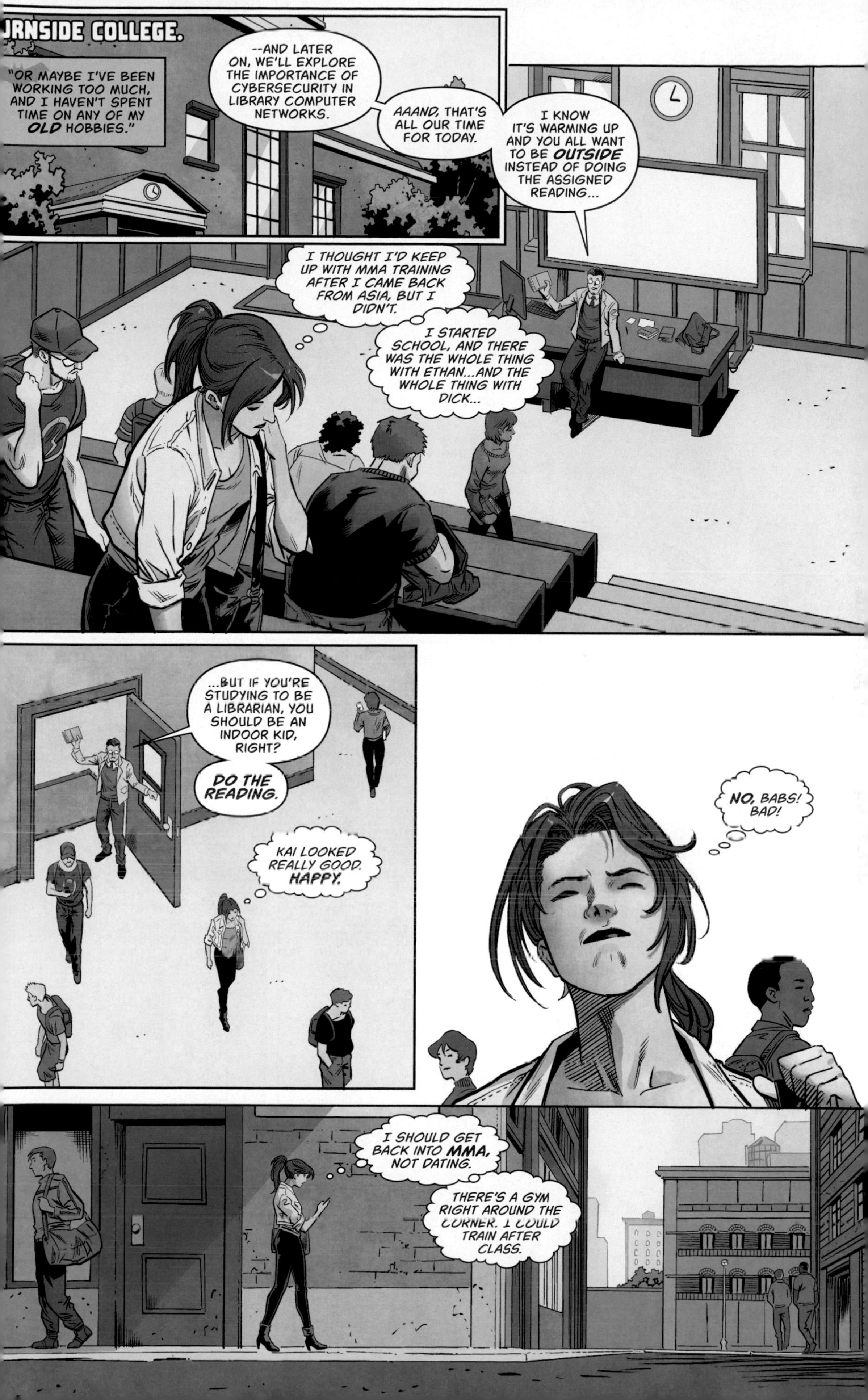

URNSIDE COLLEGE.
"OR MAYBE I'VE BEEN WORKING TOO MUCH, AND I HAVEN'T SPENT TIME ON ANY OF MY OLD HOBBIES."
--AND LATER ON, WE'LL EXPLORE THE IMPORTANCE OF CYBERSECURITY IN LIBRARY COMPUTER NETWORKS.
AAAND, THAT'S ALL OUR TIME FOR TODAY.
I KNOW IT'S WARMING UP AND YOU ALL WANT TO BE OUTSIDE INSTEAD OF DOING THE ASSIGNED READING...
I THOUGHT I'D KEEP UP WITH MMA TRAINING AFTER I CAME BACK FROM ASIA, BUT I DIDN'T.
I STARTED SCHOOL, AND THERE WAS THE WHOLE THING WITH ETHAN...AND THE WHOLE THING WITH DICK...
...BUT IF YOU'RE STUDYING TO BE A LIBRARIAN, YOU SHOULD BE AN INDOOR KID, RIGHT?
DO THE READING.
KAI LOOKED REALLY GOOD. HAPPY.
NO, BABS! BAD!
I SHOULD GET BACK INTO MMA, NOT DATING.
THERE'S A GYM RIGHT AROUND THE CORNER. I COULD TRAIN AFTER CLASS.

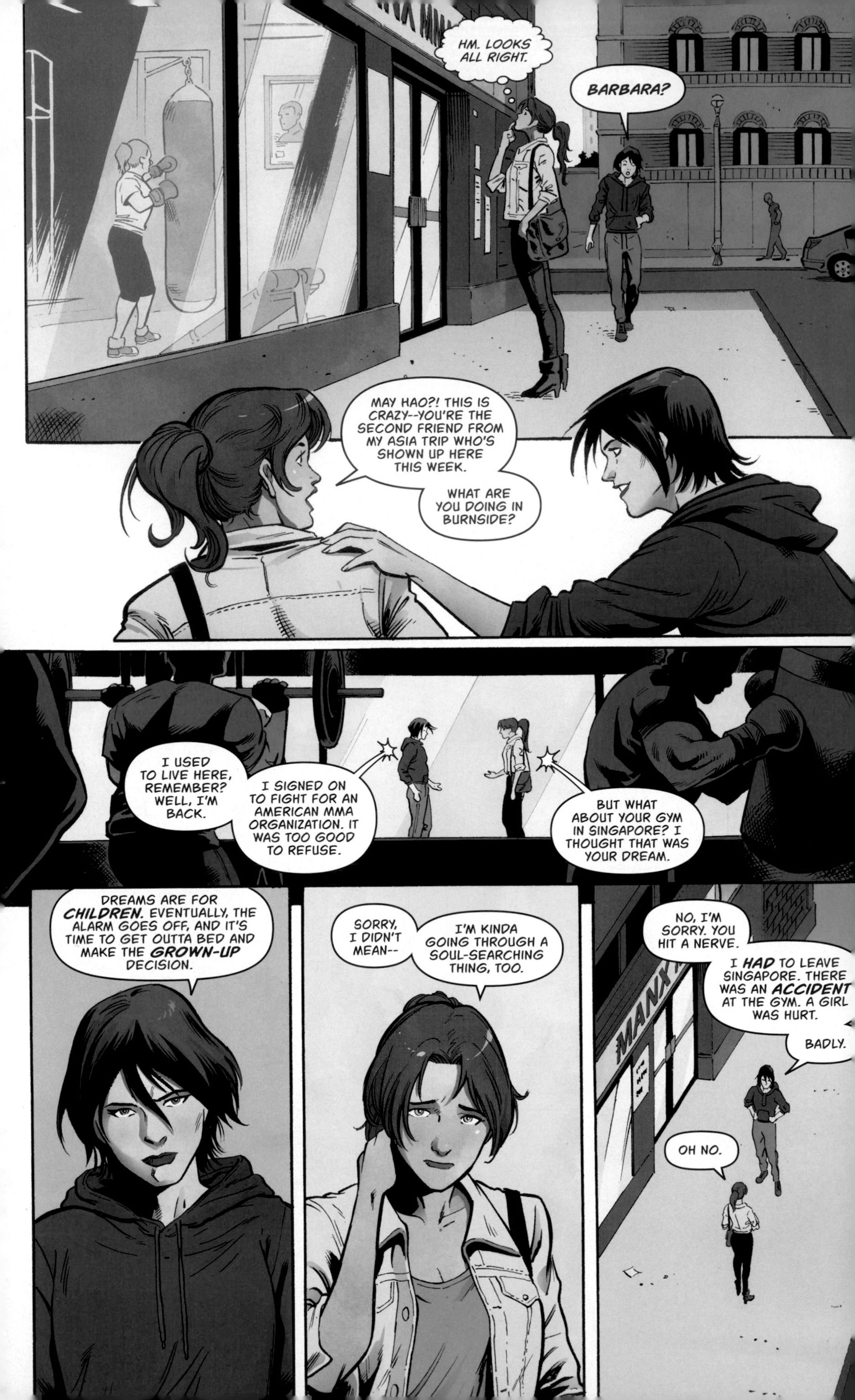
HM. LOOKS ALL RIGHT.
BARBARA?
MAY HAO?! THIS IS CRAZY--YOU'RE THE SECOND FRIEND FROM MY ASIA TRIP WHO'S SHOWN UP HERE THIS WEEK.
WHAT ARE YOU DOING IN BURNSIDE?
I USED TO LIVE HERE, REMEMBER? WELL, I'M BACK.
I SIGNED ON TO FIGHT FOR AN AMERICAN MMA ORGANIZATION. IT WAS TOO GOOD TO REFUSE.
BUT WHAT ABOUT YOUR GYM IN SINGAPORE? I THOUGHT THAT WAS YOUR DREAM.
DREAMS ARE FOR **CHILDREN.** EVENTUALLY, THE ALARM GOES OFF, AND IT'S TIME TO GET OUTTA BED AND MAKE THE **GROWN-UP** DECISION.
SORRY, I DIDN'T MEAN--
I'M KINDA GOING THROUGH A SOUL-SEARCHING THING, TOO.
NO, I'M SORRY. YOU HIT A NERVE.
I **HAD** TO LEAVE SINGAPORE. THERE WAS AN **ACCIDENT** AT THE GYM. A GIRL WAS HURT.
BADLY.
OH NO.

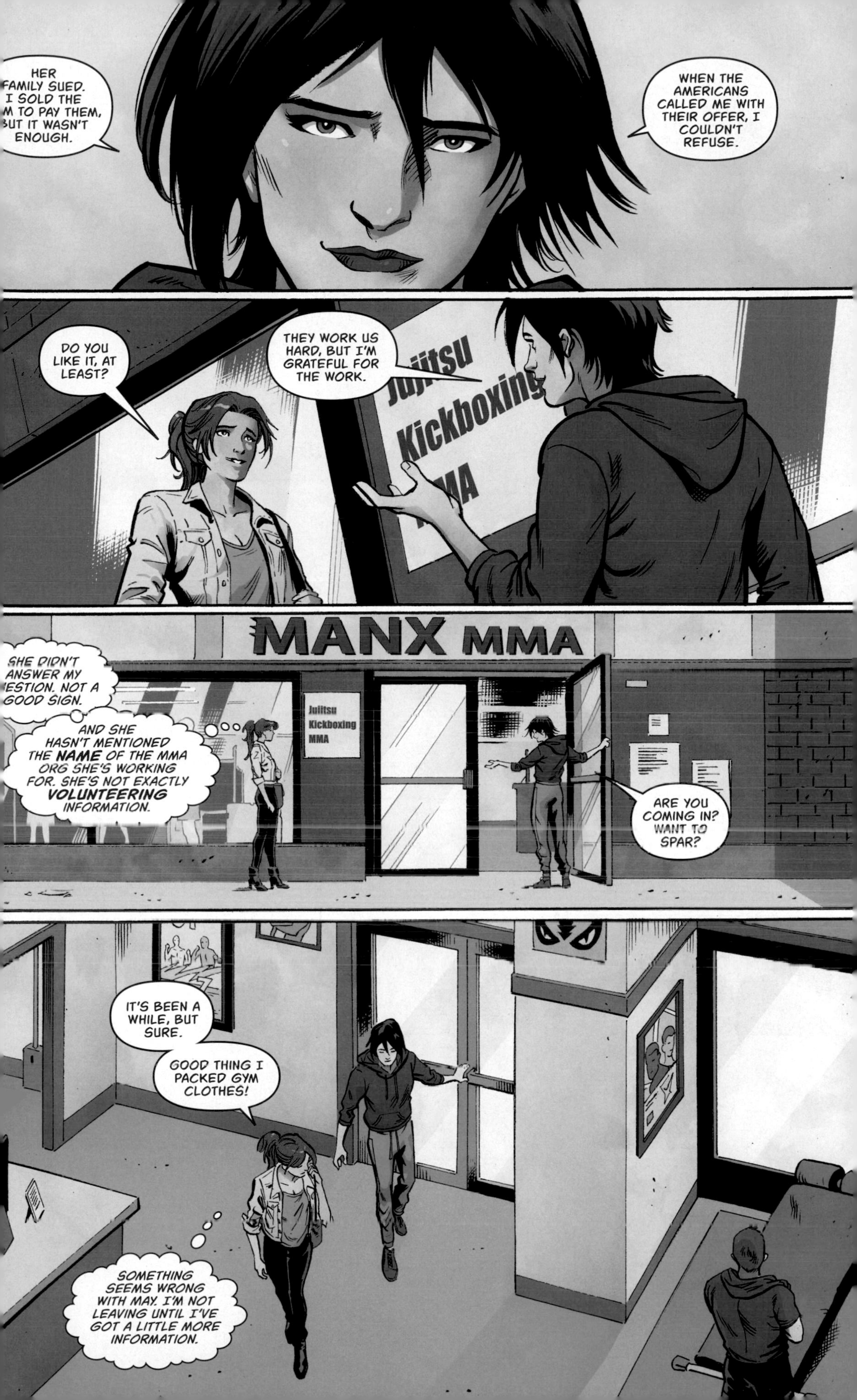
HER FAMILY SUED. I SOLD THE M TO PAY THEM, UT IT WASN'T ENOUGH.
WHEN THE AMERICANS CALLED ME WITH THEIR OFFER, I COULDN'T REFUSE.
DO YOU LIKE IT, AT LEAST?
THEY WORK US HARD, BUT I'M GRATEFUL FOR THE WORK.
Jujitsu
Kickboxing
MANX MMA
SHE DIDN'T ANSWER MY ESTION. NOT A GOOD SIGN.
AND SHE HASN'T MENTIONED THE NAME OF THE MMA ORG SHE'S WORKING FOR. SHE'S NOT EXACTLY VOLUNTEERING INFORMATION.
Jujitsu
Kickboxing
MMA
ARE YOU COMING IN? WANT TO SPAR?
IT'S BEEN A WHILE, BUT SURE.
GOOD THING I PACKED GYM CLOTHES!
SOMETHING SEEMS WRONG WITH MAY. I'M NOT LEAVING UNTIL I'VE GOT A LITTLE MORE INFORMATION.

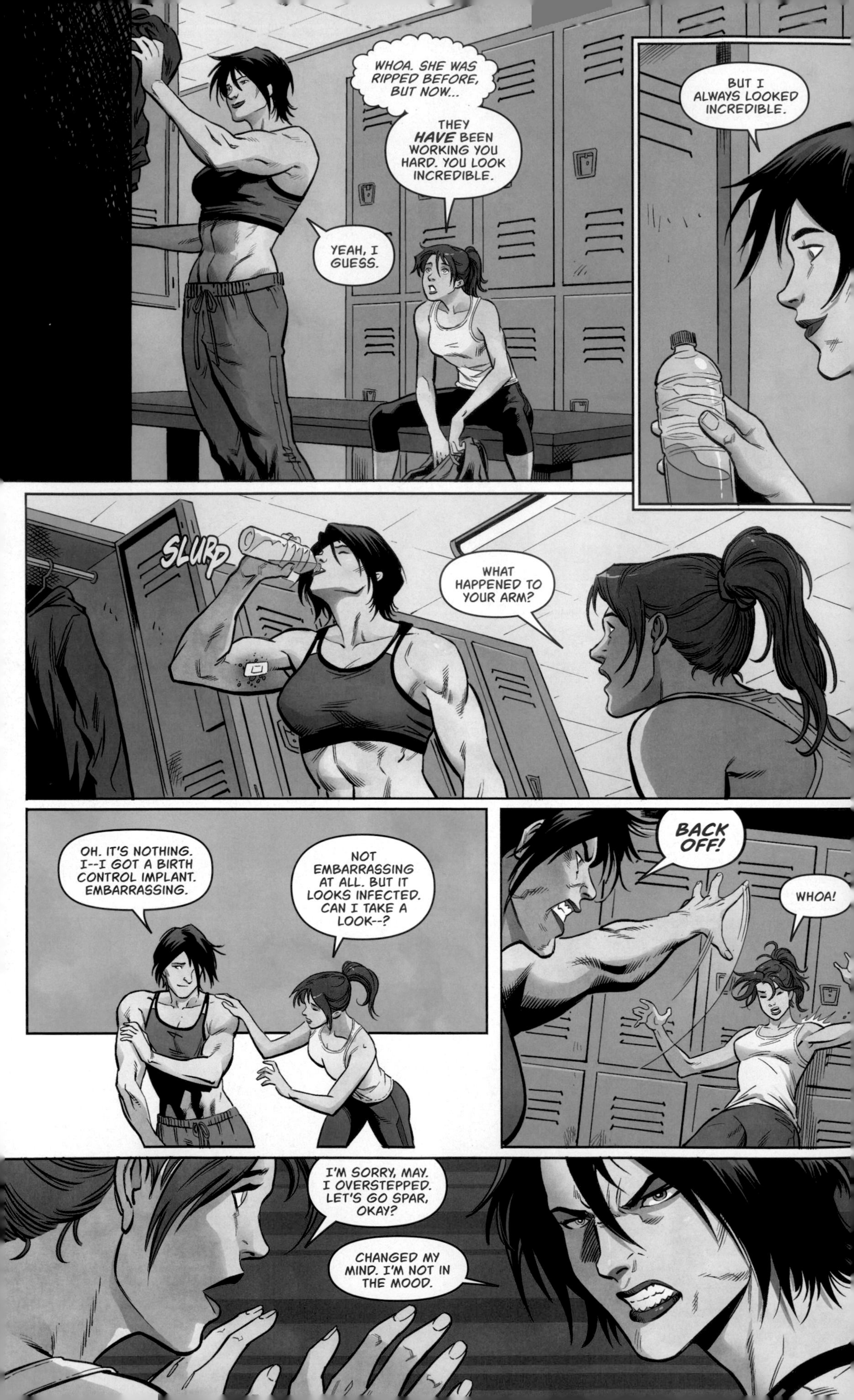
WHOA. SHE WAS RIPPED BEFORE, BUT NOW...
THEY HAVE BEEN WORKING YOU HARD. YOU LOOK INCREDIBLE.
YEAH, I GUESS.
BUT I ALWAYS LOOKED INCREDIBLE.
SLURP
WHAT HAPPENED TO YOUR ARM?
OH. IT'S NOTHING. I--I GOT A BIRTH CONTROL IMPLANT. EMBARRASSING.
NOT EMBARRASSING AT ALL. BUT IT LOOKS INFECTED. CAN I TAKE A LOOK--?
BACK OFF!
WHOA!
I'M SORRY, MAY. I OVERSTEPPED. LET'S GO SPAR, OKAY?
CHANGED MY MIND. I'M NOT IN THE MOOD.

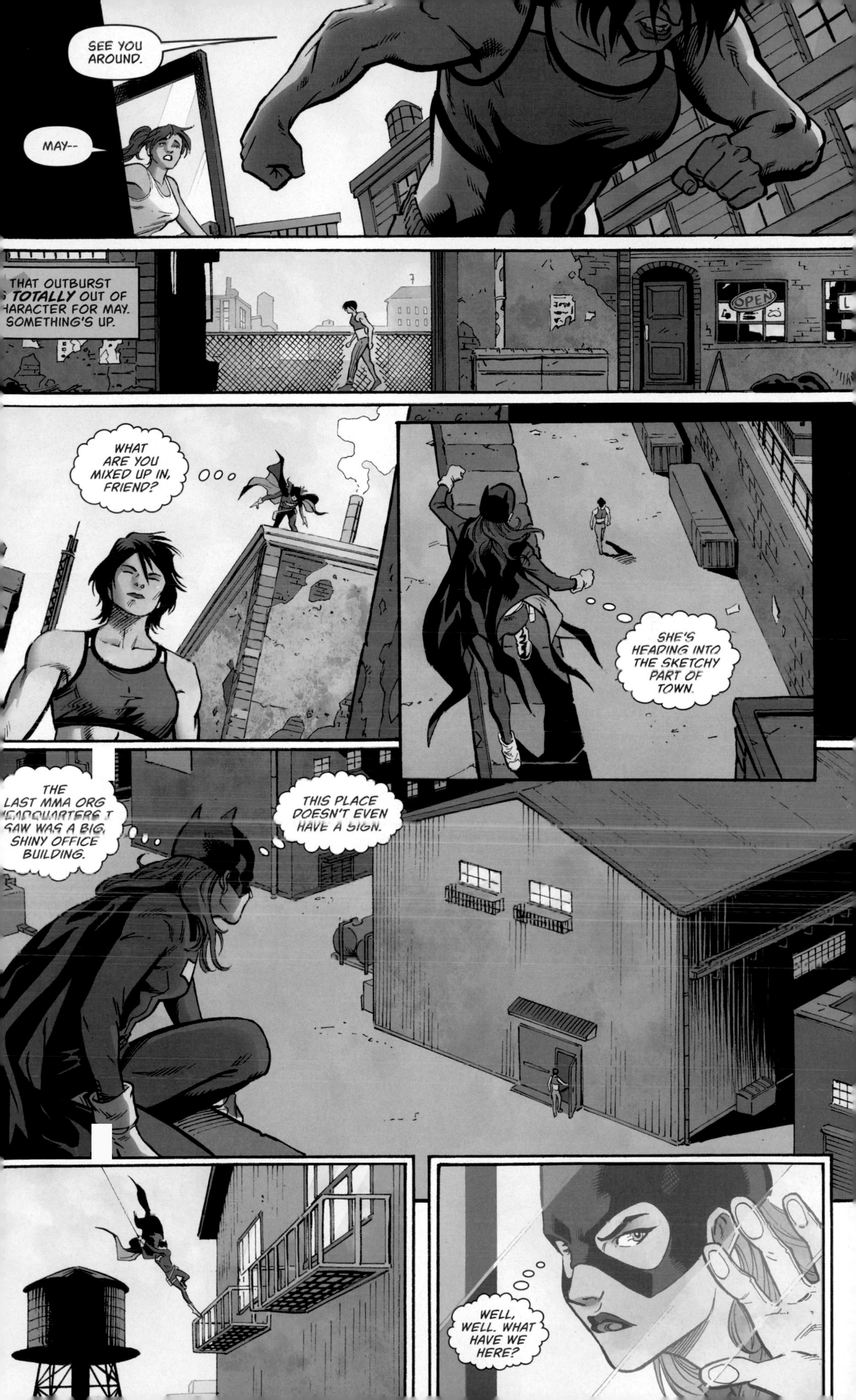
SEE YOU AROUND.
MAY--
THAT OUTBURST
S TOTALLY OUT OF
HARACTER FOR MAY.
SOMETHING'S UP.
OPEN
WHAT ARE YOU MIXED UP IN, FRIEND?
SHE'S HEADING INTO THE SKETCHY PART OF TOWN.
THE LAST MMA ORG EADQUARTERS I SAW WAS A BIG, SHINY OFFICE BUILDING.
THIS PLACE DOESN'T EVEN HAVE A SIGN.
WELL, WELL. WHAT HAVE WE HERE?

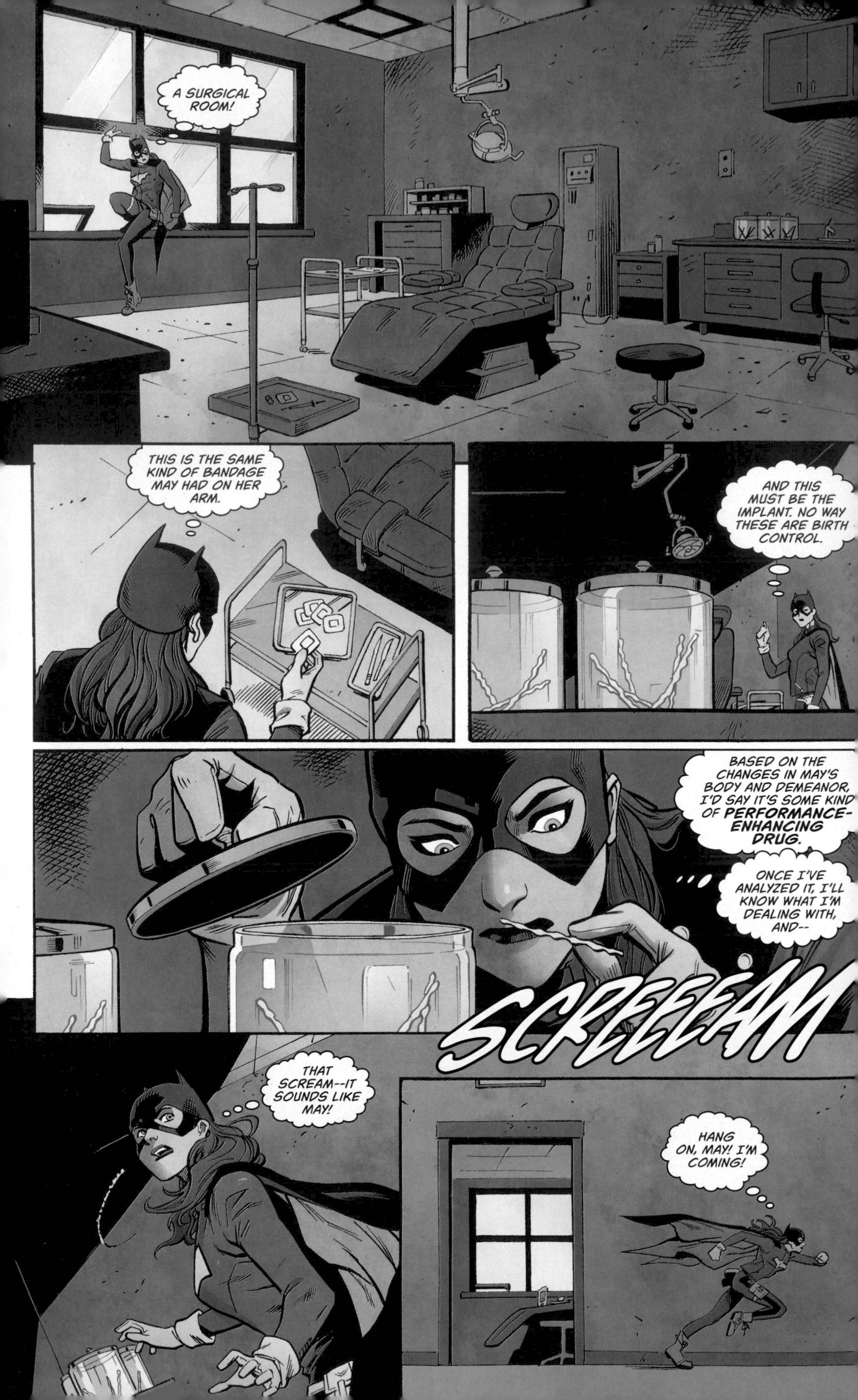
A SURGICAL ROOM!
THIS IS THE SAME KIND OF BANDAGE MAY HAD ON HER ARM.
AND THIS MUST BE THE IMPLANT. NO WAY THESE ARE BIRTH CONTROL.
BASED ON THE CHANGES IN MAY'S BODY AND DEMEANOR, I'D SAY IT'S SOME KIND OF PERFORMANCE-ENHANCING DRUG.
...
ONCE I'VE ANALYZED IT, I'LL KNOW WHAT I'M DEALING WITH, AND--
SCREEEAM
THAT SCREAM--IT SOUNDS LIKE MAY!
HANG ON, MAY! I'M COMING!

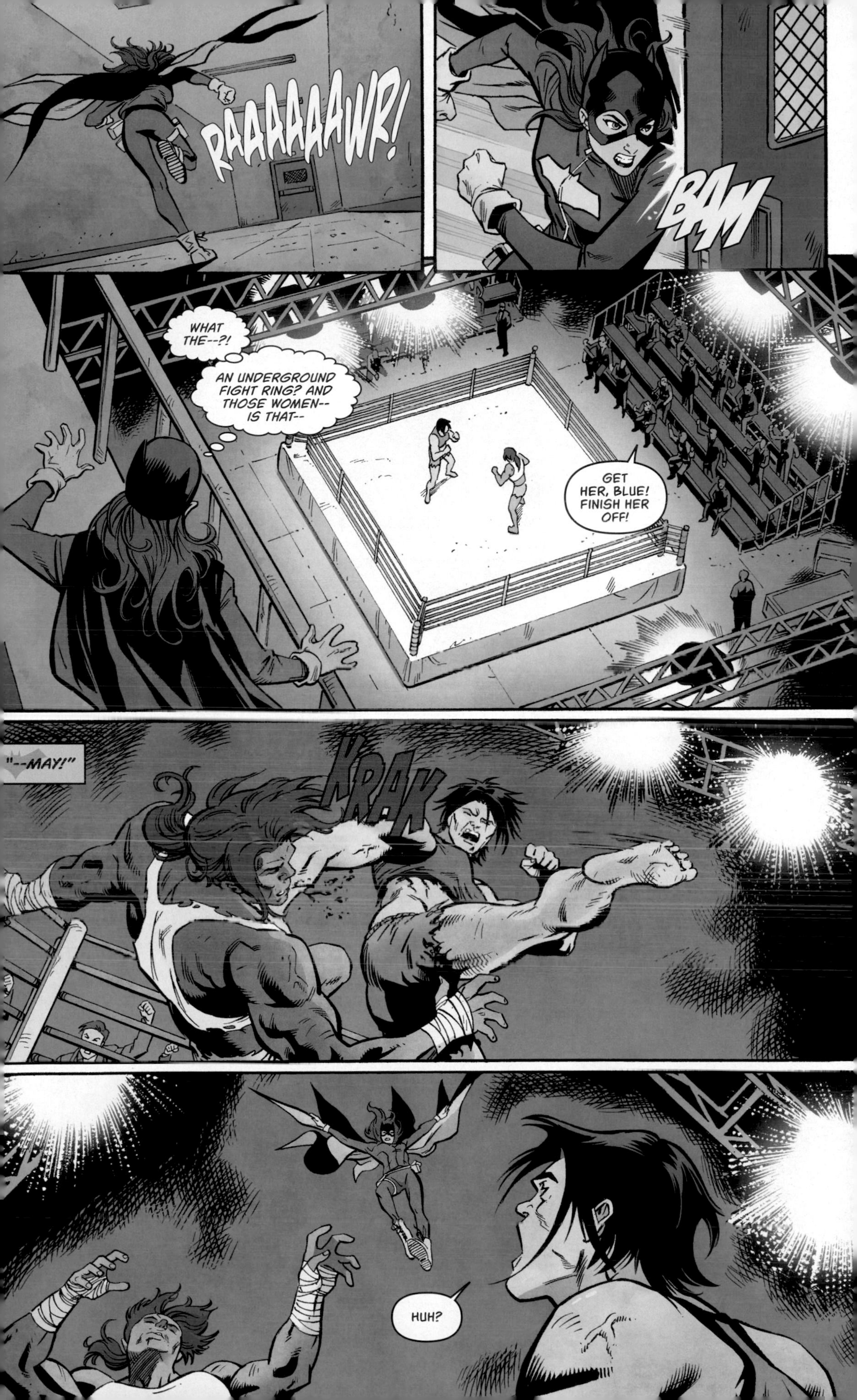
RAAAAAAWR!
BAM
WHAT THE--?!
AN UNDERGROUND FIGHT RING? AND THOSE WOMEN-- IS THAT--
GET HER, BLUE! FINISH HER OFF!
"--MAY!"
KRAK
HUH?

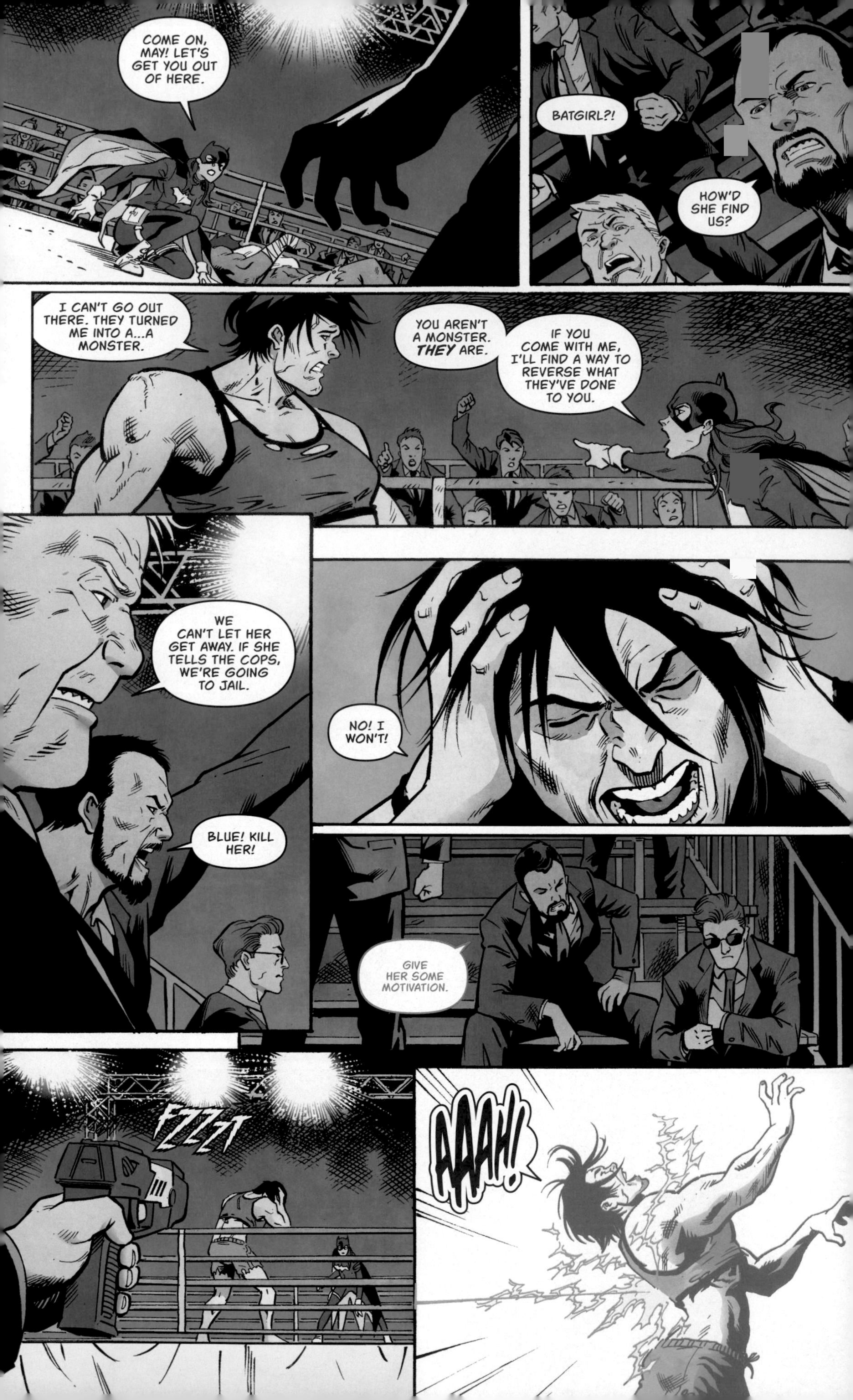
COME ON, MAY! LET'S GET YOU OUT OF HERE.
BATGIRL?!
HOW'D SHE FIND US?
I CAN'T GO OUT THERE. THEY TURNED ME INTO A...A MONSTER.
YOU AREN'T A MONSTER. THEY ARE.
IF YOU COME WITH ME, I'LL FIND A WAY TO REVERSE WHAT THEY'VE DONE TO YOU.
WE CAN'T LET HER GET AWAY. IF SHE TELLS THE COPS, WE'RE GOING TO JAIL.
BLUE! KILL HER!
NO! I WON'T!
GIVE HER SOME MOTIVATION.
FZZZT
AAAH!

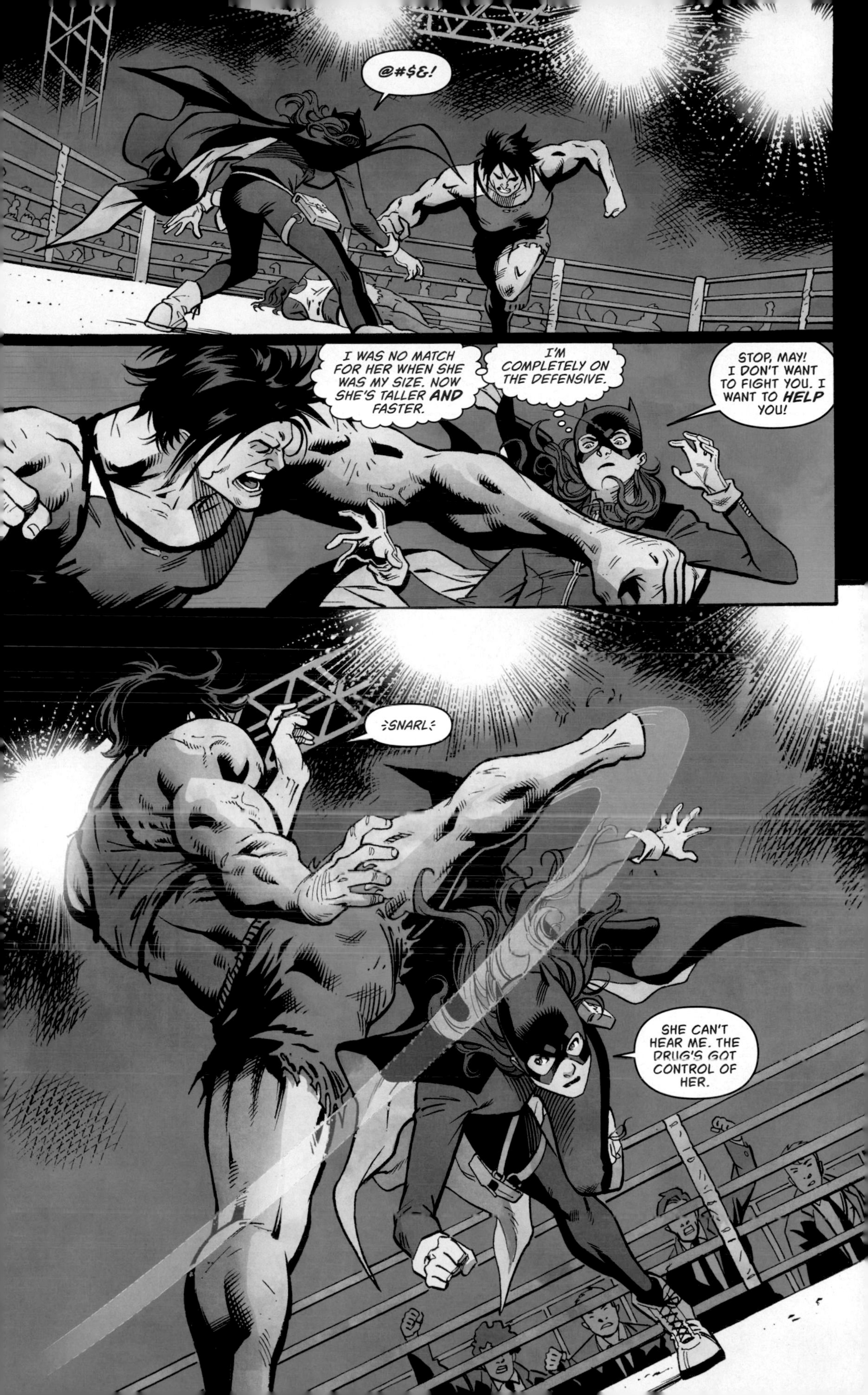
@#$&!
I WAS NO MATCH FOR HER WHEN SHE WAS MY SIZE. NOW SHE'S TALLER **AND** FASTER.
I'M COMPLETELY ON THE DEFENSIVE.
STOP, MAY! I DON'T WANT TO FIGHT YOU. I WANT TO **HELP** YOU!
SNARL
SHE CAN'T HEAR ME. THE DRUG'S GOT CONTROL OF HER.

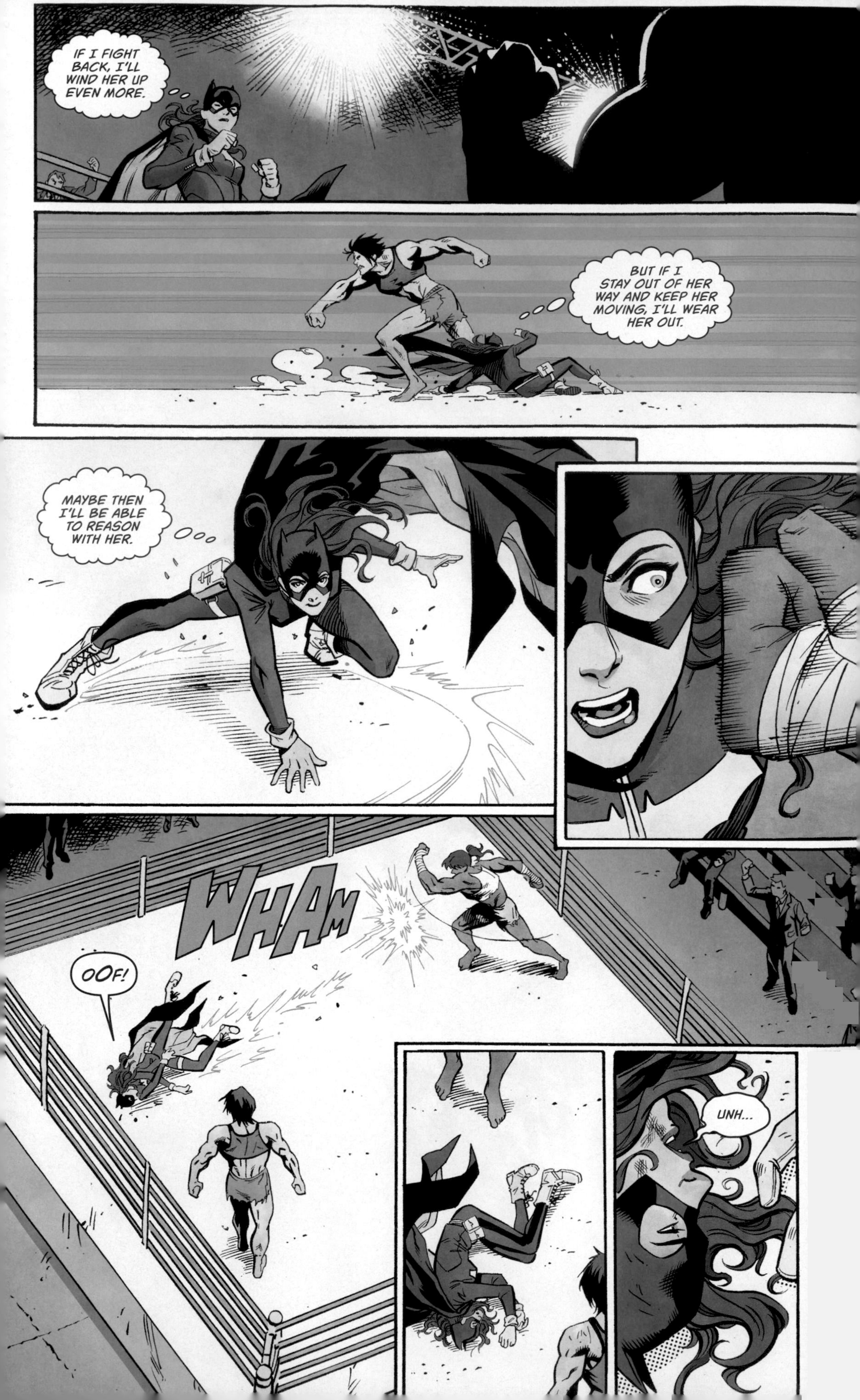
IF I FIGHT BACK, I'LL WIND HER UP EVEN MORE.
BUT IF I STAY OUT OF HER WAY AND KEEP HER MOVING, I'LL WEAR HER OUT.
MAYBE THEN I'LL BE ABLE TO REASON WITH HER.
WHAM
OOF!
UNH...

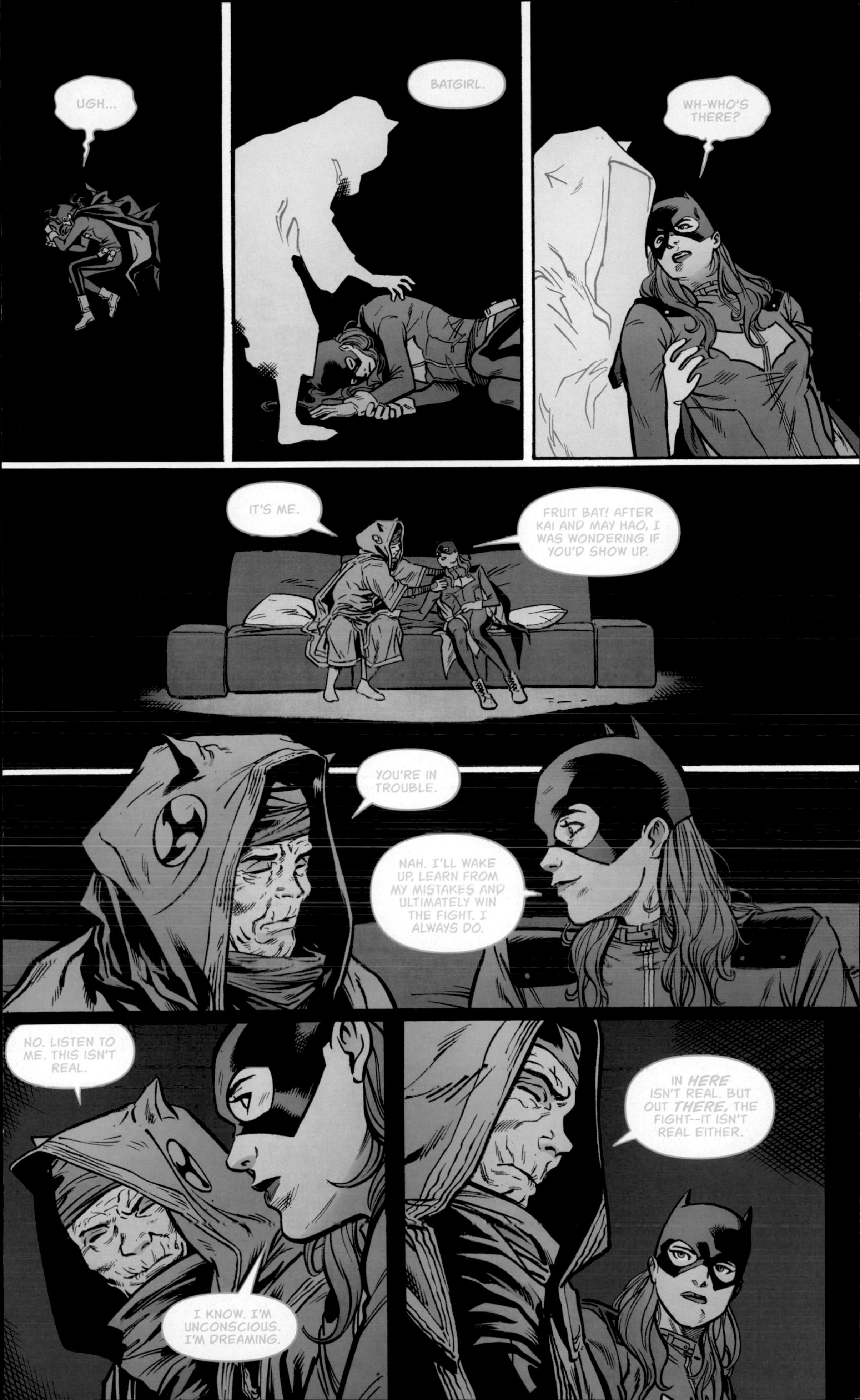
UGH...
BATGIRL.
WH-WHO'S THERE?
IT'S ME.
FRUIT BAT! AFTER KAI AND MAY HAO, I WAS WONDERING IF YOU'D SHOW UP.
YOU'RE IN TROUBLE.
NAH. I'LL WAKE UP, LEARN FROM MY MISTAKES AND ULTIMATELY WIN THE FIGHT. I ALWAYS DO.
NO. LISTEN TO ME. THIS ISN'T REAL.
I KNOW. I'M UNCONSCIOUS. I'M DREAMING.
IN HERE ISN'T REAL. BUT OUT THERE, THE FIGHT--IT ISN'T REAL EITHER.

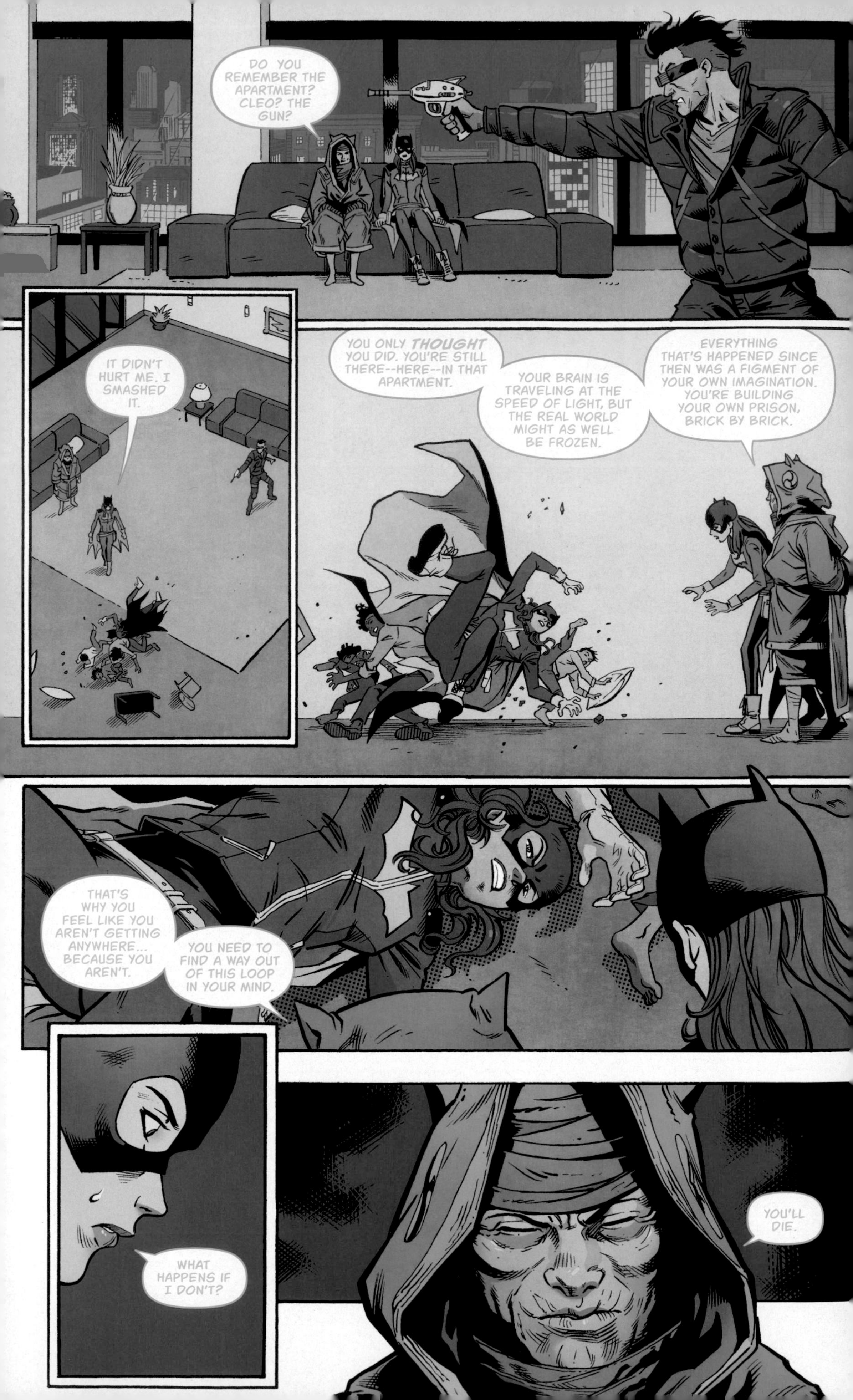
DO YOU REMEMBER THE APARTMENT? CLEO? THE GUN?
IT DIDN'T HURT ME. I SMASHED IT.
YOU ONLY *THOUGHT* YOU DID. YOU'RE STILL THERE--HERE--IN THAT APARTMENT.
YOUR BRAIN IS TRAVELING AT THE SPEED OF LIGHT, BUT THE REAL WORLD MIGHT AS WELL BE FROZEN.
EVERYTHING THAT'S HAPPENED SINCE THEN WAS A FIGMENT OF YOUR OWN IMAGINATION. YOU'RE BUILDING YOUR OWN PRISON, BRICK BY BRICK.
THAT'S WHY YOU FEEL LIKE YOU AREN'T GETTING ANYWHERE... BECAUSE YOU AREN'T.
YOU NEED TO FIND A WAY OUT OF THIS LOOP IN YOUR MIND.
WHAT HAPPENS IF I DON'T?
YOU'LL DIE.

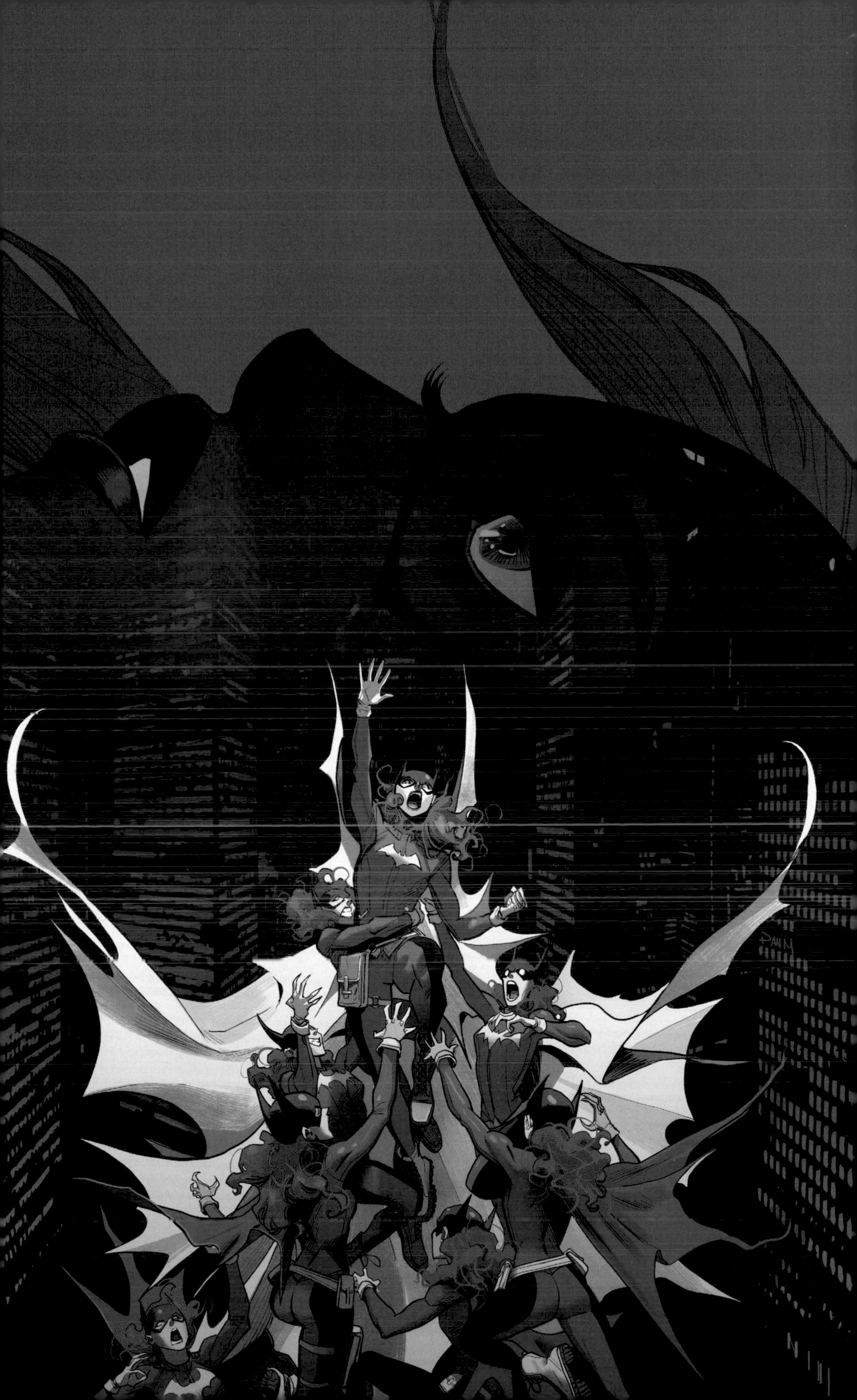

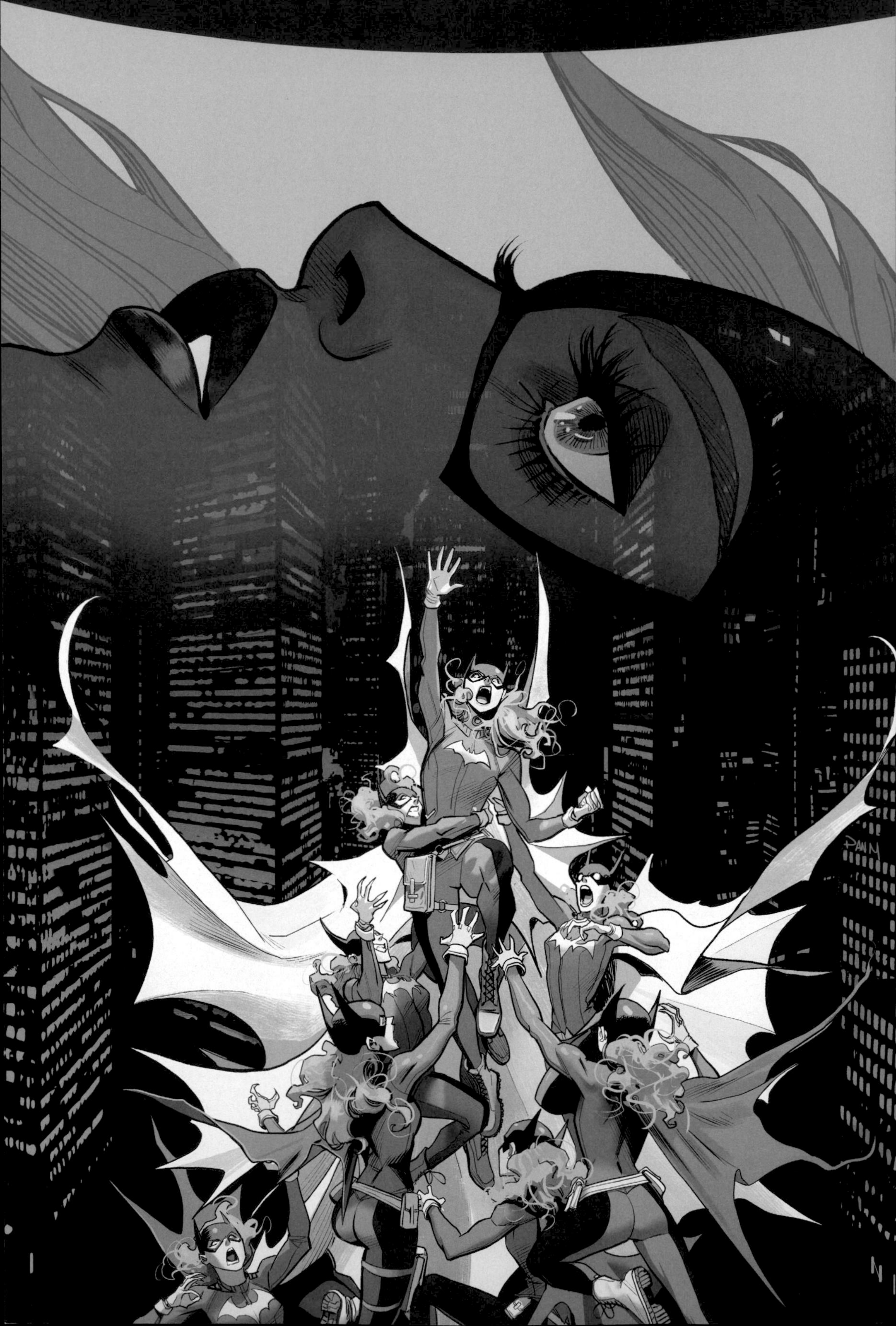

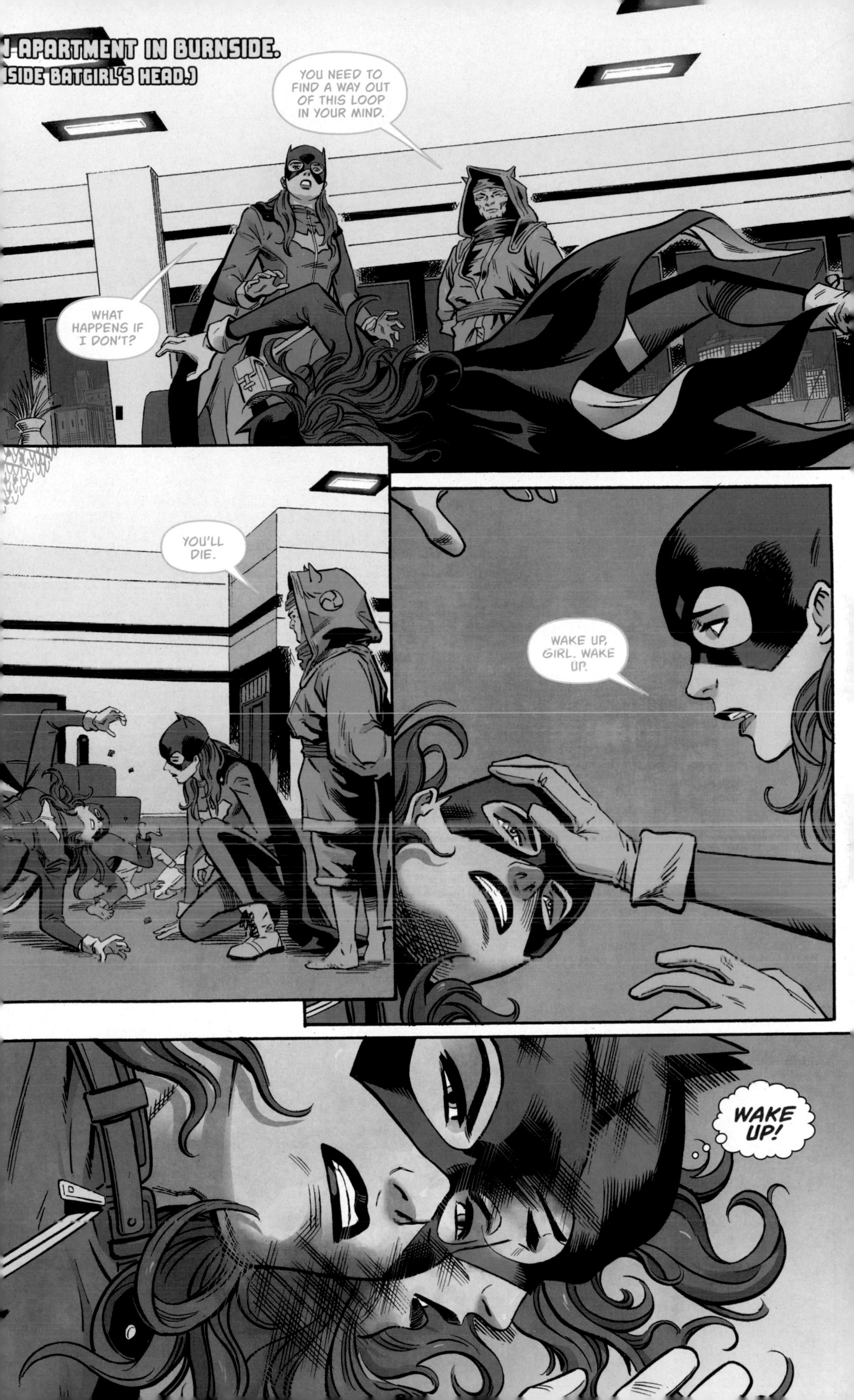

-APARTMENT IN BURNSIDE.
SIDE BATGIRL'S HEAD.)
YOU NEED TO FIND A WAY OUT OF THIS LOOP IN YOUR MIND.
WHAT HAPPENS IF I DON'T?
YOU'LL DIE.
WAKE UP, GIRL. WAKE UP.
WAKE UP!

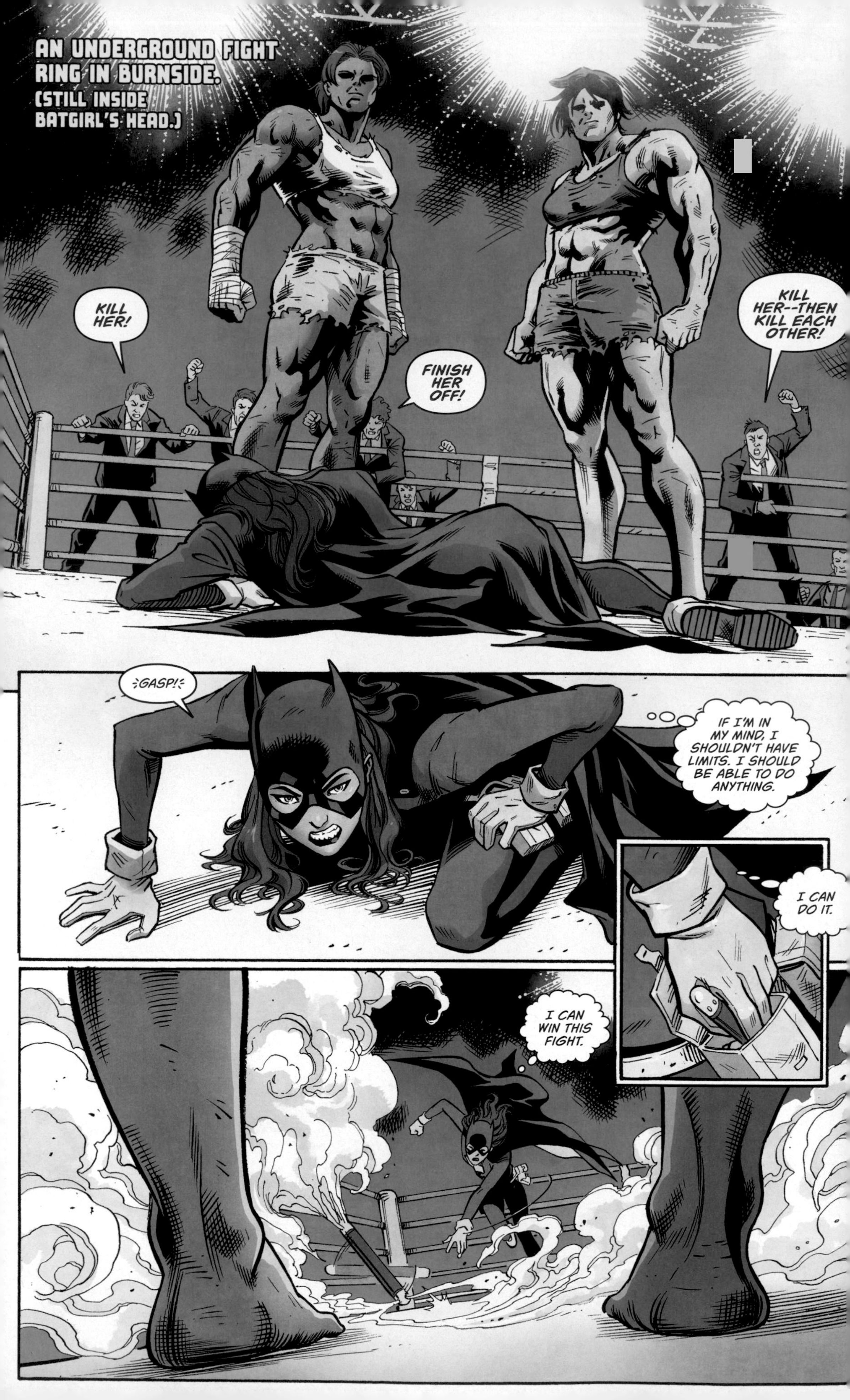
AN UNDERGROUND FIGHT RING IN BURNSIDE.
(STILL INSIDE BATGIRL'S HEAD.)
KILL HER!
FINISH HER OFF!
KILL HER--THEN KILL EACH OTHER!
GASP!
IF I'M IN MY MIND, I SHOULDN'T HAVE LIMITS. I SHOULD BE ABLE TO DO ANYTHING.
I CAN DO IT.
I CAN WIN THIS FIGHT.

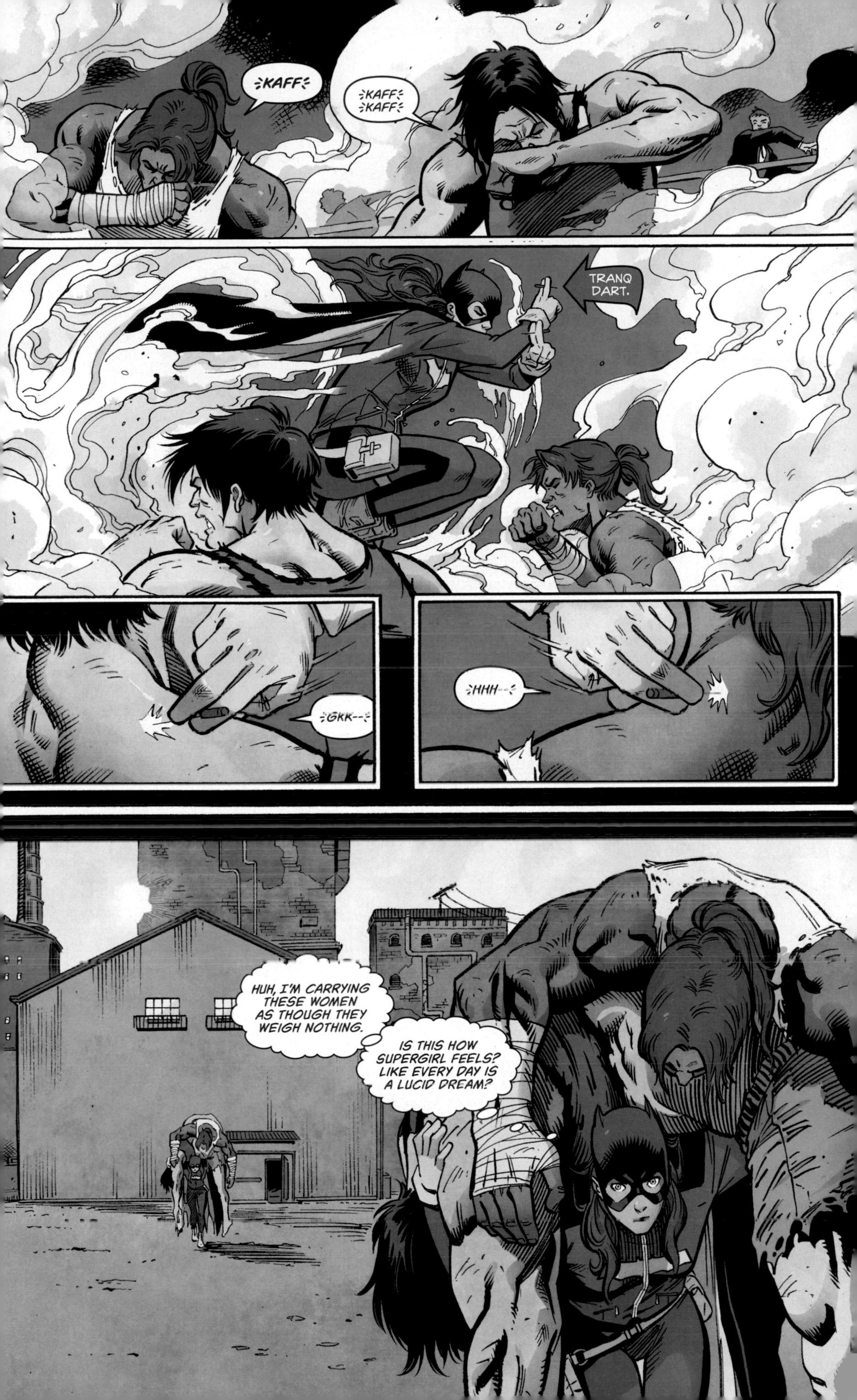
KAFF
KAFF KAFF
TRANQ DART.
GKK--
HHH--
HUH, I'M CARRYING THESE WOMEN AS THOUGH THEY WEIGH NOTHING.
IS THIS HOW SUPERGIRL FEELS? LIKE EVERY DAY IS A LUCID DREAM?

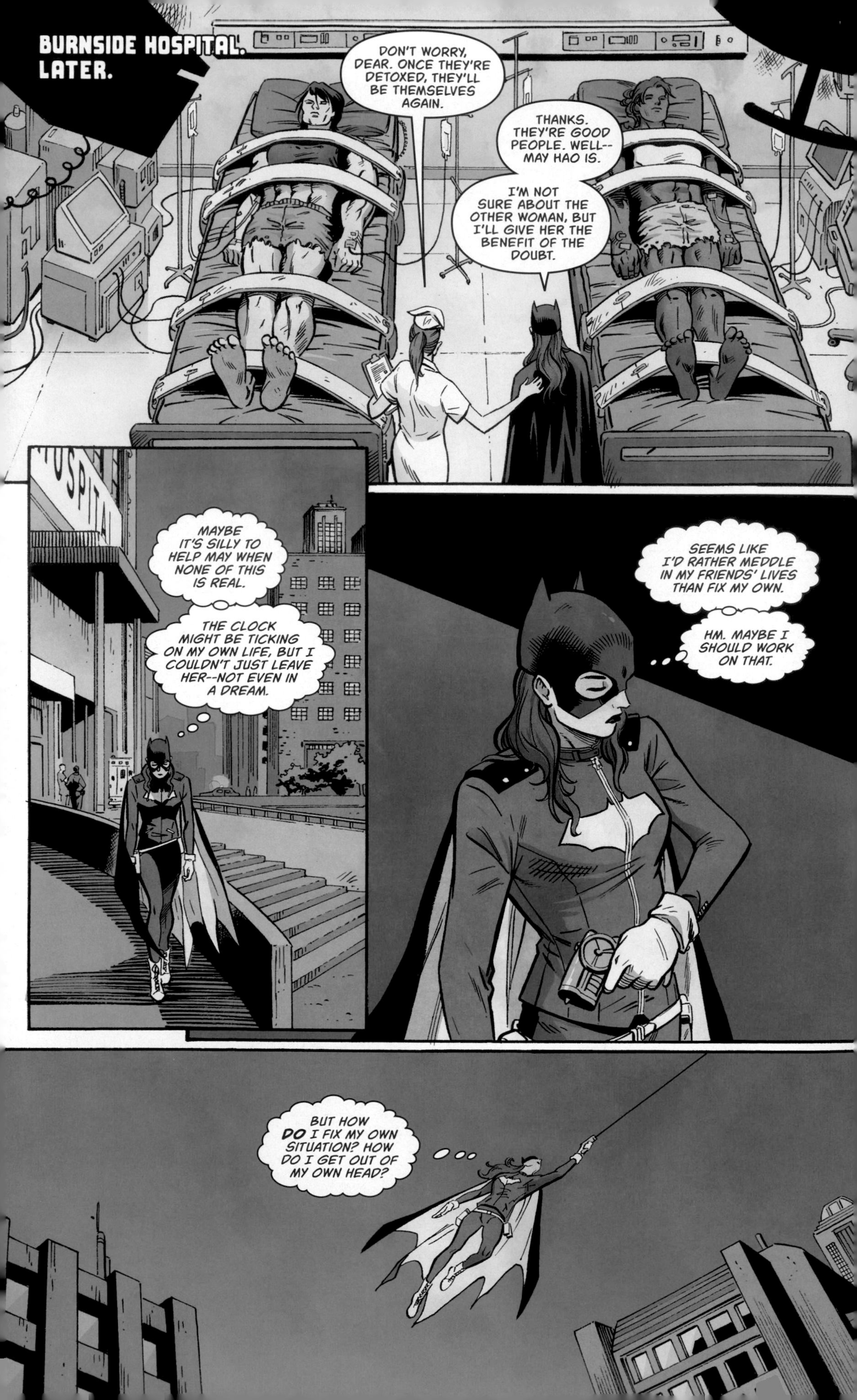
BURNSIDE HOSPITAL. LATER.
DON'T WORRY, DEAR. ONCE THEY'RE DETOXED, THEY'LL BE THEMSELVES AGAIN.
THANKS. THEY'RE GOOD PEOPLE. WELL-- MAY HAO IS.
I'M NOT SURE ABOUT THE OTHER WOMAN, BUT I'LL GIVE HER THE BENEFIT OF THE DOUBT.
MAYBE IT'S SILLY TO HELP MAY WHEN NONE OF THIS IS REAL.
THE CLOCK MIGHT BE TICKING ON MY OWN LIFE, BUT I COULDN'T JUST LEAVE HER--NOT EVEN IN A DREAM.
SEEMS LIKE I'D RATHER MEDDLE IN MY FRIENDS' LIVES THAN FIX MY OWN.
HM. MAYBE I SHOULD WORK ON THAT.
BUT HOW DO I FIX MY OWN SITUATION? HOW DO I GET OUT OF MY OWN HEAD?

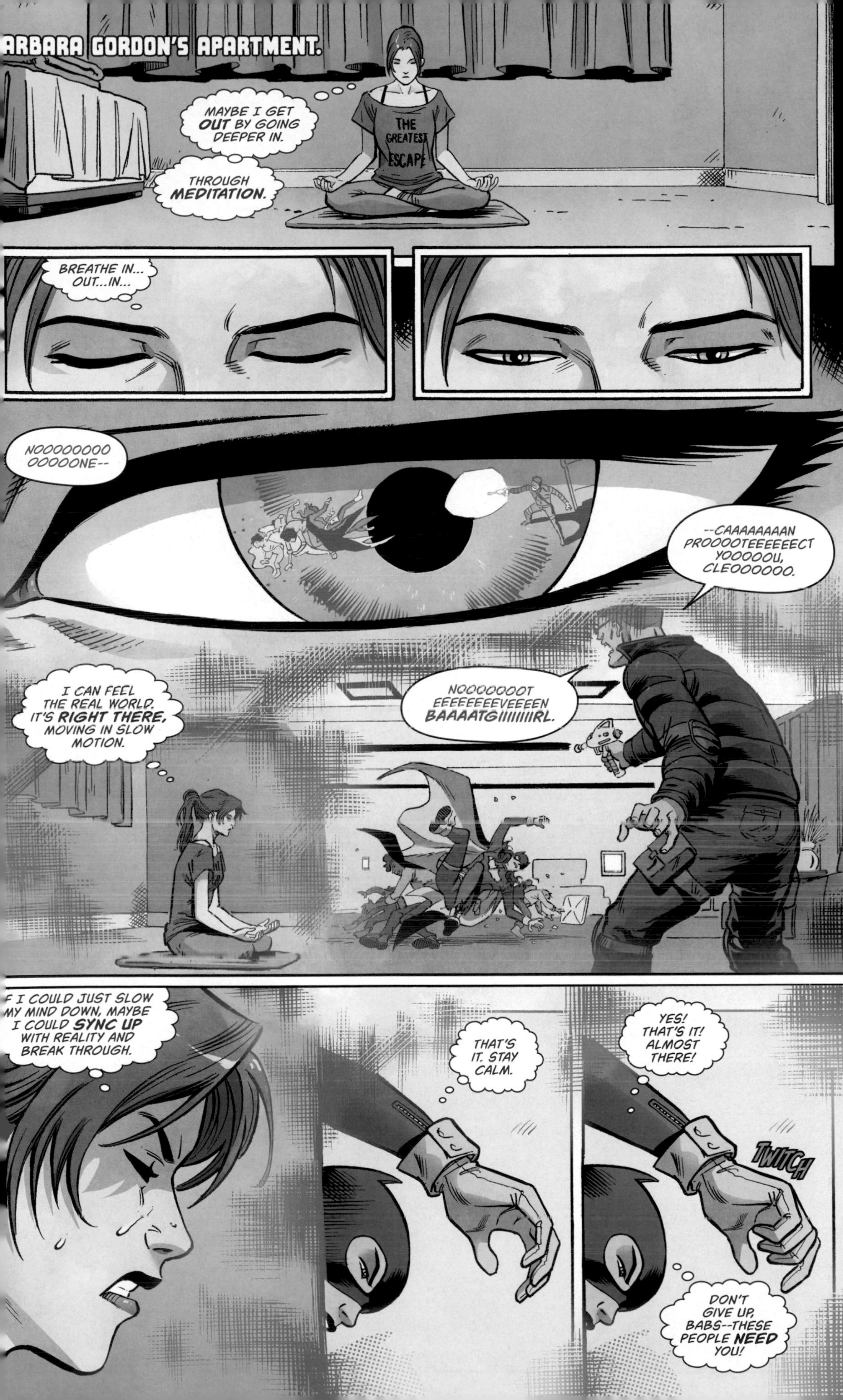
ARBARA GORDON'S APARTMENT.
MAYBE I GET OUT BY GOING DEEPER IN.
THROUGH MEDITATION.
THE GREATEST ESCAPE
BREATHE IN... OUT...IN...
NOOOOOOOO OOOOONE--
--CAAAAAAAAN PROOOOTEEEEEECT YOOOOOU, CLEOOOOOO.
I CAN FEEL THE REAL WORLD. IT'S RIGHT THERE, MOVING IN SLOW MOTION.
NOOOOOOOT EEEEEEEEVEEEEN BAAAATGIIIIIIIRL.
F I COULD JUST SLOW MY MIND DOWN, MAYBE I COULD SYNC UP WITH REALITY AND BREAK THROUGH.
THAT'S IT. STAY CALM.
YES! THAT'S IT! ALMOST THERE!
TWITCH
DON'T GIVE UP, BABS--THESE PEOPLE NEED YOU!

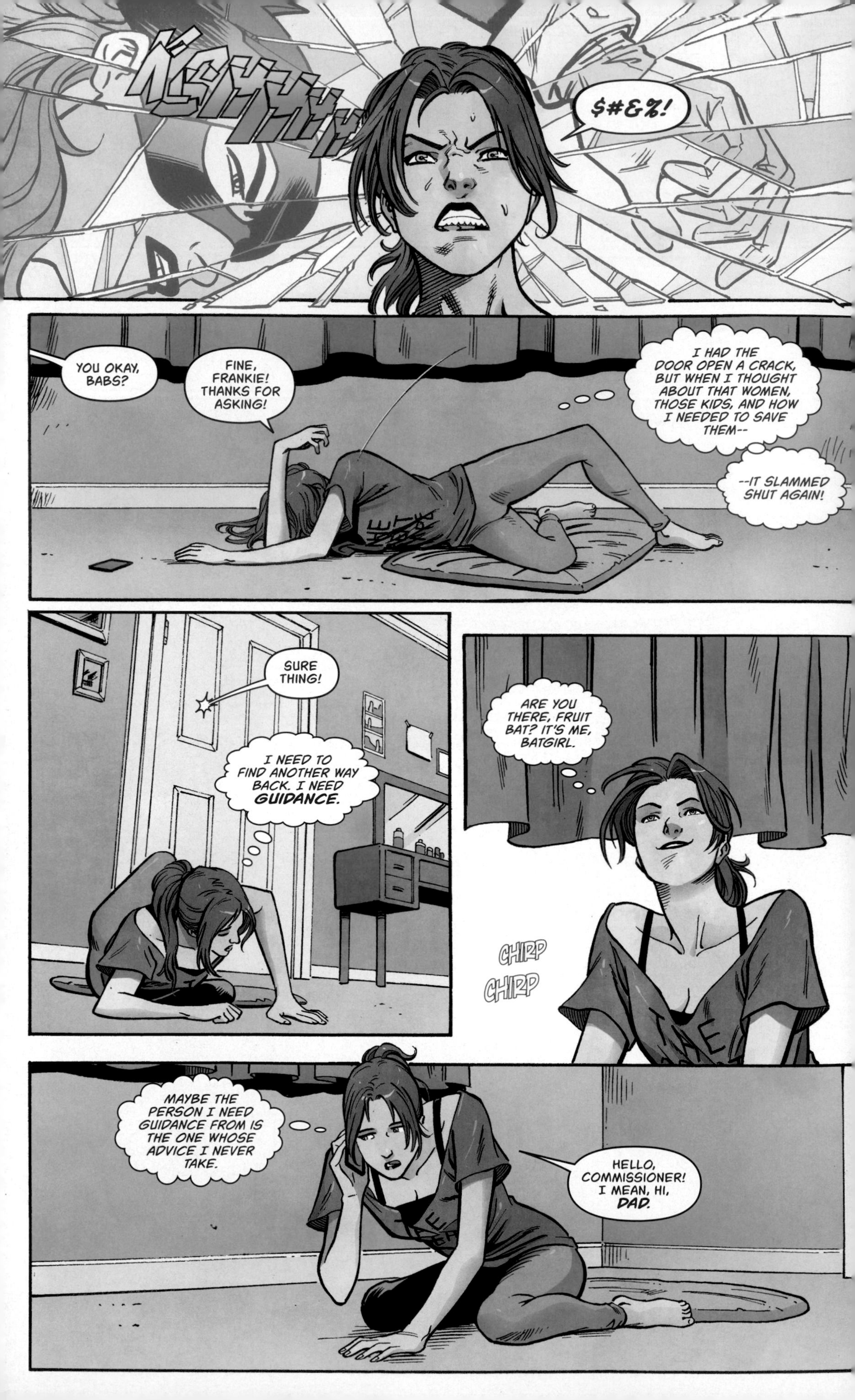
$#&%!
YOU OKAY, BABS?
FINE, FRANKIE! THANKS FOR ASKING!
I HAD THE DOOR OPEN A CRACK, BUT WHEN I THOUGHT ABOUT THAT WOMEN, THOSE KIDS, AND HOW I NEEDED TO SAVE THEM--
--IT SLAMMED SHUT AGAIN!
SURE THING!
I NEED TO FIND ANOTHER WAY BACK. I NEED GUIDANCE.
ARE YOU THERE, FRUIT BAT? IT'S ME, BATGIRL.
CHIRP
CHIRP
MAYBE THE PERSON I NEED GUIDANCE FROM IS THE ONE WHOSE ADVICE I NEVER TAKE.
HELLO, COMMISSIONER! I MEAN, HI, DAD.

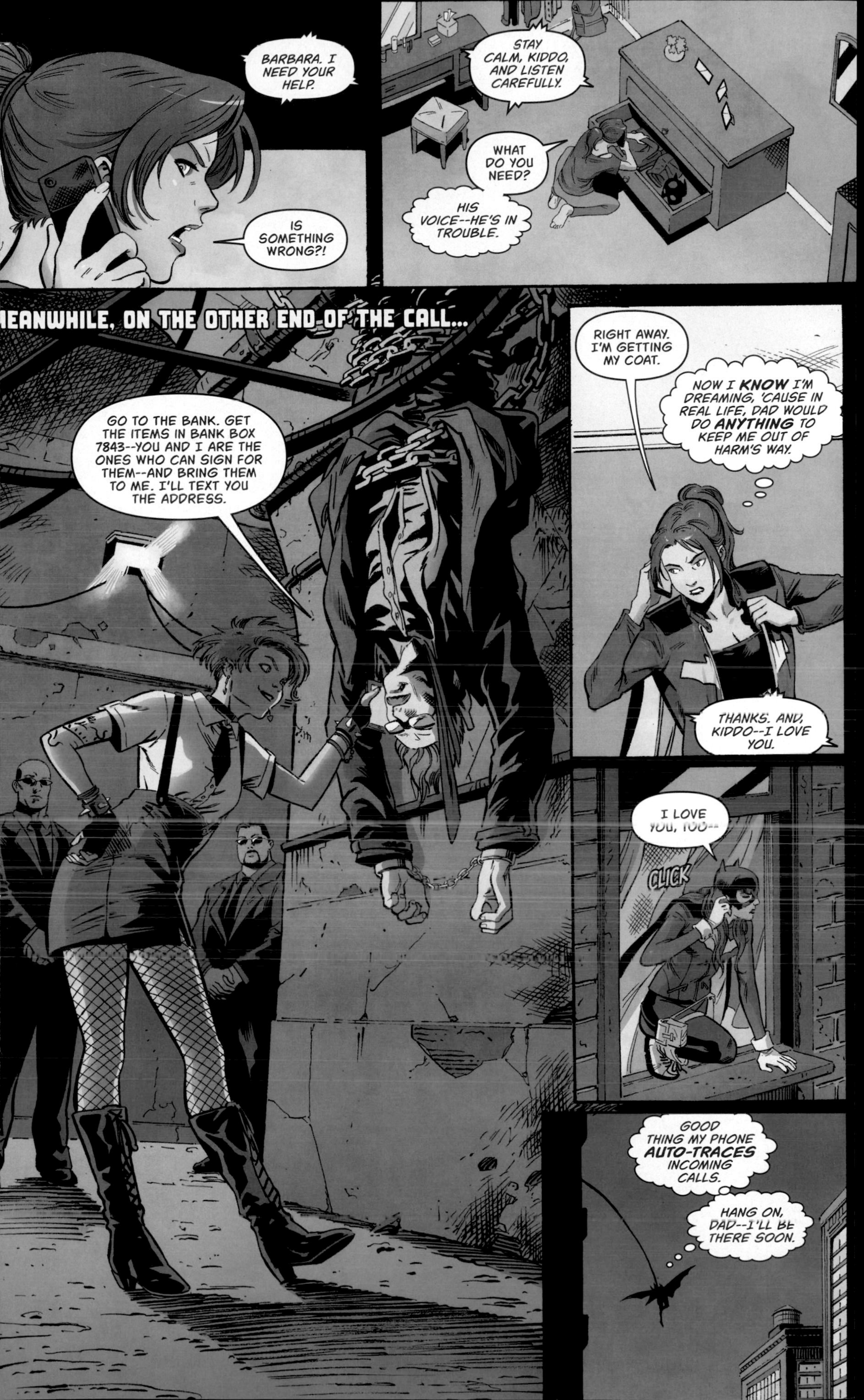
BARBARA. I NEED YOUR HELP.
IS SOMETHING WRONG?!
STAY CALM, KIDDO, AND LISTEN CAREFULLY.
WHAT DO YOU NEED?
HIS VOICE--HE'S IN TROUBLE.
MEANWHILE, ON THE OTHER END OF THE CALL...
GO TO THE BANK. GET THE ITEMS IN BANK BOX 7843--YOU AND I ARE THE ONES WHO CAN SIGN FOR THEM--AND BRING THEM TO ME. I'LL TEXT YOU THE ADDRESS.
RIGHT AWAY. I'M GETTING MY COAT.
NOW I KNOW I'M DREAMING, 'CAUSE IN REAL LIFE, DAD WOULD DO ANYTHING TO KEEP ME OUT OF HARM'S WAY.
THANKS. AND, KIDDO--I LOVE YOU.
I LOVE YOU, TOO--
CLICK
GOOD THING MY PHONE AUTO-TRACES INCOMING CALLS.
HANG ON, DAD--I'LL BE THERE SOON.

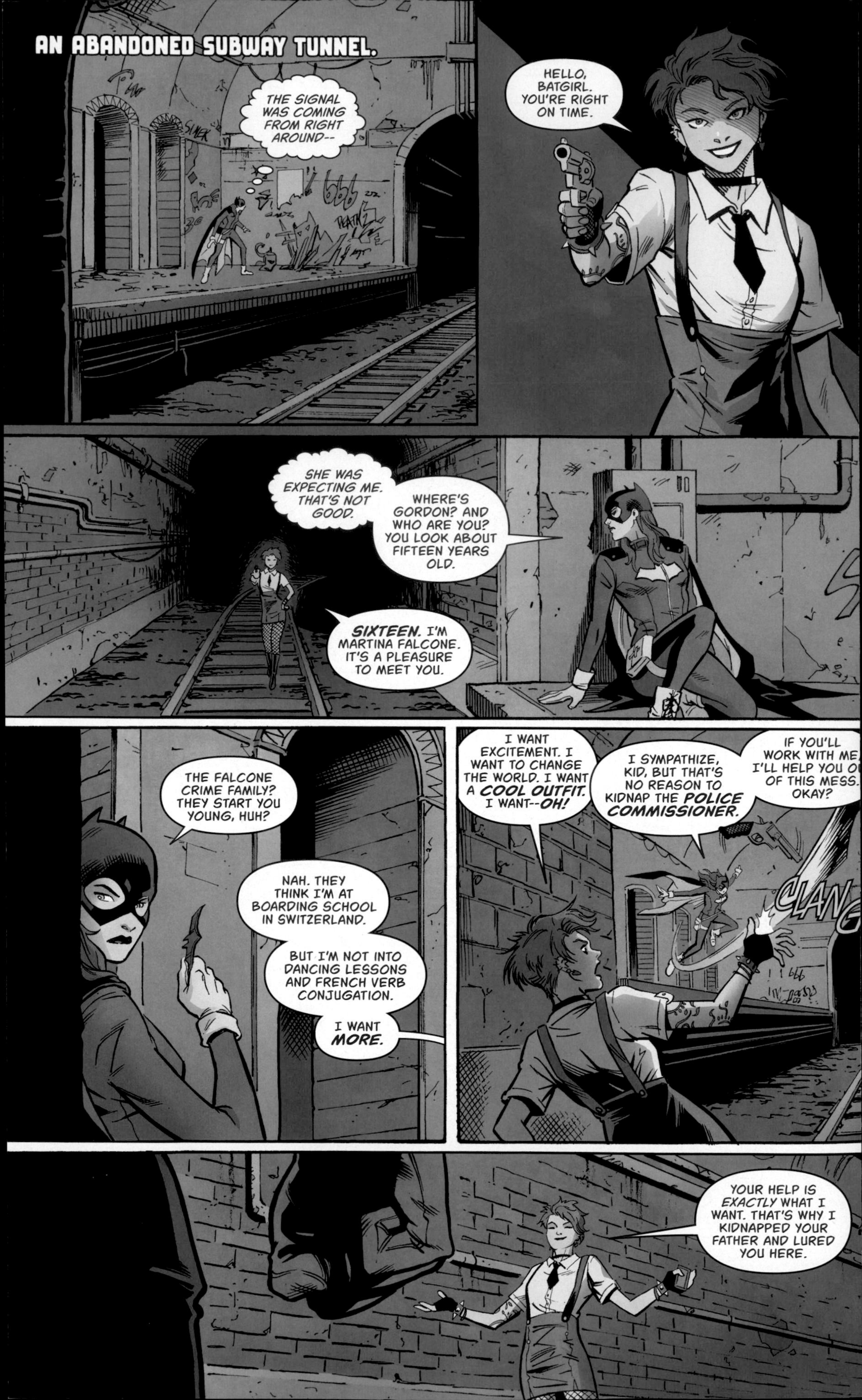

AN ABANDONED SUBWAY TUNNEL.
THE SIGNAL WAS COMING FROM RIGHT AROUND--
HELLO, BATGIRL. YOU'RE RIGHT ON TIME.
SHE WAS EXPECTING ME. THAT'S NOT GOOD.
WHERE'S GORDON? AND WHO ARE YOU? YOU LOOK ABOUT FIFTEEN YEARS OLD.
SIXTEEN. I'M MARTINA FALCONE. IT'S A PLEASURE TO MEET YOU.
THE FALCONE CRIME FAMILY? THEY START YOU YOUNG, HUH?
NAH. THEY THINK I'M AT BOARDING SCHOOL IN SWITZERLAND.
BUT I'M NOT INTO DANCING LESSONS AND FRENCH VERB CONJUGATION.
I WANT MORE.
I WANT EXCITEMENT. I WANT TO CHANGE THE WORLD. I WANT A COOL OUTFIT. I WANT--OH!
I SYMPATHIZE, KID, BUT THAT'S NO REASON TO KIDNAP THE POLICE COMMISSIONER.
YOUR HELP IS EXACTLY WHAT I WANT. THAT'S WHY I KIDNAPPED YOUR FATHER AND LURED YOU HERE.

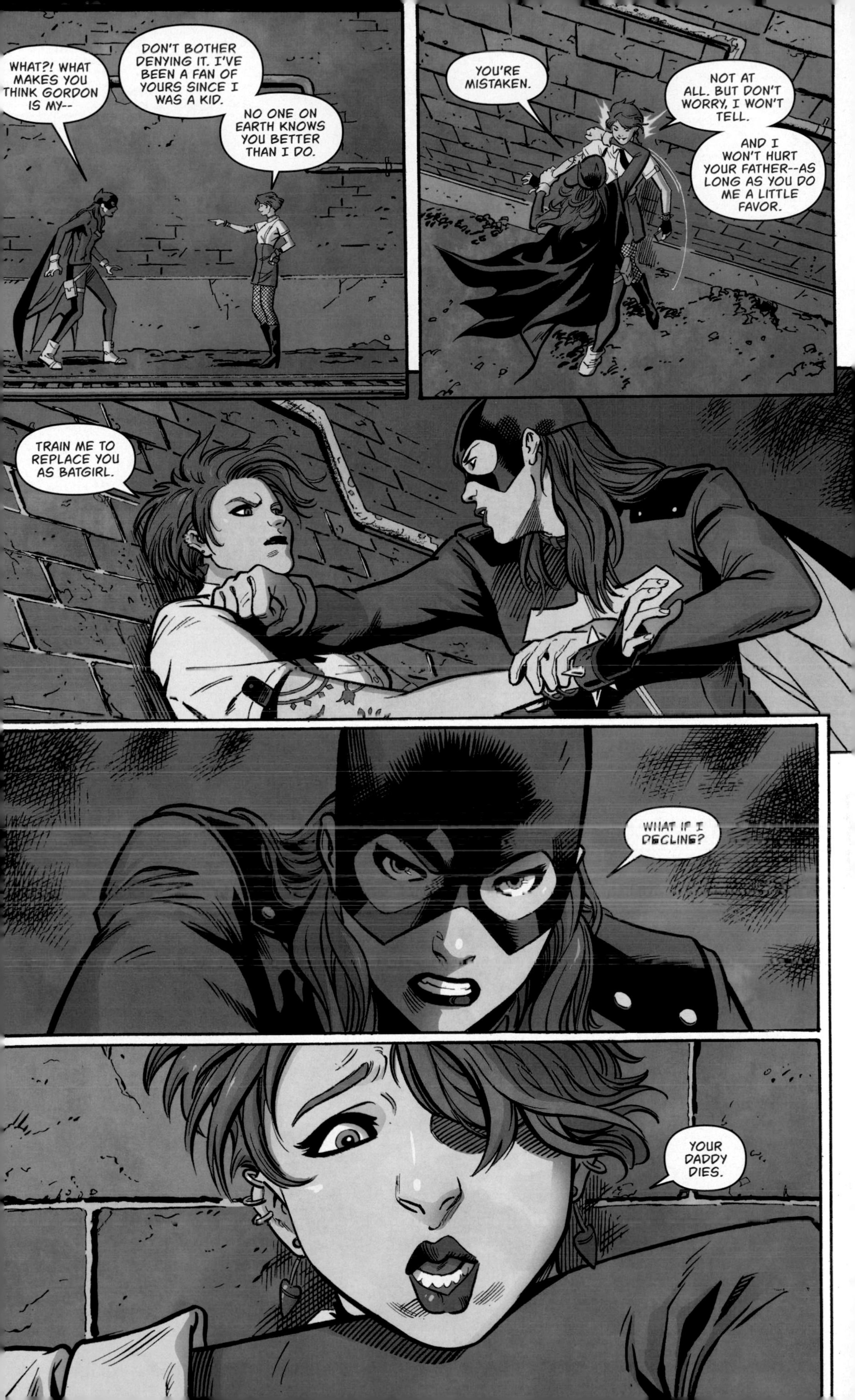
WHAT?! WHAT MAKES YOU THINK GORDON IS MY--
DON'T BOTHER DENYING IT. I'VE BEEN A FAN OF YOURS SINCE I WAS A KID.
NO ONE ON EARTH KNOWS YOU BETTER THAN I DO.
YOU'RE MISTAKEN.
NOT AT ALL. BUT DON'T WORRY, I WON'T TELL.
AND I WON'T HURT YOUR FATHER--AS LONG AS YOU DO ME A LITTLE FAVOR.
TRAIN ME TO REPLACE YOU AS BATGIRL.
WHAT IF I DECLINE?
YOUR DADDY DIES.

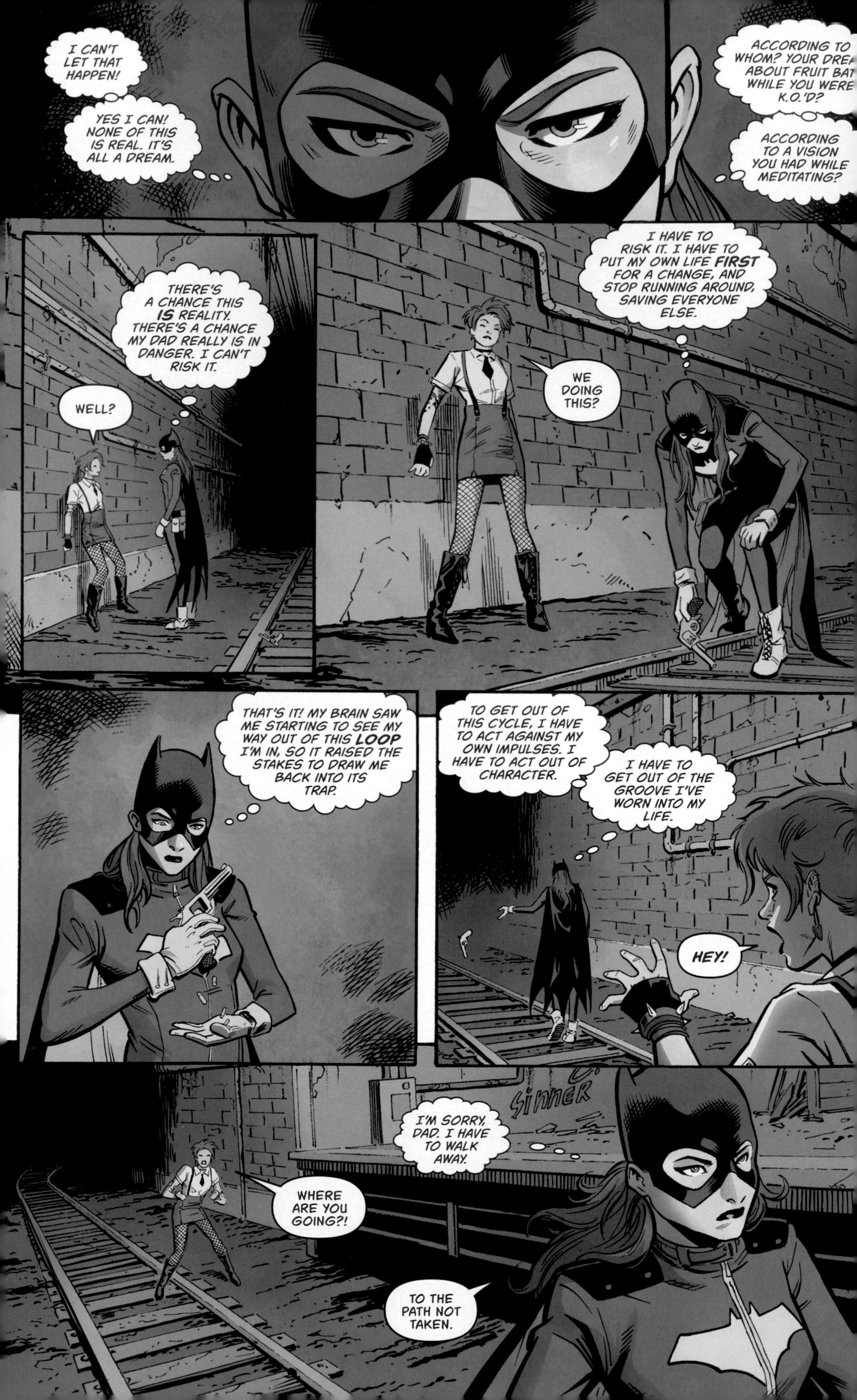
I CAN'T LET THAT HAPPEN!
YES I CAN! NONE OF THIS IS REAL. IT'S ALL A DREAM.
ACCORDING TO WHOM? YOUR DREA ABOUT FRUIT BAT WHILE YOU WERE K.O.'D?
ACCORDING TO A VISION YOU HAD WHILE MEDITATING?
THERE'S A CHANCE THIS IS REALITY. THERE'S A CHANCE MY DAD REALLY IS IN DANGER. I CAN'T RISK IT.
WELL?
I HAVE TO RISK IT. I HAVE TO PUT MY OWN LIFE FIRST FOR A CHANGE, AND STOP RUNNING AROUND, SAVING EVERYONE ELSE.
WE DOING THIS?
THAT'S IT! MY BRAIN SAW ME STARTING TO SEE MY WAY OUT OF THIS LOOP I'M IN, SO IT RAISED THE STAKES TO DRAW ME BACK INTO ITS TRAP.
TO GET OUT OF THIS CYCLE, I HAVE TO ACT AGAINST MY OWN IMPULSES. I HAVE TO ACT OUT OF CHARACTER.
I HAVE TO GET OUT OF THE GROOVE I'VE WORN INTO MY LIFE.
HEY!
SINNER
I'M SORRY, DAD. I HAVE TO WALK AWAY.
WHERE ARE YOU GOING?!
TO THE PATH NOT TAKEN.

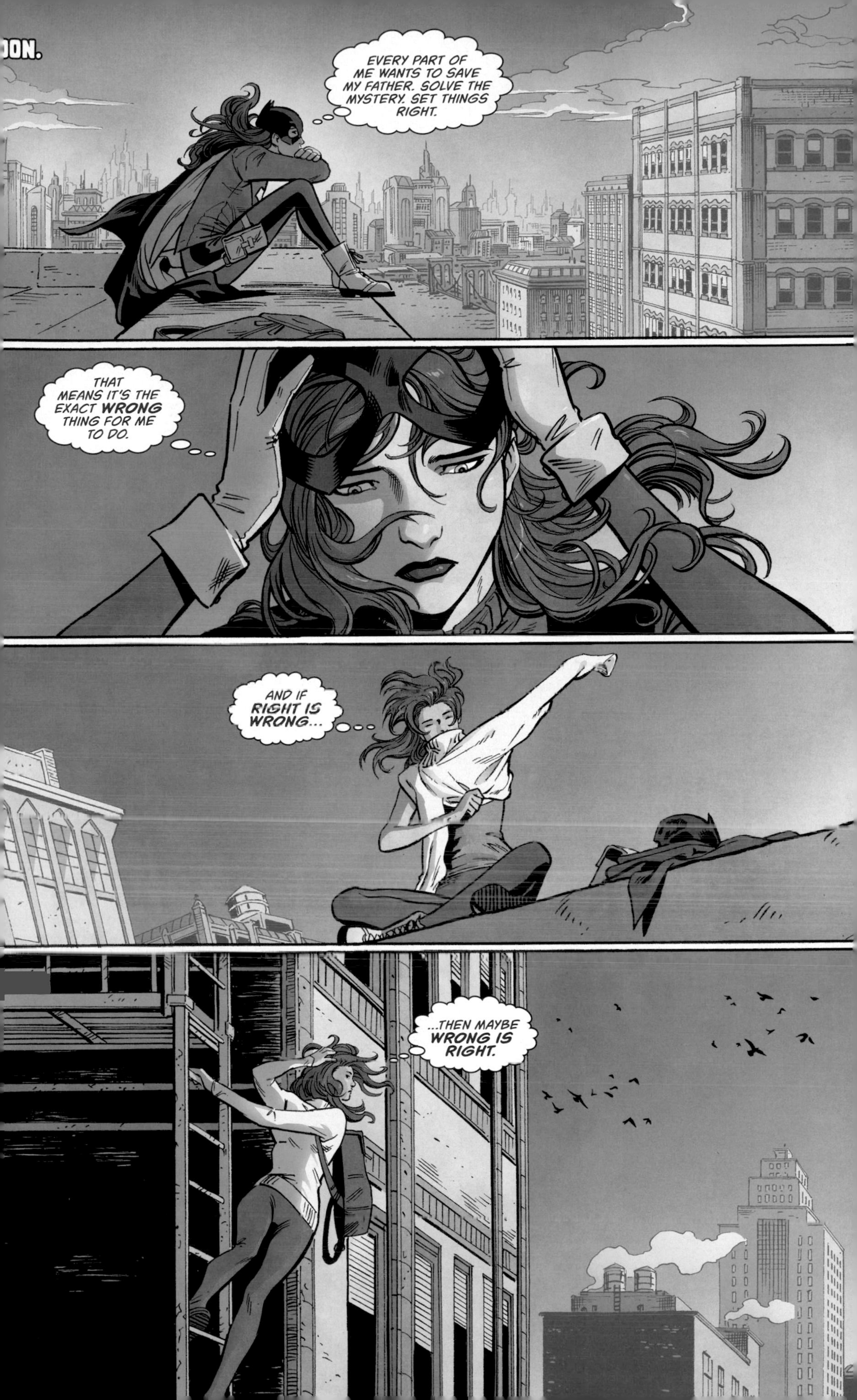

DON.
EVERY PART OF ME WANTS TO SAVE MY FATHER. SOLVE THE MYSTERY. SET THINGS RIGHT.
THAT MEANS IT'S THE EXACT WRONG THING FOR ME TO DO.
AND IF RIGHT IS WRONG...
...THEN MAYBE WRONG IS RIGHT.

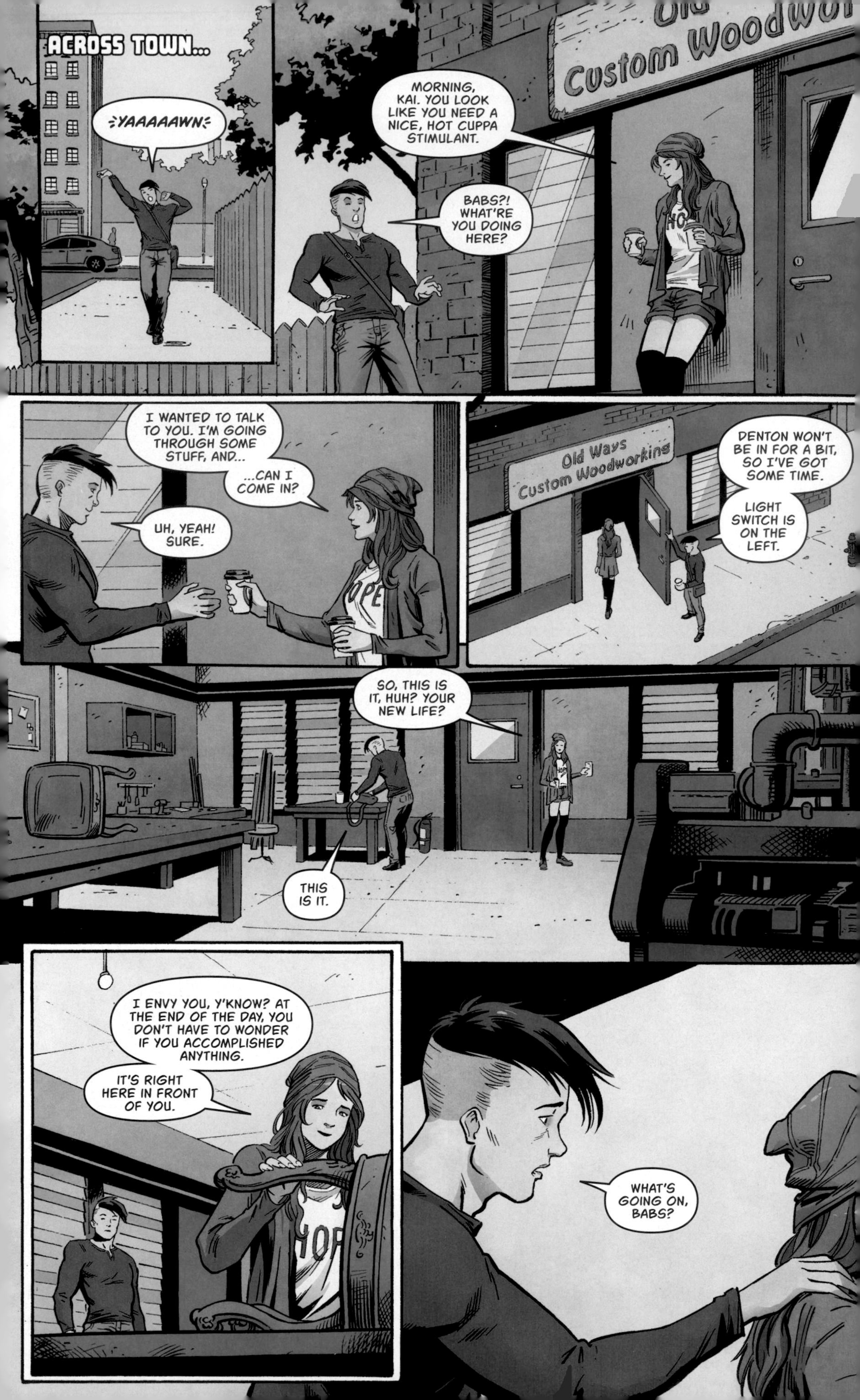
ACROSS TOWN...
YAAAAAWN
MORNING, KAI. YOU LOOK LIKE YOU NEED A NICE, HOT CUPPA STIMULANT.
BABS?! WHAT'RE YOU DOING HERE?
Custom Woodwor
I WANTED TO TALK TO YOU. I'M GOING THROUGH SOME STUFF, AND...
...CAN I COME IN?
UH, YEAH! SURE.
HOPE
Old Ways Custom Woodworking
DENTON WON'T BE IN FOR A BIT, SO I'VE GOT SOME TIME.
LIGHT SWITCH IS ON THE LEFT.
SO, THIS IS IT, HUH? YOUR NEW LIFE?
THIS IS IT.
I ENVY YOU, Y'KNOW? AT THE END OF THE DAY, YOU DON'T HAVE TO WONDER IF YOU ACCOMPLISHED ANYTHING.
IT'S RIGHT HERE IN FRONT OF YOU.
WHAT'S GOING ON, BABS?

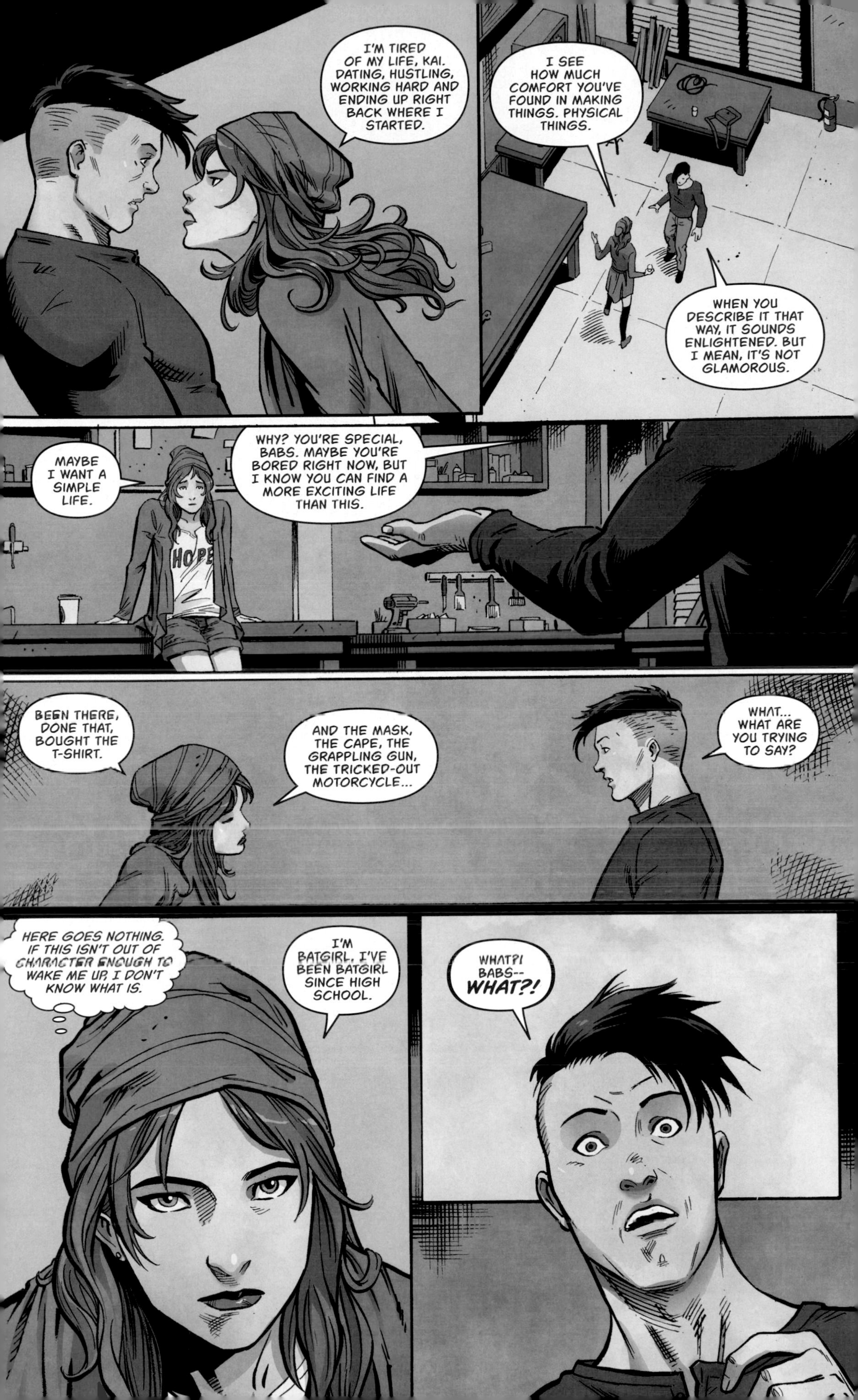
I'M TIRED OF MY LIFE, KAI. DATING, HUSTLING, WORKING HARD AND ENDING UP RIGHT BACK WHERE I STARTED.
I SEE HOW MUCH COMFORT YOU'VE FOUND IN MAKING THINGS. PHYSICAL THINGS.
WHEN YOU DESCRIBE IT THAT WAY, IT SOUNDS ENLIGHTENED. BUT I MEAN, IT'S NOT GLAMOROUS.
MAYBE I WANT A SIMPLE LIFE.
WHY? YOU'RE SPECIAL, BABS. MAYBE YOU'RE BORED RIGHT NOW, BUT I KNOW YOU CAN FIND A MORE EXCITING LIFE THAN THIS.
HOPE
BEEN THERE, DONE THAT, BOUGHT THE T-SHIRT.
AND THE MASK, THE CAPE, THE GRAPPLING GUN, THE TRICKED-OUT MOTORCYCLE...
WHAT... WHAT ARE YOU TRYING TO SAY?
HERE GOES NOTHING. IF THIS ISN'T OUT OF CHARACTER ENOUGH TO WAKE ME UP, I DON'T KNOW WHAT IS.
I'M BATGIRL. I'VE BEEN BATGIRL SINCE HIGH SCHOOL.
WHAT?! BABS-- WHAT?!

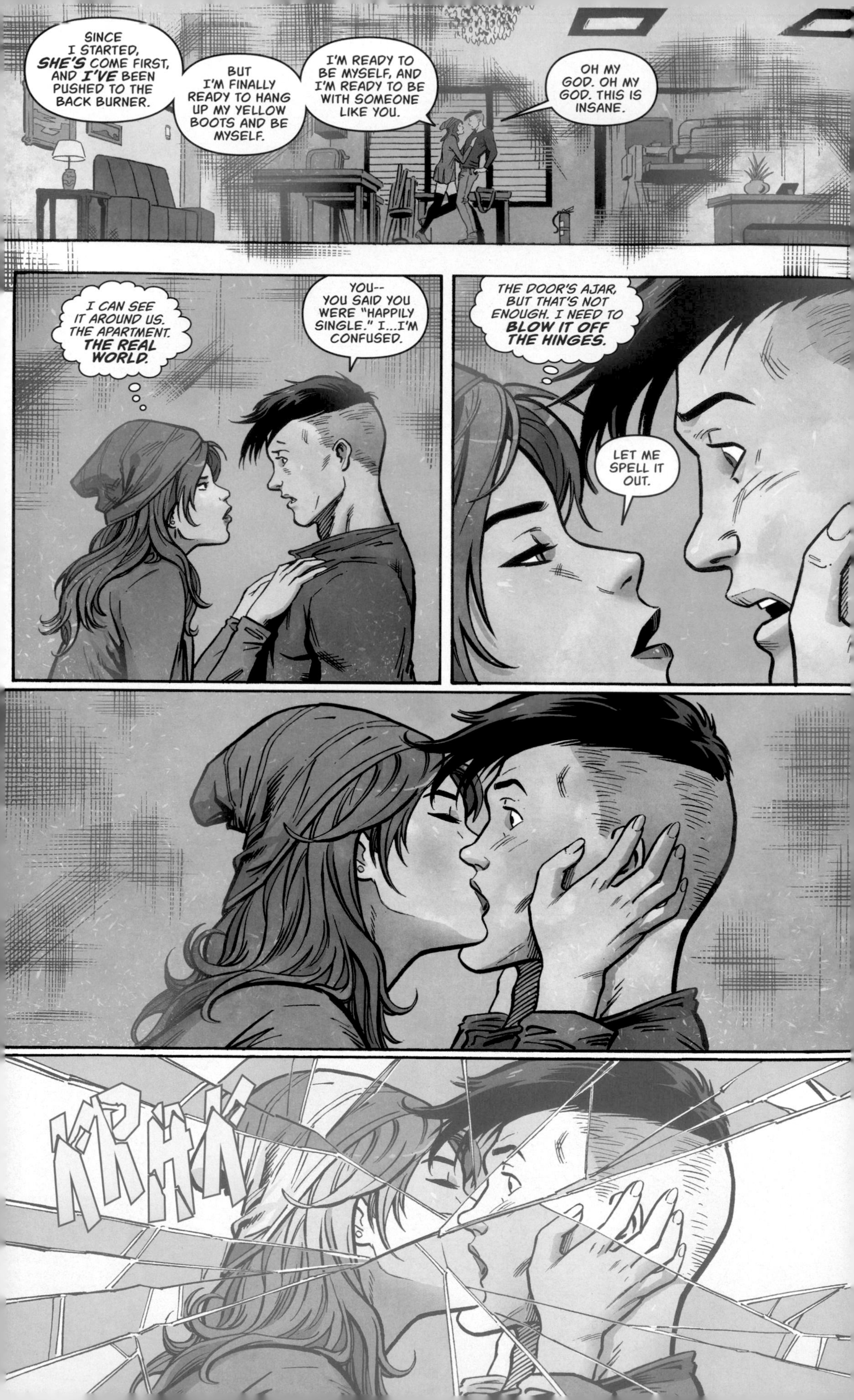
SINCE I STARTED, SHE'S COME FIRST, AND I'VE BEEN PUSHED TO THE BACK BURNER.
BUT I'M FINALLY READY TO HANG UP MY YELLOW BOOTS AND BE MYSELF.
I'M READY TO BE MYSELF, AND I'M READY TO BE WITH SOMEONE LIKE YOU.
OH MY GOD. OH MY GOD. THIS IS INSANE.
I CAN SEE IT AROUND US. THE APARTMENT. THE REAL WORLD.
YOU-- YOU SAID YOU WERE "HAPPILY SINGLE." I...I'M CONFUSED.
THE DOOR'S AJAR, BUT THAT'S NOT ENOUGH. I NEED TO BLOW IT OFF THE HINGES.
LET ME SPELL IT OUT.
KRAK

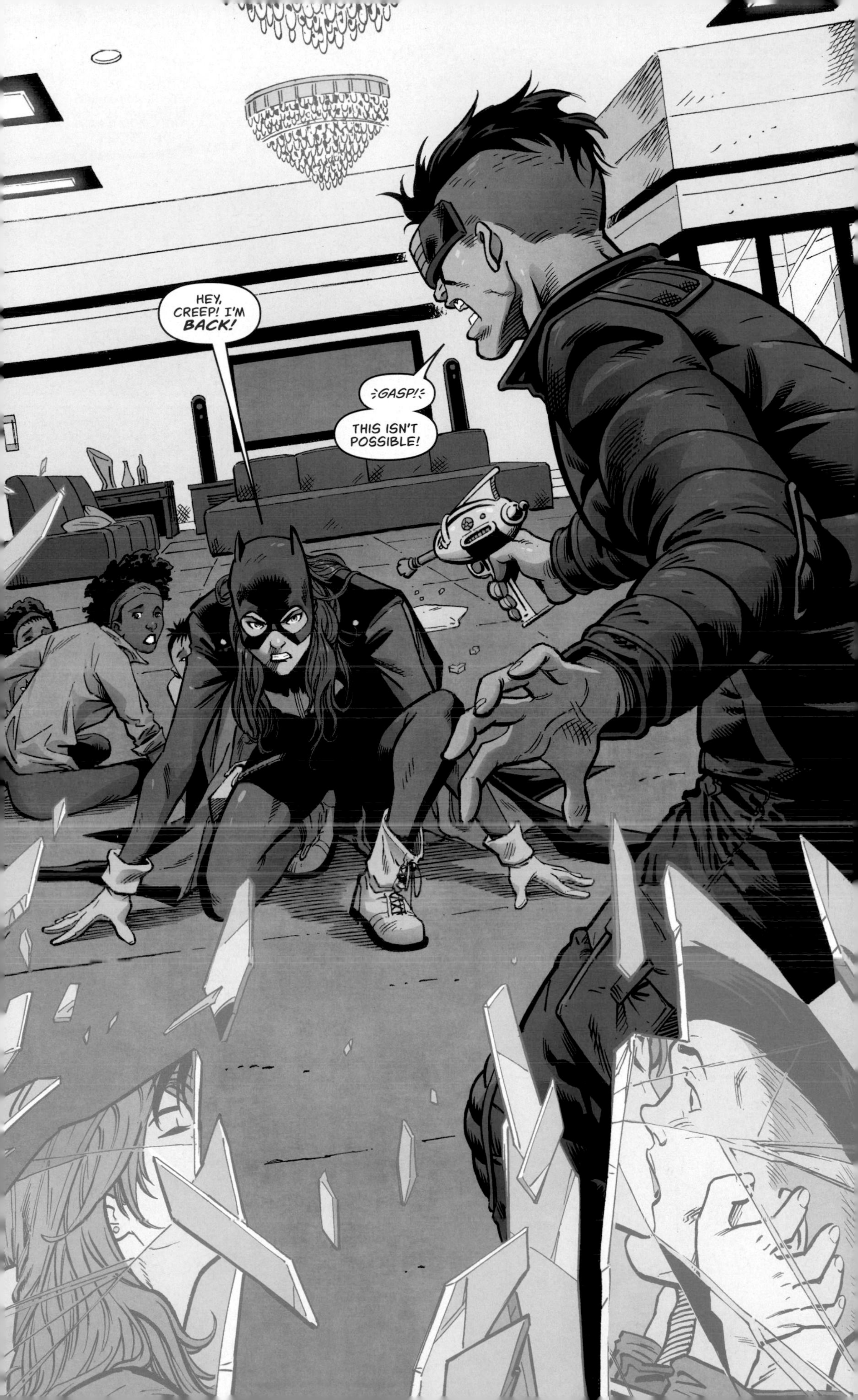
HEY, CREEP! I'M BACK!
GASP!
THIS ISN'T POSSIBLE!

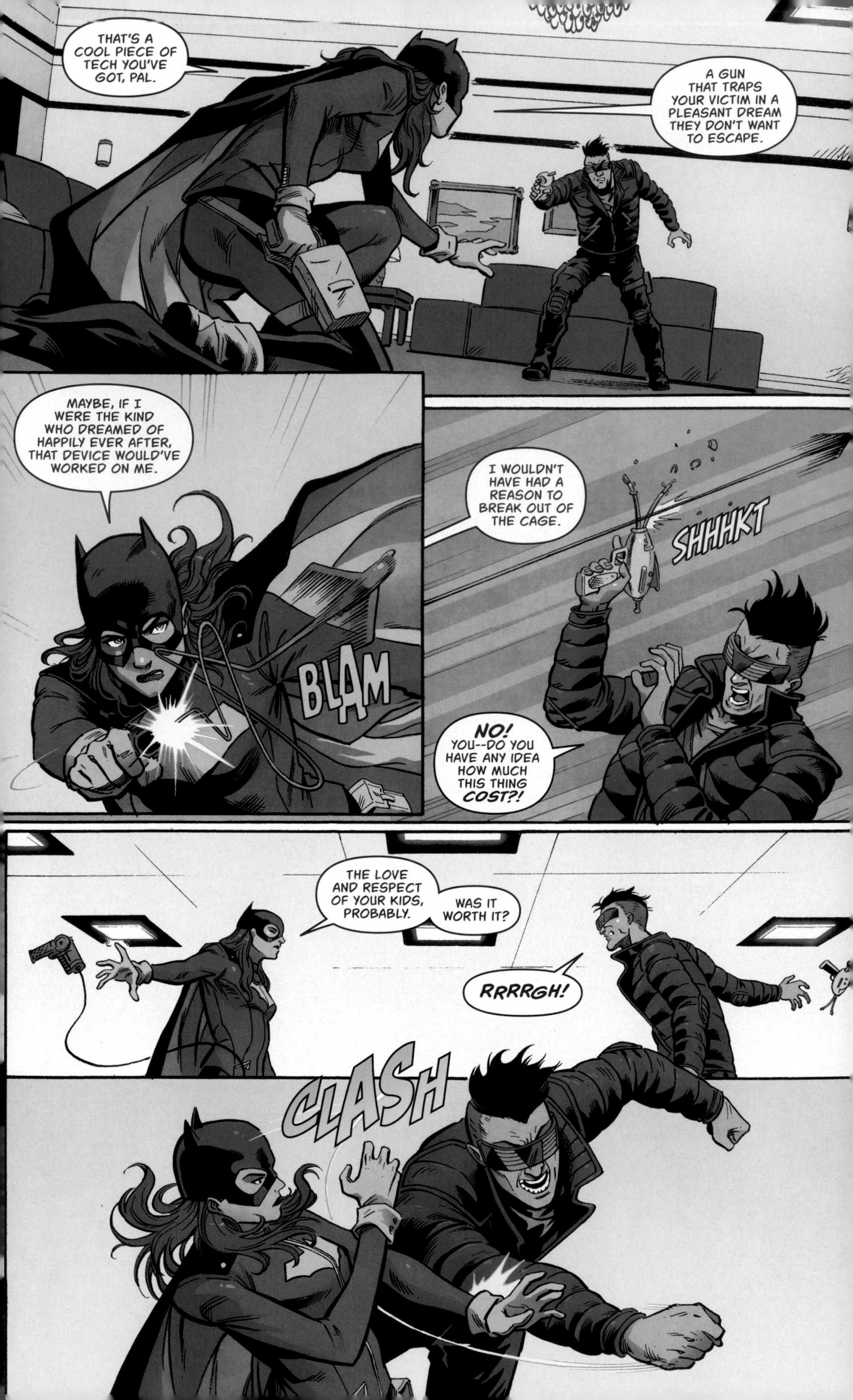
THAT'S A COOL PIECE OF TECH YOU'VE GOT, PAL.
A GUN THAT TRAPS YOUR VICTIM IN A PLEASANT DREAM THEY DON'T WANT TO ESCAPE.
MAYBE, IF I WERE THE KIND WHO DREAMED OF HAPPILY EVER AFTER, THAT DEVICE WOULD'VE WORKED ON ME.
BLAM
I WOULDN'T HAVE HAD A REASON TO BREAK OUT OF THE CAGE.
SHHHKT
NO! YOU--DO YOU HAVE ANY IDEA HOW MUCH THIS THING COST?!
THE LOVE AND RESPECT OF YOUR KIDS, PROBABLY.
WAS IT WORTH IT?
RRRRGH!
CLASH

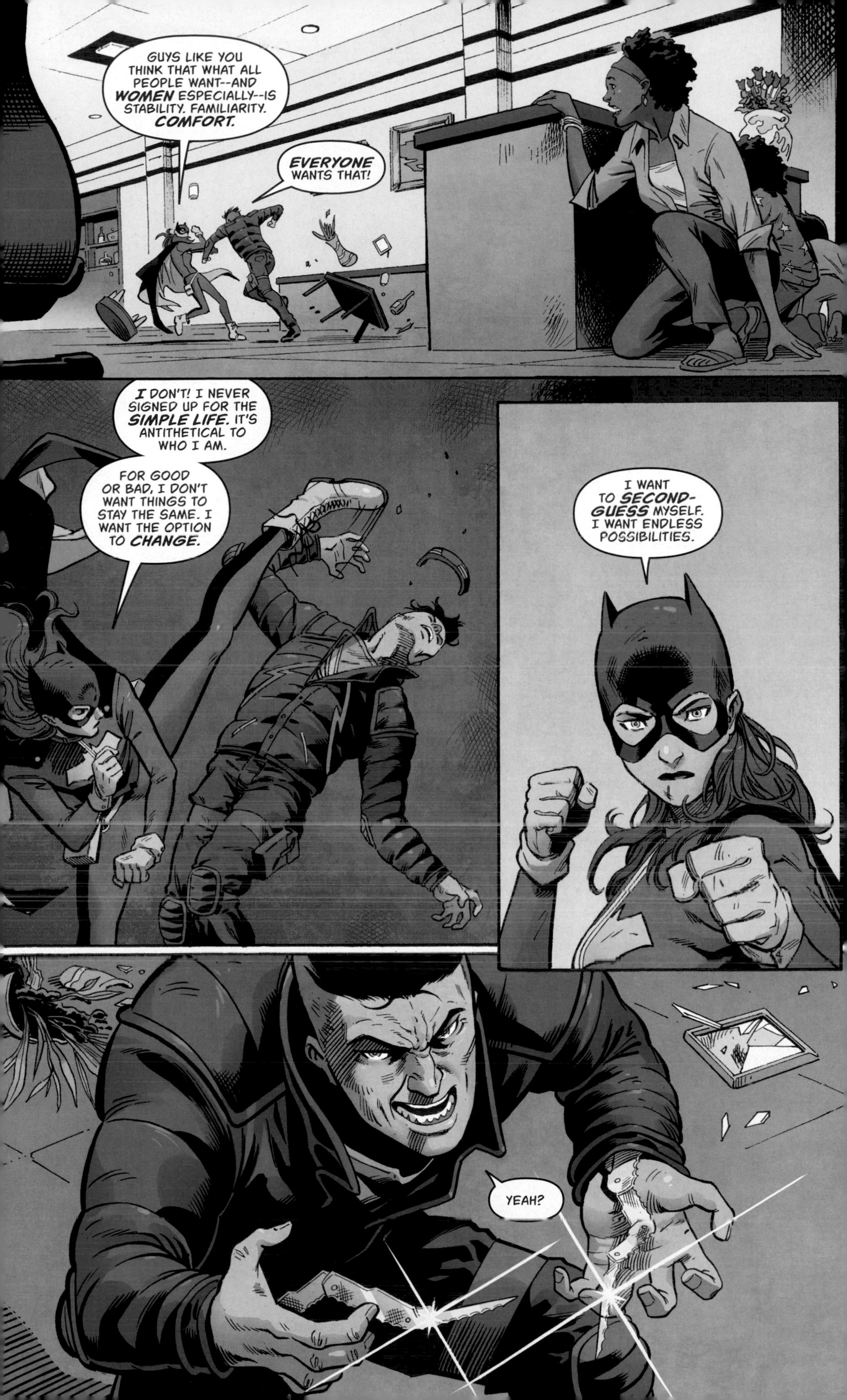
GUYS LIKE YOU THINK THAT WHAT ALL PEOPLE WANT--AND WOMEN ESPECIALLY--IS STABILITY. FAMILIARITY. COMFORT.
EVERYONE WANTS THAT!
I DON'T! I NEVER SIGNED UP FOR THE SIMPLE LIFE. IT'S ANTITHETICAL TO WHO I AM.
FOR GOOD OR BAD, I DON'T WANT THINGS TO STAY THE SAME. I WANT THE OPTION TO CHANGE.
I WANT TO SECOND-GUESS MYSELF. I WANT ENDLESS POSSIBILITIES.
YEAH?

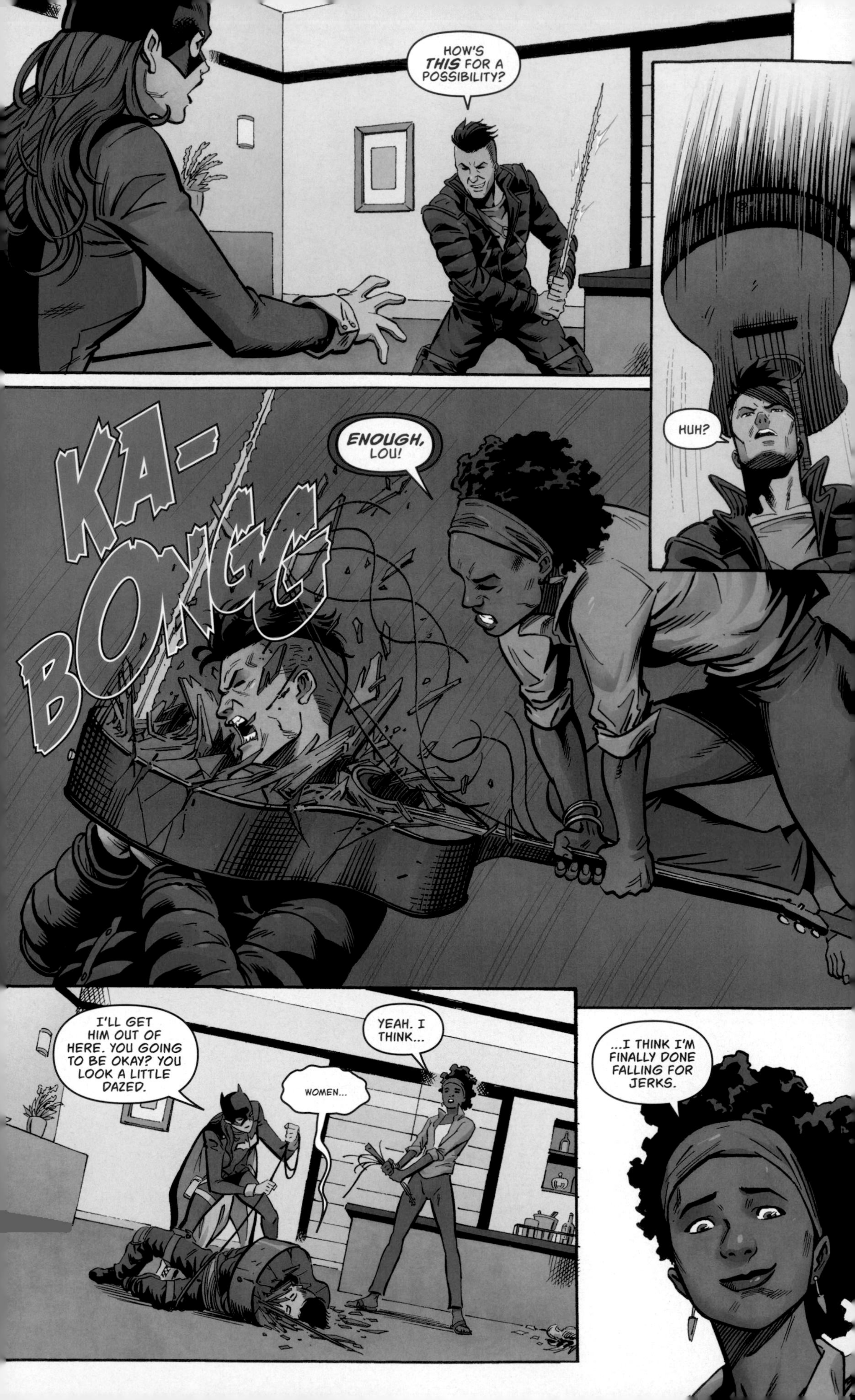
HOW'S THIS FOR A POSSIBILITY?
HUH?
KA-BONG
ENOUGH, LOU!
I'LL GET HIM OUT OF HERE. YOU GOING TO BE OKAY? YOU LOOK A LITTLE DAZED.
WOMEN...
YEAH. I THINK...
...I THINK I'M FINALLY DONE FALLING FOR JERKS.

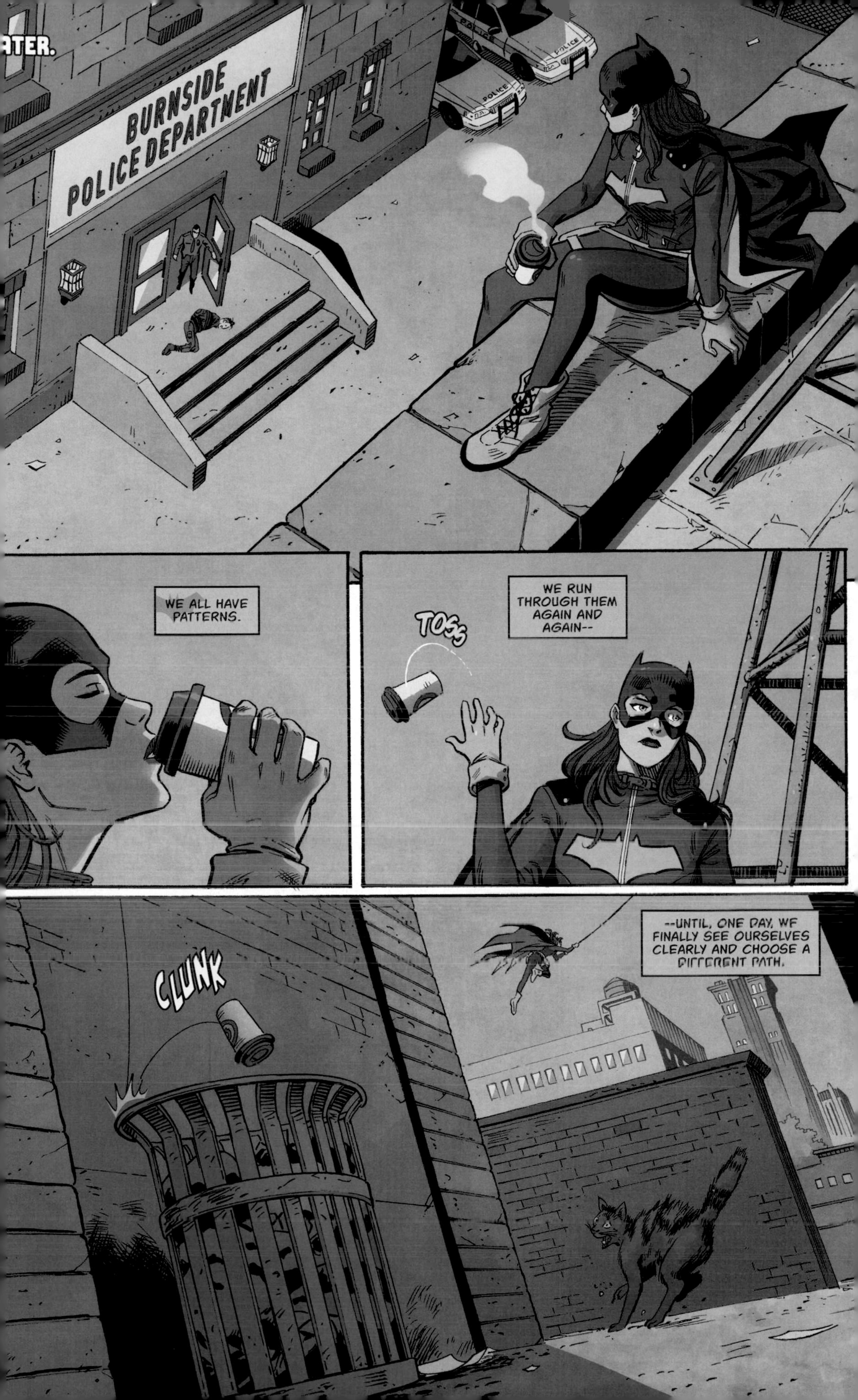

…ATER.
BURNSIDE POLICE DEPARTMENT
POLICE
WE ALL HAVE PATTERNS.
TOSS
WE RUN THROUGH THEM AGAIN AND AGAIN--
--UNTIL, ONE DAY, WE FINALLY SEE OURSELVES CLEARLY AND CHOOSE A DIFFERENT PATH.
CLUNK

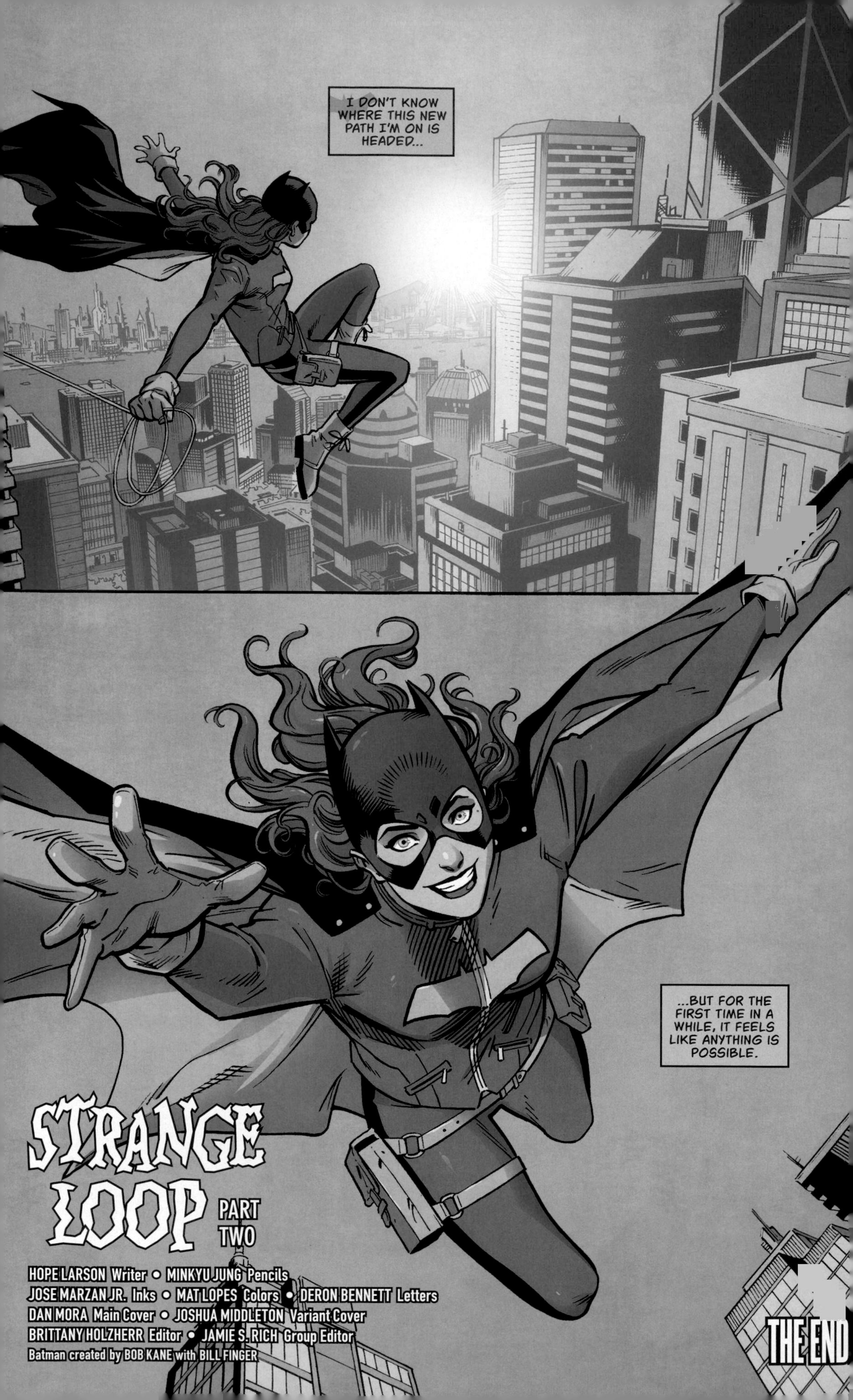
I DON'T KNOW WHERE THIS NEW PATH I'M ON IS HEADED...
...BUT FOR THE FIRST TIME IN A WHILE, IT FEELS LIKE ANYTHING IS POSSIBLE.
STRANGE LOOP PART TWO
HOPE LARSON Writer • MINKYU JUNG Pencils
JOSE MARZAN JR. Inks • MAT LOPES Colors • DERON BENNETT Letters
DAN MORA Main Cover • JOSHUA MIDDLETON Variant Cover
BRITTANY HOLZHERR Editor • JAMIE S. RICH Group Editor
Batman created by BOB KANE with BILL FINGER
THE END

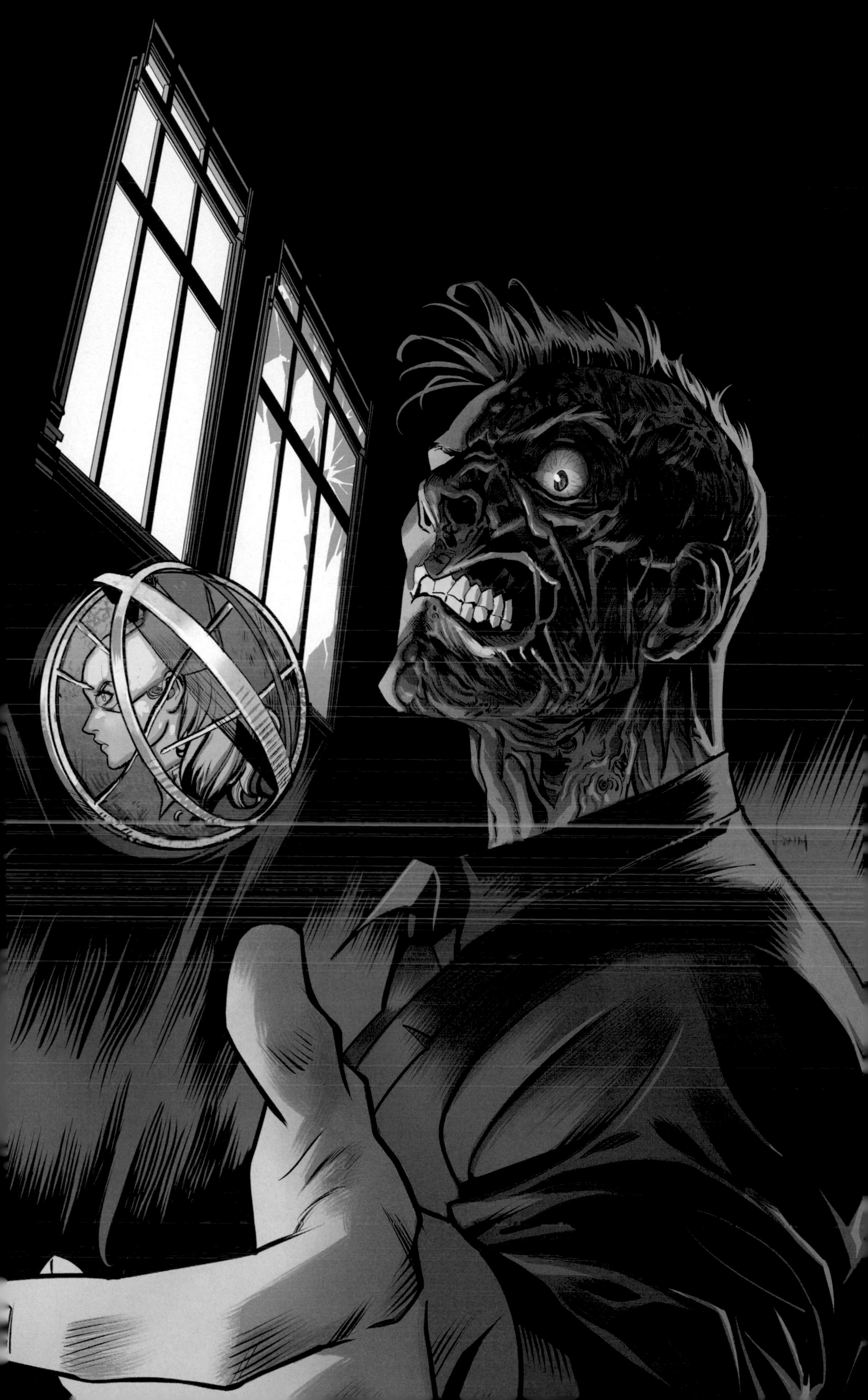

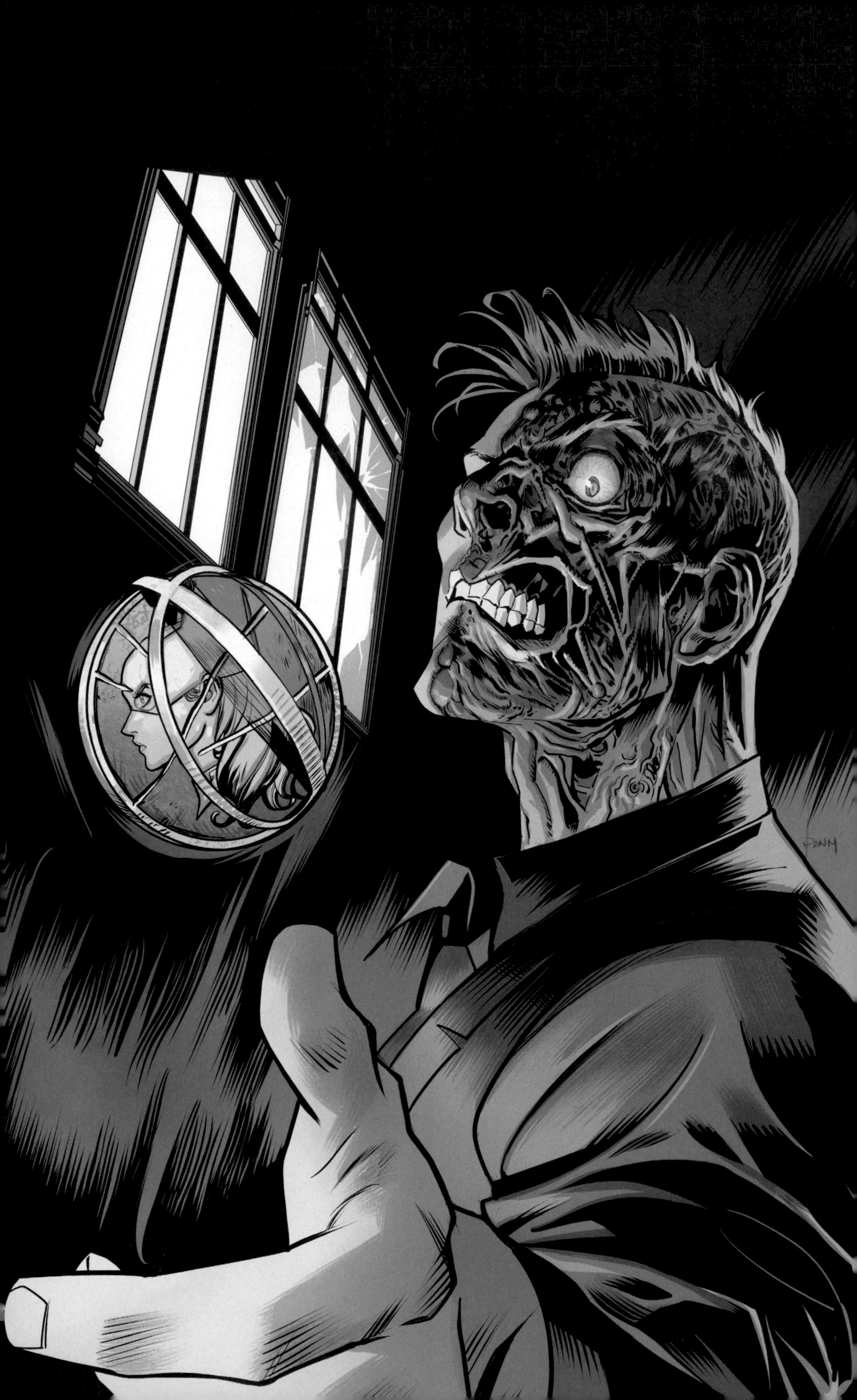

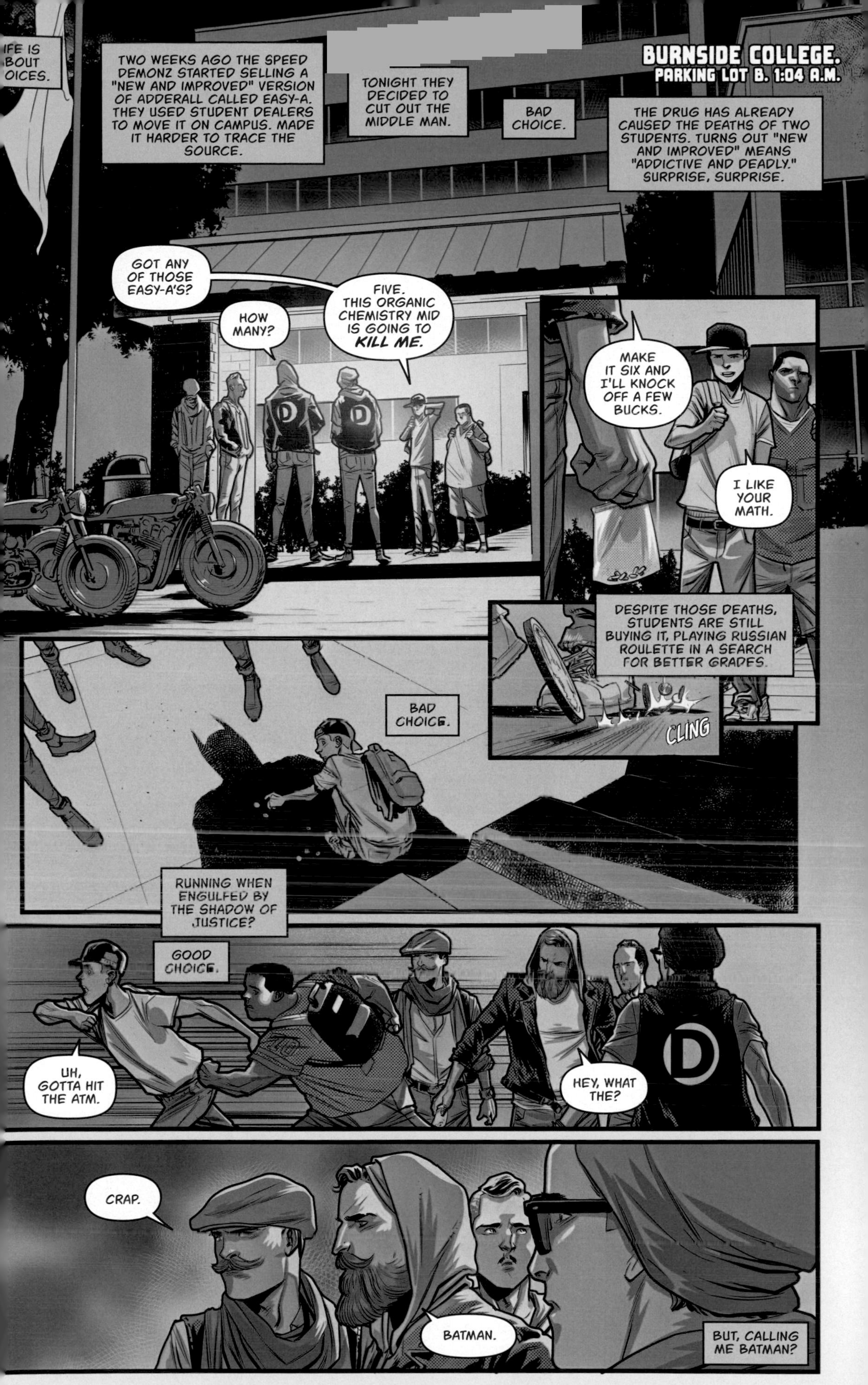
IFE IS
BOUT
OICES.
TWO WEEKS AGO THE SPEED DEMONZ STARTED SELLING A "NEW AND IMPROVED" VERSION OF ADDERALL CALLED EASY-A. THEY USED STUDENT DEALERS TO MOVE IT ON CAMPUS. MADE IT HARDER TO TRACE THE SOURCE.
TONIGHT THEY DECIDED TO CUT OUT THE MIDDLE MAN.
BAD CHOICE.
BURNSIDE COLLEGE.
PARKING LOT B. 1:04 A.M.
THE DRUG HAS ALREADY CAUSED THE DEATHS OF TWO STUDENTS. TURNS OUT "NEW AND IMPROVED" MEANS "ADDICTIVE AND DEADLY." SURPRISE, SURPRISE.
GOT ANY OF THOSE EASY-A'S?
HOW MANY?
FIVE. THIS ORGANIC CHEMISTRY MID IS GOING TO KILL ME.
MAKE IT SIX AND I'LL KNOCK OFF A FEW BUCKS.
I LIKE YOUR MATH.
DESPITE THOSE DEATHS, STUDENTS ARE STILL BUYING IT, PLAYING RUSSIAN ROULETTE IN A SEARCH FOR BETTER GRADES.
CLING
BAD CHOICE.
RUNNING WHEN ENGULFED BY THE SHADOW OF JUSTICE?
GOOD CHOICE.
UH, GOTTA HIT THE ATM.
HEY, WHAT THE?
CRAP.
BATMAN.
BUT, CALLING ME BATMAN?

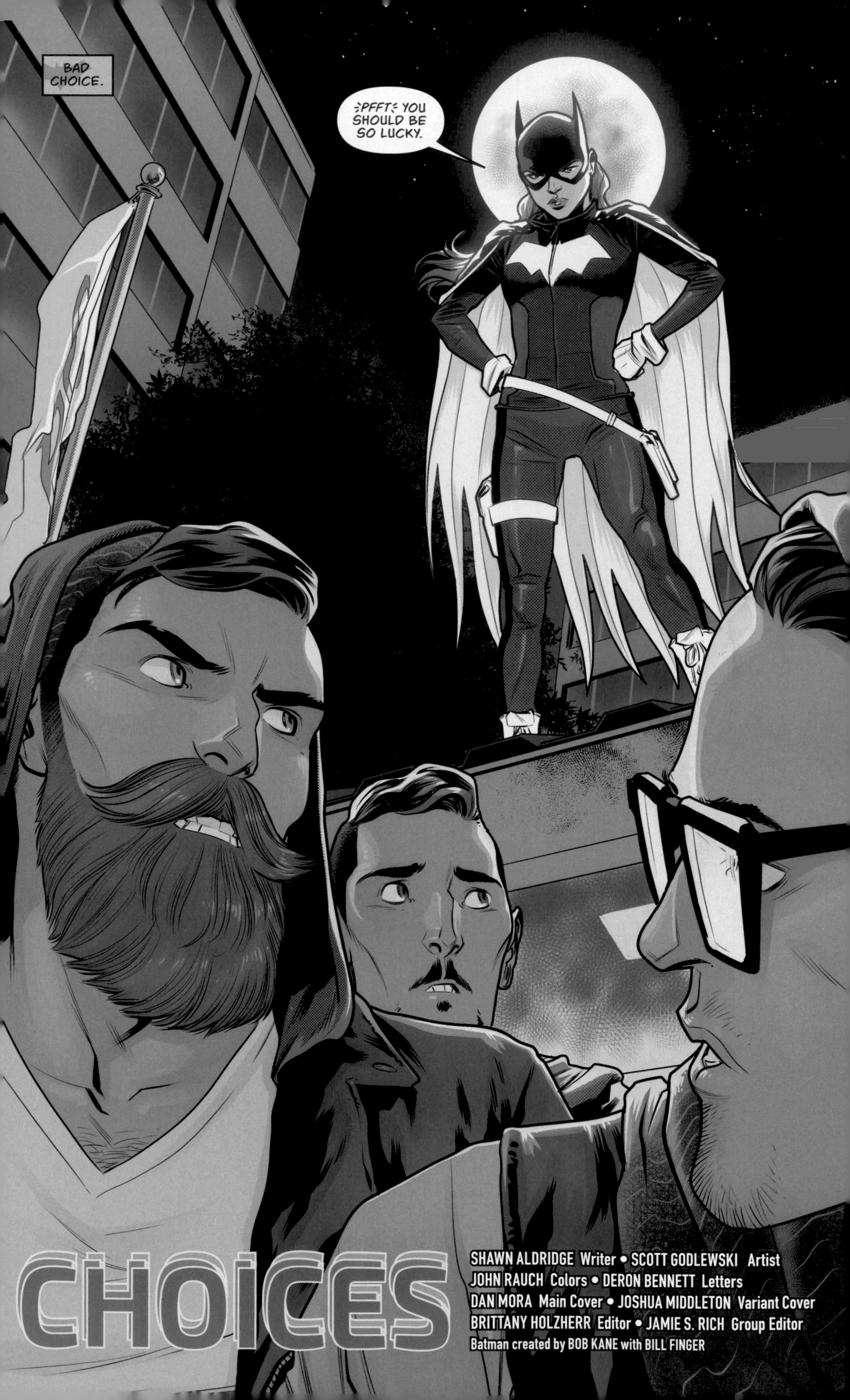
BAD CHOICE.
=PFFT= YOU SHOULD BE SO LUCKY.
CHOICES
SHAWN ALDRIDGE Writer • SCOTT GODLEWSKI Artist
JOHN RAUCH Colors • DERON BENNETT Letters
DAN MORA Main Cover • JOSHUA MIDDLETON Variant Cover
BRITTANY HOLZHERR Editor • JAMIE S. RICH Group Editor
Batman created by BOB KANE with BILL FINGER

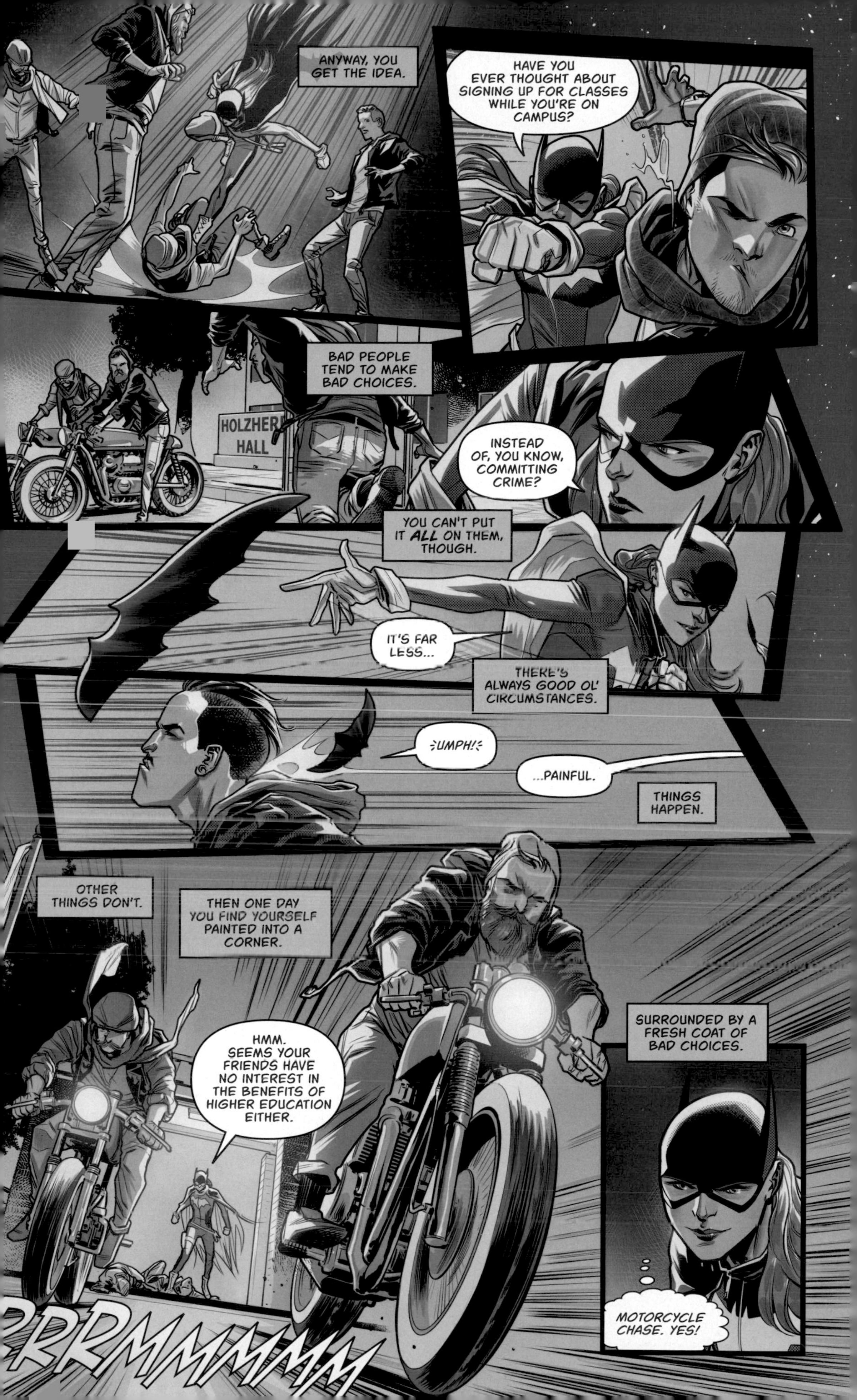
ANYWAY, YOU GET THE IDEA.
HAVE YOU EVER THOUGHT ABOUT SIGNING UP FOR CLASSES WHILE YOU'RE ON CAMPUS?
BAD PEOPLE TEND TO MAKE BAD CHOICES.
HOLZHER HALL
INSTEAD OF, YOU KNOW, COMMITTING CRIME?
YOU CAN'T PUT IT ALL ON THEM, THOUGH.
IT'S FAR LESS...
THERE'S ALWAYS GOOD OL' CIRCUMSTANCES.
UMPH!
...PAINFUL.
THINGS HAPPEN.
OTHER THINGS DON'T.
THEN ONE DAY YOU FIND YOURSELF PAINTED INTO A CORNER.
HMM. SEEMS YOUR FRIENDS HAVE NO INTEREST IN THE BENEFITS OF HIGHER EDUCATION EITHER.
SURROUNDED BY A FRESH COAT OF BAD CHOICES.
MOTORCYCLE CHASE. YES!
RRRMMMMMM

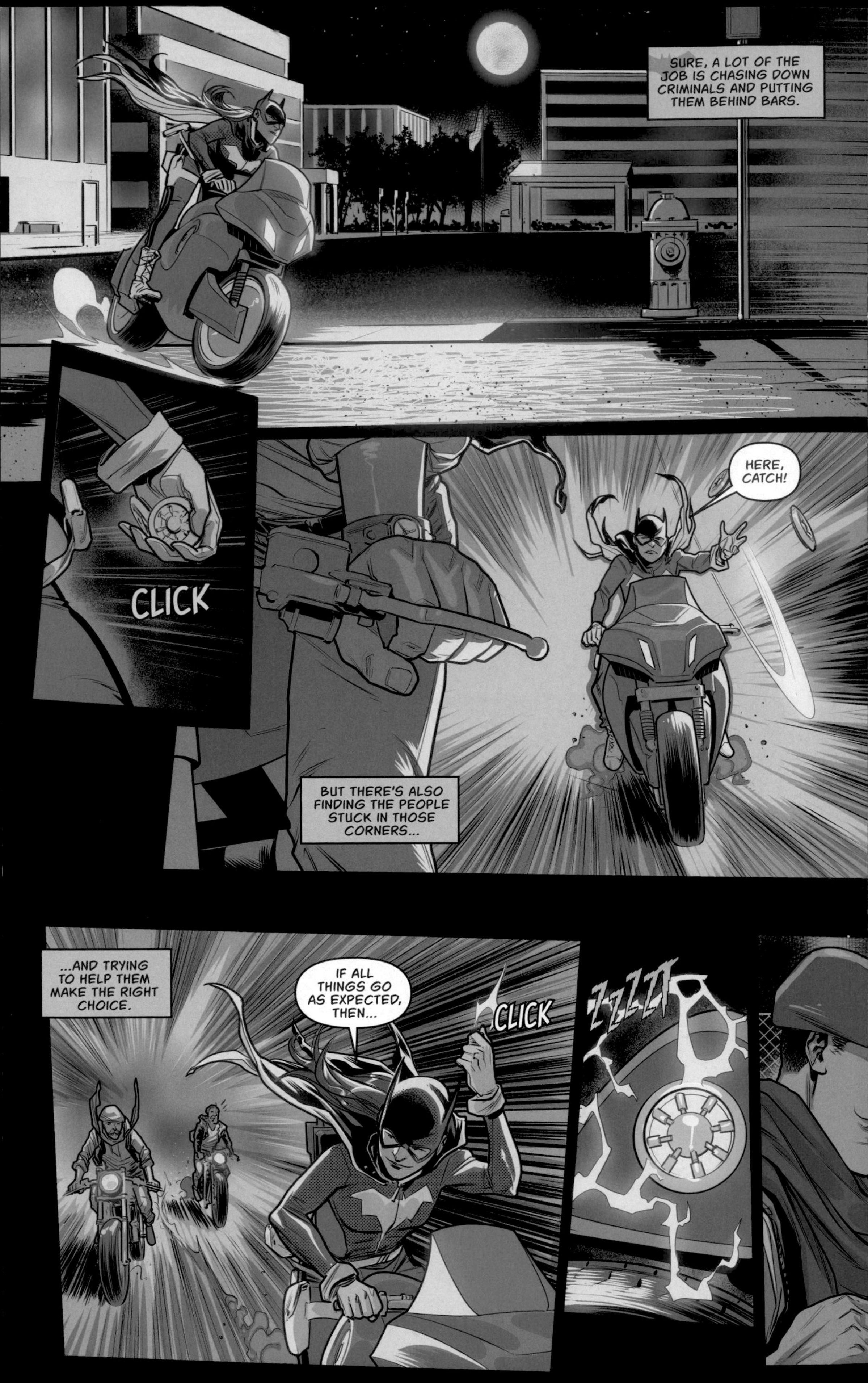
SURE, A LOT OF THE JOB IS CHASING DOWN CRIMINALS AND PUTTING THEM BEHIND BARS.
CLICK
HERE, CATCH!
BUT THERE'S ALSO FINDING THE PEOPLE STUCK IN THOSE CORNERS...
...AND TRYING TO HELP THEM MAKE THE RIGHT CHOICE.
IF ALL THINGS GO AS EXPECTED, THEN...
CLICK
ZZZZT

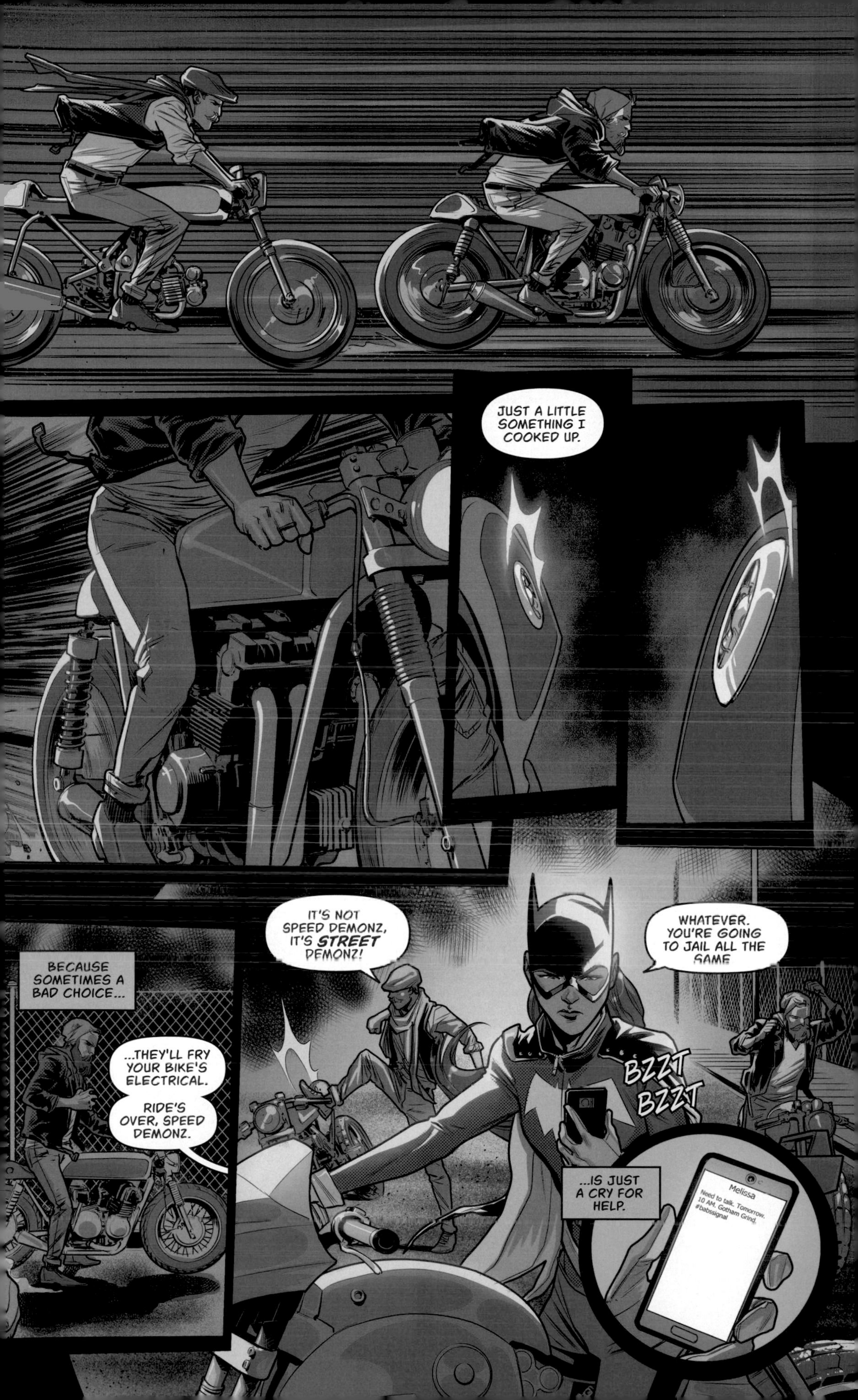
JUST A LITTLE SOMETHING I COOKED UP.
BECAUSE SOMETIMES A BAD CHOICE...
...THEY'LL FRY YOUR BIKE'S ELECTRICAL.
RIDE'S OVER, SPEED DEMONZ.
IT'S NOT SPEED DEMONZ, IT'S STREET DEMONZ!
WHATEVER. YOU'RE GOING TO JAIL ALL THE SAME.
BZZT
BZZT
...IS JUST A CRY FOR HELP.
Melissa
Need to talk. Tomorrow, 10 AM, Gotham Grind. #babssignal

GOTHAM GRIND COFFEE SHOP.
10:07 A.M.

NOT SURE I'VE EVER SEEN ANYONE ORDER A COFFEE WITH FIVE SHOTS BEFORE. LONG NIGHT?

THEY'RE ALL *LONG NIGHTS.*

HOURS
MONDAY 7am-1pm
TUESDAY 7am-1pm
WEDNESDAY 7am-1pm
THURSDAY 7am-1pm
FRIDAY 7am-1pm
SATURDAY 7am-1pm
SUNDAY 8am-10pm

HAHA. YOU STILL GOING TO BURNSIDE COLLEGE?

YEAH, LIBRARY SCIENCES. BUT I'M THINKING OF CHANGING.

YOU?

GOTHAM U. PRE-MED.

SO...ABOUT THE TEXT?

YEAH, THAT, THE REASON FOR THE BABS-SIGNAL...

WELL, YOU SAID TO USE IT IF WE WERE EVER IN TROUBLE. WITH YOUR DAD BEING COMMISSIONER AND ALL THAT, YOU COULD...

MELISSA, IF YOU'RE IN...

IT'S NOT ME. YOU REMEMBER JACOB CESARO FROM MR. CARLSON'S COMPUTER CLASS?

YEAH, SECOND-BEST CODER IN OUR HIGH SCHOOL.

WELL, I VOLUNTEER AT THE HOSPITAL A FEW NIGHTS A WEEK.

HE WAS BROUGH[T] IN THE OTHER NIGH[T] LOOKED LIKE HEL[L] LIKE HE'D GONE TEN ROUNDS WIT[H] MUHAMMAD ALI.

THING IS, TH[IS] IS LIKE THE THIRD TIME A MONTH.

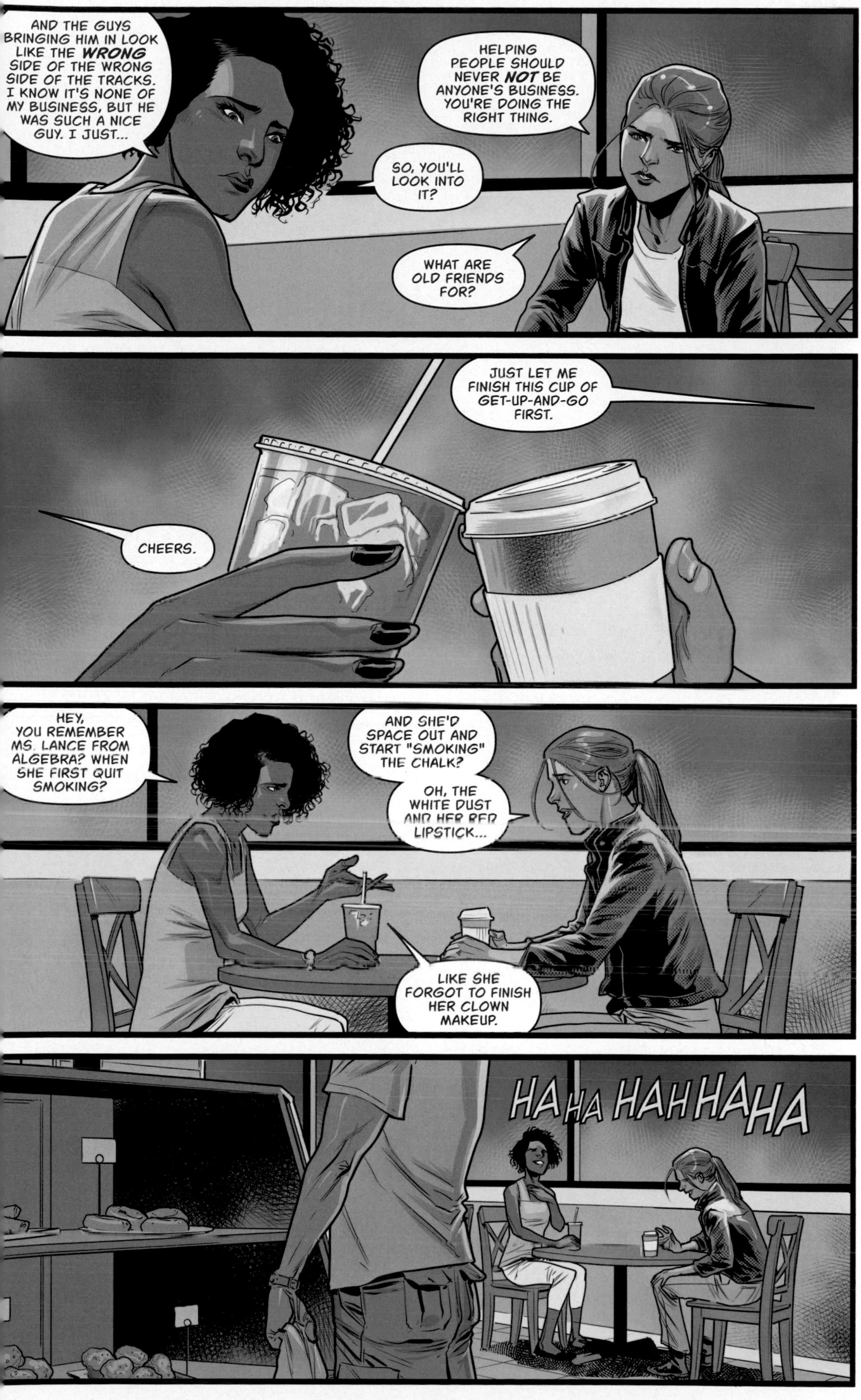

AND THE GUYS BRINGING HIM IN LOOK LIKE THE WRONG SIDE OF THE WRONG SIDE OF THE TRACKS. I KNOW IT'S NONE OF MY BUSINESS, BUT HE WAS SUCH A NICE GUY. I JUST...
HELPING PEOPLE SHOULD NEVER NOT BE ANYONE'S BUSINESS. YOU'RE DOING THE RIGHT THING.
SO, YOU'LL LOOK INTO IT?
WHAT ARE OLD FRIENDS FOR?
JUST LET ME FINISH THIS CUP OF GET-UP-AND-GO FIRST.
CHEERS.
HEY, YOU REMEMBER MS. LANCE FROM ALGEBRA? WHEN SHE FIRST QUIT SMOKING?
AND SHE'D SPACE OUT AND START "SMOKING" THE CHALK?
OH, THE WHITE DUST AND HER RED LIPSTICK...
LIKE SHE FORGOT TO FINISH HER CLOWN MAKEUP.
HAHA HAHHAHAHA

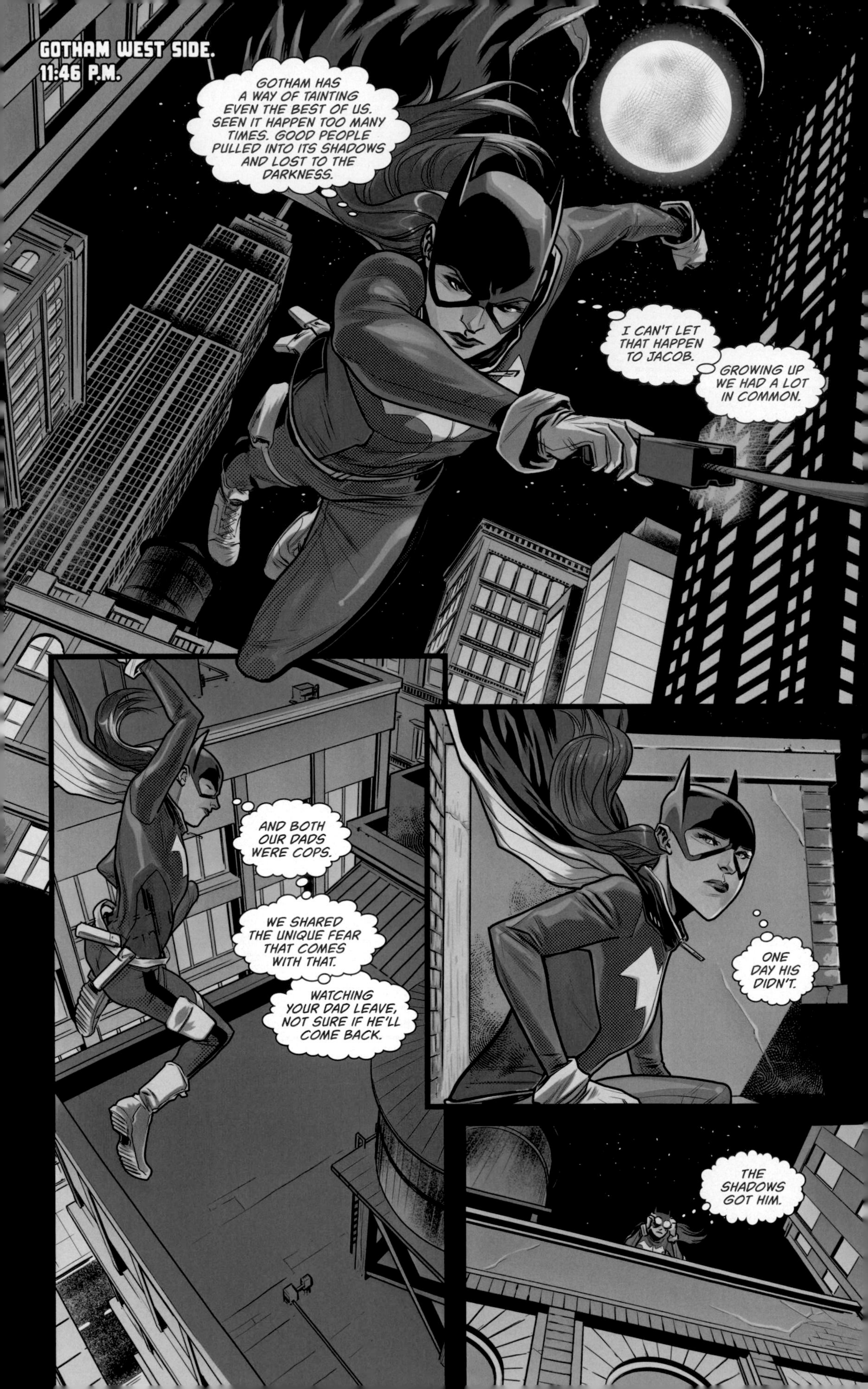

GOTHAM WEST SIDE. 11:46 P.M.
GOTHAM HAS A WAY OF TAINTING EVEN THE BEST OF US. SEEN IT HAPPEN TOO MANY TIMES. GOOD PEOPLE PULLED INTO ITS SHADOWS AND LOST TO THE DARKNESS.
I CAN'T LET THAT HAPPEN TO JACOB.
GROWING UP WE HAD A LOT IN COMMON.
AND BOTH OUR DADS WERE COPS.
WE SHARED THE UNIQUE FEAR THAT COMES WITH THAT.
WATCHING YOUR DAD LEAVE, NOT SURE IF HE'LL COME BACK.
ONE DAY HIS DIDN'T.
THE SHADOWS GOT HIM.

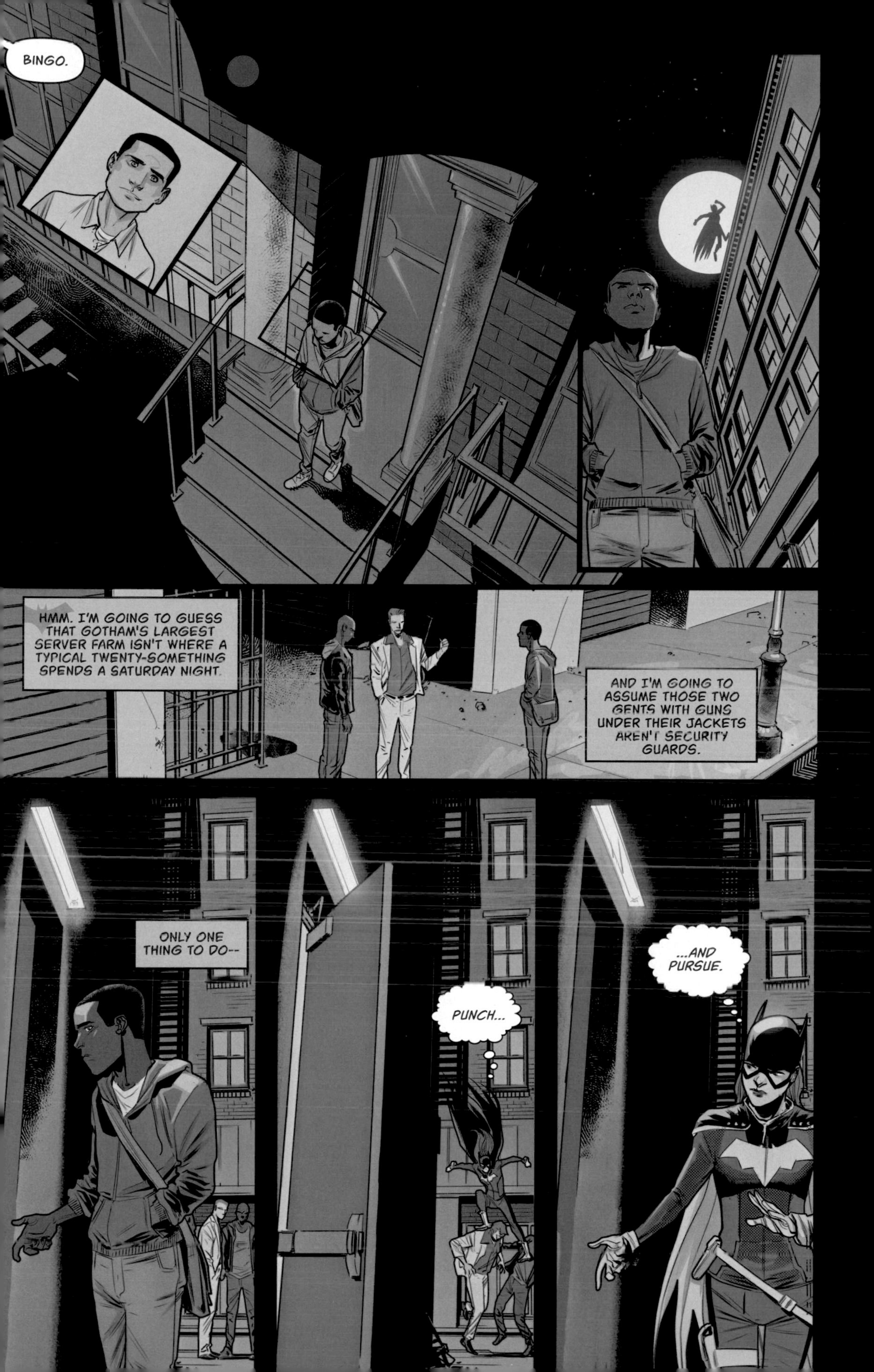
BINGO.
HMM. I'M GOING TO GUESS THAT GOTHAM'S LARGEST SERVER FARM ISN'T WHERE A TYPICAL TWENTY-SOMETHING SPENDS A SATURDAY NIGHT.
AND I'M GOING TO ASSUME THOSE TWO GENTS WITH GUNS UNDER THEIR JACKETS AREN'T SECURITY GUARDS.
ONLY ONE THING TO DO--
PUNCH...
...AND PURSUE.

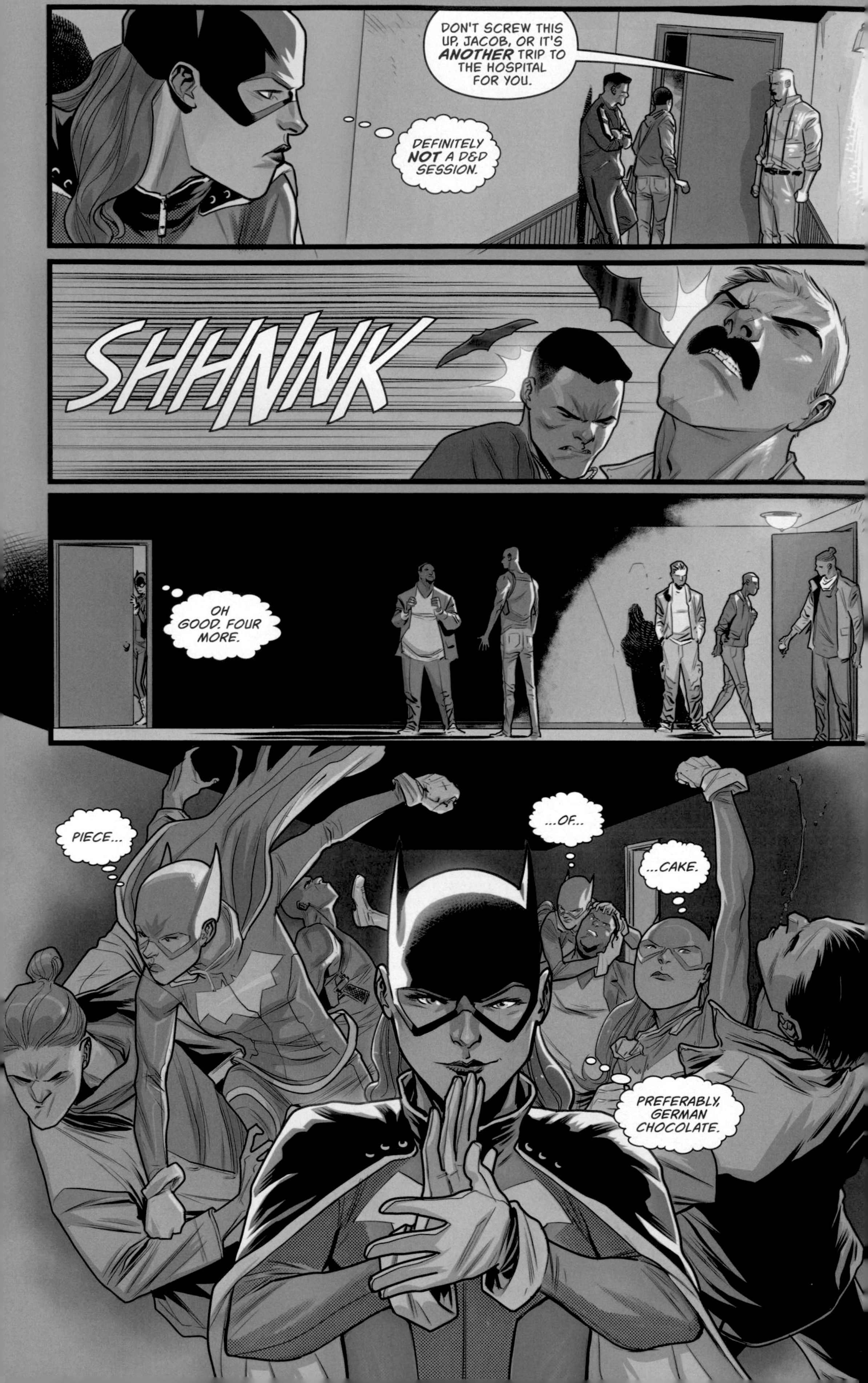
DON'T SCREW THIS UP, JACOB, OR IT'S ANOTHER TRIP TO THE HOSPITAL FOR YOU.
DEFINITELY NOT A D&D SESSION.
SHHNNK
OH GOOD. FOUR MORE.
PIECE...
...OF...
...CAKE.
PREFERABLY, GERMAN CHOCOLATE.

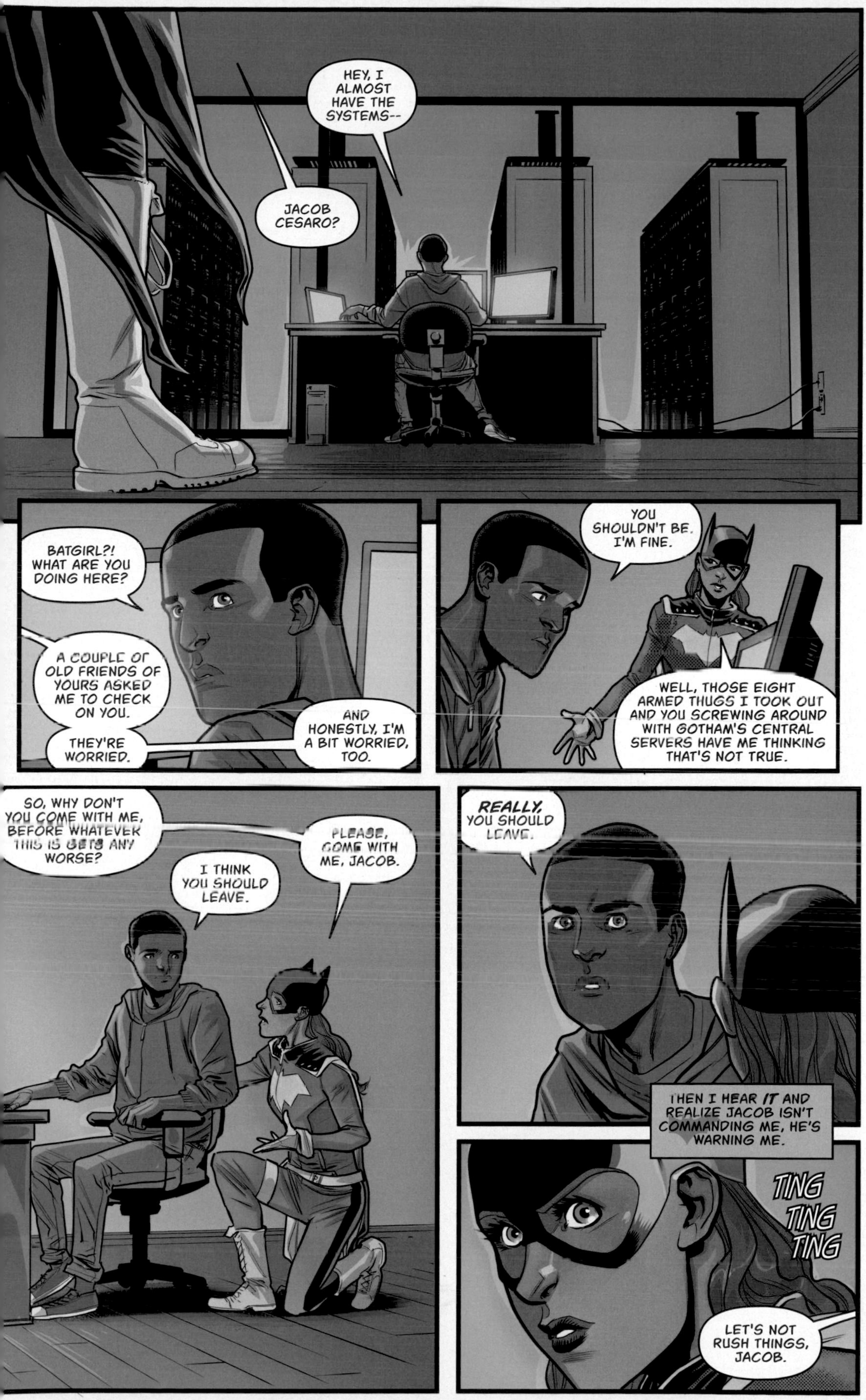
HEY, I ALMOST HAVE THE SYSTEMS--
JACOB CESARO?
BATGIRL?! WHAT ARE YOU DOING HERE?
A COUPLE OF OLD FRIENDS OF YOURS ASKED ME TO CHECK ON YOU.
THEY'RE WORRIED.
AND HONESTLY, I'M A BIT WORRIED, TOO.
YOU SHOULDN'T BE. I'M FINE.
WELL, THOSE EIGHT ARMED THUGS I TOOK OUT AND YOU SCREWING AROUND WITH GOTHAM'S CENTRAL SERVERS HAVE ME THINKING THAT'S NOT TRUE.
SO, WHY DON'T YOU COME WITH ME, BEFORE WHATEVER THIS IS GETS ANY WORSE?
I THINK YOU SHOULD LEAVE.
PLEASE, COME WITH ME, JACOB.
REALLY, YOU SHOULD LEAVE.
THEN I HEAR IT AND REALIZE JACOB ISN'T COMMANDING ME, HE'S WARNING ME.
TING TING TING
LET'S NOT RUSH THINGS, JACOB.

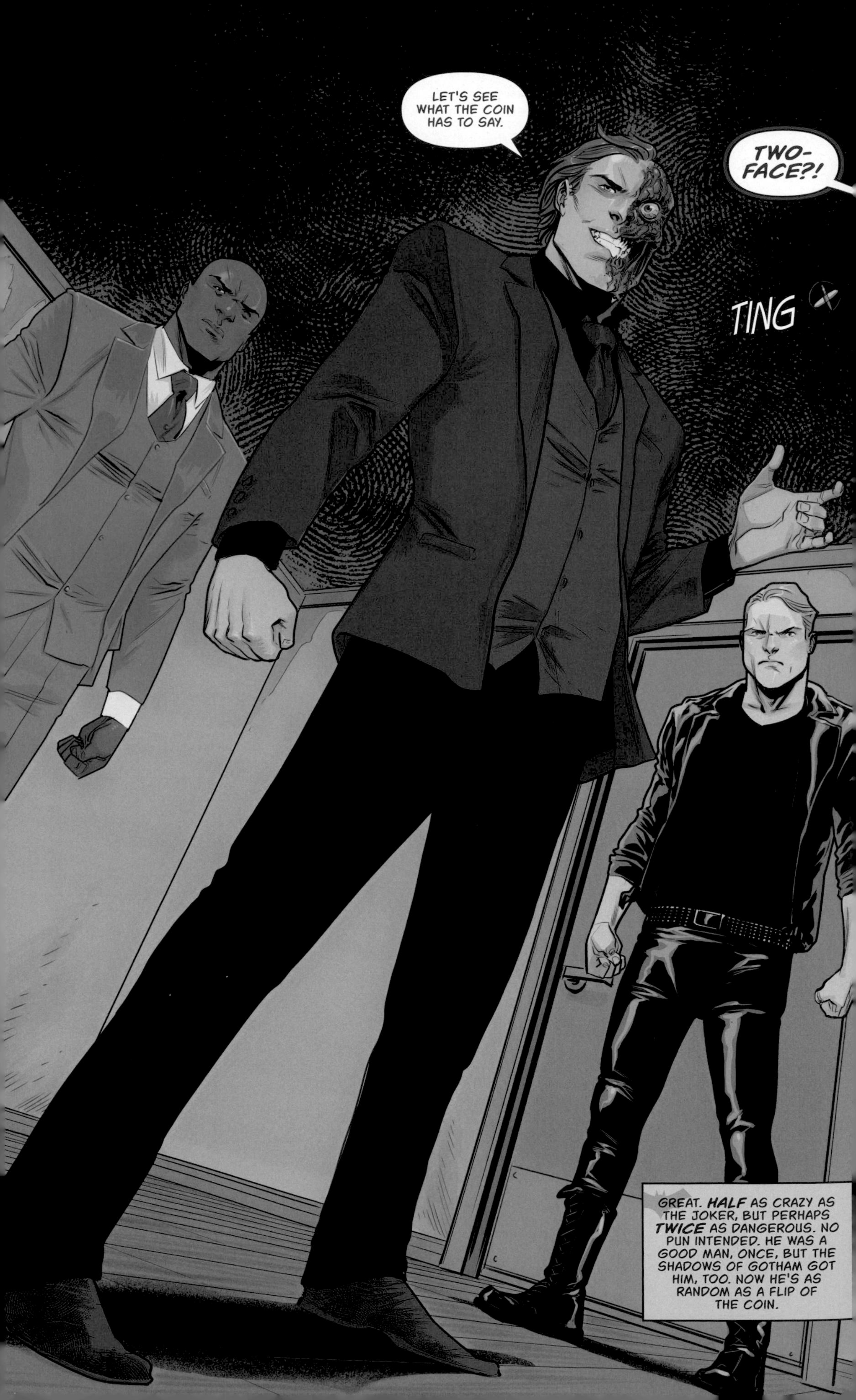
LET'S SEE WHAT THE COIN HAS TO SAY.
TWO-FACE?!
TING
GREAT. HALF AS CRAZY AS THE JOKER, BUT PERHAPS TWICE AS DANGEROUS. NO PUN INTENDED. HE WAS A GOOD MAN, ONCE, BUT THE SHADOWS OF GOTHAM GOT HIM, TOO. NOW HE'S AS RANDOM AS A FLIP OF THE COIN.

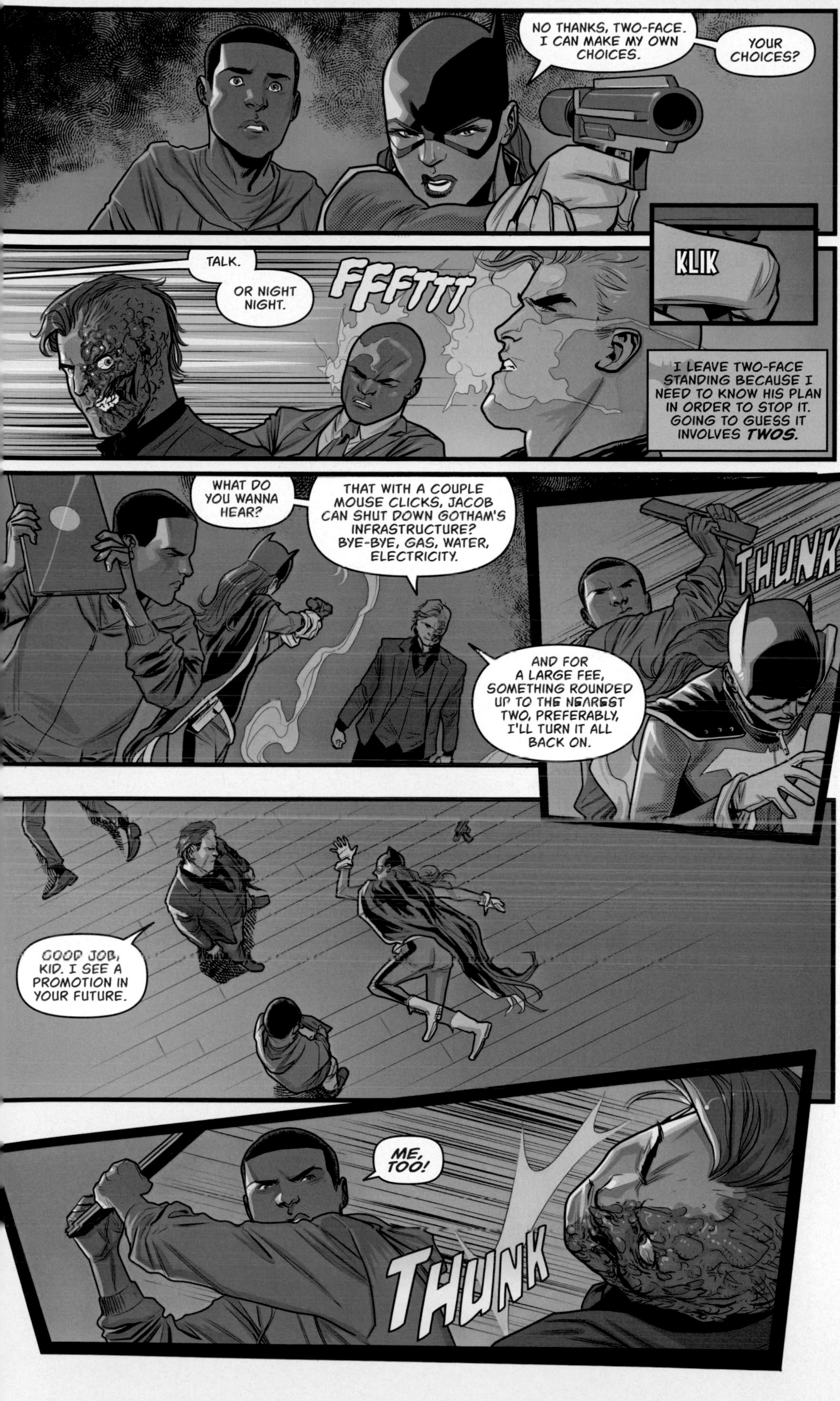
NO THANKS, TWO-FACE. I CAN MAKE MY OWN CHOICES.
YOUR CHOICES?
KLIK
TALK.
OR NIGHT NIGHT.
FFFTTTT
I LEAVE TWO-FACE STANDING BECAUSE I NEED TO KNOW HIS PLAN IN ORDER TO STOP IT. GOING TO GUESS IT INVOLVES TWOS.
WHAT DO YOU WANNA HEAR?
THAT WITH A COUPLE MOUSE CLICKS, JACOB CAN SHUT DOWN GOTHAM'S INFRASTRUCTURE? BYE-BYE, GAS, WATER, ELECTRICITY.
AND FOR A LARGE FEE, SOMETHING ROUNDED UP TO THE NEAREST TWO, PREFERABLY, I'LL TURN IT ALL BACK ON.
THUNK
GOOD JOB, KID. I SEE A PROMOTION IN YOUR FUTURE.
ME, TOO!
THUNK

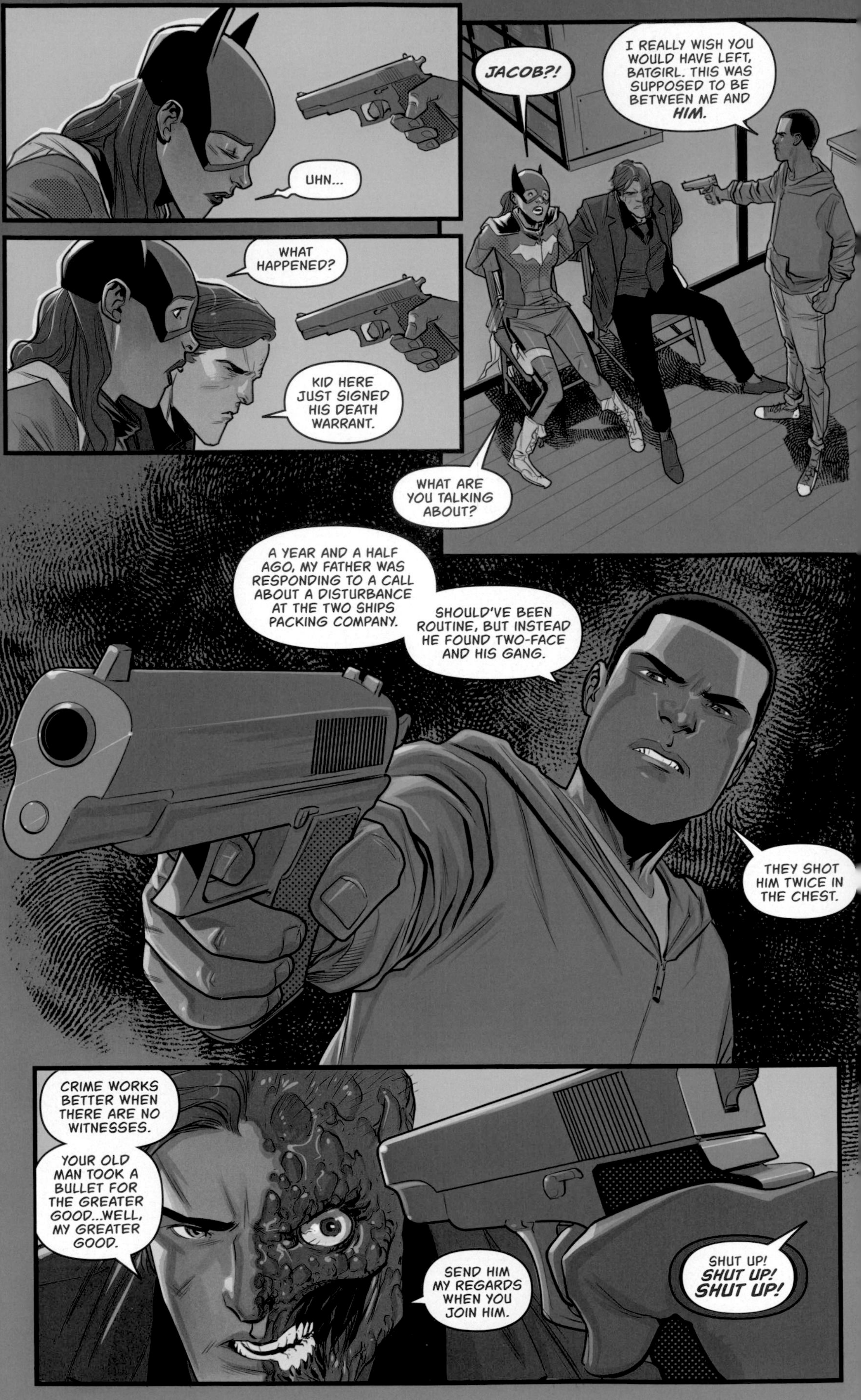
UHN...
JACOB?!
I REALLY WISH YOU WOULD HAVE LEFT, BATGIRL. THIS WAS SUPPOSED TO BE BETWEEN ME AND HIM.
WHAT HAPPENED?
KID HERE JUST SIGNED HIS DEATH WARRANT.
WHAT ARE YOU TALKING ABOUT?
A YEAR AND A HALF AGO, MY FATHER WAS RESPONDING TO A CALL ABOUT A DISTURBANCE AT THE TWO SHIPS PACKING COMPANY.
SHOULD'VE BEEN ROUTINE, BUT INSTEAD HE FOUND TWO-FACE AND HIS GANG.
THEY SHOT HIM TWICE IN THE CHEST.
CRIME WORKS BETTER WHEN THERE ARE NO WITNESSES.
YOUR OLD MAN TOOK A BULLET FOR THE GREATER GOOD...WELL, MY GREATER GOOD.
SEND HIM MY REGARDS WHEN YOU JOIN HIM.
SHUT UP! SHUT UP! SHUT UP!

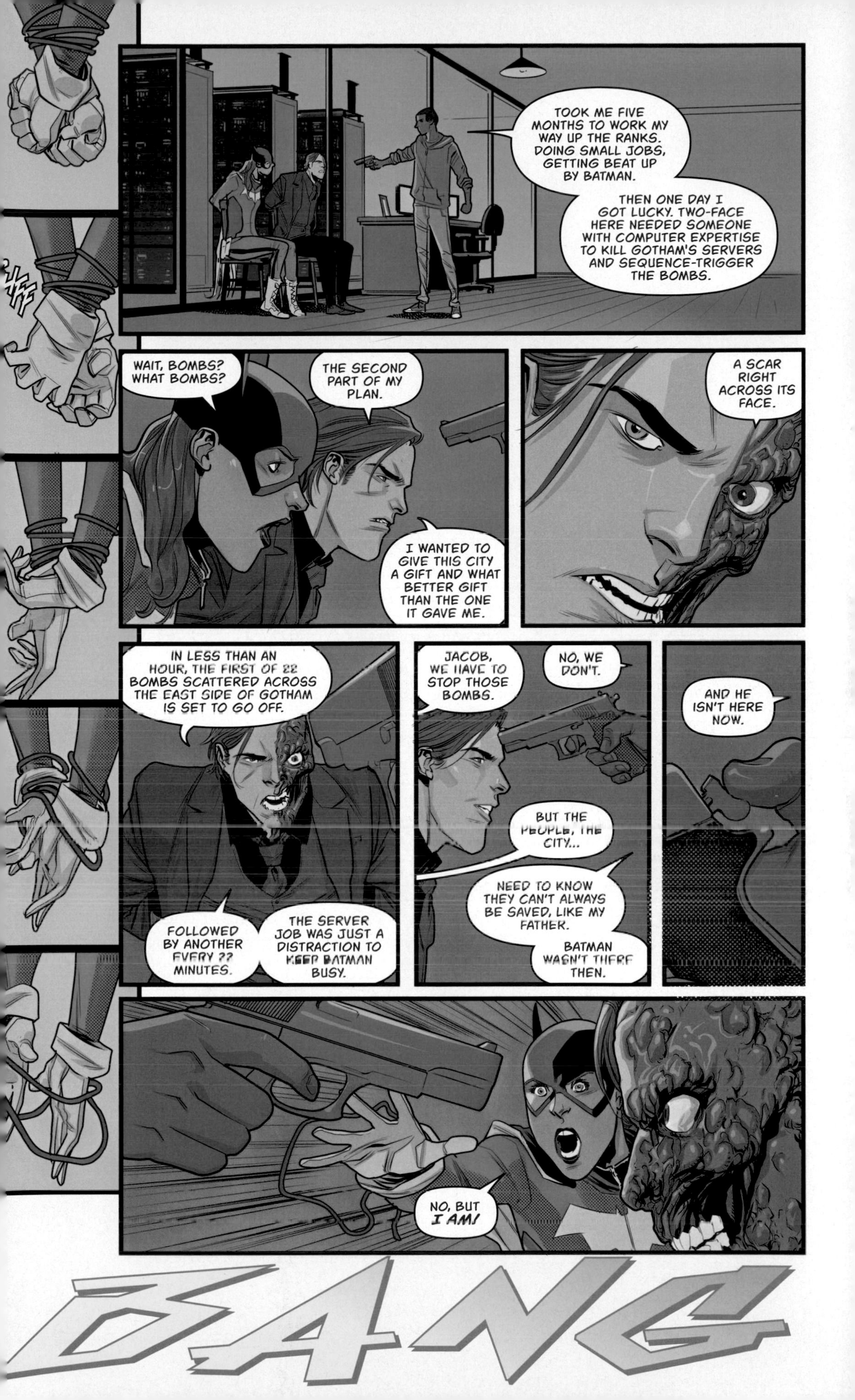

TOOK ME FIVE MONTHS TO WORK MY WAY UP THE RANKS. DOING SMALL JOBS, GETTING BEAT UP BY BATMAN.
THEN ONE DAY I GOT LUCKY. TWO-FACE HERE NEEDED SOMEONE WITH COMPUTER EXPERTISE TO KILL GOTHAM'S SERVERS AND SEQUENCE-TRIGGER THE BOMBS.
WAIT, BOMBS? WHAT BOMBS?
THE SECOND PART OF MY PLAN.
I WANTED TO GIVE THIS CITY A GIFT AND WHAT BETTER GIFT THAN THE ONE IT GAVE ME.
A SCAR RIGHT ACROSS ITS FACE.
IN LESS THAN AN HOUR, THE FIRST OF 22 BOMBS SCATTERED ACROSS THE EAST SIDE OF GOTHAM IS SET TO GO OFF.
FOLLOWED BY ANOTHER EVERY 22 MINUTES.
THE SERVER JOB WAS JUST A DISTRACTION TO KEEP BATMAN BUSY.
JACOB, WE HAVE TO STOP THOSE BOMBS.
NO, WE DON'T.
BUT THE PEOPLE, THE CITY...
NEED TO KNOW THEY CAN'T ALWAYS BE SAVED, LIKE MY FATHER.
BATMAN WASN'T THERE THEN.
AND HE ISN'T HERE NOW.
NO, BUT I AM!
BANG

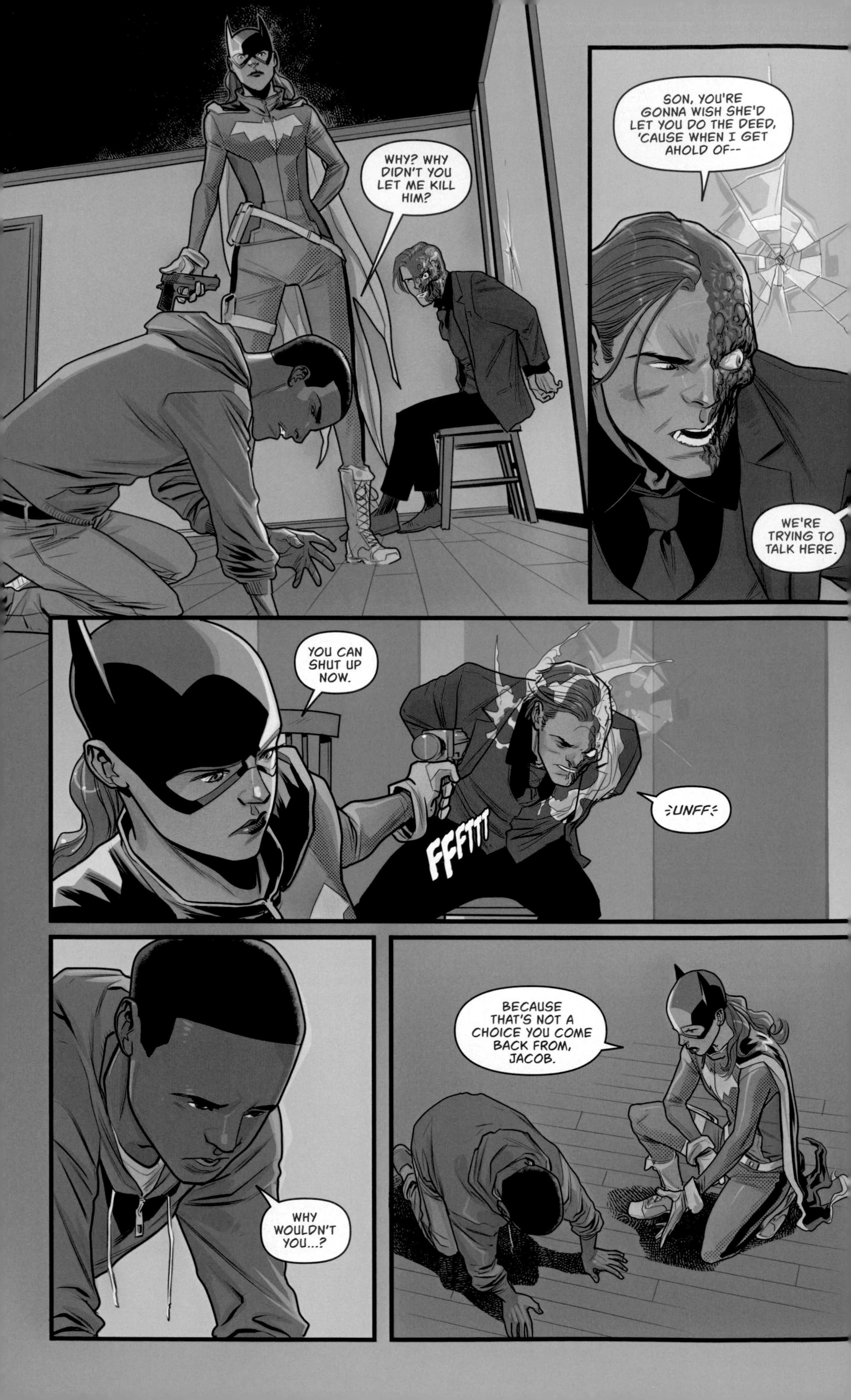
WHY? WHY DIDN'T YOU LET ME KILL HIM?
SON, YOU'RE GONNA WISH SHE'D LET YOU DO THE DEED, 'CAUSE WHEN I GET AHOLD OF--
WE'RE TRYING TO TALK HERE.
YOU CAN SHUT UP NOW.
FFFTTTT
UNFF
WHY WOULDN'T YOU...?
BECAUSE THAT'S NOT A CHOICE YOU COME BACK FROM, JACOB.

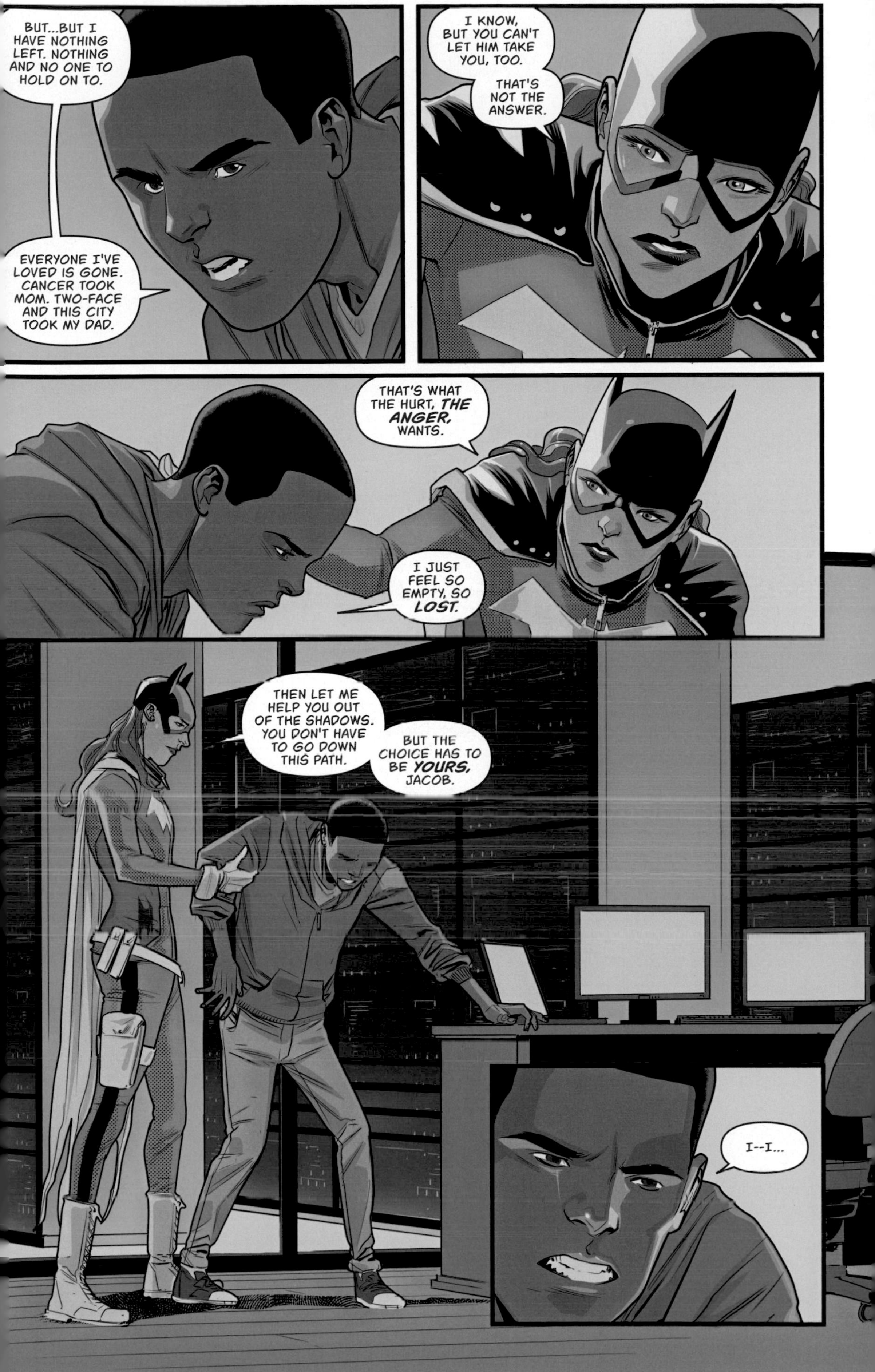
BUT...BUT I HAVE NOTHING LEFT. NOTHING AND NO ONE TO HOLD ON TO.
EVERYONE I'VE LOVED IS GONE. CANCER TOOK MOM. TWO-FACE AND THIS CITY TOOK MY DAD.
I KNOW, BUT YOU CAN'T LET HIM TAKE YOU, TOO.
THAT'S NOT THE ANSWER.
THAT'S WHAT THE HURT, *THE ANGER,* WANTS.
I JUST FEEL SO EMPTY, SO *LOST.*
THEN LET ME HELP YOU OUT OF THE SHADOWS. YOU DON'T HAVE TO GO DOWN THIS PATH.
BUT THE CHOICE HAS TO BE *YOURS,* JACOB.
I--I...

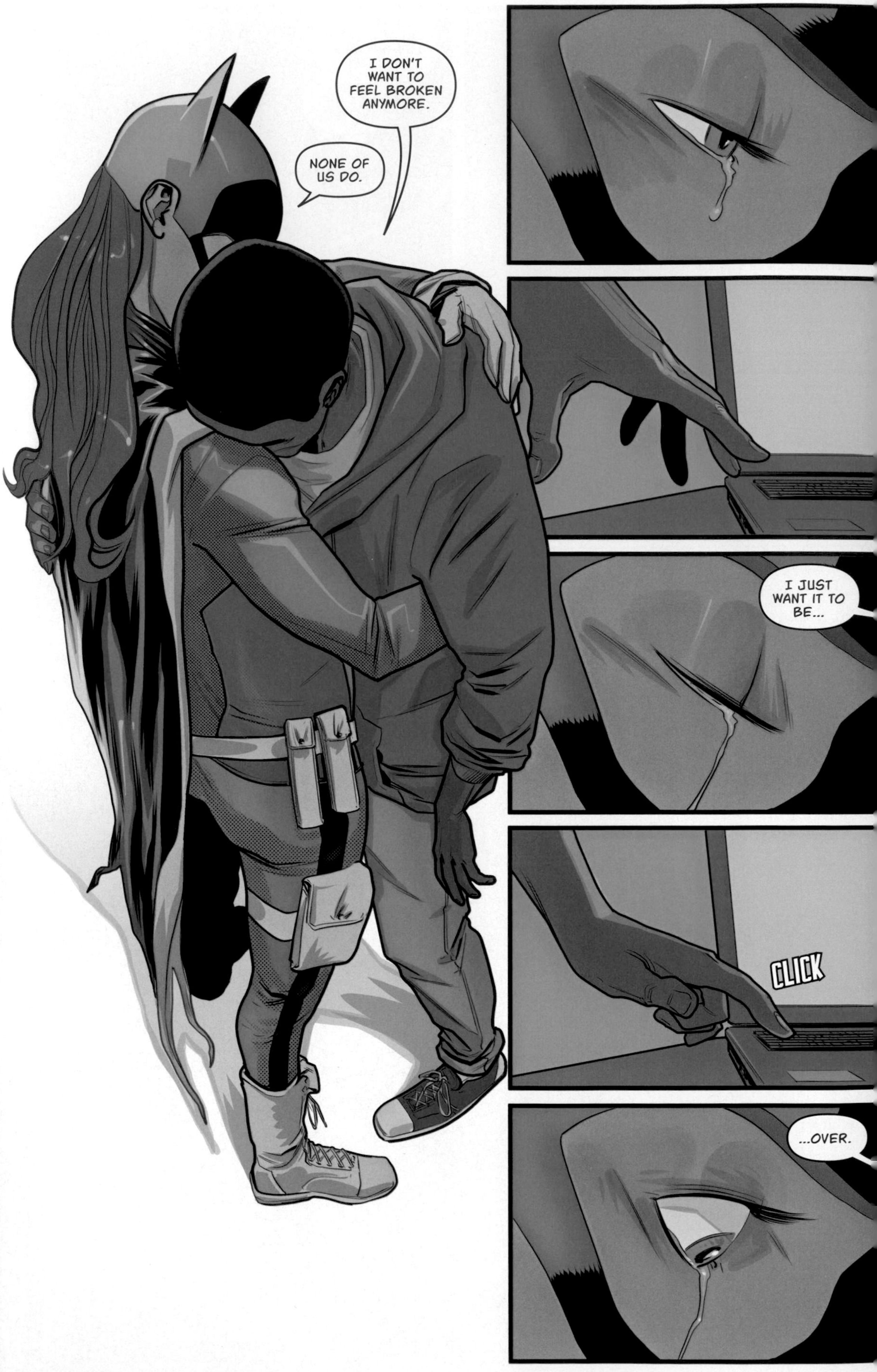
I DON'T WANT TO FEEL BROKEN ANYMORE.
NONE OF US DO.
I JUST WANT IT TO BE...
CLICK
...OVER.

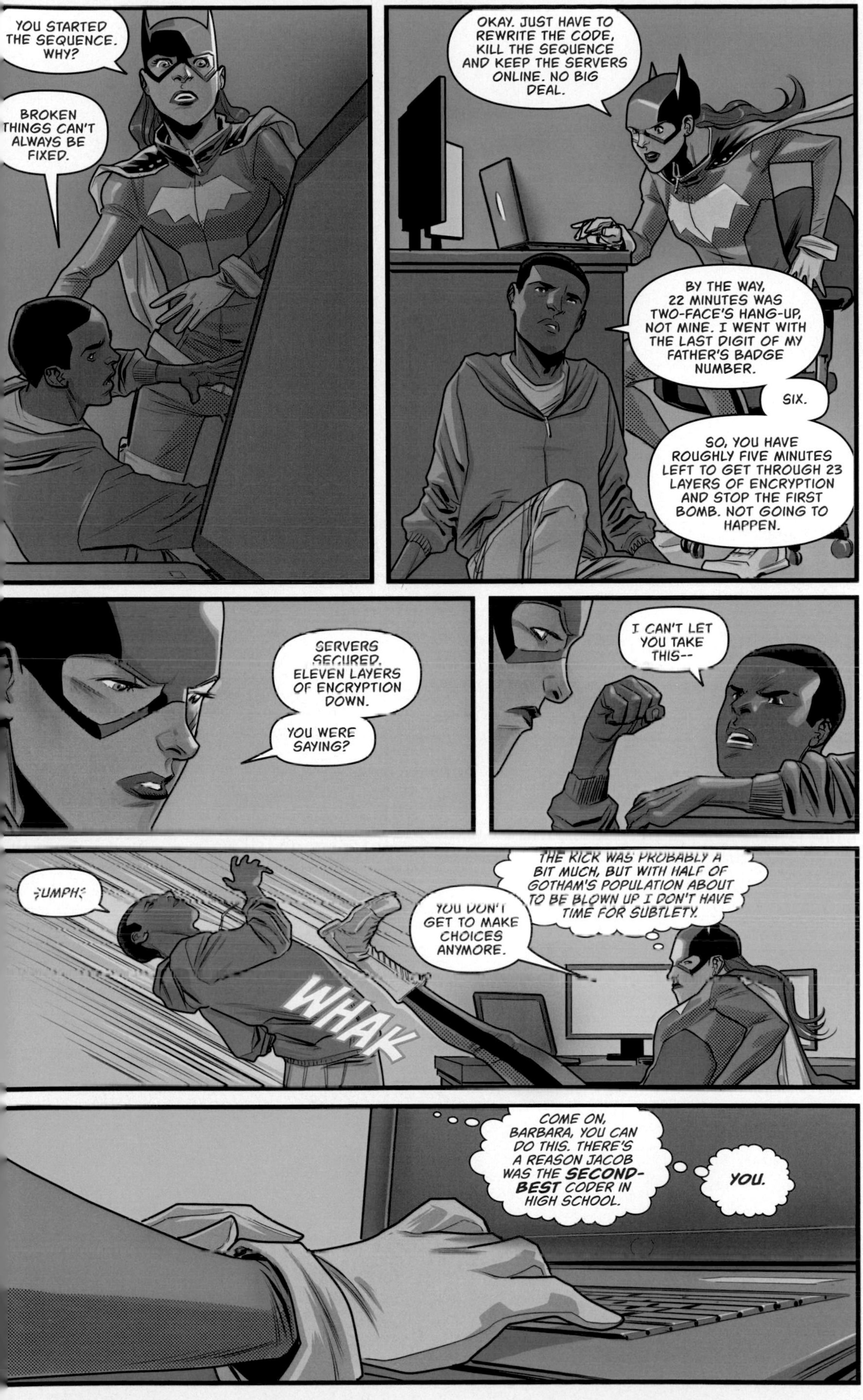
YOU STARTED THE SEQUENCE. WHY?
BROKEN THINGS CAN'T ALWAYS BE FIXED.
OKAY. JUST HAVE TO REWRITE THE CODE, KILL THE SEQUENCE AND KEEP THE SERVERS ONLINE. NO BIG DEAL.
BY THE WAY, 22 MINUTES WAS TWO-FACE'S HANG-UP, NOT MINE. I WENT WITH THE LAST DIGIT OF MY FATHER'S BADGE NUMBER.
SIX.
SO, YOU HAVE ROUGHLY FIVE MINUTES LEFT TO GET THROUGH 23 LAYERS OF ENCRYPTION AND STOP THE FIRST BOMB. NOT GOING TO HAPPEN.
SERVERS SECURED. ELEVEN LAYERS OF ENCRYPTION DOWN.
YOU WERE SAYING?
I CAN'T LET YOU TAKE THIS--
UMPH!
WHAK
YOU DON'T GET TO MAKE CHOICES ANYMORE.
THE KICK WAS PROBABLY A BIT MUCH, BUT WITH HALF OF GOTHAM'S POPULATION ABOUT TO BE BLOWN UP I DON'T HAVE TIME FOR SUBTLETY.
COME ON, BARBARA, YOU CAN DO THIS. THERE'S A REASON JACOB WAS THE SECOND-BEST CODER IN HIGH SCHOOL.
YOU.

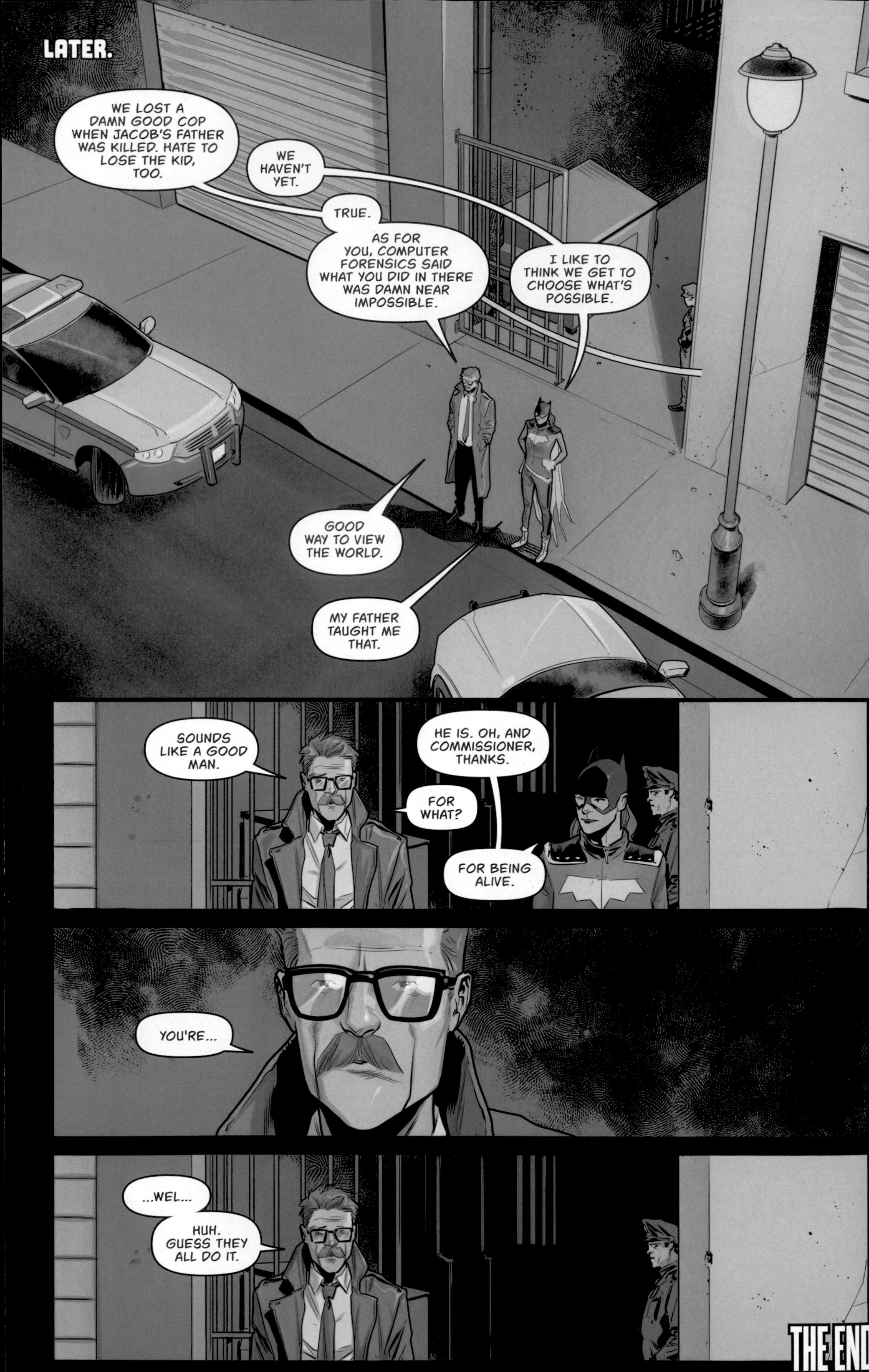
LATER.
WE LOST A DAMN GOOD COP WHEN JACOB'S FATHER WAS KILLED. HATE TO LOSE THE KID, TOO.
WE HAVEN'T YET.
TRUE.
AS FOR YOU, COMPUTER FORENSICS SAID WHAT YOU DID IN THERE WAS DAMN NEAR IMPOSSIBLE.
I LIKE TO THINK WE GET TO CHOOSE WHAT'S POSSIBLE.
GOOD WAY TO VIEW THE WORLD.
MY FATHER TAUGHT ME THAT.
SOUNDS LIKE A GOOD MAN.
HE IS. OH, AND COMMISSIONER, THANKS.
FOR WHAT?
FOR BEING ALIVE.
YOU'RE...
...WEL...
HUH. GUESS THEY ALL DO IT.
THE END

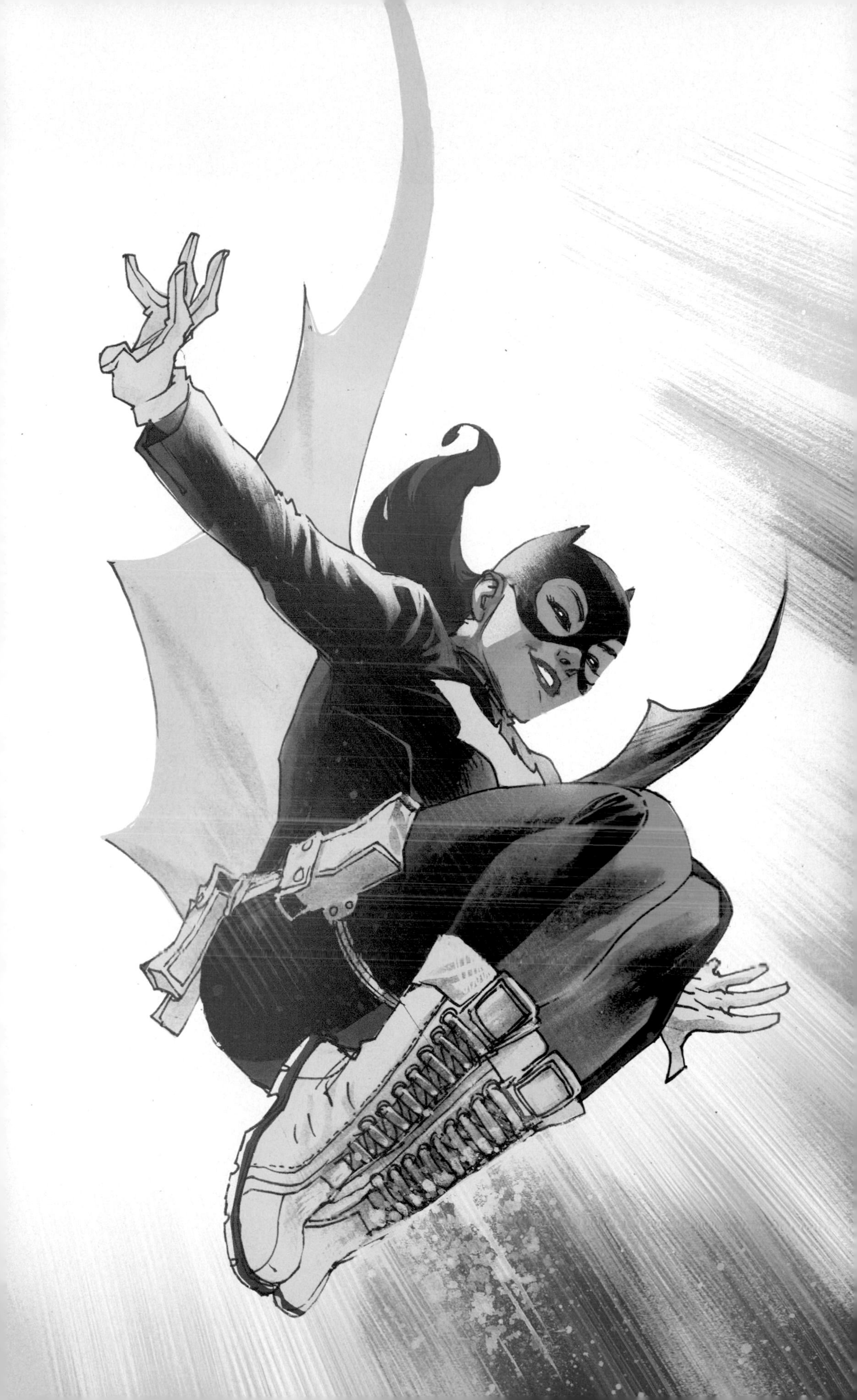

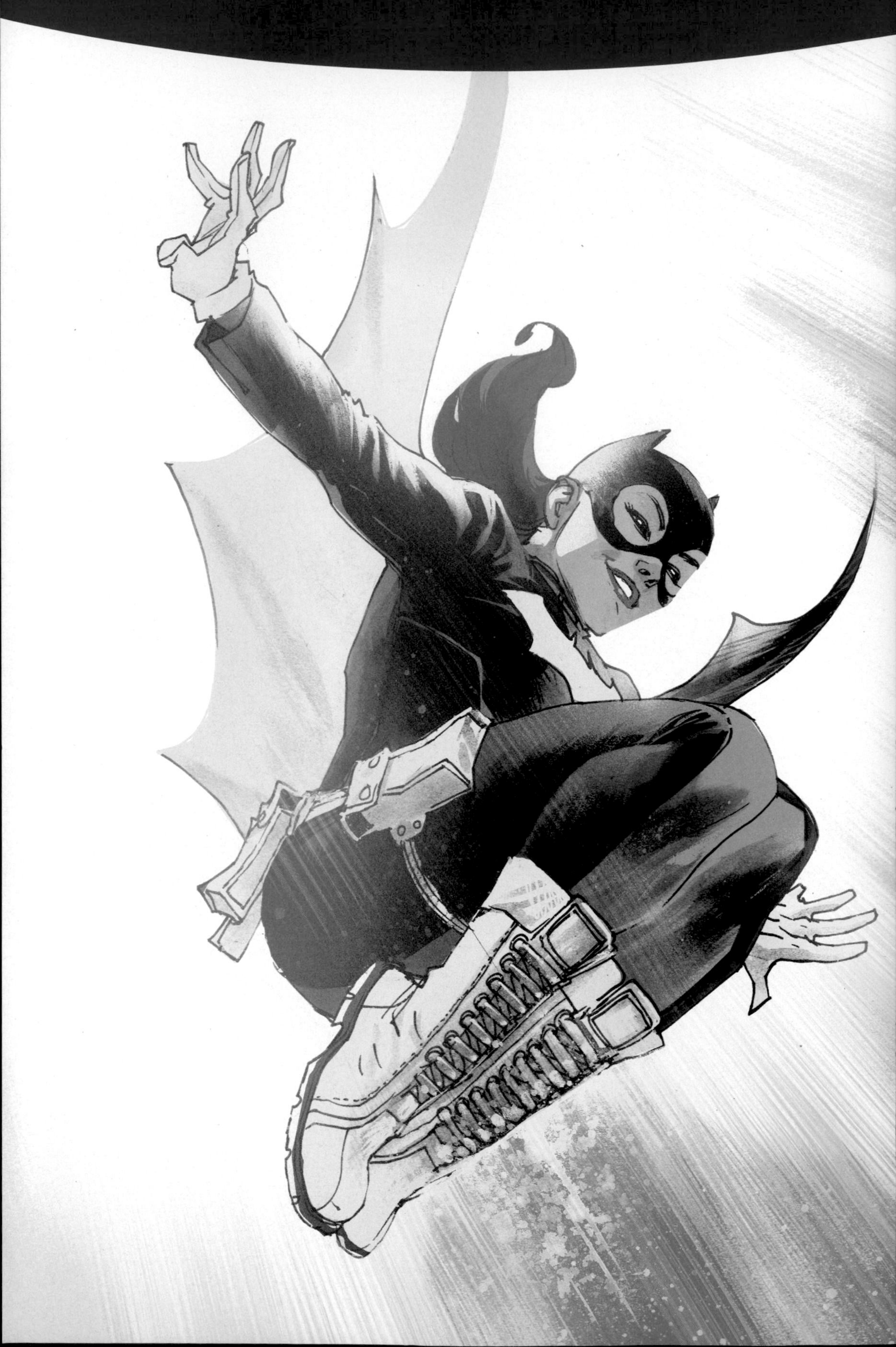

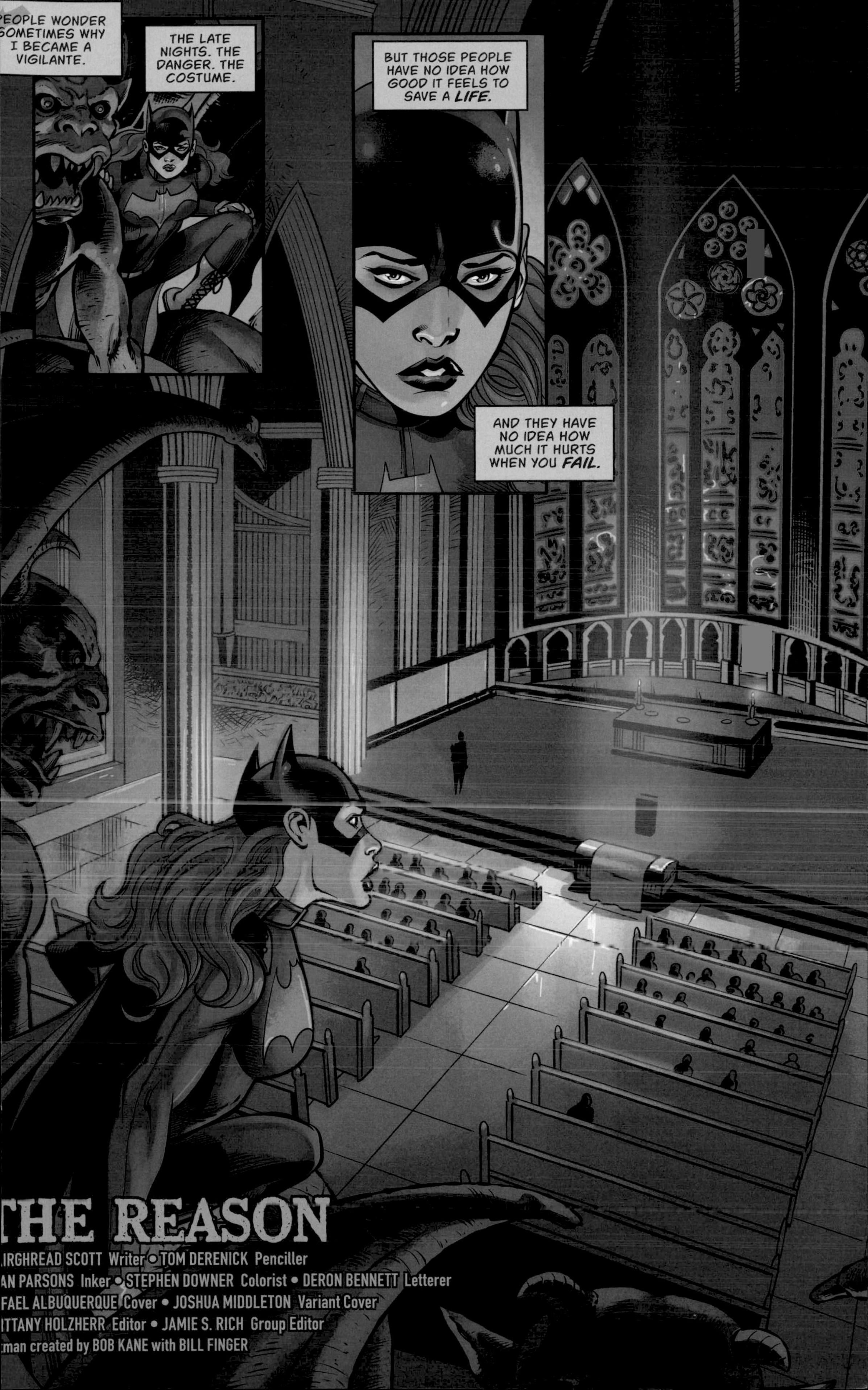
PEOPLE WONDER SOMETIMES WHY I BECAME A VIGILANTE.
THE LATE NIGHTS. THE DANGER. THE COSTUME.
BUT THOSE PEOPLE HAVE NO IDEA HOW GOOD IT FEELS TO SAVE A LIFE.
AND THEY HAVE NO IDEA HOW MUCH IT HURTS WHEN YOU FAIL.
THE REASON
IRGHREAD SCOTT Writer • TOM DERENICK Penciller
AN PARSONS Inker • STEPHEN DOWNER Colorist • DERON BENNETT Letterer
FAEL ALBUQUERQUE Cover • JOSHUA MIDDLETON Variant Cover
ITTANY HOLZHERR Editor • JAMIE S. RICH Group Editor
tman created by BOB KANE with BILL FINGER

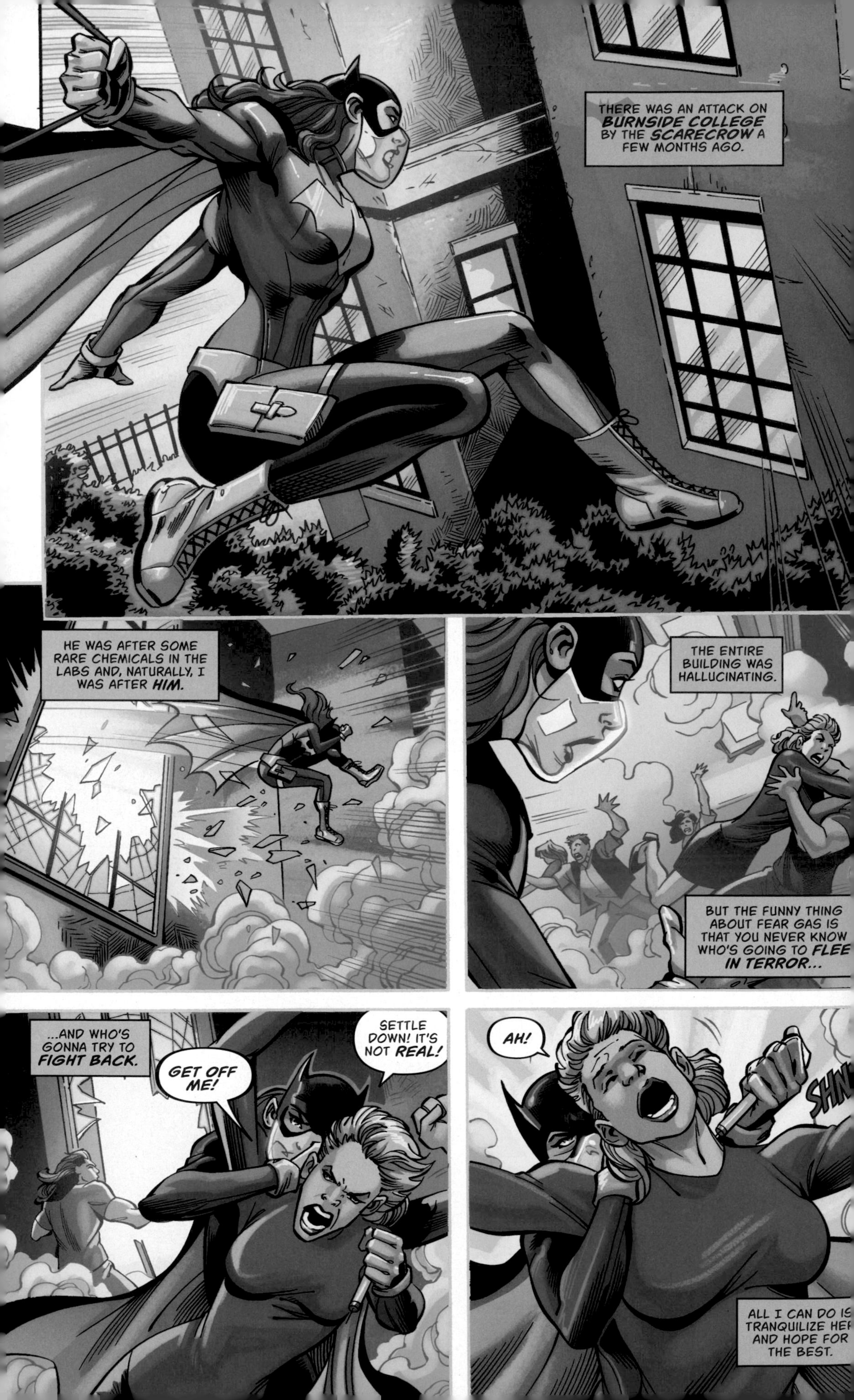
THERE WAS AN ATTACK ON BURNSIDE COLLEGE BY THE SCARECROW A FEW MONTHS AGO.
HE WAS AFTER SOME RARE CHEMICALS IN THE LABS AND, NATURALLY, I WAS AFTER HIM.
THE ENTIRE BUILDING WAS HALLUCINATING.
BUT THE FUNNY THING ABOUT FEAR GAS IS THAT YOU NEVER KNOW WHO'S GOING TO FLEE IN TERROR...
...AND WHO'S GONNA TRY TO FIGHT BACK.
GET OFF ME!
SETTLE DOWN! IT'S NOT REAL!
AH!
ALL I CAN DO IS TRANQUILIZE HER AND HOPE FOR THE BEST.

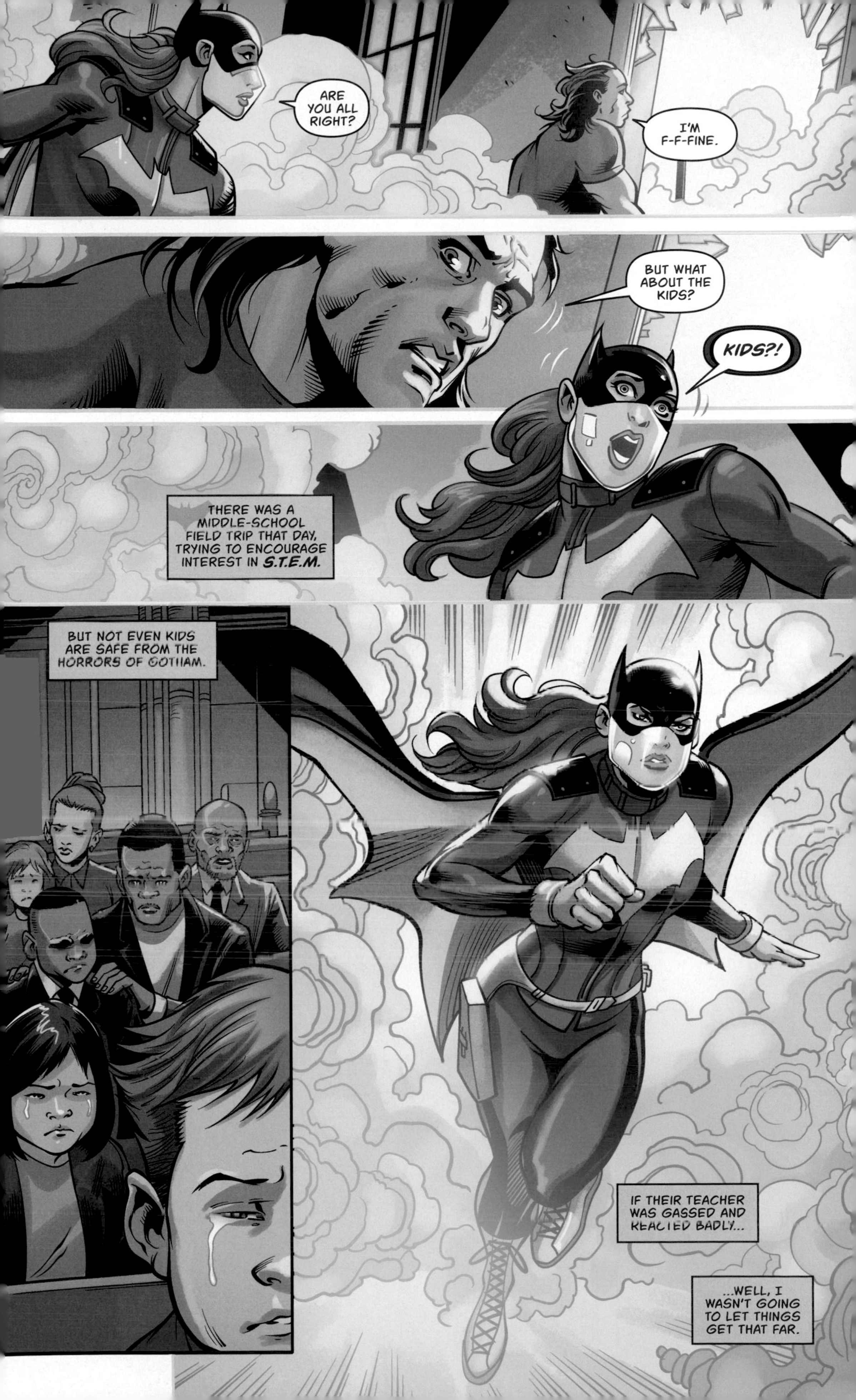

ARE YOU ALL RIGHT?
I'M F-F-FINE.
BUT WHAT ABOUT THE KIDS?
KIDS?!
THERE WAS A MIDDLE-SCHOOL FIELD TRIP THAT DAY, TRYING TO ENCOURAGE INTEREST IN S.T.E.M.
BUT NOT EVEN KIDS ARE SAFE FROM THE HORRORS OF GOTHAM.
IF THEIR TEACHER WAS GASSED AND REACTED BADLY...
...WELL, I WASN'T GOING TO LET THINGS GET THAT FAR.

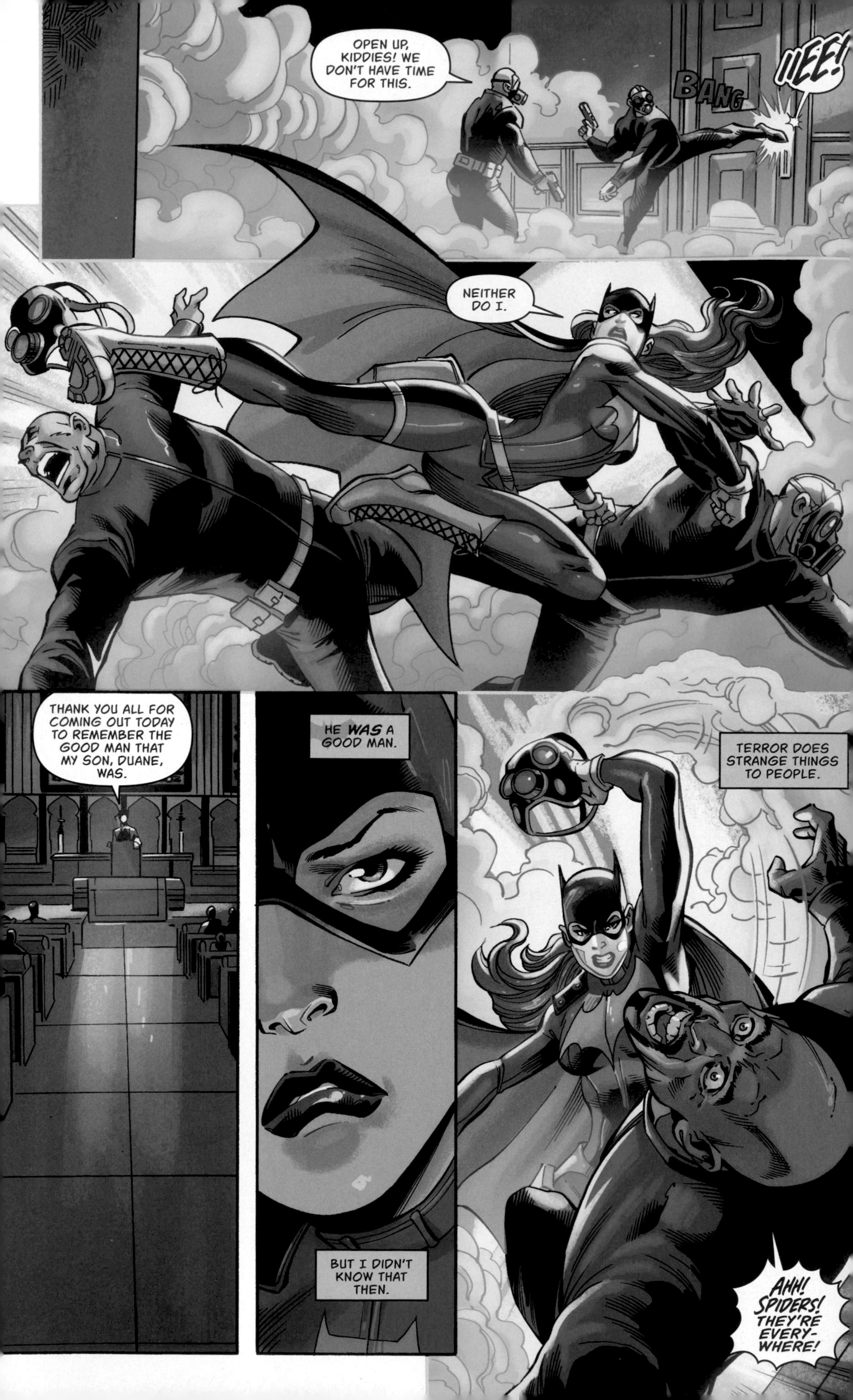
OPEN UP, KIDDIES! WE DON'T HAVE TIME FOR THIS.
BANG
IIEE!
NEITHER DO I.
THANK YOU ALL FOR COMING OUT TODAY TO REMEMBER THE GOOD MAN THAT MY SON, DUANE, WAS.
HE WAS A GOOD MAN.
BUT I DIDN'T KNOW THAT THEN.
TERROR DOES STRANGE THINGS TO PEOPLE.
AHH! SPIDERS! THEY'RE EVERY-WHERE!

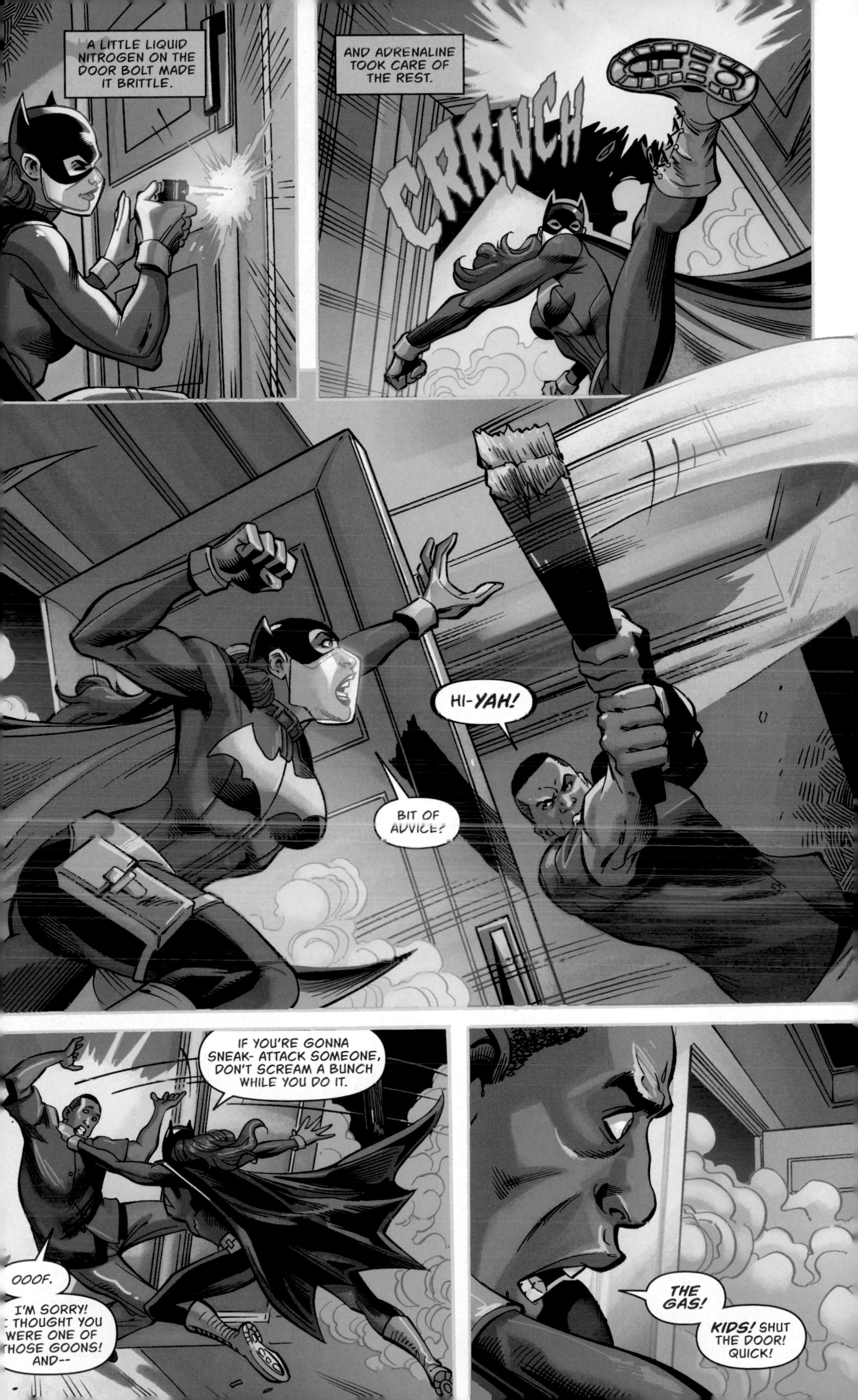
A LITTLE LIQUID NITROGEN ON THE DOOR BOLT MADE IT BRITTLE.
AND ADRENALINE TOOK CARE OF THE REST.
CRRNCH
HI-YAH!
BIT OF ADVICE?
IF YOU'RE GONNA SNEAK- ATTACK SOMEONE, DON'T SCREAM A BUNCH WHILE YOU DO IT.
OOOF.
I'M SORRY! I THOUGHT YOU WERE ONE OF THOSE GOONS! AND--
THE GAS!
KIDS! SHUT THE DOOR! QUICK!

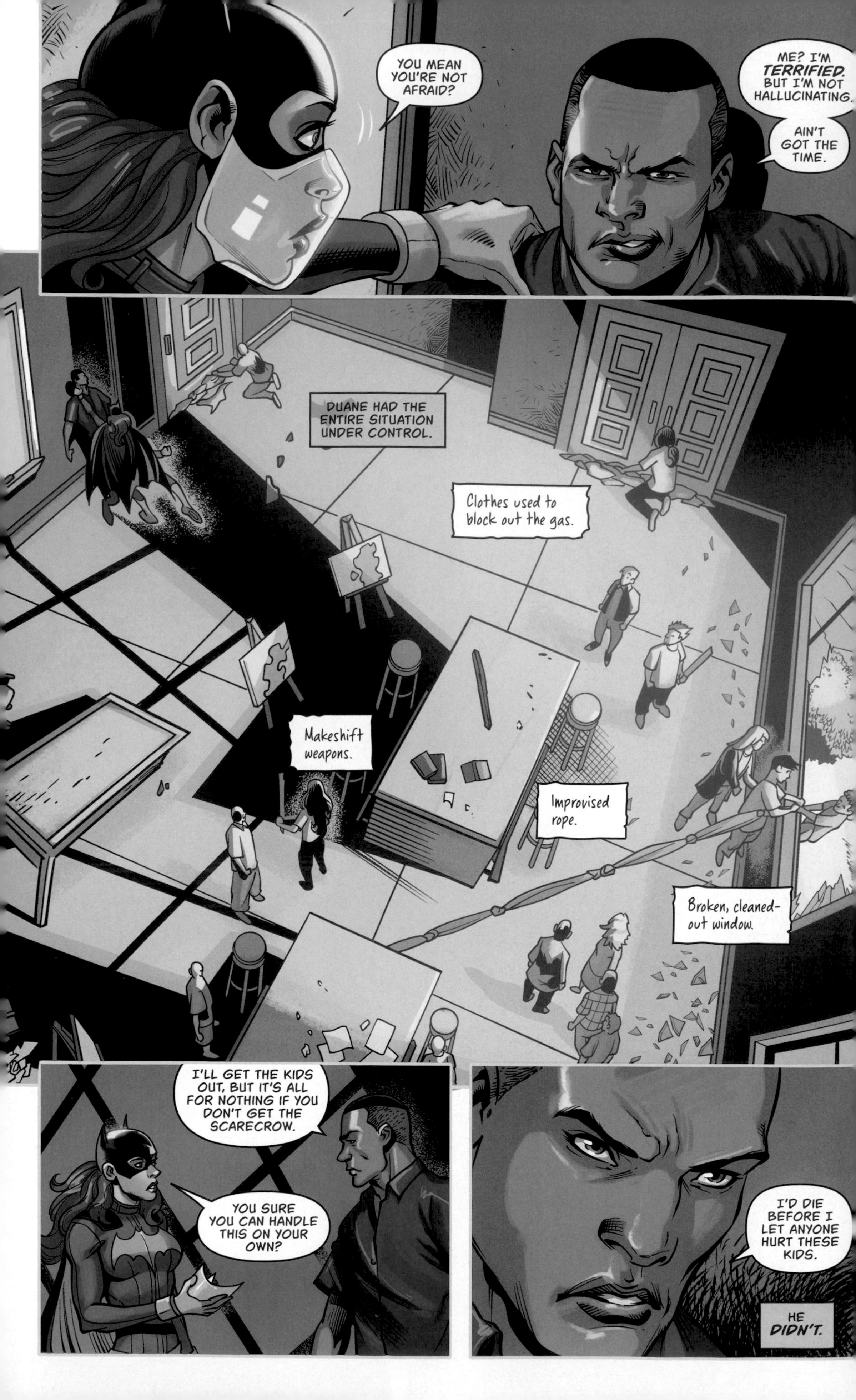
YOU MEAN YOU'RE NOT AFRAID?
ME? I'M TERRIFIED. BUT I'M NOT HALLUCINATING.
AIN'T GOT THE TIME.
DUANE HAD THE ENTIRE SITUATION UNDER CONTROL.
Clothes used to block out the gas.
Makeshift weapons.
Improvised rope.
Broken, cleaned-out window.
I'LL GET THE KIDS OUT, BUT IT'S ALL FOR NOTHING IF YOU DON'T GET THE SCARECROW.
YOU SURE YOU CAN HANDLE THIS ON YOUR OWN?
I'D DIE BEFORE I LET ANYONE HURT THESE KIDS.
HE DIDN'T.

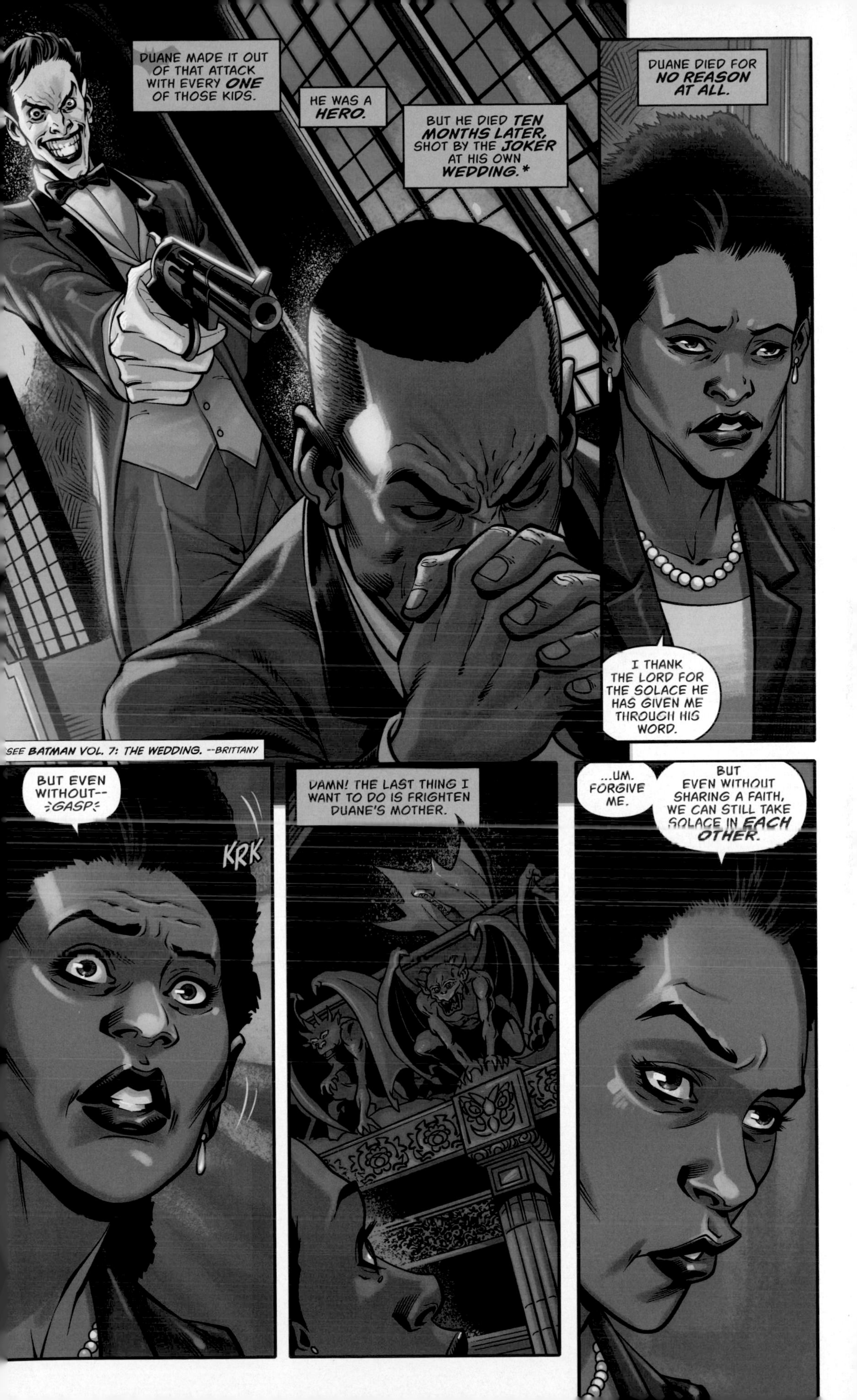
DUANE MADE IT OUT OF THAT ATTACK WITH EVERY ONE OF THOSE KIDS.
HE WAS A HERO.
BUT HE DIED TEN MONTHS LATER, SHOT BY THE JOKER AT HIS OWN WEDDING.*
DUANE DIED FOR NO REASON AT ALL.
I THANK THE LORD FOR THE SOLACE HE HAS GIVEN ME THROUGH HIS WORD.
*SEE BATMAN VOL. 7: THE WEDDING. --BRITTANY
BUT EVEN WITHOUT-- ⁓GASP⁓
KRK
DAMN! THE LAST THING I WANT TO DO IS FRIGHTEN DUANE'S MOTHER.
...UM. FORGIVE ME.
BUT EVEN WITHOUT SHARING A FAITH, WE CAN STILL TAKE SOLACE IN EACH OTHER.

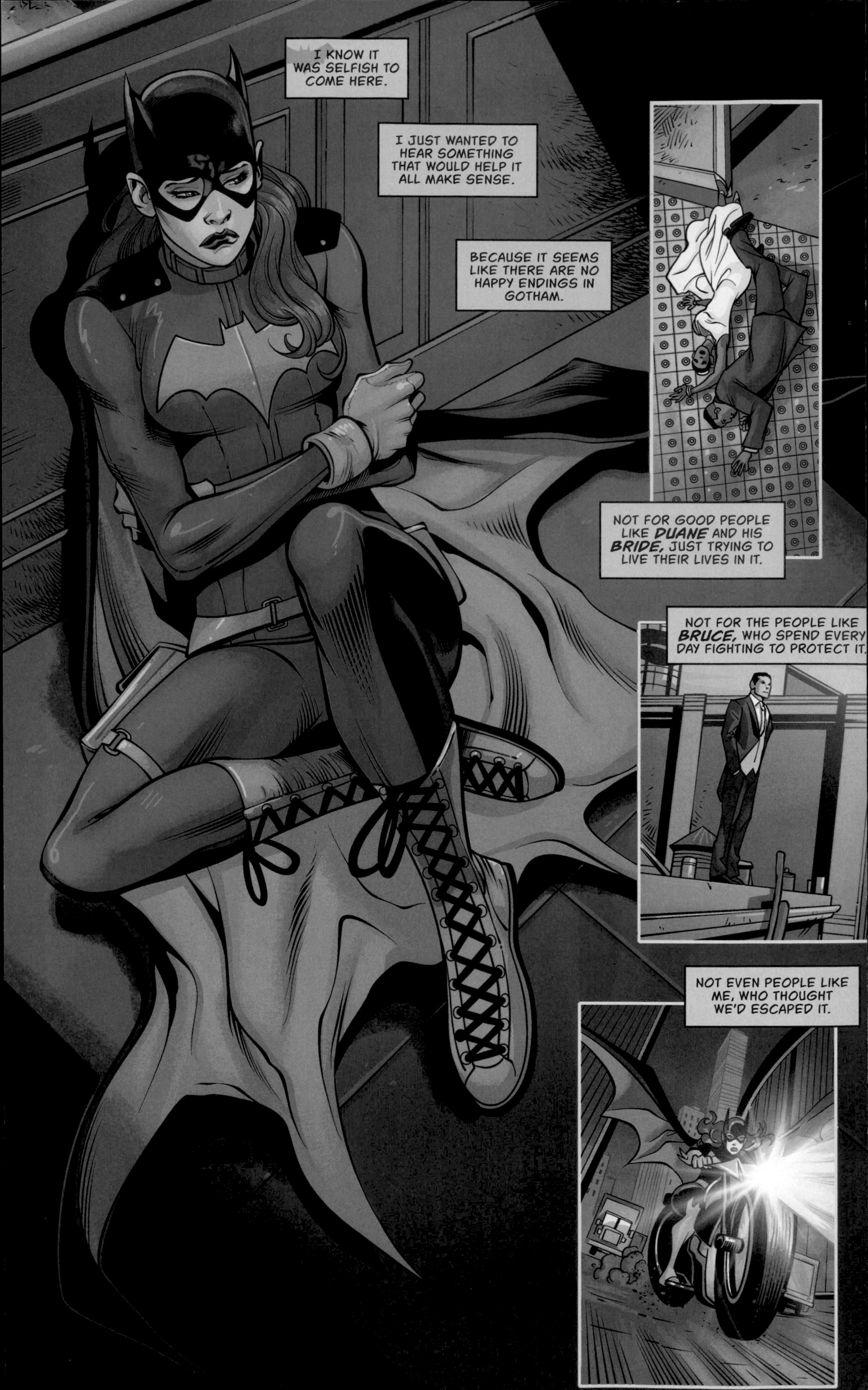
I KNOW IT WAS SELFISH TO COME HERE.
I JUST WANTED TO HEAR SOMETHING THAT WOULD HELP IT ALL MAKE SENSE.
BECAUSE IT SEEMS LIKE THERE ARE NO HAPPY ENDINGS IN GOTHAM.
NOT FOR GOOD PEOPLE LIKE DUANE AND HIS BRIDE, JUST TRYING TO LIVE THEIR LIVES IN IT.
NOT FOR THE PEOPLE LIKE BRUCE, WHO SPEND EVERY DAY FIGHTING TO PROTECT IT.
NOT EVEN PEOPLE LIKE ME, WHO THOUGHT WE'D ESCAPED IT.

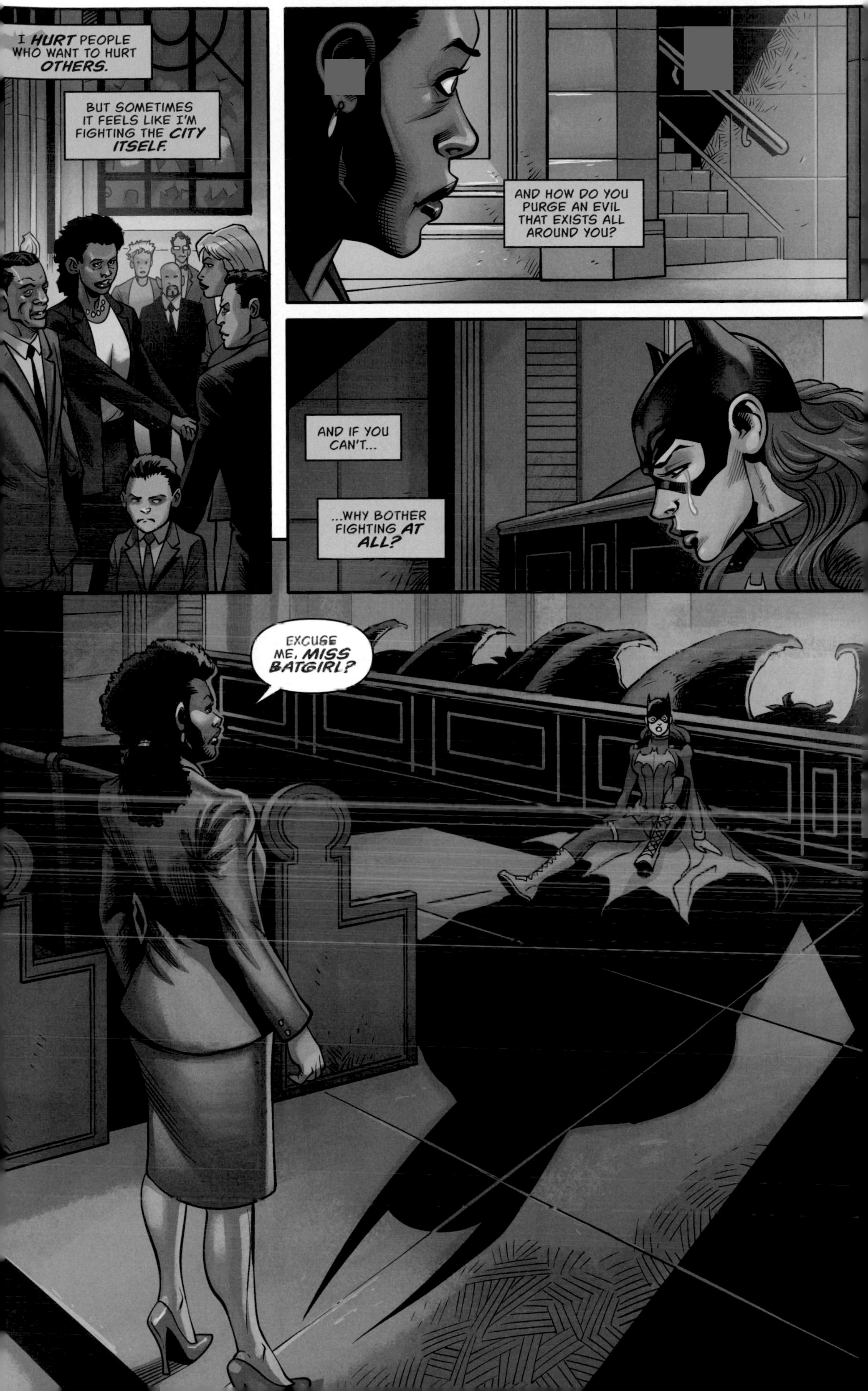
I HURT PEOPLE WHO WANT TO HURT OTHERS.
BUT SOMETIMES IT FEELS LIKE I'M FIGHTING THE CITY ITSELF.
AND HOW DO YOU PURGE AN EVIL THAT EXISTS ALL AROUND YOU?
AND IF YOU CAN'T...
...WHY BOTHER FIGHTING AT ALL?
EXCUSE ME, MISS BATGIRL?

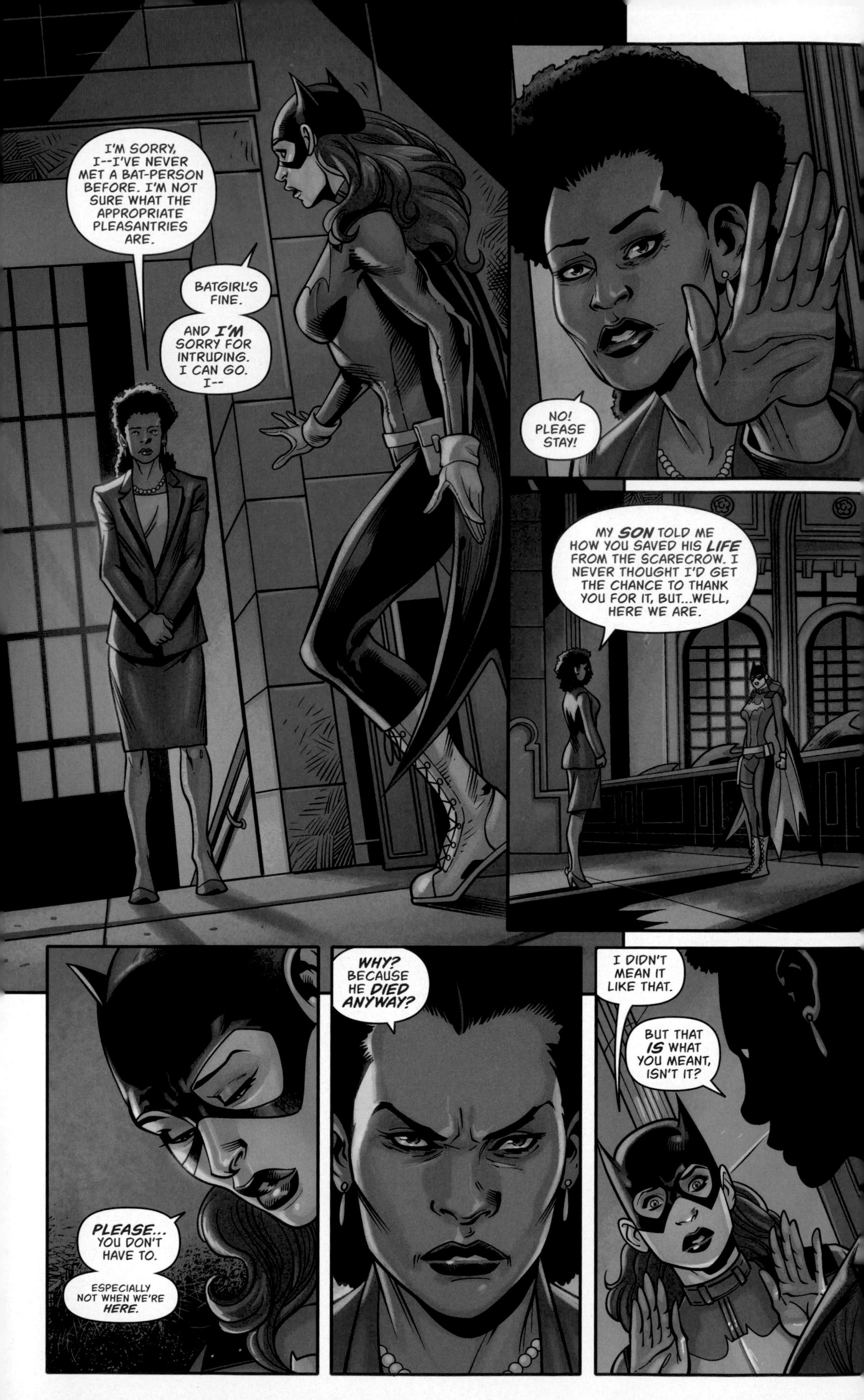
I'M SORRY, I--I'VE NEVER MET A BAT-PERSON BEFORE. I'M NOT SURE WHAT THE APPROPRIATE PLEASANTRIES ARE.
BATGIRL'S FINE.
AND I'M SORRY FOR INTRUDING. I CAN GO. I--
NO! PLEASE STAY!
MY SON TOLD ME HOW YOU SAVED HIS LIFE FROM THE SCARECROW. I NEVER THOUGHT I'D GET THE CHANCE TO THANK YOU FOR IT, BUT...WELL, HERE WE ARE.
PLEASE... YOU DON'T HAVE TO.
ESPECIALLY NOT WHEN WE'RE HERE.
WHY? BECAUSE HE DIED ANYWAY?
I DIDN'T MEAN IT LIKE THAT.
BUT THAT IS WHAT YOU MEANT, ISN'T IT?

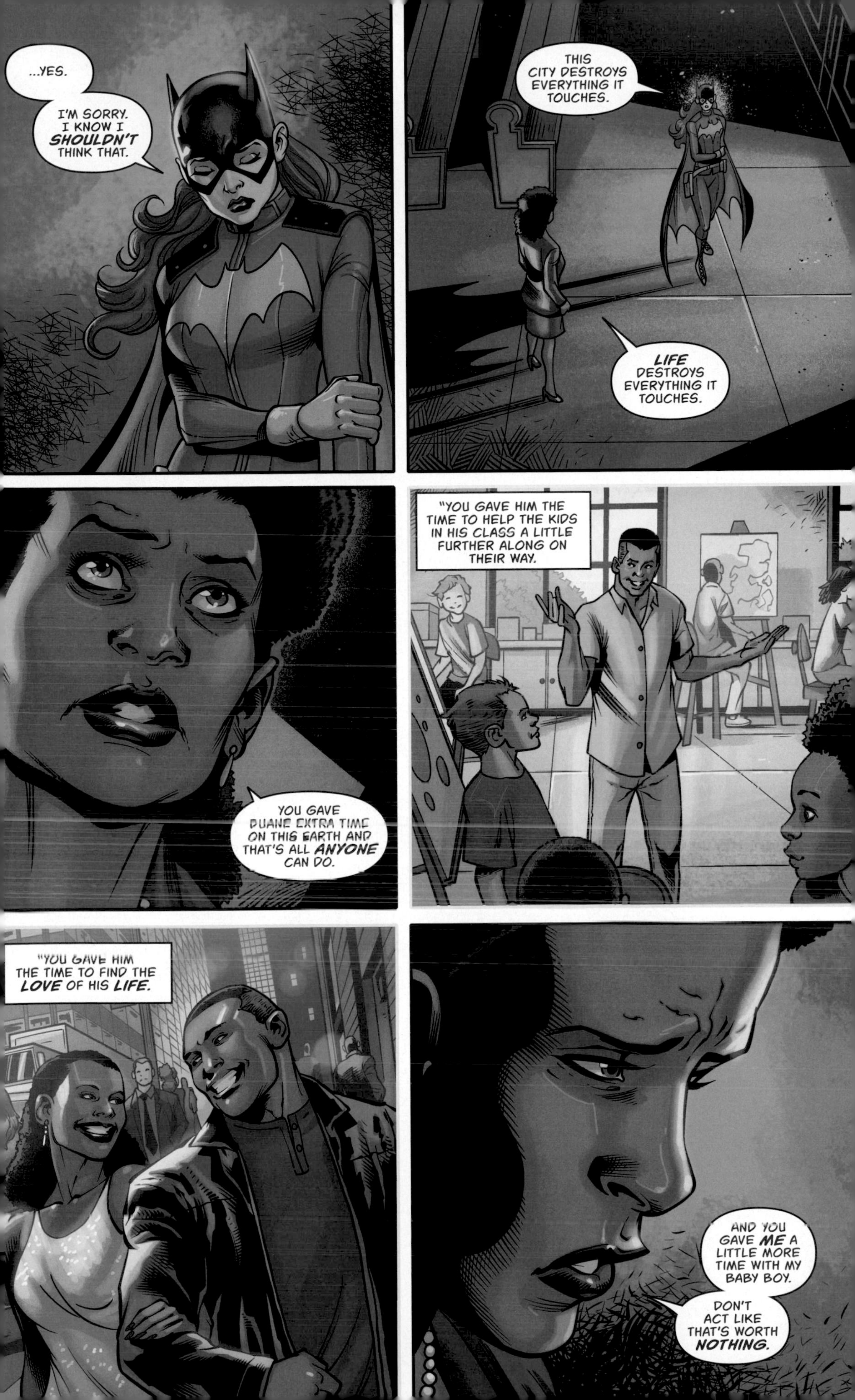
...YES.
I'M SORRY. I KNOW I SHOULDN'T THINK THAT.
THIS CITY DESTROYS EVERYTHING IT TOUCHES.
LIFE DESTROYS EVERYTHING IT TOUCHES.
YOU GAVE DUANE EXTRA TIME ON THIS EARTH AND THAT'S ALL ANYONE CAN DO.
"YOU GAVE HIM THE TIME TO HELP THE KIDS IN HIS CLASS A LITTLE FURTHER ALONG ON THEIR WAY.
"YOU GAVE HIM THE TIME TO FIND THE LOVE OF HIS LIFE.
AND YOU GAVE ME A LITTLE MORE TIME WITH MY BABY BOY.
DON'T ACT LIKE THAT'S WORTH NOTHING.

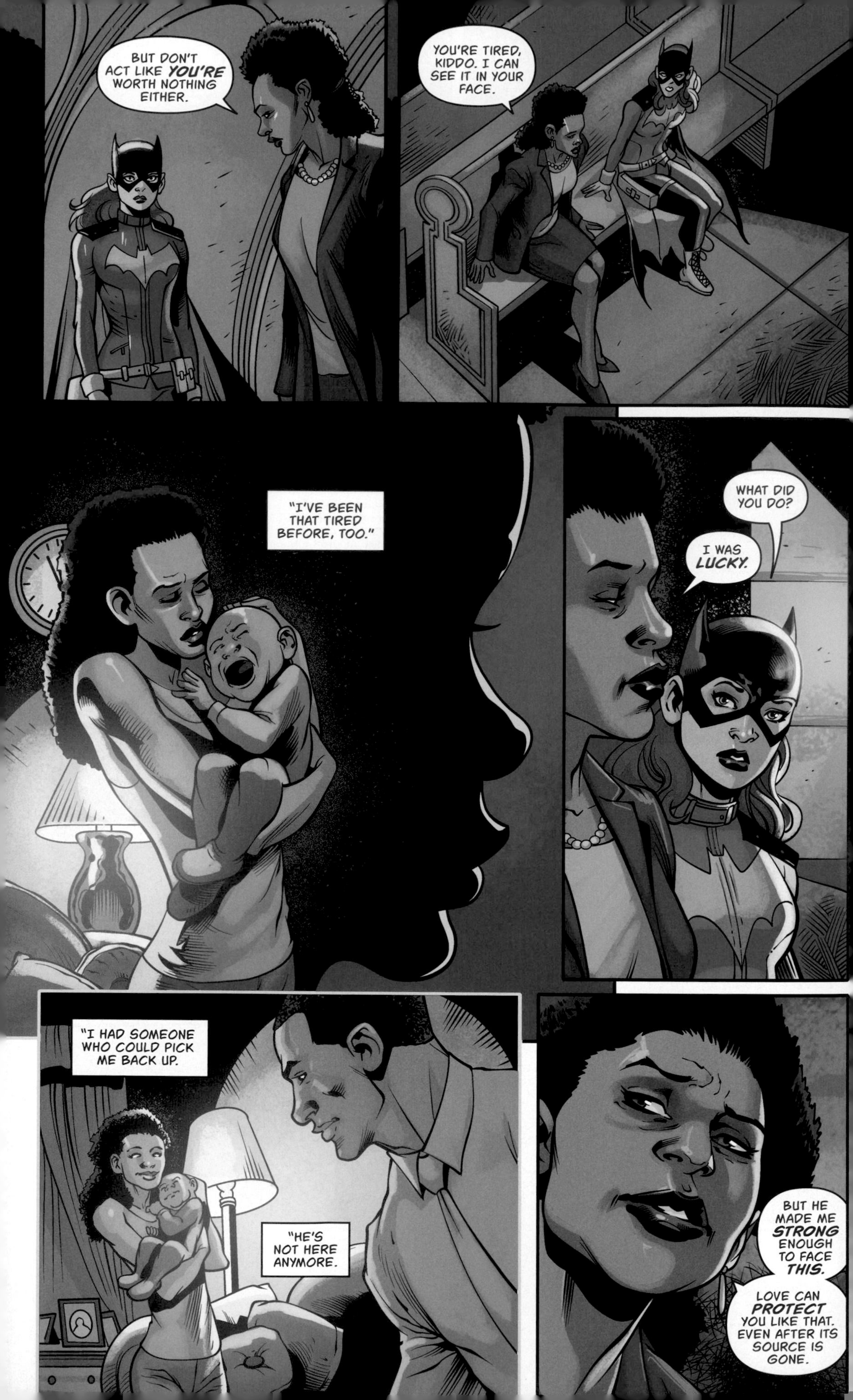
BUT DON'T ACT LIKE YOU'RE WORTH NOTHING EITHER.
YOU'RE TIRED, KIDDO. I CAN SEE IT IN YOUR FACE.
"I'VE BEEN THAT TIRED BEFORE, TOO."
WHAT DID YOU DO?
I WAS LUCKY.
"I HAD SOMEONE WHO COULD PICK ME BACK UP.
"HE'S NOT HERE ANYMORE.
BUT HE MADE ME STRONG ENOUGH TO FACE THIS.
LOVE CAN PROTECT YOU LIKE THAT. EVEN AFTER ITS SOURCE IS GONE.

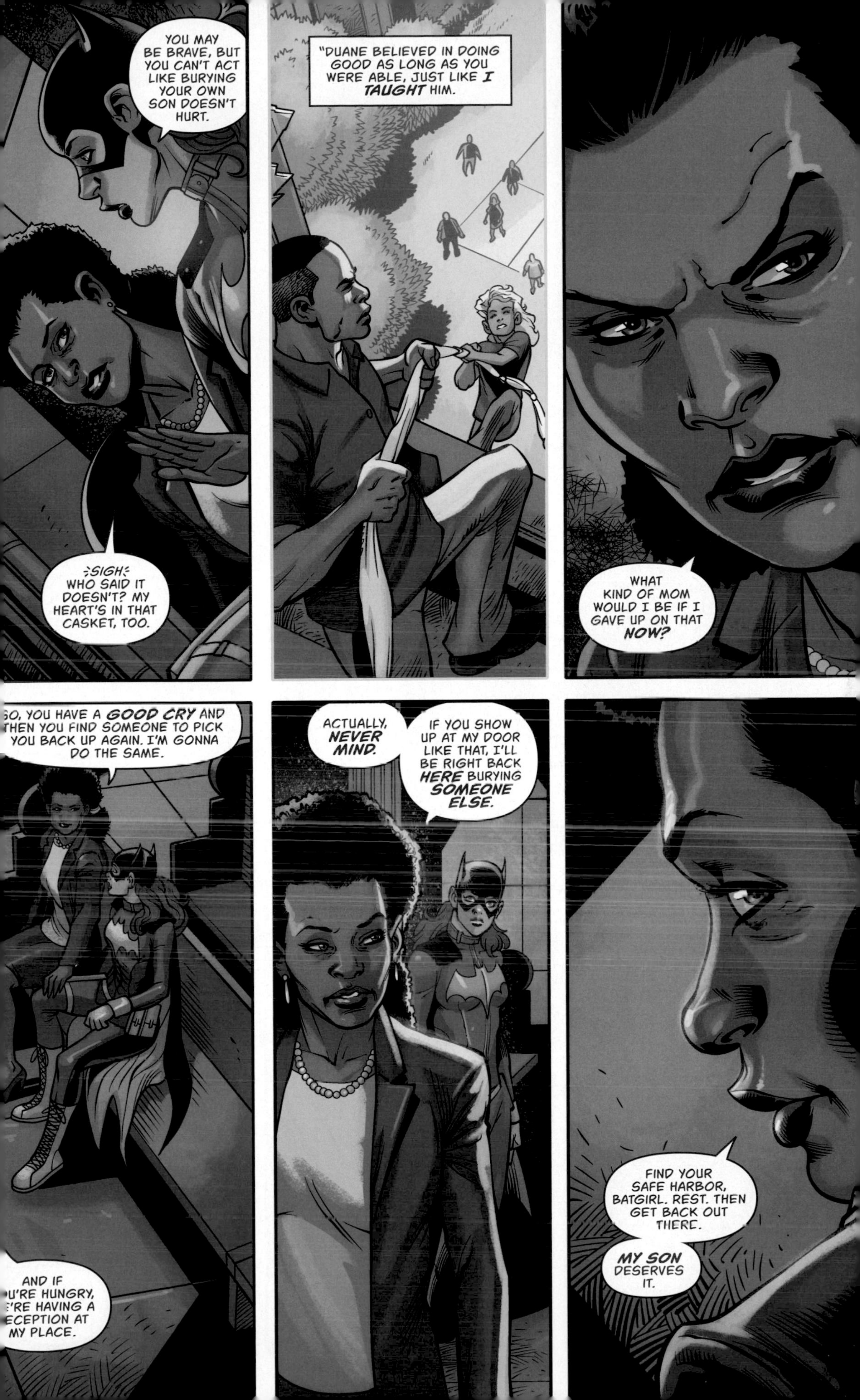
YOU MAY BE BRAVE, BUT YOU CAN'T ACT LIKE BURYING YOUR OWN SON DOESN'T HURT.
SIGH
WHO SAID IT DOESN'T? MY HEART'S IN THAT CASKET, TOO.
"DUANE BELIEVED IN DOING GOOD AS LONG AS YOU WERE ABLE, JUST LIKE I TAUGHT HIM.
WHAT KIND OF MOM WOULD I BE IF I GAVE UP ON THAT NOW?
SO, YOU HAVE A GOOD CRY AND THEN YOU FIND SOMEONE TO PICK YOU BACK UP AGAIN. I'M GONNA DO THE SAME.
AND IF ...U'RE HUNGRY, ...E'RE HAVING A ...ECEPTION AT MY PLACE.
ACTUALLY, NEVER MIND.
IF YOU SHOW UP AT MY DOOR LIKE THAT, I'LL BE RIGHT BACK HERE BURYING SOMEONE ELSE.
FIND YOUR SAFE HARBOR, BATGIRL. REST. THEN GET BACK OUT THERE.
MY SON DESERVES IT.

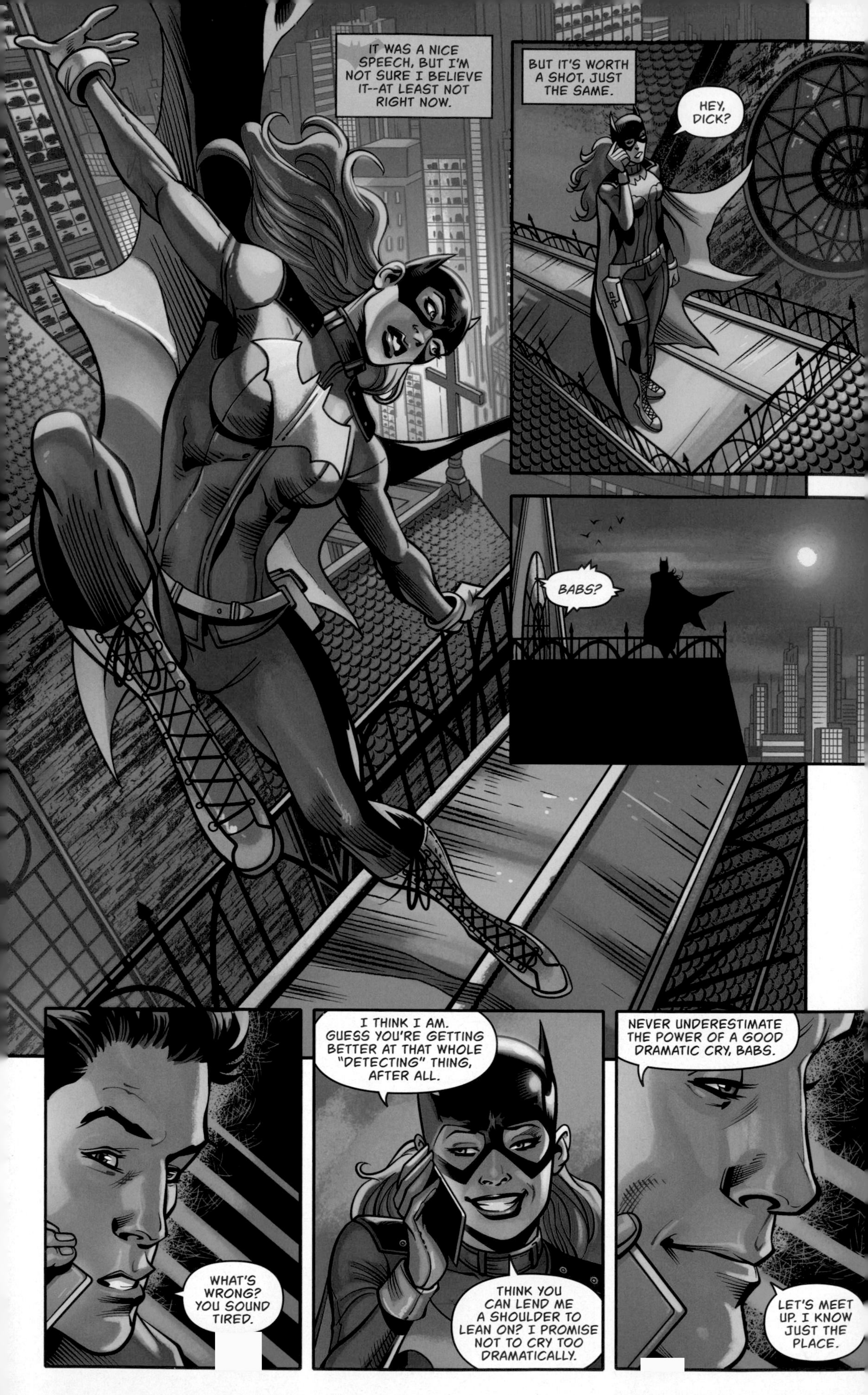

IT WAS A NICE SPEECH, BUT I'M NOT SURE I BELIEVE IT--AT LEAST NOT RIGHT NOW.
BUT IT'S WORTH A SHOT, JUST THE SAME.
HEY, DICK?
BABS?
WHAT'S WRONG? YOU SOUND TIRED.
I THINK I AM. GUESS YOU'RE GETTING BETTER AT THAT WHOLE "DETECTING" THING, AFTER ALL.
THINK YOU CAN LEND ME A SHOULDER TO LEAN ON? I PROMISE NOT TO CRY TOO DRAMATICALLY.
NEVER UNDERESTIMATE THE POWER OF A GOOD DRAMATIC CRY, BABS.
LET'S MEET UP. I KNOW JUST THE PLACE.

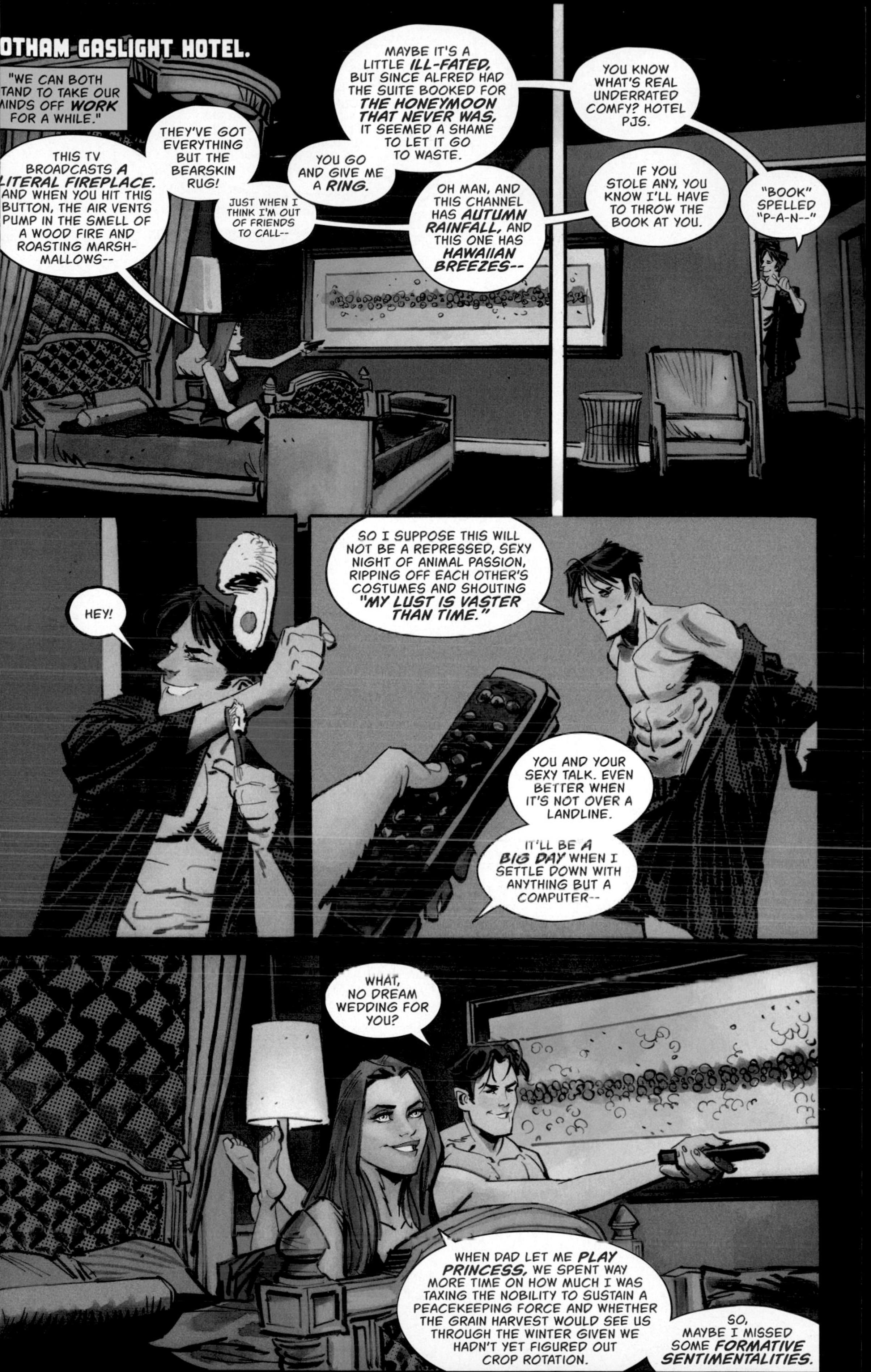
OTHAM GASLIGHT HOTEL.
"WE CAN BOTH TAND TO TAKE OUR MINDS OFF WORK FOR A WHILE."
THIS TV BROADCASTS A LITERAL FIREPLACE. AND WHEN YOU HIT THIS BUTTON, THE AIR VENTS PUMP IN THE SMELL OF A WOOD FIRE AND ROASTING MARSH-MALLOWS--
THEY'VE GOT EVERYTHING BUT THE BEARSKIN RUG!
JUST WHEN I THINK I'M OUT OF FRIENDS TO CALL--
YOU GO AND GIVE ME A RING.
MAYBE IT'S A LITTLE ILL-FATED, BUT SINCE ALFRED HAD THE SUITE BOOKED FOR THE HONEYMOON THAT NEVER WAS, IT SEEMED A SHAME TO LET IT GO TO WASTE.
OH MAN, AND THIS CHANNEL HAS AUTUMN RAINFALL, AND THIS ONE HAS HAWAIIAN BREEZES--
YOU KNOW WHAT'S REAL UNDERRATED COMFY? HOTEL PJS.
IF YOU STOLE ANY, YOU KNOW I'LL HAVE TO THROW THE BOOK AT YOU.
"BOOK" SPELLED "P-A-N--"
HEY!
SO I SUPPOSE THIS WILL NOT BE A REPRESSED, SEXY NIGHT OF ANIMAL PASSION, RIPPING OFF EACH OTHER'S COSTUMES AND SHOUTING "MY LUST IS VASTER THAN TIME."
YOU AND YOUR SEXY TALK. EVEN BETTER WHEN IT'S NOT OVER A LANDLINE.
IT'LL BE A BIG DAY WHEN I SETTLE DOWN WITH ANYTHING BUT A COMPUTER--
WHAT, NO DREAM WEDDING FOR YOU?
WHEN DAD LET ME PLAY PRINCESS, WE SPENT WAY MORE TIME ON HOW MUCH I WAS TAXING THE NOBILITY TO SUSTAIN A PEACEKEEPING FORCE AND WHETHER THE GRAIN HARVEST WOULD SEE US THROUGH THE WINTER GIVEN WE HADN'T YET FIGURED OUT CROP ROTATION.
SO, MAYBE I MISSED SOME FORMATIVE SENTIMENTALITIES.

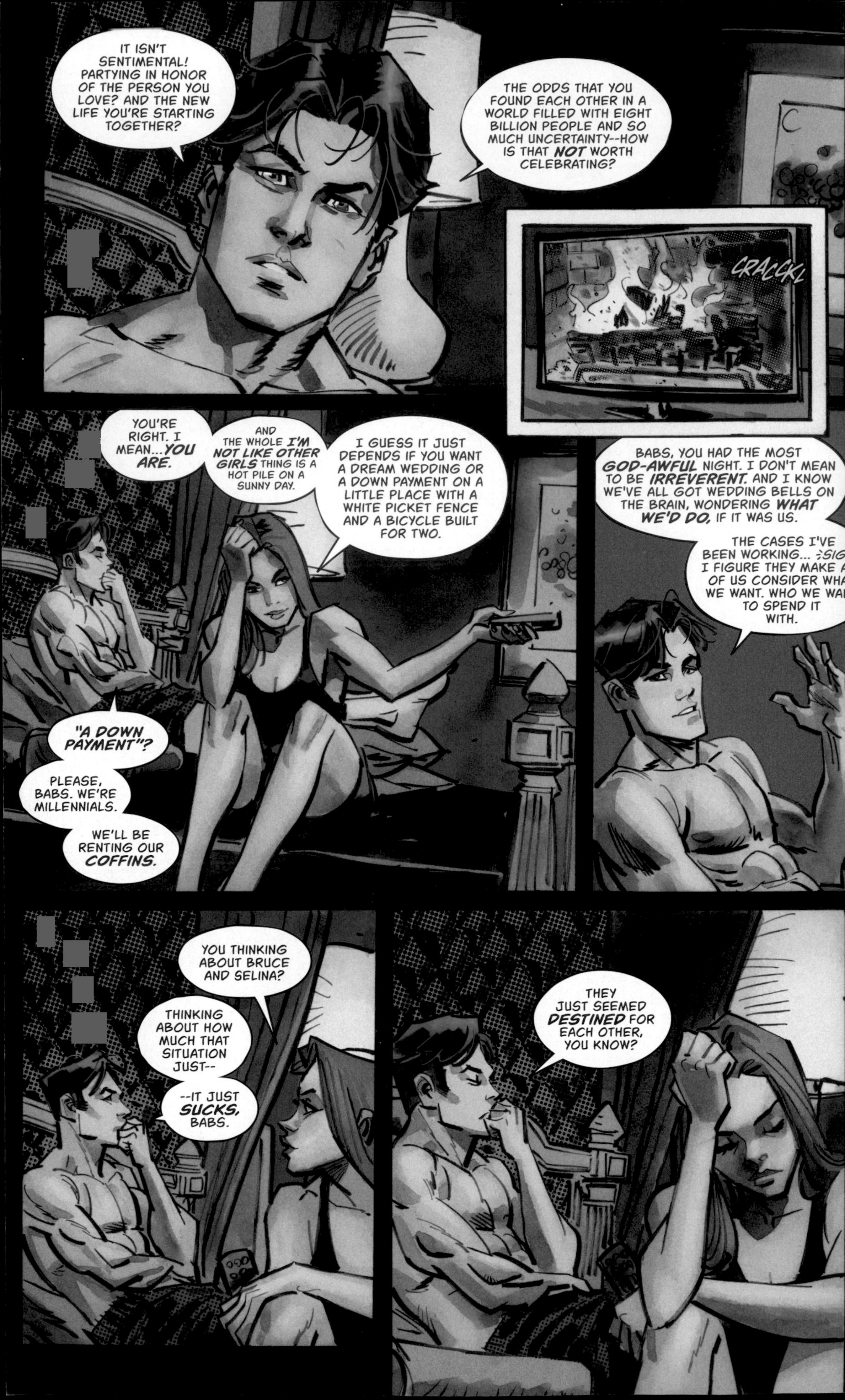

IT ISN'T SENTIMENTAL! PARTYING IN HONOR OF THE PERSON YOU LOVE? AND THE NEW LIFE YOU'RE STARTING TOGETHER?
THE ODDS THAT YOU FOUND EACH OTHER IN A WORLD FILLED WITH EIGHT BILLION PEOPLE AND SO MUCH UNCERTAINTY--HOW IS THAT NOT WORTH CELEBRATING?
CRACCKL
YOU'RE RIGHT. I MEAN...YOU ARE.
AND THE WHOLE I'M NOT LIKE OTHER GIRLS THING IS A HOT PILE ON A SUNNY DAY.
I GUESS IT JUST DEPENDS IF YOU WANT A DREAM WEDDING OR A DOWN PAYMENT ON A LITTLE PLACE WITH A WHITE PICKET FENCE AND A BICYCLE BUILT FOR TWO.
"A DOWN PAYMENT"?
PLEASE, BABS. WE'RE MILLENNIALS.
WE'LL BE RENTING OUR COFFINS.
BABS, YOU HAD THE MOST GOD-AWFUL NIGHT. I DON'T MEAN TO BE IRREVERENT. AND I KNOW WE'VE ALL GOT WEDDING BELLS ON THE BRAIN, WONDERING WHAT WE'D DO, IF IT WAS US.
THE CASES I'VE BEEN WORKING... I FIGURE THEY MAKE OF US CONSIDER WE WANT. WHO WE TO SPEND IT WITH.
YOU THINKING ABOUT BRUCE AND SELINA?
THINKING ABOUT HOW MUCH THAT SITUATION JUST--
--IT JUST SUCKS, BABS.
THEY JUST SEEMED DESTINED FOR EACH OTHER, YOU KNOW?

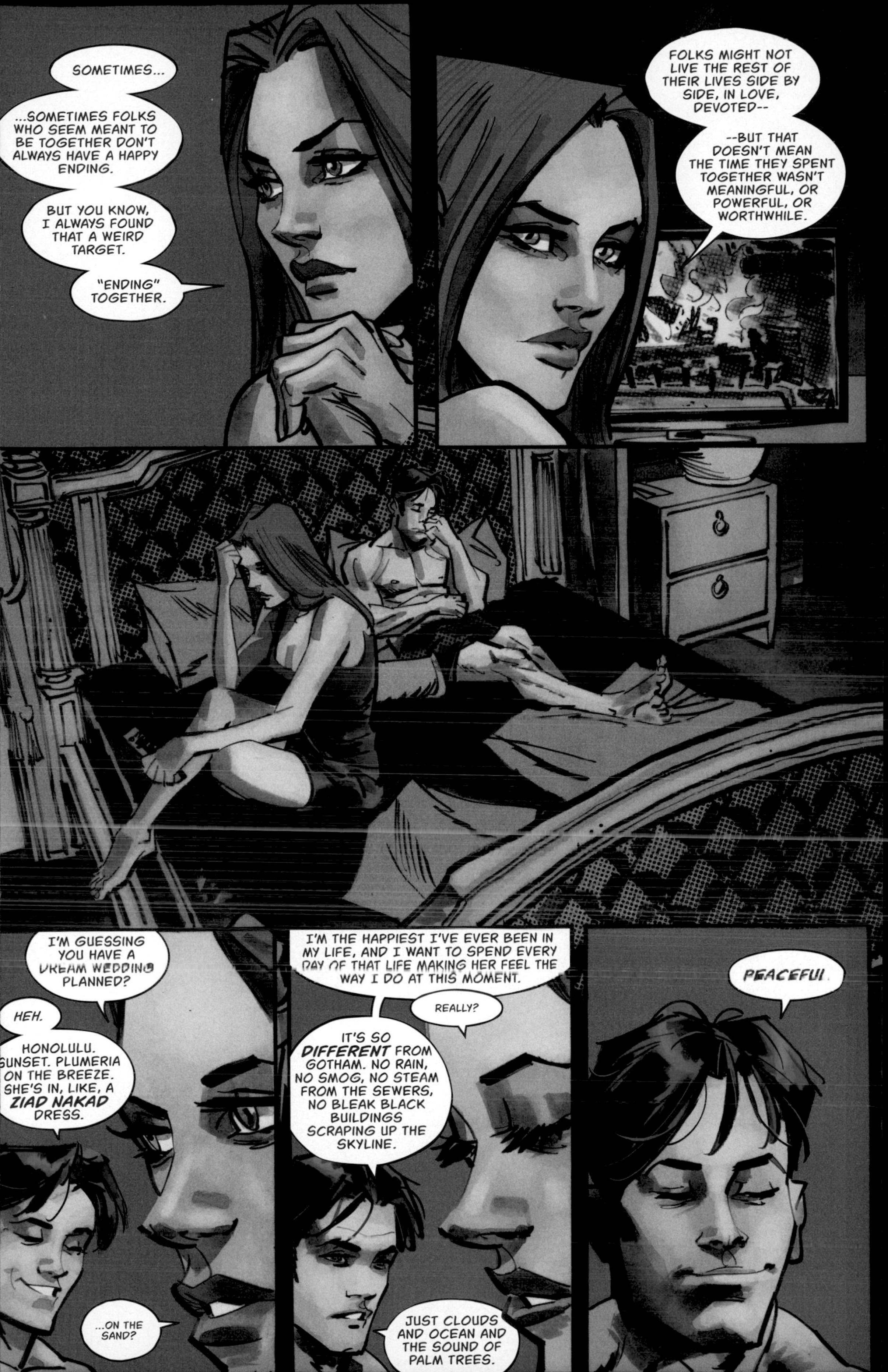
SOMETIMES...
...SOMETIMES FOLKS WHO SEEM MEANT TO BE TOGETHER DON'T ALWAYS HAVE A HAPPY ENDING.
BUT YOU KNOW, I ALWAYS FOUND THAT A WEIRD TARGET.
"ENDING" TOGETHER.
FOLKS MIGHT NOT LIVE THE REST OF THEIR LIVES SIDE BY SIDE, IN LOVE, DEVOTED--
--BUT THAT DOESN'T MEAN THE TIME THEY SPENT TOGETHER WASN'T MEANINGFUL, OR POWERFUL, OR WORTHWHILE.
I'M GUESSING YOU HAVE A DREAM WEDDING PLANNED?
HEH.
HONOLULU. SUNSET. PLUMERIA ON THE BREEZE. SHE'S IN, LIKE, A ZIAD NAKAD DRESS.
...ON THE SAND?
I'M THE HAPPIEST I'VE EVER BEEN IN MY LIFE, AND I WANT TO SPEND EVERY DAY OF THAT LIFE MAKING HER FEEL THE WAY I DO AT THIS MOMENT.
REALLY?
IT'S SO DIFFERENT FROM GOTHAM. NO RAIN, NO SMOG, NO STEAM FROM THE SEWERS, NO BLEAK BLACK BUILDINGS SCRAPING UP THE SKYLINE.
JUST CLOUDS AND OCEAN AND THE SOUND OF PALM TREES.
PEACEFUL.

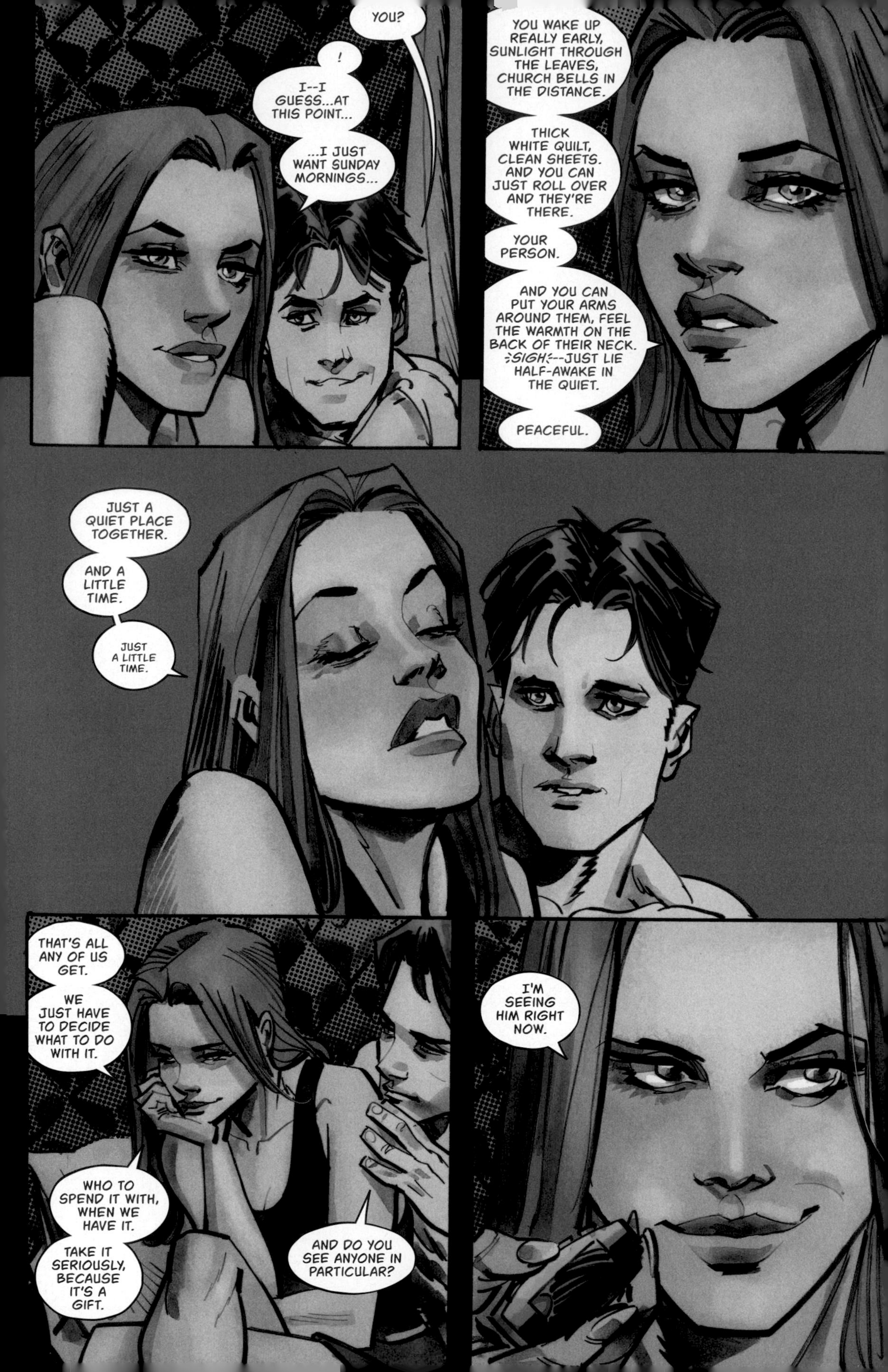
YOU?
!
I--I GUESS...AT THIS POINT...
...I JUST WANT SUNDAY MORNINGS...
YOU WAKE UP REALLY EARLY, SUNLIGHT THROUGH THE LEAVES, CHURCH BELLS IN THE DISTANCE.
THICK WHITE QUILT, CLEAN SHEETS. AND YOU CAN JUST ROLL OVER AND THEY'RE THERE.
YOUR PERSON.
AND YOU CAN PUT YOUR ARMS AROUND THEM, FEEL THE WARMTH ON THE BACK OF THEIR NECK. *SIGH*--JUST LIE HALF-AWAKE IN THE QUIET.
PEACEFUL.
JUST A QUIET PLACE TOGETHER.
AND A LITTLE TIME.
JUST A LITTLE TIME.
THAT'S ALL ANY OF US GET.
WE JUST HAVE TO DECIDE WHAT TO DO WITH IT.
WHO TO SPEND IT WITH, WHEN WE HAVE IT.
TAKE IT SERIOUSLY, BECAUSE IT'S A GIFT.
AND DO YOU SEE ANYONE IN PARTICULAR?
I'M SEEING HIM RIGHT NOW.

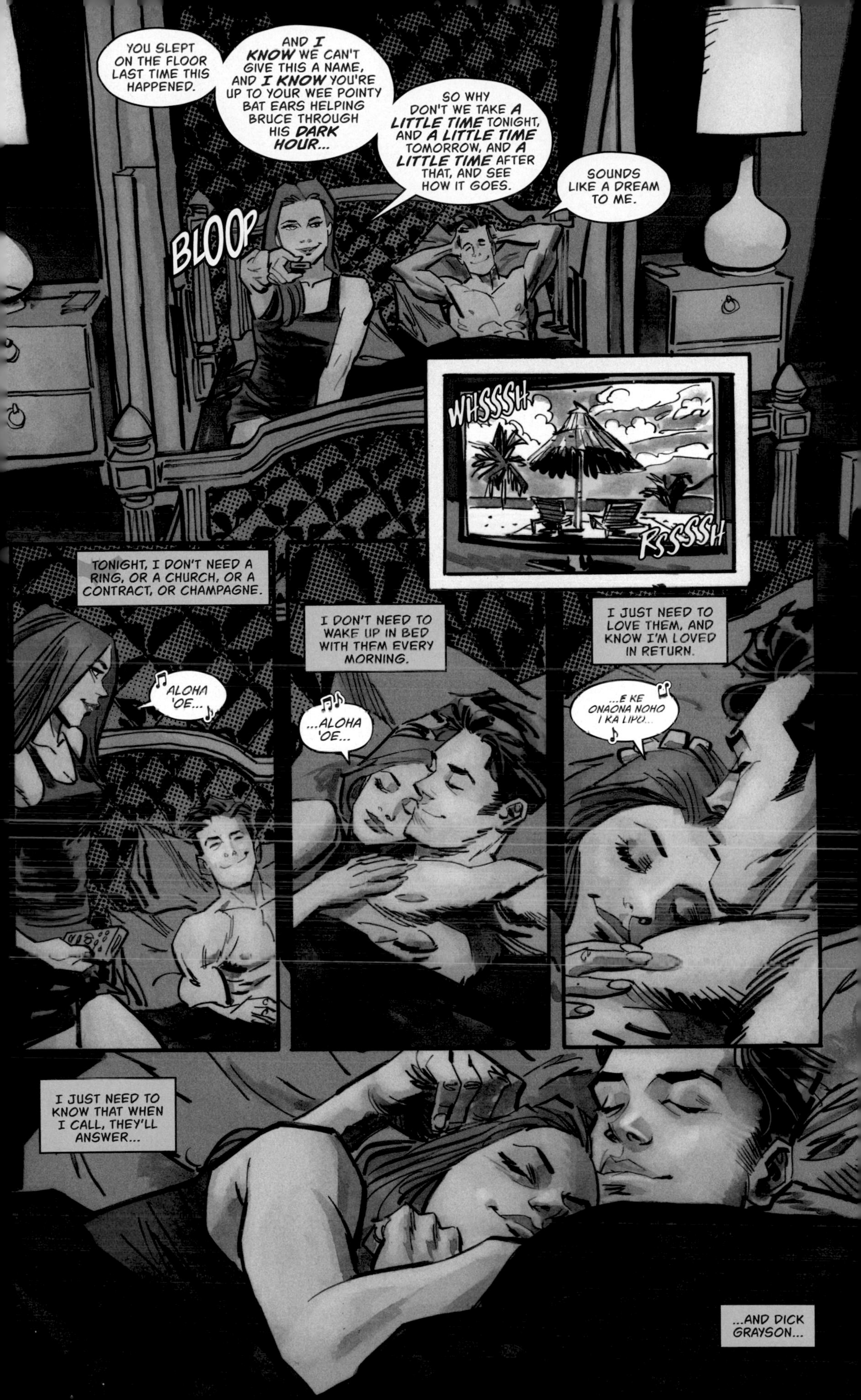

YOU SLEPT ON THE FLOOR LAST TIME THIS HAPPENED.
AND I KNOW WE CAN'T GIVE THIS A NAME, AND I KNOW YOU'RE UP TO YOUR WEE POINTY BAT EARS HELPING BRUCE THROUGH HIS DARK HOUR...
SO WHY DON'T WE TAKE A LITTLE TIME TONIGHT, AND A LITTLE TIME TOMORROW, AND A LITTLE TIME AFTER THAT, AND SEE HOW IT GOES.
SOUNDS LIKE A DREAM TO ME.
BLOOP
WHSSSSH
RSSSSSH
TONIGHT, I DON'T NEED A RING, OR A CHURCH, OR A CONTRACT, OR CHAMPAGNE.
ALOHA 'OE...
I DON'T NEED TO WAKE UP IN BED WITH THEM EVERY MORNING.
...ALOHA 'OE...
I JUST NEED TO LOVE THEM, AND KNOW I'M LOVED IN RETURN.
...E KE ONAONA NOHO I KA LIPO...
I JUST NEED TO KNOW THAT WHEN I CALL, THEY'LL ANSWER...
...AND DICK GRAYSON...

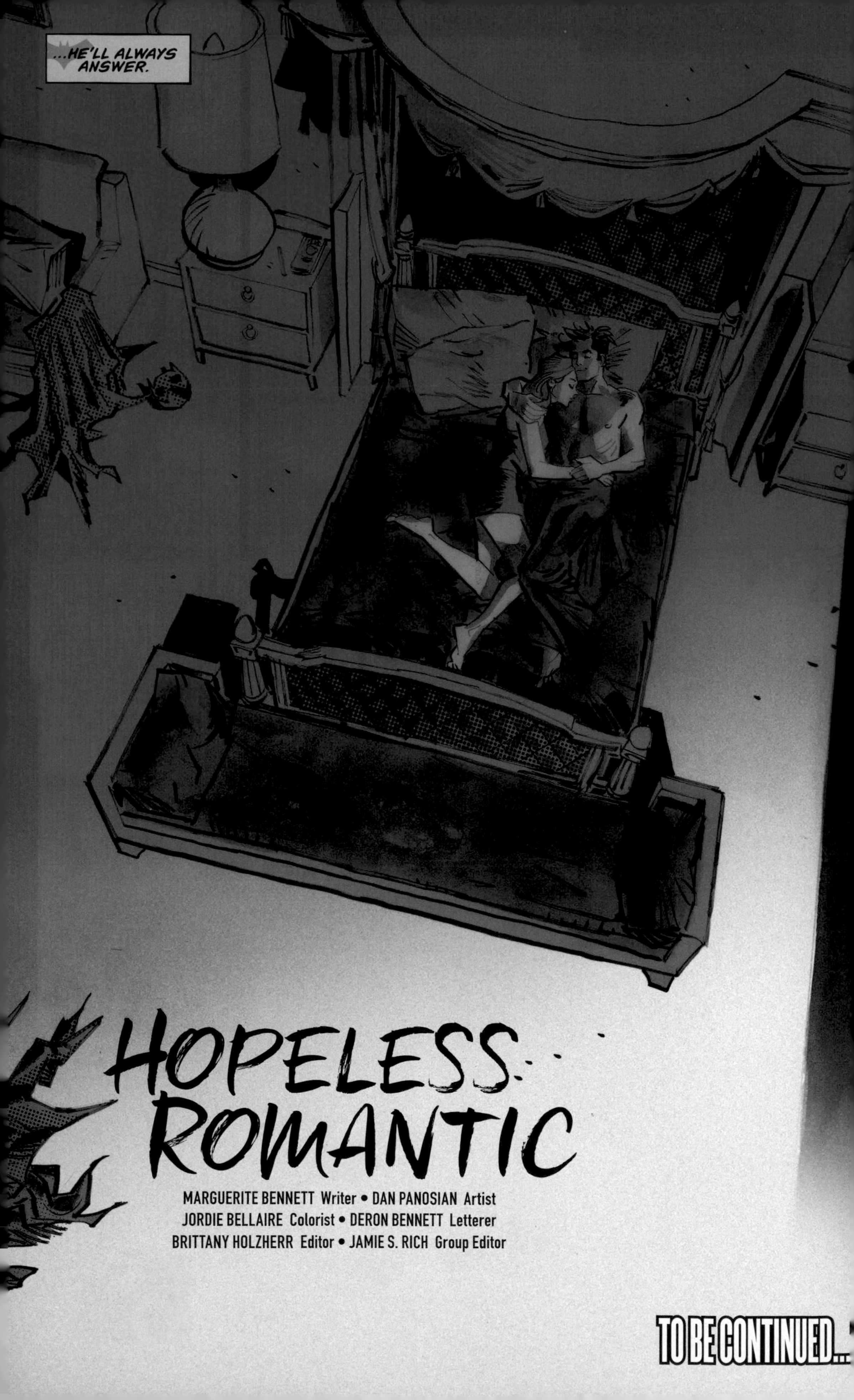
...HE'LL ALWAYS ANSWER.
HOPELESS ROMANTIC
MARGUERITE BENNETT Writer • DAN PANOSIAN Artist
JORDIE BELLAIRE Colorist • DERON BENNETT Letterer
BRITTANY HOLZHERR Editor • JAMIE S. RICH Group Editor
TO BE CONTINUED...

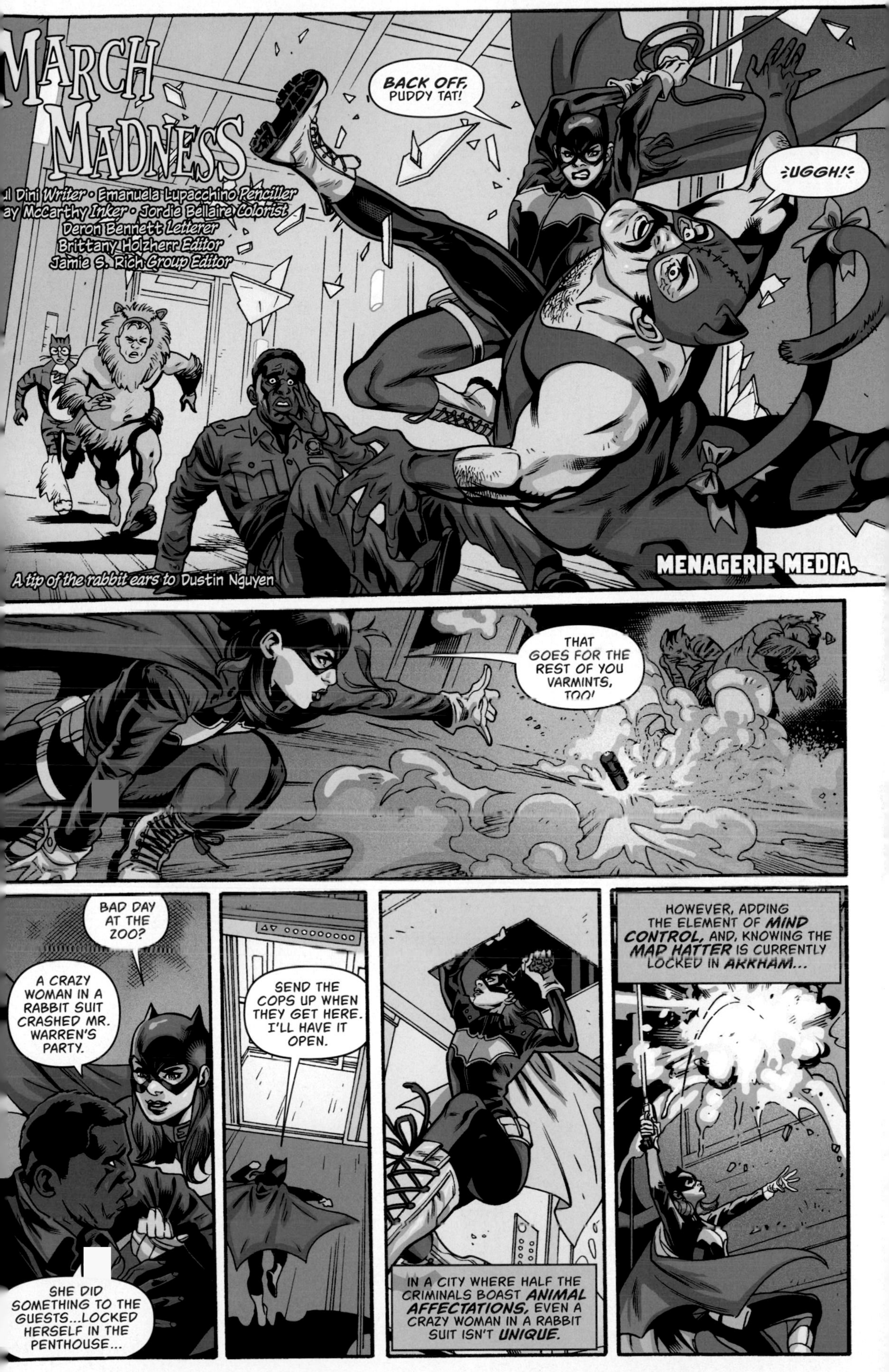
MARCH MADNESS
ul Dini Writer • Emanuela Lupacchino Penciller
ay McCarthy Inker • Jordie Bellaire Colorist
Deron Bennett Letterer
Brittany Holzherr Editor
Jamie S. Rich Group Editor
BACK OFF, PUDDY TAT!
UGGH!
MENAGERIE MEDIA.
A tip of the rabbit ears to Dustin Nguyen
THAT GOES FOR THE REST OF YOU VARMINTS, TOO!
BAD DAY AT THE ZOO?
A CRAZY WOMAN IN A RABBIT SUIT CRASHED MR. WARREN'S PARTY.
SHE DID SOMETHING TO THE GUESTS...LOCKED HERSELF IN THE PENTHOUSE...
SEND THE COPS UP WHEN THEY GET HERE. I'LL HAVE IT OPEN.
IN A CITY WHERE HALF THE CRIMINALS BOAST ANIMAL AFFECTATIONS, EVEN A CRAZY WOMAN IN A RABBIT SUIT ISN'T UNIQUE.
HOWEVER, ADDING THE ELEMENT OF MIND CONTROL, AND, KNOWING THE MAD HATTER IS CURRENTLY LOCKED IN ARKHAM...

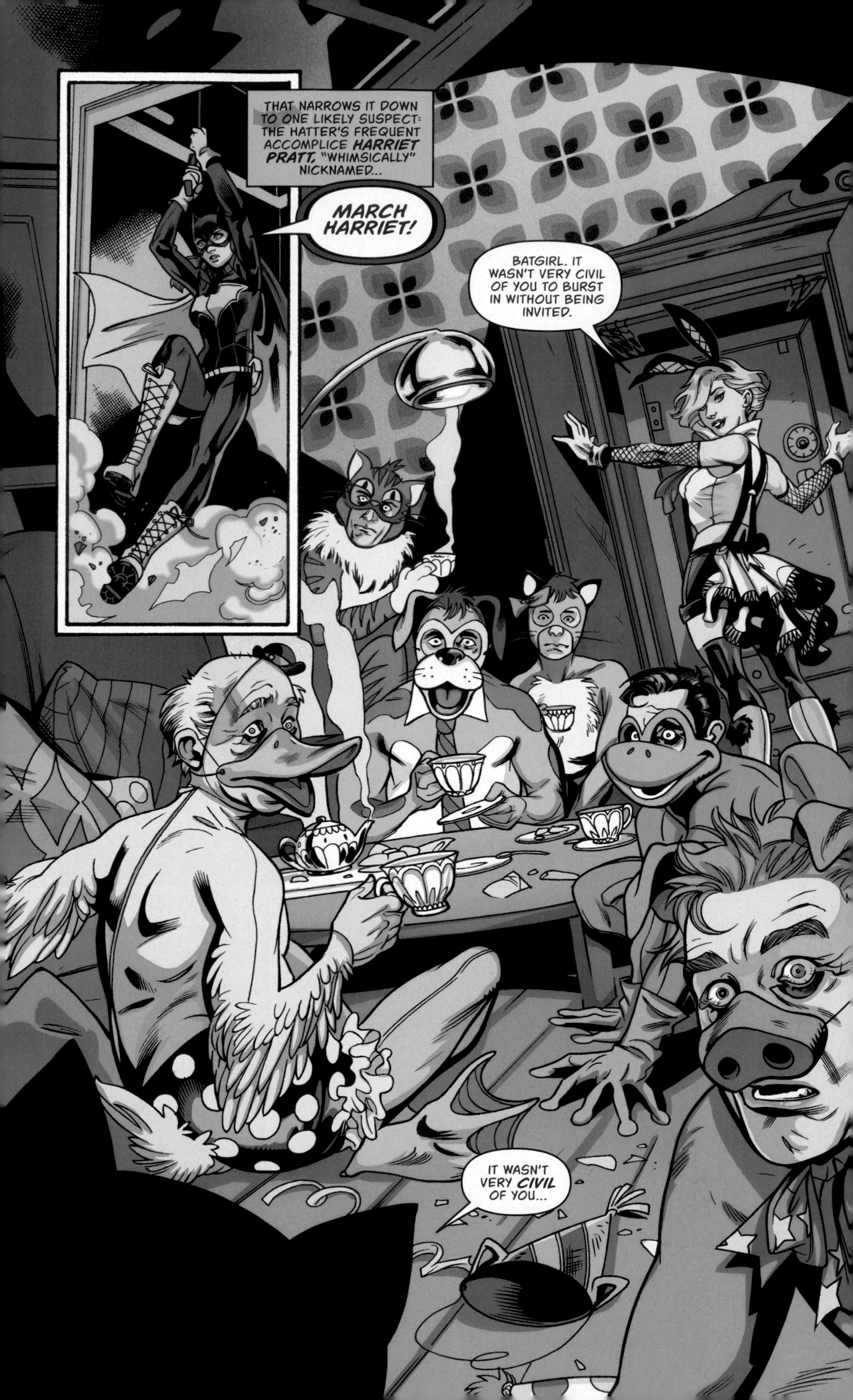

THAT NARROWS IT DOWN TO ONE LIKELY SUSPECT: THE HATTER'S FREQUENT ACCOMPLICE HARRIET PRATT, "WHIMSICALLY" NICKNAMED...
MARCH HARRIET!
BATGIRL. IT WASN'T VERY CIVIL OF YOU TO BURST IN WITHOUT BEING INVITED.
IT WASN'T VERY CIVIL OF YOU...

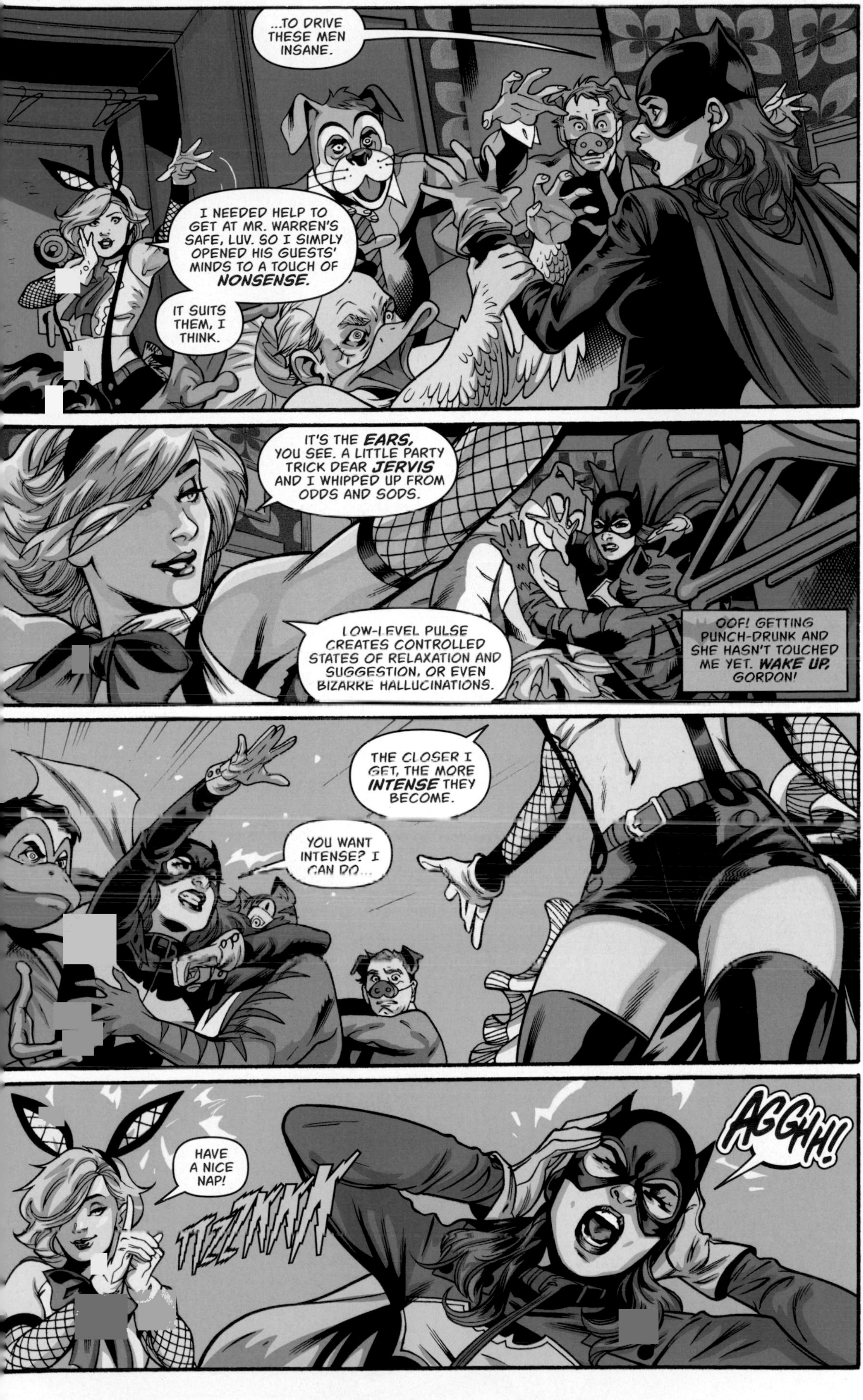
...TO DRIVE THESE MEN INSANE.
I NEEDED HELP TO GET AT MR. WARREN'S SAFE, LUV. SO I SIMPLY OPENED HIS GUESTS' MINDS TO A TOUCH OF NONSENSE.
IT SUITS THEM, I THINK.
IT'S THE EARS, YOU SEE. A LITTLE PARTY TRICK DEAR JERVIS AND I WHIPPED UP FROM ODDS AND SODS.
LOW-LEVEL PULSE CREATES CONTROLLED STATES OF RELAXATION AND SUGGESTION, OR EVEN BIZARRE HALLUCINATIONS.
OOF! GETTING PUNCH-DRUNK AND SHE HASN'T TOUCHED ME YET. WAKE UP, GORDON!
THE CLOSER I GET, THE MORE INTENSE THEY BECOME.
YOU WANT INTENSE? I CAN DO...
HAVE A NICE NAP!
AGGHH!

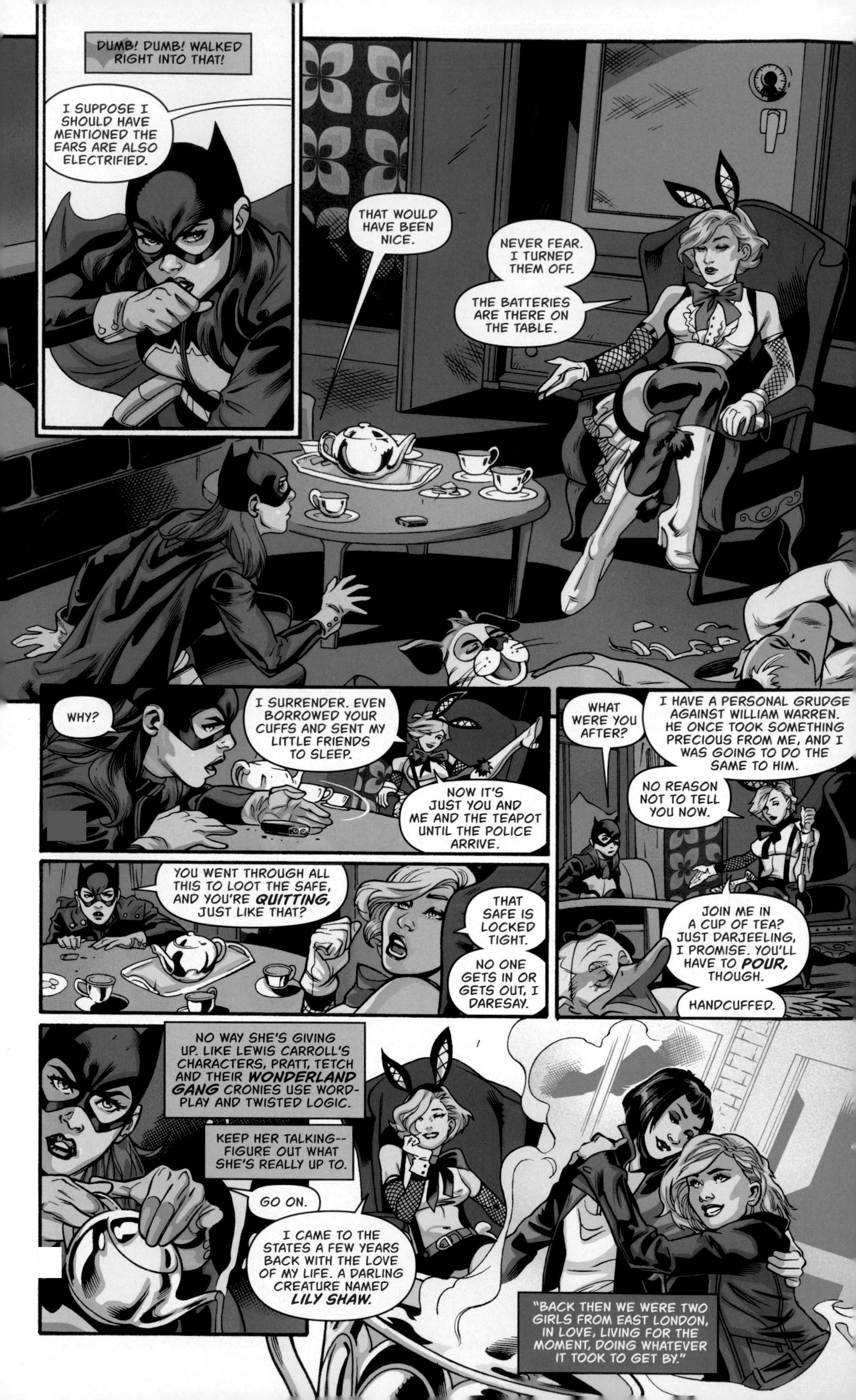
DUMB! DUMB! WALKED RIGHT INTO THAT!
I SUPPOSE I SHOULD HAVE MENTIONED THE EARS ARE ALSO ELECTRIFIED.
THAT WOULD HAVE BEEN NICE.
NEVER FEAR. I TURNED THEM OFF.
THE BATTERIES ARE THERE ON THE TABLE.
WHY?
I SURRENDER. EVEN BORROWED YOUR CUFFS AND SENT MY LITTLE FRIENDS TO SLEEP.
NOW IT'S JUST YOU AND ME AND THE TEAPOT UNTIL THE POLICE ARRIVE.
YOU WENT THROUGH ALL THIS TO LOOT THE SAFE, AND YOU'RE QUITTING, JUST LIKE THAT?
THAT SAFE IS LOCKED TIGHT.
NO ONE GETS IN OR GETS OUT, I DARESAY.
WHAT WERE YOU AFTER?
I HAVE A PERSONAL GRUDGE AGAINST WILLIAM WARREN. HE ONCE TOOK SOMETHING PRECIOUS FROM ME, AND I WAS GOING TO DO THE SAME TO HIM.
NO REASON NOT TO TELL YOU NOW.
JOIN ME IN A CUP OF TEA? JUST DARJEELING, I PROMISE. YOU'LL HAVE TO POUR, THOUGH.
HANDCUFFED.
NO WAY SHE'S GIVING UP. LIKE LEWIS CARROLL'S CHARACTERS, PRATT, TETCH AND THEIR WONDERLAND GANG CRONIES USE WORD-PLAY AND TWISTED LOGIC.
KEEP HER TALKING-- FIGURE OUT WHAT SHE'S REALLY UP TO.
GO ON.
I CAME TO THE STATES A FEW YEARS BACK WITH THE LOVE OF MY LIFE. A DARLING CREATURE NAMED LILY SHAW.
"BACK THEN WE WERE TWO GIRLS FROM EAST LONDON, IN LOVE, LIVING FOR THE MOMENT, DOING WHATEVER IT TOOK TO GET BY."

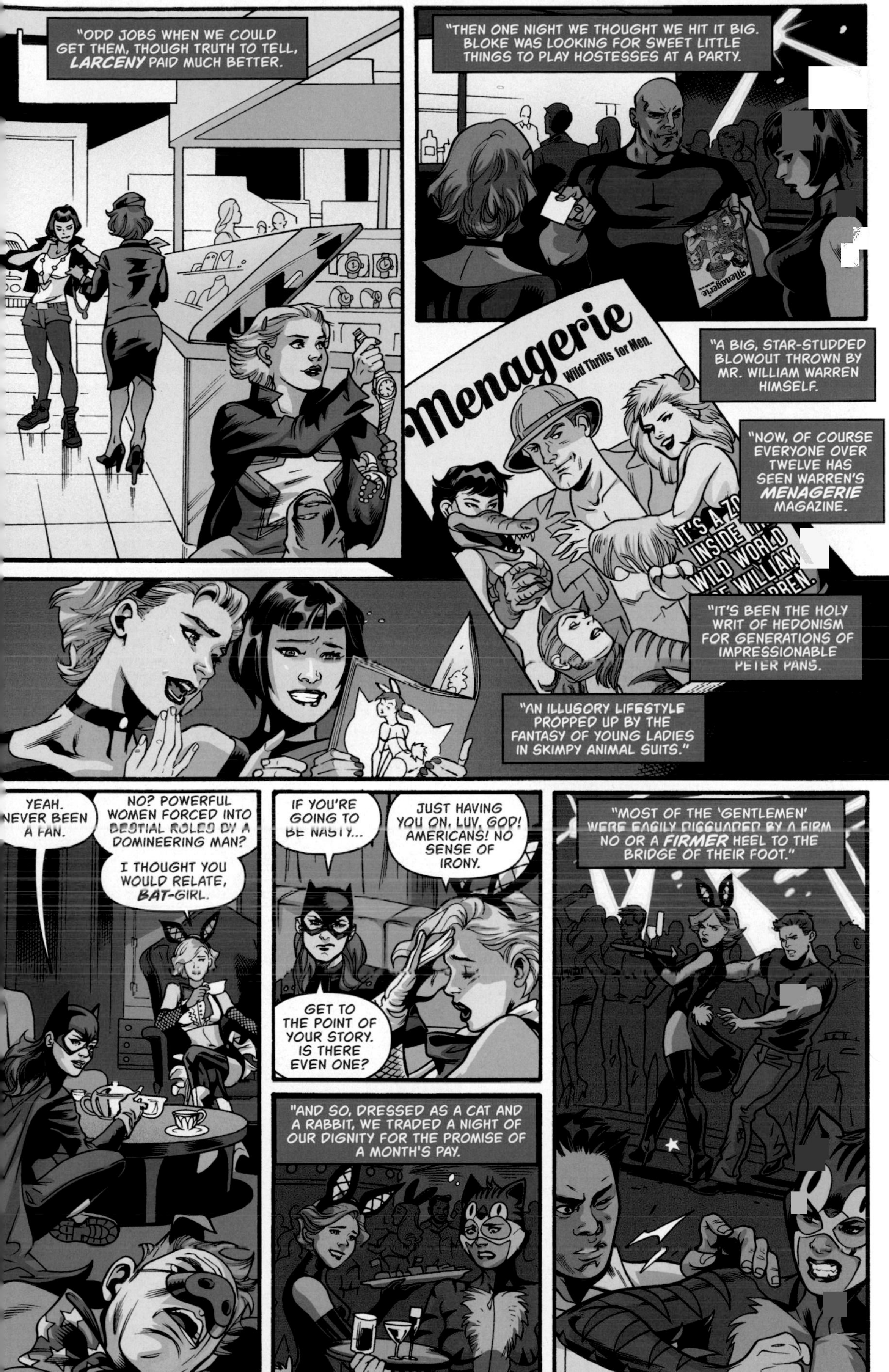
"ODD JOBS WHEN WE COULD GET THEM, THOUGH TRUTH TO TELL, LARCENY PAID MUCH BETTER.
"THEN ONE NIGHT WE THOUGHT WE HIT IT BIG. BLOKE WAS LOOKING FOR SWEET LITTLE THINGS TO PLAY HOSTESSES AT A PARTY.
Menagerie
Wild Thrills for Men.
"A BIG, STAR-STUDDED BLOWOUT THROWN BY MR. WILLIAM WARREN HIMSELF.
"NOW, OF COURSE EVERYONE OVER TWELVE HAS SEEN WARREN'S MENAGERIE MAGAZINE.
"IT'S BEEN THE HOLY WRIT OF HEDONISM FOR GENERATIONS OF IMPRESSIONABLE PETER PANS.
"AN ILLUSORY LIFESTYLE PROPPED UP BY THE FANTASY OF YOUNG LADIES IN SKIMPY ANIMAL SUITS."
YEAH. NEVER BEEN A FAN.
NO? POWERFUL WOMEN FORCED INTO BESTIAL ROLES BY A DOMINEERING MAN?
I THOUGHT YOU WOULD RELATE, BAT-GIRL.
IF YOU'RE GOING TO BE NASTY...
JUST HAVING YOU ON, LUV. GOD! AMERICANS! NO SENSE OF IRONY.
GET TO THE POINT OF YOUR STORY. IS THERE EVEN ONE?
"AND SO, DRESSED AS A CAT AND A RABBIT, WE TRADED A NIGHT OF OUR DIGNITY FOR THE PROMISE OF A MONTH'S PAY.
"MOST OF THE 'GENTLEMEN' WERE EASILY DISSUADED BY A FIRM NO OR A FIRMER HEEL TO THE BRIDGE OF THEIR FOOT."

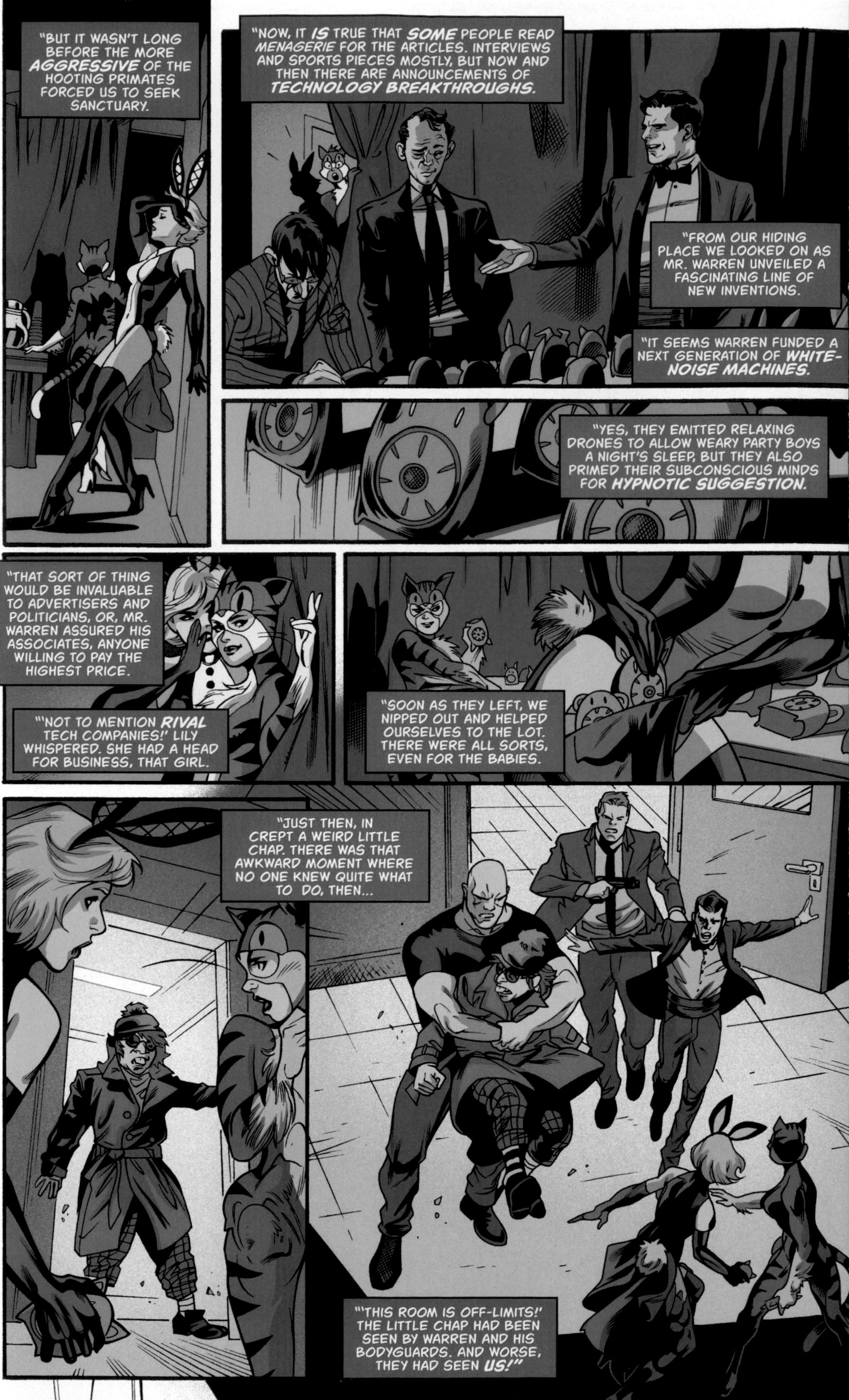
"BUT IT WASN'T LONG BEFORE THE MORE AGGRESSIVE OF THE HOOTING PRIMATES FORCED US TO SEEK SANCTUARY.
"NOW, IT IS TRUE THAT SOME PEOPLE READ MENAGERIE FOR THE ARTICLES. INTERVIEWS AND SPORTS PIECES MOSTLY, BUT NOW AND THEN THERE ARE ANNOUNCEMENTS OF TECHNOLOGY BREAKTHROUGHS.
"FROM OUR HIDING PLACE WE LOOKED ON AS MR. WARREN UNVEILED A FASCINATING LINE OF NEW INVENTIONS.
"IT SEEMS WARREN FUNDED A NEXT GENERATION OF WHITE-NOISE MACHINES.
"YES, THEY EMITTED RELAXING DRONES TO ALLOW WEARY PARTY BOYS A NIGHT'S SLEEP, BUT THEY ALSO PRIMED THEIR SUBCONSCIOUS MINDS FOR HYPNOTIC SUGGESTION.
"THAT SORT OF THING WOULD BE INVALUABLE TO ADVERTISERS AND POLITICIANS, OR, MR. WARREN ASSURED HIS ASSOCIATES, ANYONE WILLING TO PAY THE HIGHEST PRICE.
"'NOT TO MENTION RIVAL TECH COMPANIES!' LILY WHISPERED. SHE HAD A HEAD FOR BUSINESS, THAT GIRL.
"SOON AS THEY LEFT, WE NIPPED OUT AND HELPED OURSELVES TO THE LOT. THERE WERE ALL SORTS, EVEN FOR THE BABIES.
"JUST THEN, IN CREPT A WEIRD LITTLE CHAP. THERE WAS THAT AWKWARD MOMENT WHERE NO ONE KNEW QUITE WHAT TO DO, THEN...
"'THIS ROOM IS OFF-LIMITS!' THE LITTLE CHAP HAD BEEN SEEN BY WARREN AND HIS BODYGUARDS. AND WORSE, THEY HAD SEEN US!"

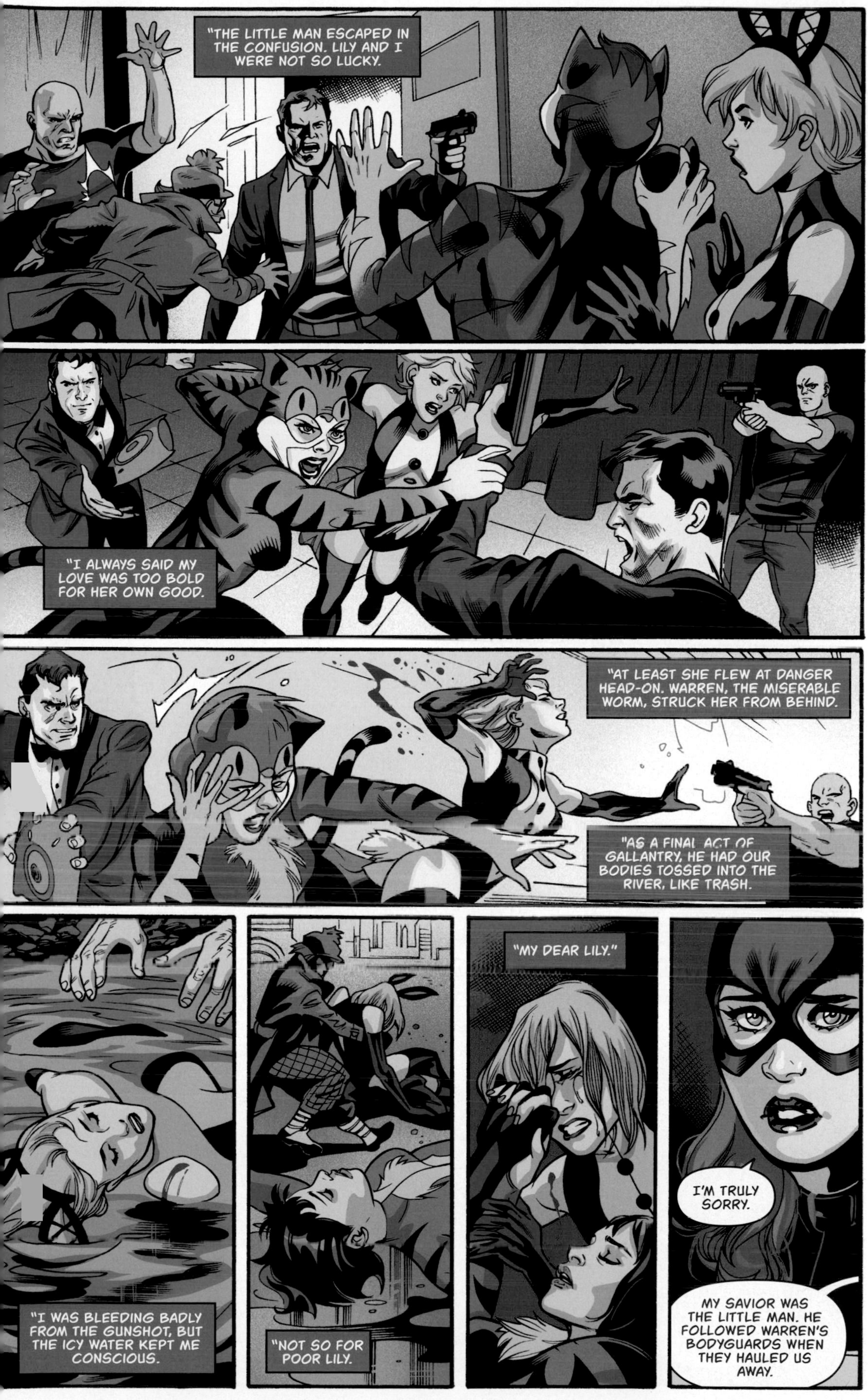
"THE LITTLE MAN ESCAPED IN THE CONFUSION. LILY AND I WERE NOT SO LUCKY.
"I ALWAYS SAID MY LOVE WAS TOO BOLD FOR HER OWN GOOD.
"AT LEAST SHE FLEW AT DANGER HEAD-ON. WARREN, THE MISERABLE WORM, STRUCK HER FROM BEHIND.
"AS A FINAL ACT OF GALLANTRY, HE HAD OUR BODIES TOSSED INTO THE RIVER, LIKE TRASH.
"I WAS BLEEDING BADLY FROM THE GUNSHOT, BUT THE ICY WATER KEPT ME CONSCIOUS.
"NOT SO FOR POOR LILY.
"MY DEAR LILY."
I'M TRULY SORRY.
MY SAVIOR WAS THE LITTLE MAN. HE FOLLOWED WARREN'S BODYGUARDS WHEN THEY HAULED US AWAY.

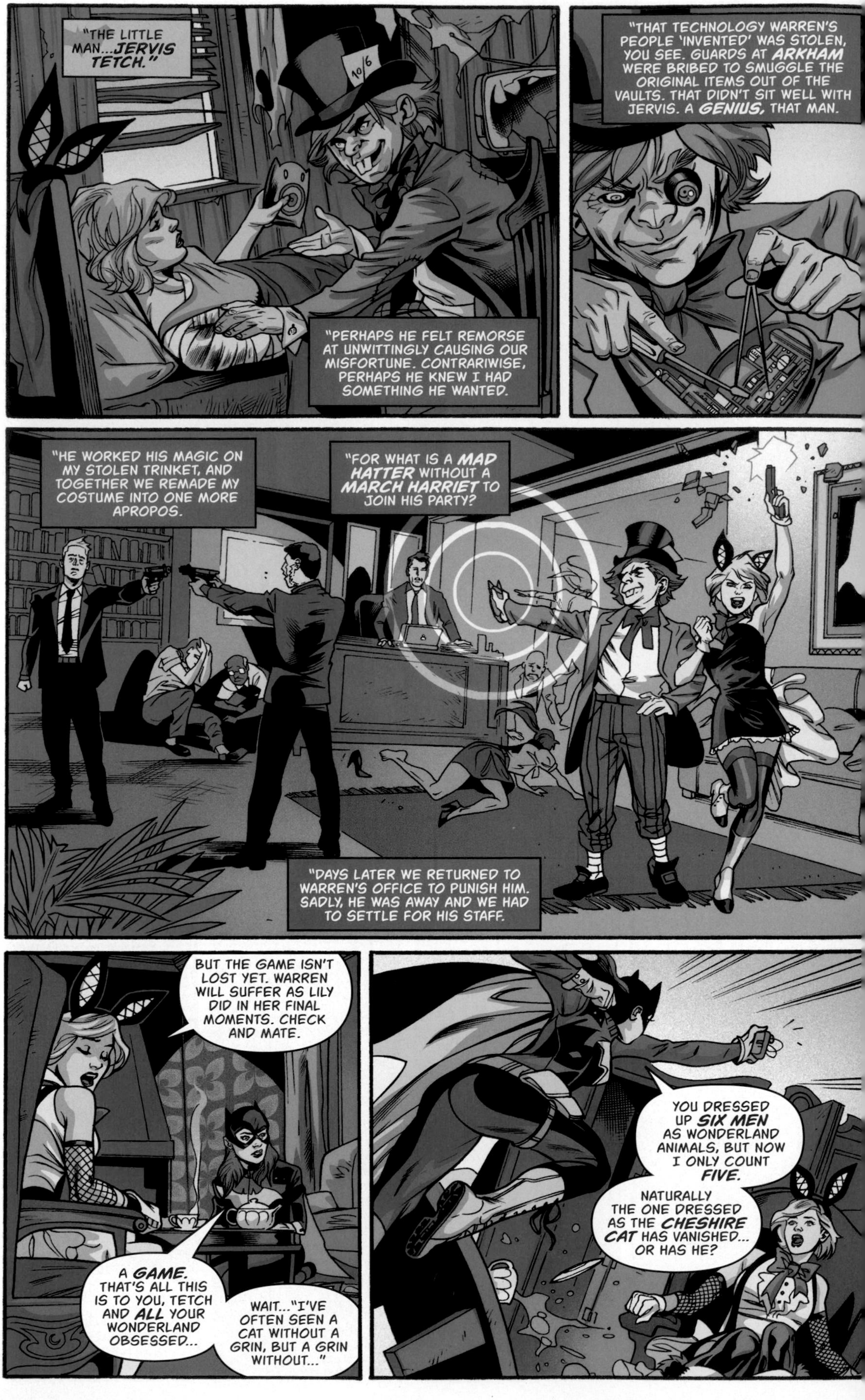
"THE LITTLE MAN...JERVIS TETCH."
"PERHAPS HE FELT REMORSE AT UNWITTINGLY CAUSING OUR MISFORTUNE. CONTRARIWISE, PERHAPS HE KNEW I HAD SOMETHING HE WANTED.
"THAT TECHNOLOGY WARREN'S PEOPLE 'INVENTED' WAS STOLEN, YOU SEE. GUARDS AT ARKHAM WERE BRIBED TO SMUGGLE THE ORIGINAL ITEMS OUT OF THE VAULTS. THAT DIDN'T SIT WELL WITH JERVIS. A GENIUS, THAT MAN.
10/6
"HE WORKED HIS MAGIC ON MY STOLEN TRINKET, AND TOGETHER WE REMADE MY COSTUME INTO ONE MORE APROPOS.
"FOR WHAT IS A MAD HATTER WITHOUT A MARCH HARRIET TO JOIN HIS PARTY?
"DAYS LATER WE RETURNED TO WARREN'S OFFICE TO PUNISH HIM. SADLY, HE WAS AWAY AND WE HAD TO SETTLE FOR HIS STAFF.
BUT THE GAME ISN'T LOST YET. WARREN WILL SUFFER AS LILY DID IN HER FINAL MOMENTS. CHECK AND MATE.
A GAME. THAT'S ALL THIS IS TO YOU, TETCH AND ALL YOUR WONDERLAND OBSESSED...
WAIT..."I'VE OFTEN SEEN A CAT WITHOUT A GRIN, BUT A GRIN WITHOUT..."
YOU DRESSED UP SIX MEN AS WONDERLAND ANIMALS, BUT NOW I ONLY COUNT FIVE.
NATURALLY THE ONE DRESSED AS THE CHESHIRE CAT HAS VANISHED... OR HAS HE?

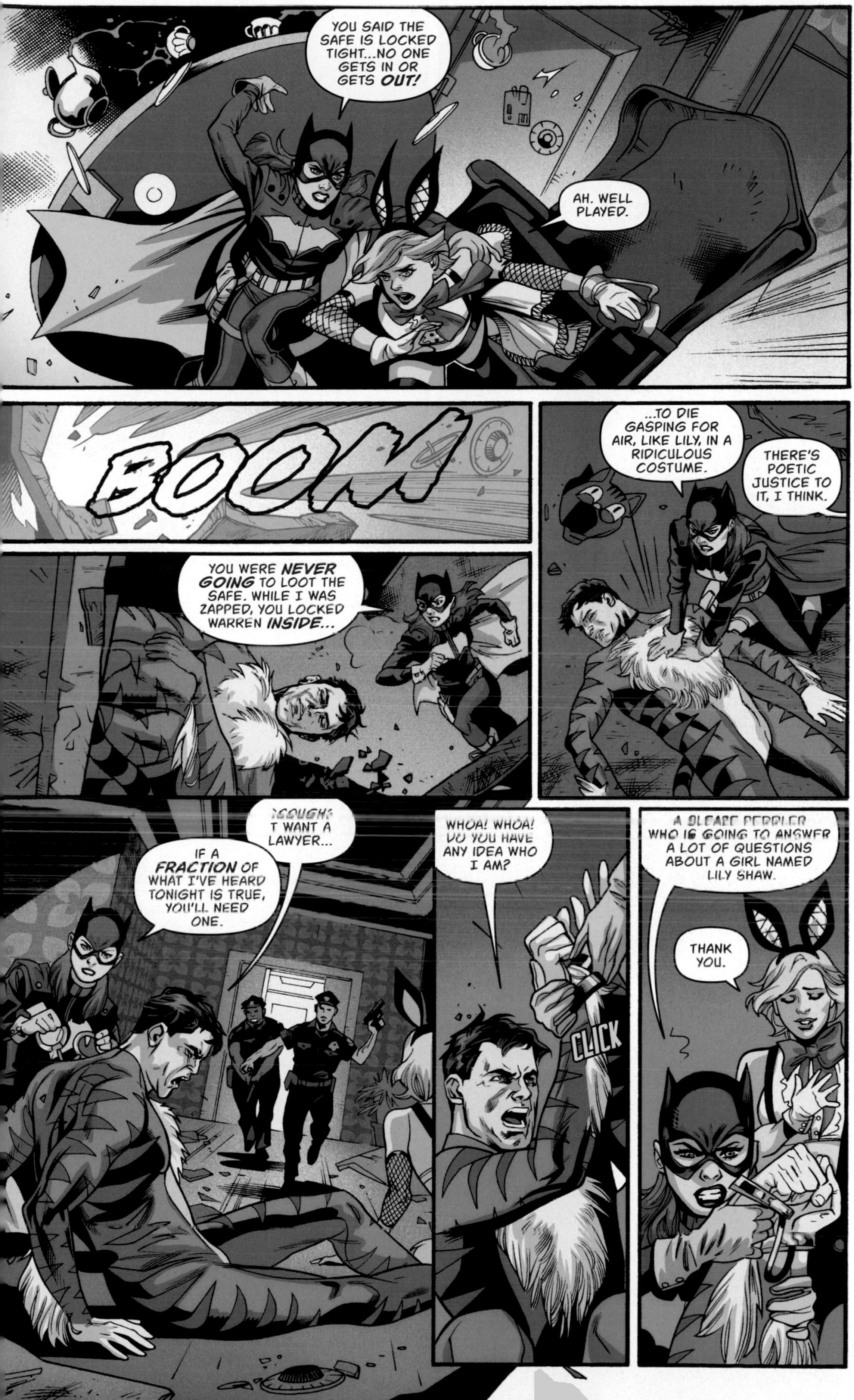
YOU SAID THE SAFE IS LOCKED TIGHT...NO ONE GETS IN OR GETS OUT!
AH. WELL PLAYED.
BOOM
...TO DIE GASPING FOR AIR, LIKE LILY, IN A RIDICULOUS COSTUME.
THERE'S POETIC JUSTICE TO IT, I THINK.
YOU WERE NEVER GOING TO LOOT THE SAFE. WHILE I WAS ZAPPED, YOU LOCKED WARREN INSIDE...
COUGH I WANT A LAWYER...
IF A FRACTION OF WHAT I'VE HEARD TONIGHT IS TRUE, YOU'LL NEED ONE.
WHOA! WHOA! DO YOU HAVE ANY IDEA WHO I AM?
CLICK
A SLEAZE PEDDLER WHO IS GOING TO ANSWER A LOT OF QUESTIONS ABOUT A GIRL NAMED LILY SHAW.
THANK YOU.

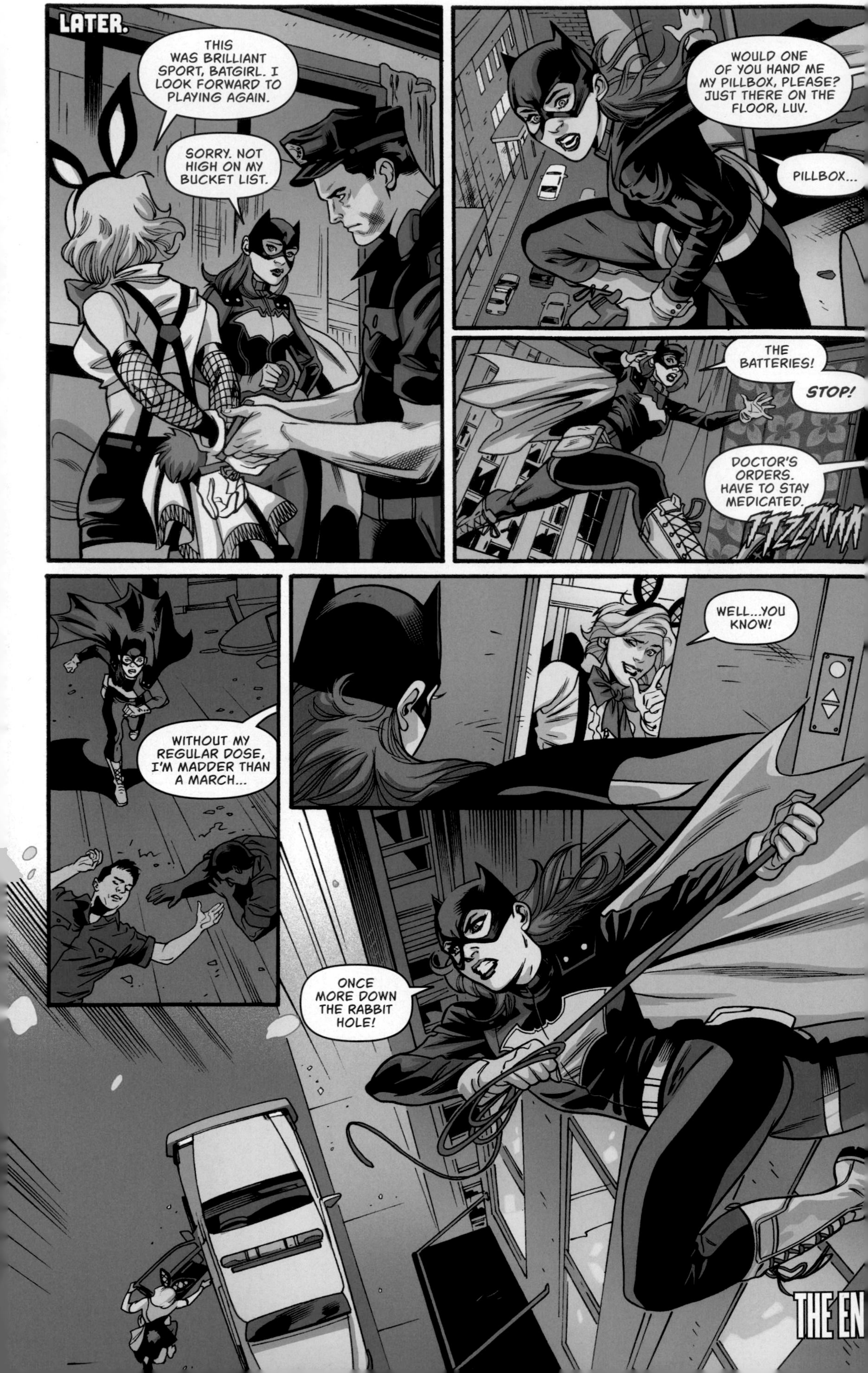
LATER.
THIS WAS BRILLIANT SPORT, BATGIRL. I LOOK FORWARD TO PLAYING AGAIN.
SORRY. NOT HIGH ON MY BUCKET LIST.
WOULD ONE OF YOU HAND ME MY PILLBOX, PLEASE? JUST THERE ON THE FLOOR, LUV.
PILLBOX...
THE BATTERIES!
STOP!
DOCTOR'S ORDERS. HAVE TO STAY MEDICATED.
WITHOUT MY REGULAR DOSE, I'M MADDER THAN A MARCH...
WELL...YOU KNOW!
ONCE MORE DOWN THE RABBIT HOLE!
THE EN

BATGIRL

VARIANT COVER GALLERY

BATGIRL #18 variant cover by JOSHUA MIDDLETON

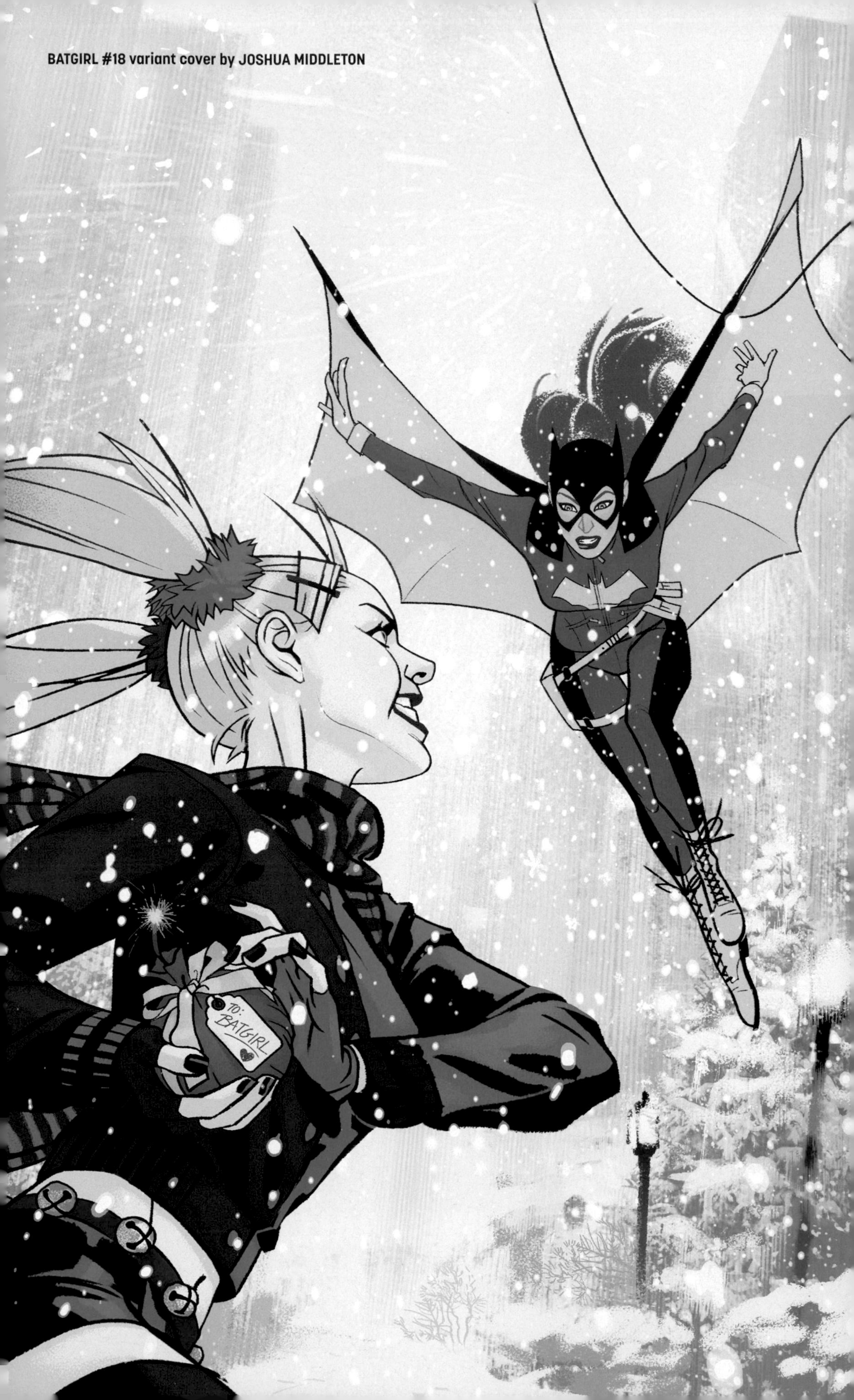
TO: BATGIRL

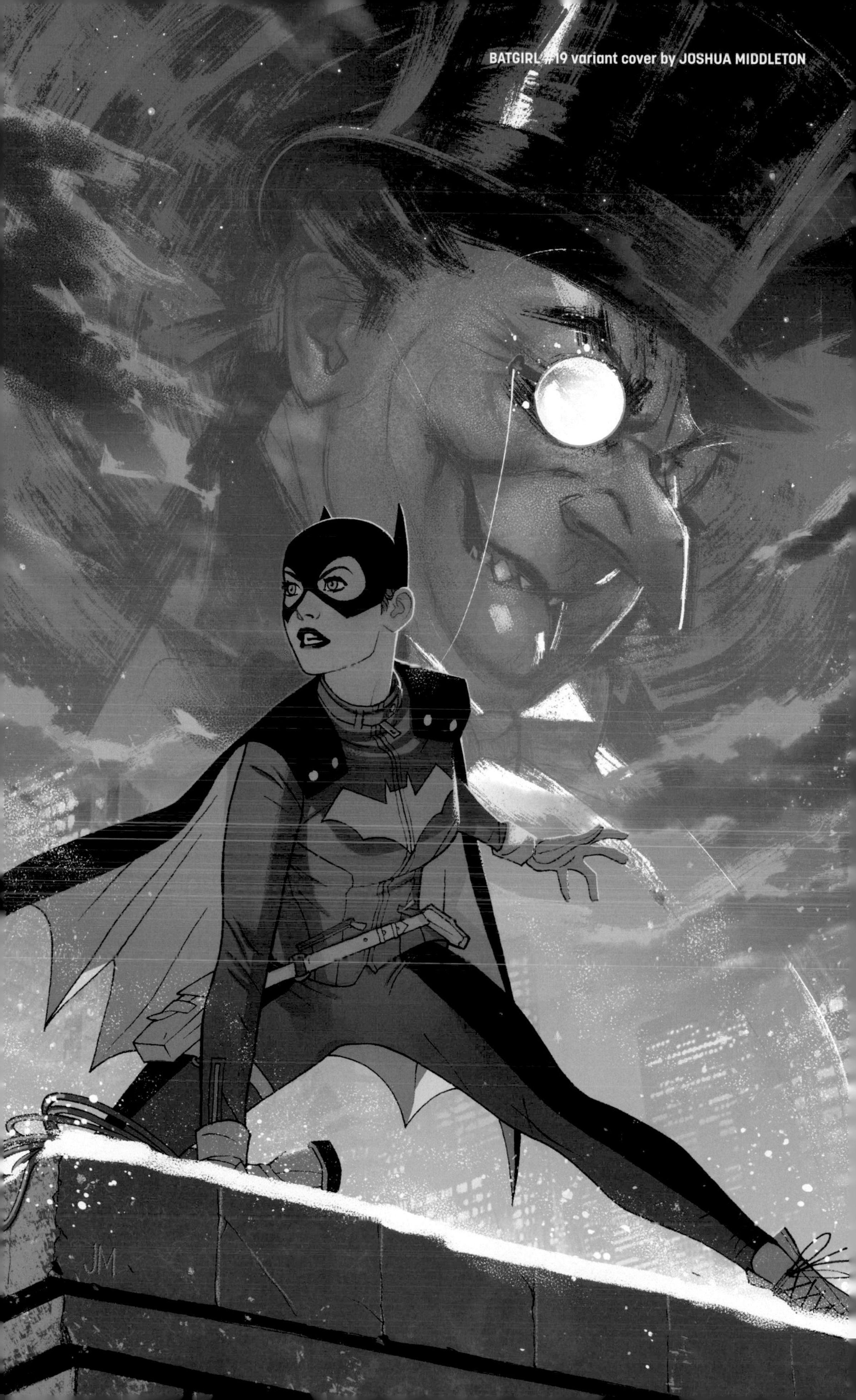

BATGIRL #19 variant cover by JOSHUA MIDDLETON

BATGIRL #20 variant cover by JOSHUA MIDDLETON

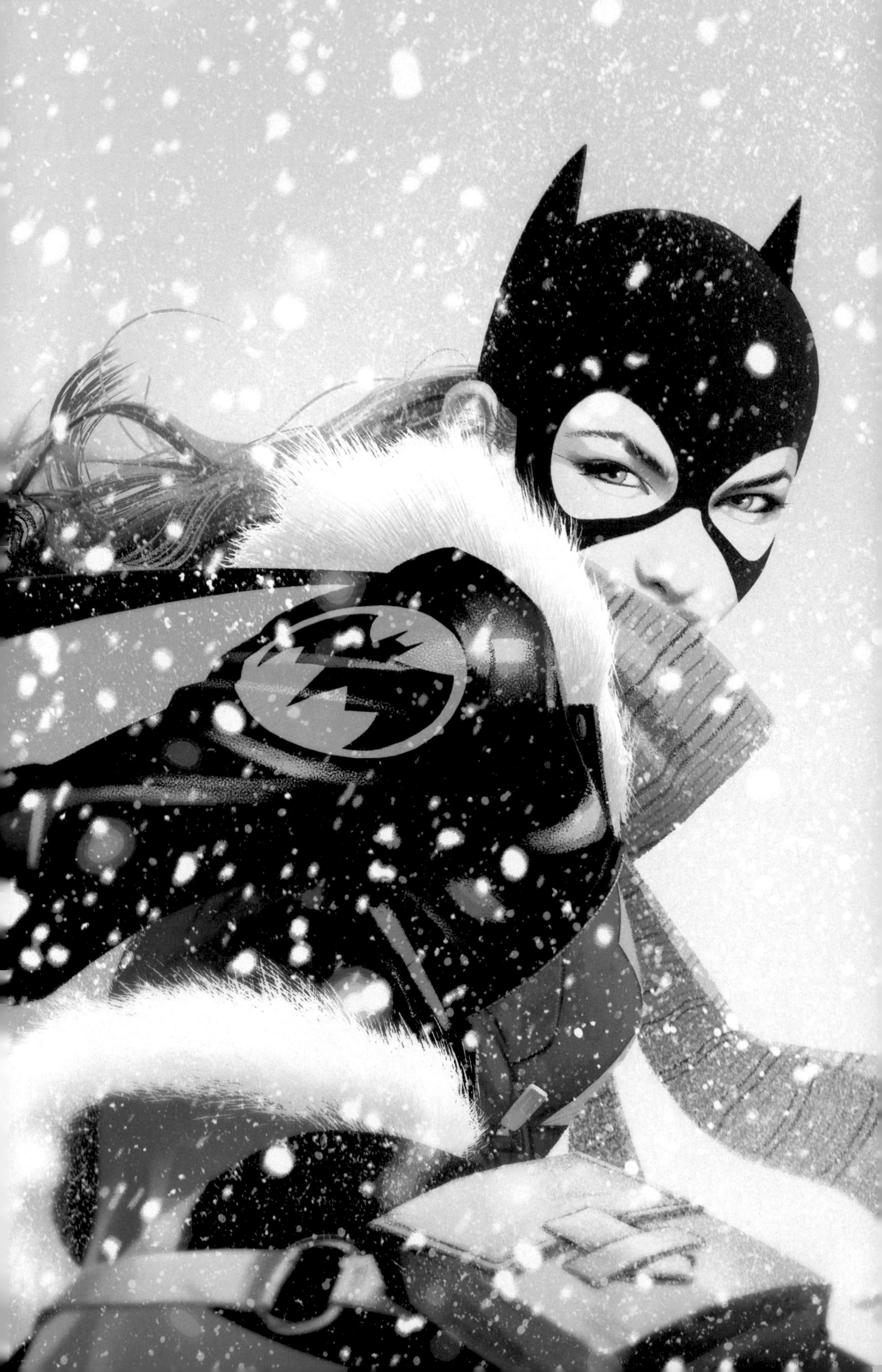

BATGIRL #21 variant cover by JOSHUA MIDDLETON

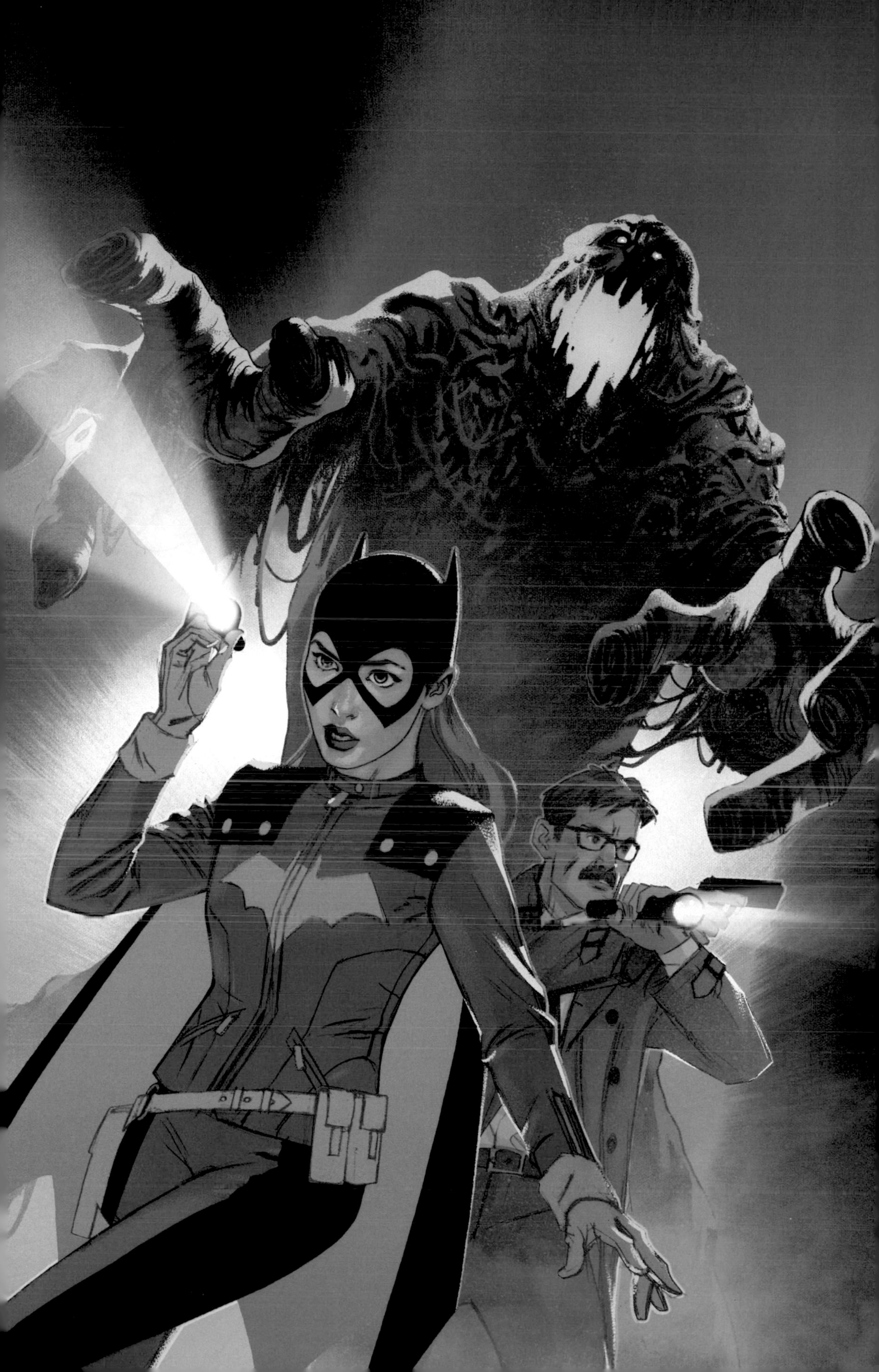

BATGIRL #22 variant cover by JOSHUA MIDDLETON

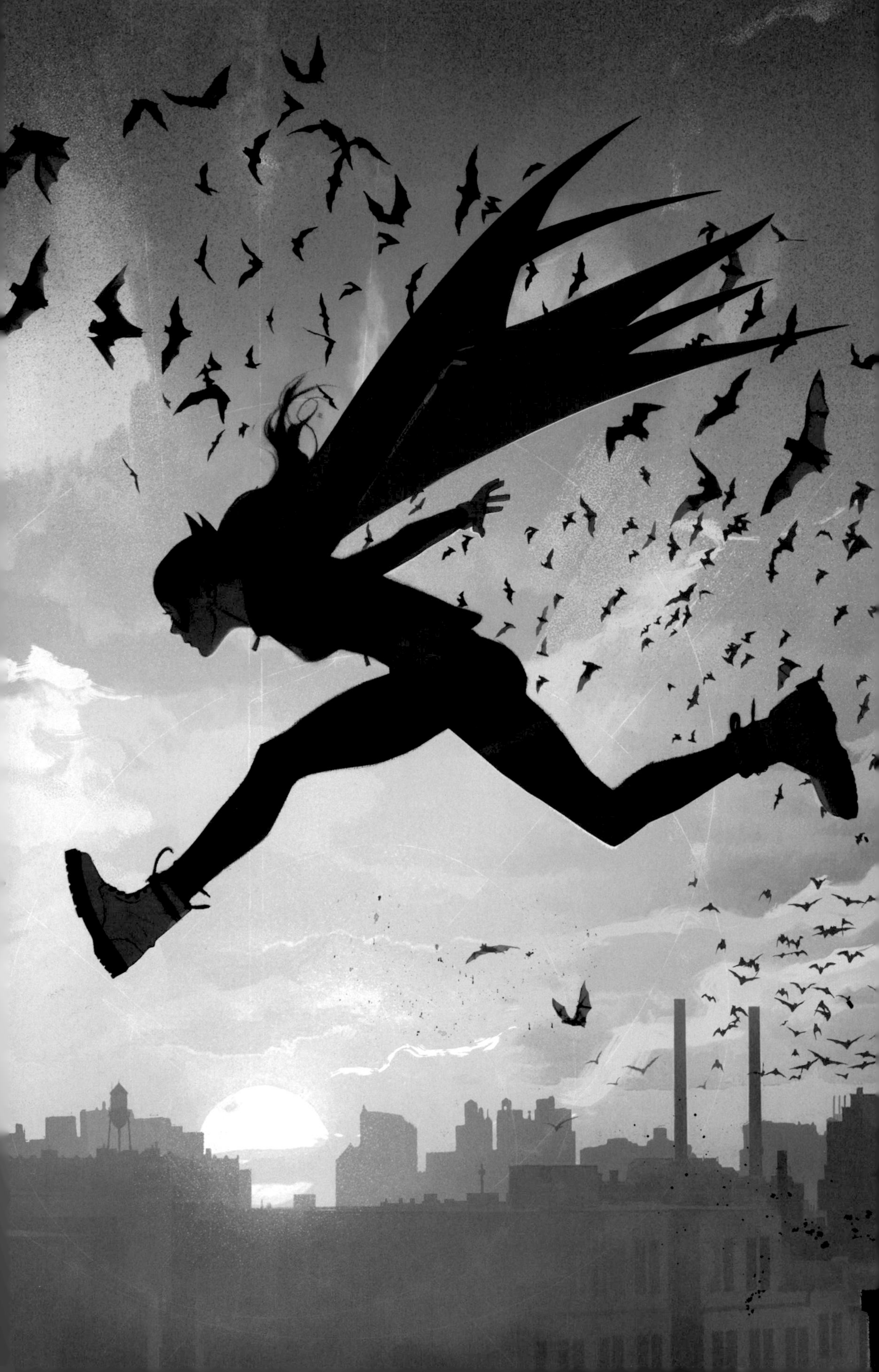

BATGIRL #23 variant cover by JOSHUA MIDDLETON

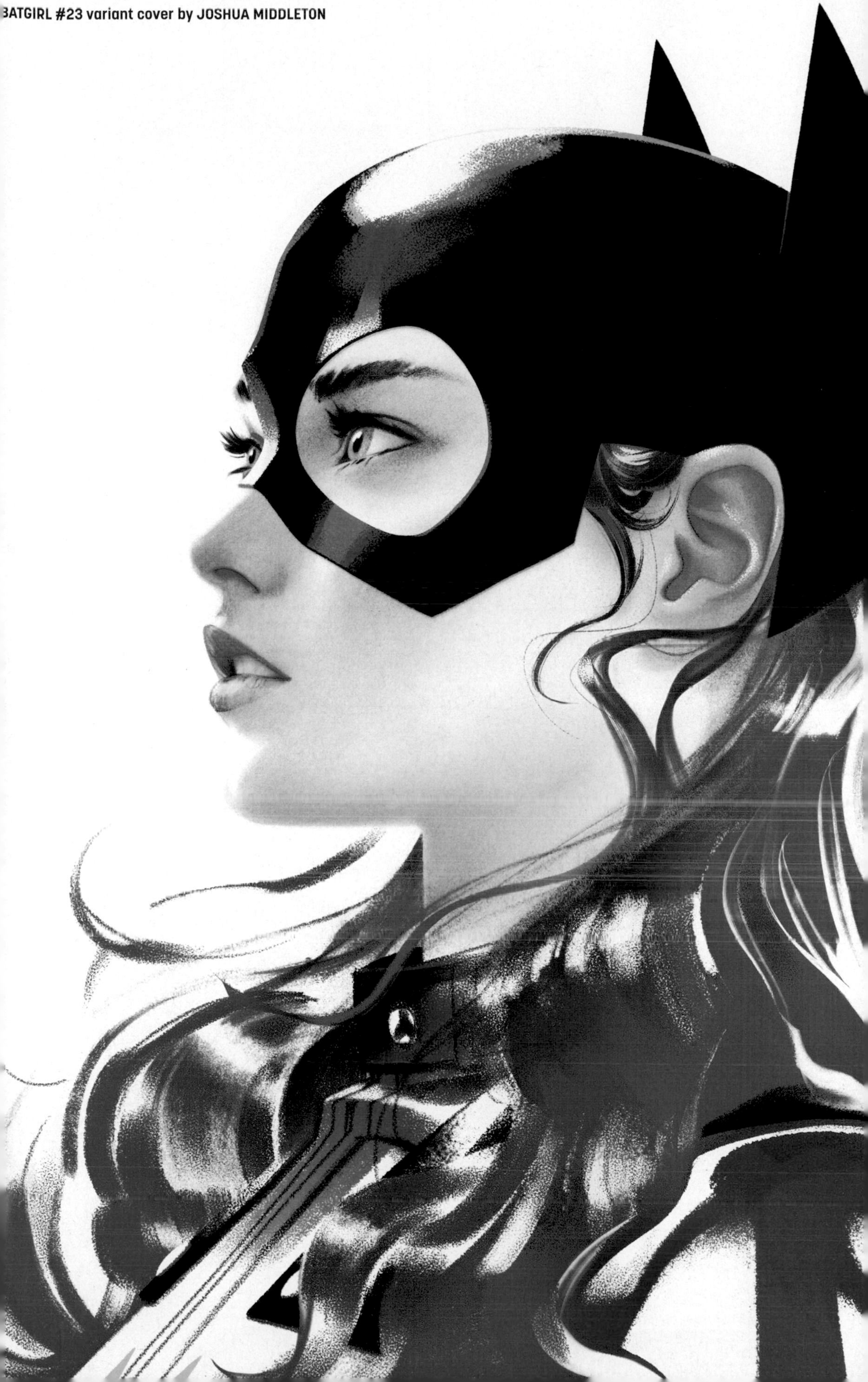

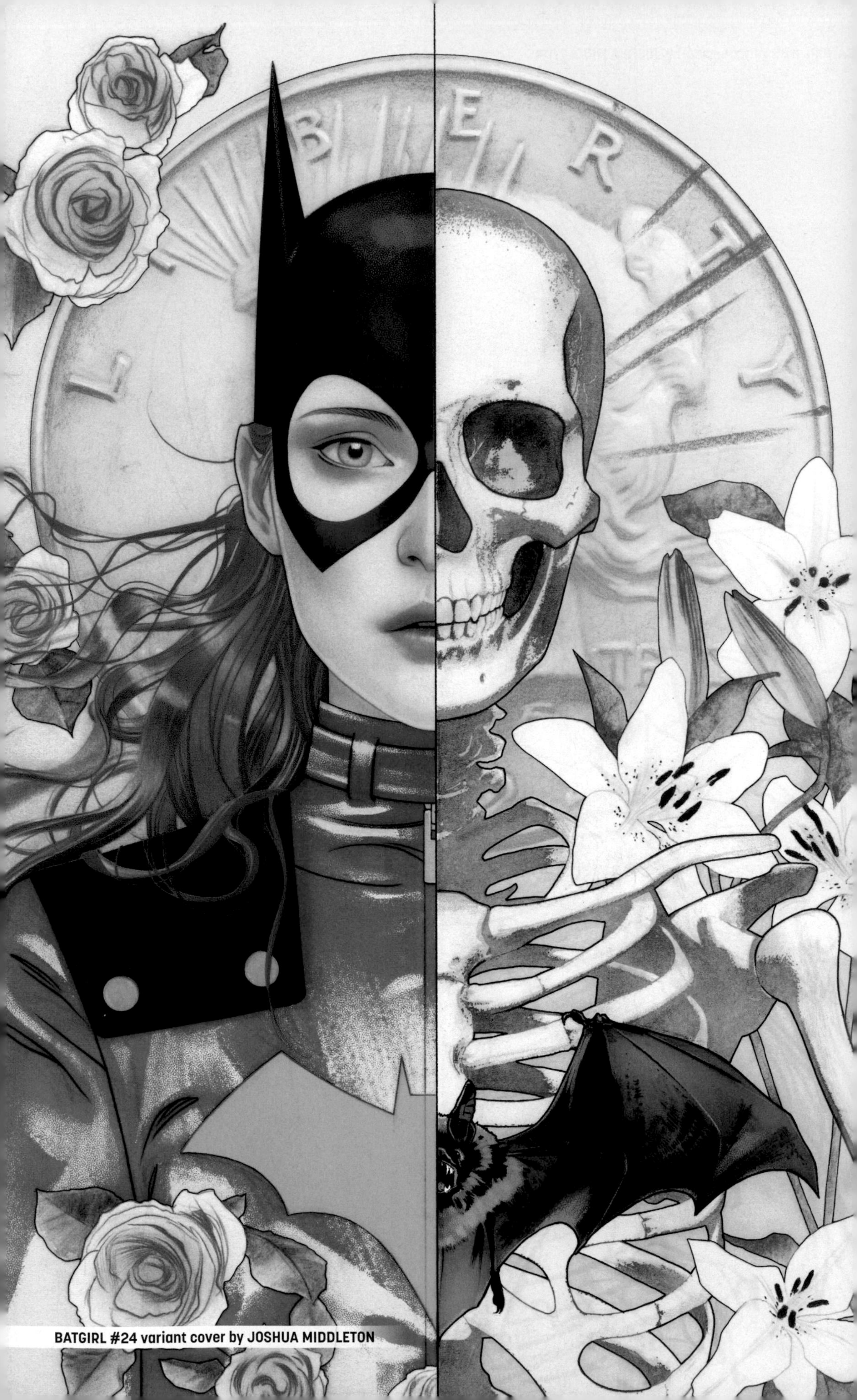

BATGIRL #24 variant cover by JOSHUA MIDDLETON

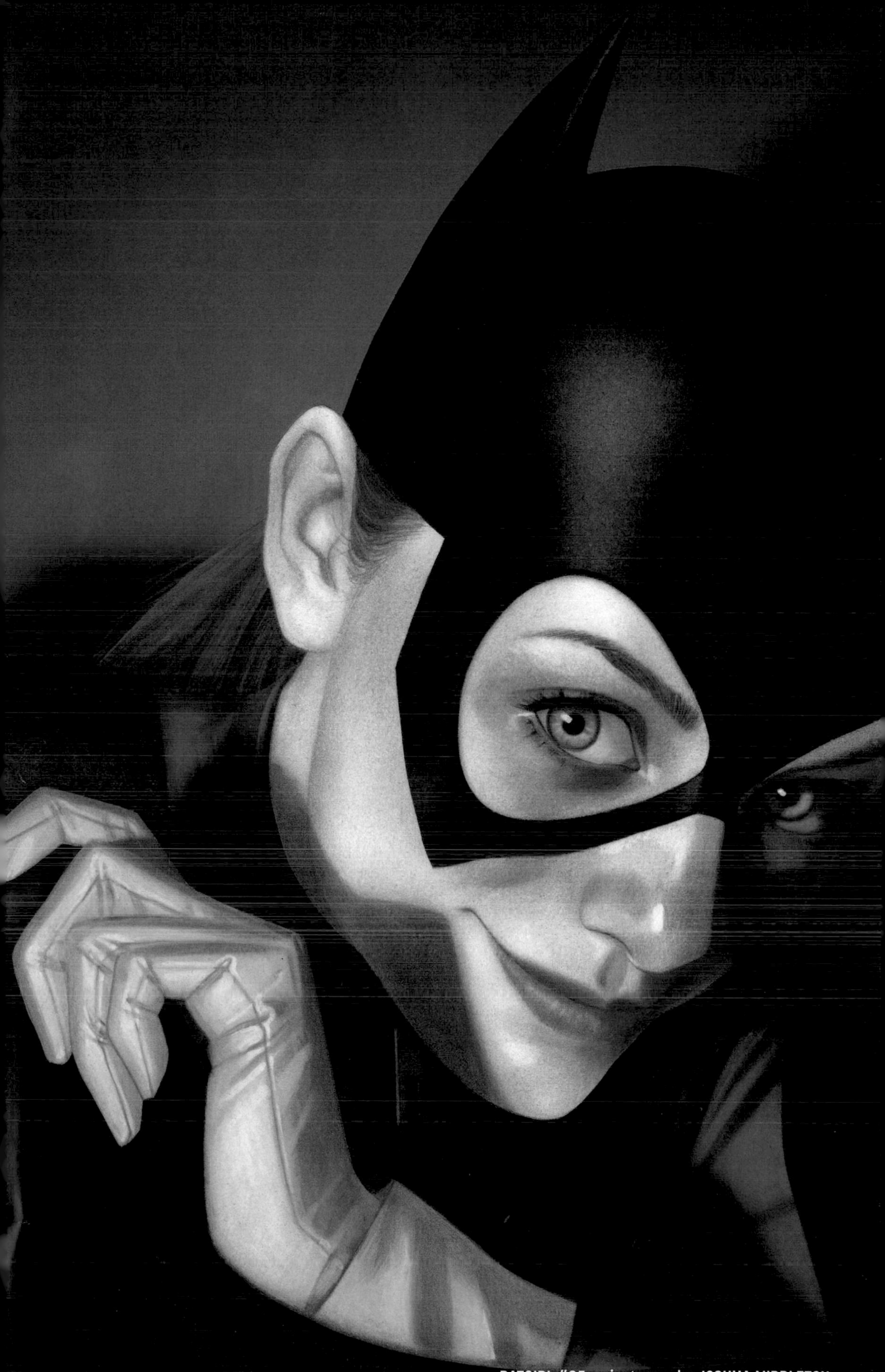

BATGIRL #25 variant cover by JOSHUA MIDDLETON

"A brand-new take on a classic, and it looks absolutely, jaw-droppingly fantastic."
– NEWSARAMA

"A whole lot of excitement and killer art."
– COMIC BOOK RESOURCES

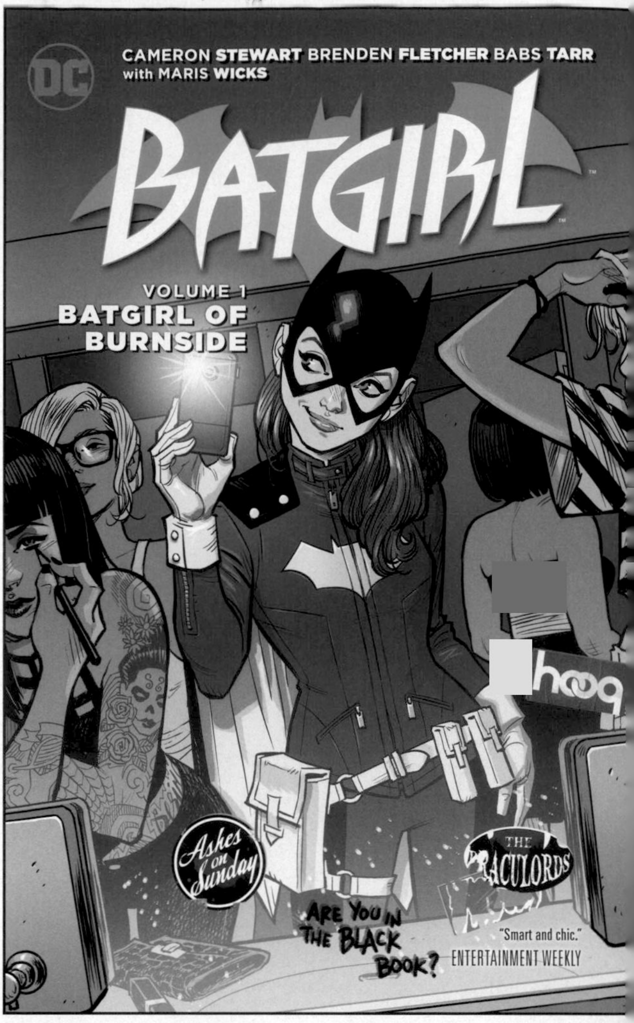
CAMERON STEWART BRENDEN FLETCHER BABS TARR
with MARIS WICKS
BATGIRL
VOLUME 1
BATGIRL OF BURNSIDE
Ashes on Sunday
THE DRACULORDS
ARE YOU IN THE BLACK BOOK?
"Smart and chic."
ENTERTAINMENT WEEKLY

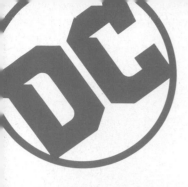

BATGIRL

VOL. 1: BATGIRL OF BURNSIDE

CAMERON STEWART &
BRENDEN FLETCHER
with BABS TARR

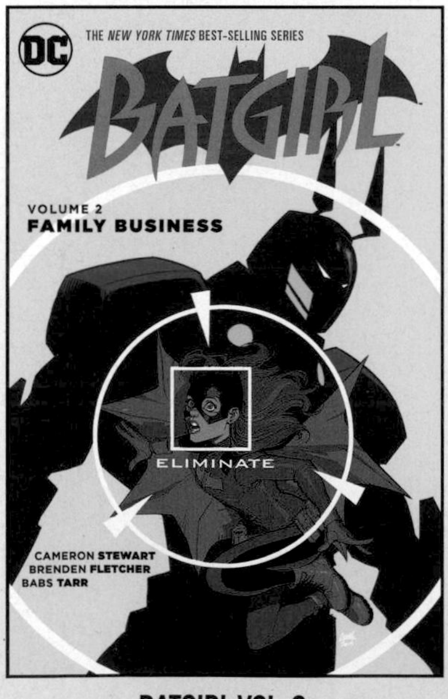
THE NEW YORK TIMES BEST-SELLING SERIES
BATGIRL
VOLUME 2
FAMILY BUSINESS
ELIMINATE
CAMERON STEWART
BRENDEN FLETCHER
BABS TARR

BATGIRL VOL. 2: FAMILY BUSINESS

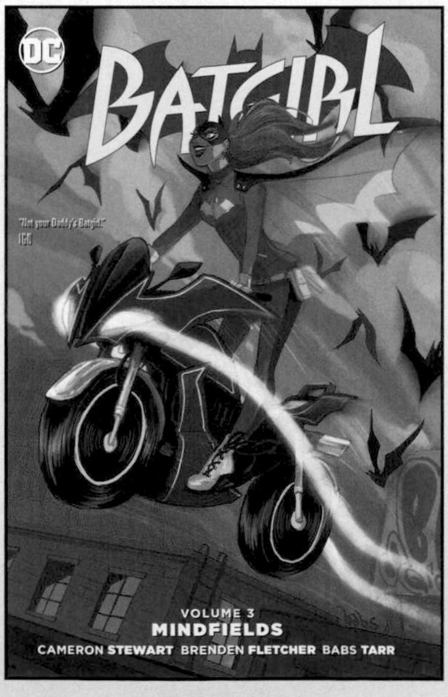
BATGIRL
VOLUME 3
MINDFIELDS
CAMERON STEWART BRENDEN FLETCHER BABS TARR

BATGIRL VOL. 3: MINDFIELDS

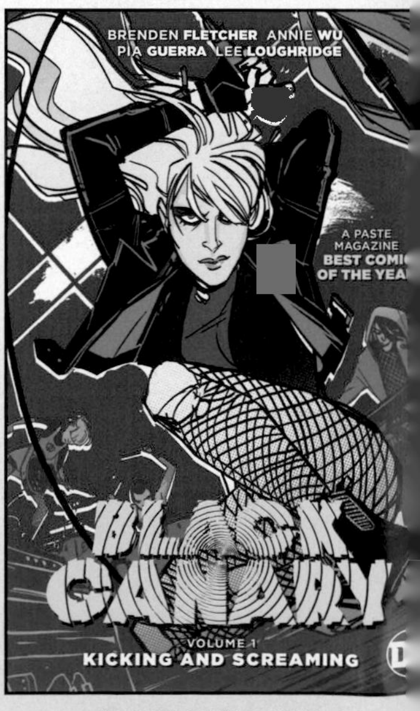
BRENDEN FLETCHER ANNIE WU
PIA GUERRA LEE LOUGHRIDGE
A PASTE MAGAZINE BEST COMI
OF THE YEA
BLACK CANARY
VOLUME 1
KICKING AND SCREAMING

BLACK CANARY VOL. 1: KICKING AND SCREAMING

Get more DC graphic novels wherever comics and books are sold!